The Master
IC Cookbook
2nd Edition

Clayton L. Hallmark
Delton T. Horn

TAB TAB BOOKS

Blue Ridge Summit, PA

Trademarks
The following are all trademarks of Motorola.

C-QUAM
MONOMAX
TRI-STATE

SECOND EDITION
FIRST PRINTING

© 1991 by **TAB BOOKS**.
TAB BOOKS is a division of McGraw-Hill, Inc.

Library of Congress Cataloging-in-Publication Data

Hallmark, Clayton L.
    The master IC cookbook / by Clayton L. Hallmark and Delton T.
Horn. — 2nd ed.
        p.   cm.
    Includes index.
    ISBN 0-8306-6550-1   ISBN 0-8306-3550-5 (pbk.)
    1. Integrated circuits.   I. Horn, Delton T.   II. Title.
TK7874.H32   1991
621.381′5—dc20   90-24382
                                                CIP

TAB BOOKS offers software for sale. For information and a catalog, please contact TAB Software Department, Blue Ridge Summit, PA 17294-0850.

Questions regarding the content of this book should be addressed to:

Reader Inquiry Branch
TAB BOOKS
Blue Ridge Summit, PA 17294-0850

Acquisitions Editor: Roland S. Phelps
Technical Editor: Andrew Yoder
Production: Katherine G. Brown
Book Design: Jaclyn J. Boone

Contents

Introduction

This revised edition of the *Master IC Cookbook* is a one-source reference for data on hundreds of different integrated circuits, both digital and linear. This book is a handy addition to any electronics workbench, whether you are a professional technician, or a hobbyist.

At this writing, all the devices discussed in this volume were available. However, remember that electronics is a rapidly growing field, and some chips might be obsolete and unavailable by the time you read this.

In each section, chips are listed in numerical order. Any prefix letters are ignored. In most cases, the prefix letters simply indicate the manufacturer. For example, National Semiconductor uses *LM*, Rohm uses *BA* and *BU*, Motorola uses *MC*, and Signetics uses *NE*. In most cases, prefix letters can be safely ignored. For instance, an LM567 is exactly the same as an NE567.

Suffix letters are used for various purposes. Sometimes they indicate a case style, an operating temperature characteristic, or an improved version. In most cases, suffix letters can also be ignored, but be aware of some exceptions. When in doubt about chip compatibility, always check the relevant specification sheets, whether in this book or those supplied by the manufacturer/supplier.

The ideal logic family should dissipate no power, have zero propagation delay, controlled rise and fall times, and have noise immunity equal to 50 percent of the logic swing. The properties of CMOS (Complementary MOS) begin to approach these ideal characteristics.

First, CMOS dissipates low power. Typically, the static power dissipation is 10 nW per gate, as a result of the flow of leakage currents. The active power depends on power supply voltage, frequency, output load and input rise time, but typically, gate dissipation at 1 MHz with a 50-pF load is less than 10 mW.

Second, the propagation delays through CMOS are short, though not quite zero. Depending on power supply voltage, the delay through a typical gate is on the order of 25 to 50 ns.

Third, rise and fall times are controlled, tending to be ramps, rather than step functions. Typically, rise and fall times tend to be 20 to 40 percent longer than the propagation delays.

Last, the noise immunity approaches 50 percent, being typically 45 percent of the full logic swing.

On a component basis, CMOS is still more expensive than TTL. However, system level cost might be lower. The power supplies in a CMOS system will be less expensive since they can be made smaller and with less regulation. Because of lower currents, the power supply distribution system can be simpler and, therefore, cheaper. Fans and other cooling equipment are not needed because of the lower dissipation. Longer rise and fall times make the transmission of digital signals simpler. This, in turn, makes transmission techniques less expensive. Finally, there is no technical reason why CMOS prices cannot approach present day TTL prices as sales volume and manufacturing experience increase. So an engineer about to start a new design should compare the system level cost of using CMOS or some other logic family. He might find that even at today's prices, CMOS is the most economical choice.

The 74C line consists of CMOS parts which are pin and functional equivalents of many of the most popular parts in the 7400 TTL series. This line is typically 50 percent faster than the 4000A series and sinks 50 percent more current. For ease of design, it is specified at TTL levels as well as CMOS levels, and there are two temperature ranges available: 54C, $-55°C$ to $+125°C$ or 74C, $-40°C$ to $+85°C$.

TTL Family

TTL devices differ widely in function, complexity and performance, but their electrical input and output characteristics are very similar and are defined and tested to guarantee compatibility. The oldest TTL product category is the gold-doped double-diffused type, which is made up of the 7400 devices. The 74H family is a high performance version of the 74 series which uses the gold-doped structure, but has higher power and faster speeds. The 74S products are fabricated with a nonsaturating Schottky clamped transistor technique. The 74S TTL products are very high performance, high-power devices. The newest and most popular TTL category is the 74LS low-power Schottky family. These products feature the performance of the 74 family using about one-quarter the power.

Absolute Maximum Ratings

The absolute maximum ratings constitute limiting values above which service-ability of the device might be impaired. Provisions should be made in system design and testing to limit voltages and currents as shown in the table.

Operating Temperature and Voltage Ranges

The nominal supply voltage (Vcc) for all TTL circuits is + 5.0 volts. Commercial grade (7400) parts are guaranteed to perform with a ± 5 percent supply toler-ance (± 250 mV) over an ambient temperature range of 0°C to 70°C. The Mili-tary grade (5400) parts are guaranteed to perform with a ± 10 percent supply tolerance (± 500 mV) over an ambient temperature range of − 55°C to + 125°C.

Input Loading and Output Drive Characteristics

The logic levels of all the TTL products are fully compatible with each other. However, the input loading and output drive characteristics of each of these fami-lies is different and must be taken into consideration when mixing the TTL fami-lies in a system.

Mixing TTL Families

Most TTL families are intended for use together, but this cannot be done indis-criminately. Each family of TTL devices has unique input and output characteris-tics optimized to get the desired speed or power features. Fast devices like 74S and 74H are designed with relatively low input and output impedances. The speed of these devices is determined primarily by fast rise and fall times inter-nally, as well as at the input and output nodes. These fast transitions cause noise of various types in the system. Power and ground line noise is generated by the large currents needed to charge and discharge the circuit and load capacitances during the switching transitions. Signal line noise is generated by the fast output transitions and the relatively low output impedances, which tend to increase reflections.

The noise generated by these 74S and 74H can only be tolerated in systems designed with very short signal leads, elaborate ground planes, and good well-decoupled power distribution networks. Mixing the slower TTL families like 74 and 74LS with the higher speed families is also possible but must be done with caution. The slower speed families are more susceptible to induced noise than the higher speed families due to their higher input and output impedances. The low power Schottky 74LS family is especially sensitive to induced noise and must be isolated as much as possible from the 74S and 74H devices. Separate or isolated power and ground systems are recommended, and the LS input signal lines should not run adjacent to lines driven by 74S or 74H devices.

Mixing 74 and 74LS is less restrictive, and the overall system design need not be so elaborate. Standard two-sided PC boards can be used with good decoupled power and ground grid systems. The signal transitions are slower and therefore generate less noise. However, good high-speed design techniques are still required, especially when working with counters, registers, or other devices with memory.

1
SECTION

TTL

In this chapter on the transistor-transistor logic, or TTL, family, you'll find the same type of information as we include in chapter 2 on CMOS chips. In addition, we occasionally give the maximum clock frequency for flip-flops, counters and registers when it is appropriate.

TTL Chip Listing

7400 Quad 2-Input NAND Gate

This device consists of four 2-input NAND gates. Each gate can be used as an inverter, or two gates can be cross-coupled to form bistable flip-flop circuits.

The NAND gate is a variation of the conventional AND gate, delivering an inverted (false) output when all inputs are true. The term *NAND* is a contraction of NOT AND. Note that the output is true when either or both of the inputs are false. Essentially, a NAND gate is the result of using an active inverting element in the gate circuitry. As with a conventional AND gate, the NAND gate can have any number of inputs.

	74S	74H	74LS	74	74L
Typ. Delay Time (ns)	3	6	9.5	10	33
Typ. Power Per Gate (mW)	19	22	2	10	1

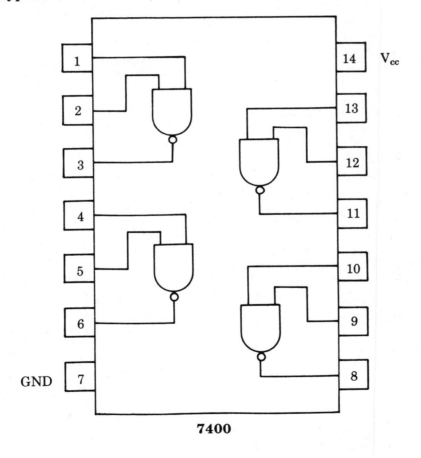

7400

7401 Quad 2-Input NAND Gate

This device consists of four 2-input NAND gates. Each gate can be used as an inverter, or two gates can be cross-coupled to form bistable flip-flop circuits.

The NAND gate is a variation of the conventional AND gate, delivering an inverted (false) output when all inputs are true. The term *NAND* is a contraction of NOT AND. Note the output is true when either or both of the inputs are false. Essentially, a NAND gate is the result of using an active inverting element in the gate circuitry. As with a conventional AND gate, the NAND gate can have any number of inputs.

	74H	74LS	74	74L
Typ. Delay Time (ns)	8	16	22	41
Typ. Power Per Gate (nW)	22	2	10	1

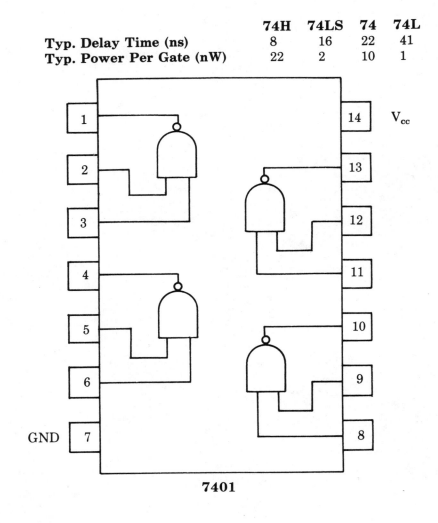

7401

Standard TTL gate outputs should not be tied together unless their logic levels will always be the same. Open-collector outputs, however, can be connected to other open-collector outputs to from additional logic. When outputs are thus tied together (OR-wired), a pullup resistor must be added between the common outputs and the positive supply. This is typically a 2.2 kΩ resistor. Open-collector outputs have a high output impedance in the high state. Furthermore, they are slow acting, especially with capacitive loading.

7402 Quad 2-Input NOR Gate

Standard TTL gate outputs should not be tied together unless their logic levels will always be the same. Open-collector outputs, however, can be connected to other open-collector outputs to form additional logic. When outputs are thus tied together (OR-wired), a pullup resistor must be added between the common outputs and the positive supply. This is typically a 2.2. $k\Omega$ resistor. Open-collector outputs have a high output impedance in the high state. Furthermore, they are slow acting, especially with capacitive loading.

	74S	74LS	74	74L
Typ. Delay Time (ns)	3.5	10	10	33
Typ. Power Per Gate (mW)	29	2.75	14	1.5

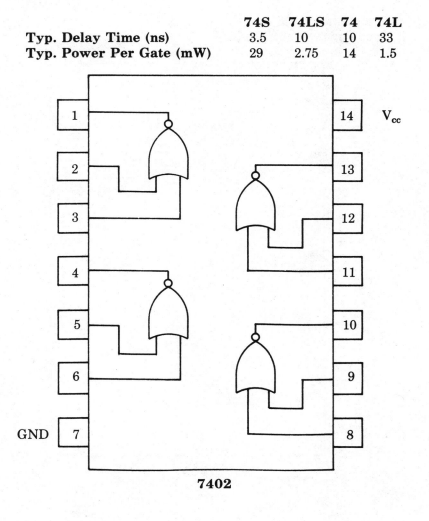

7402

7403 Quad 2-Input NAND Gate (O.C.)

The NAND gate is a variation of the conventional AND gate, delivering an inverted (false) output when all inputs are true. The term *NAND* is a contraction of NOT AND. Note that the output is true when either or both of the inputs are false. Essentially, a NAND gate is the result of using an active inserting element in the gate circuitry. As with a conventional AND gate, the NAND gate can have any number of inputs.

	74S	74LS	74	74L
Typ. Delay Time (ns)	5	16	22	41
Typ. Power Per Gate (mW)	17.2	2	10	1

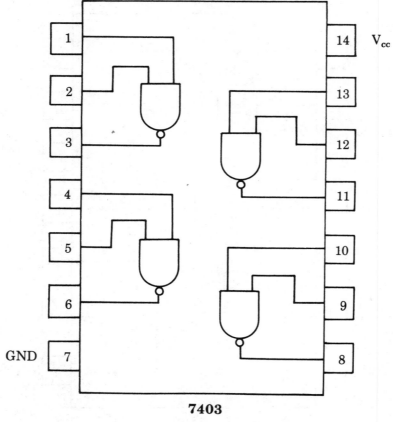

7403

7404 Hex Inverter

As logic elements are combined in series to perform logic functions, voltage levels tend to degrade. Thus, amplifiers are sometimes needed to restore voltages or currents to proper levels. Assuming no inversion is encountered, a true input will produce a true output, and a false input will produce a false output. When inversion occurs, an inversion is placed at the output, and the symbol is usually termed an inverter.

	74S	74H	74LS	74	74L
Typ. Delay Time (ns)	3	6	9.5	10	33
Typ. Power Per Gate (mW)	19	22	2	10	1

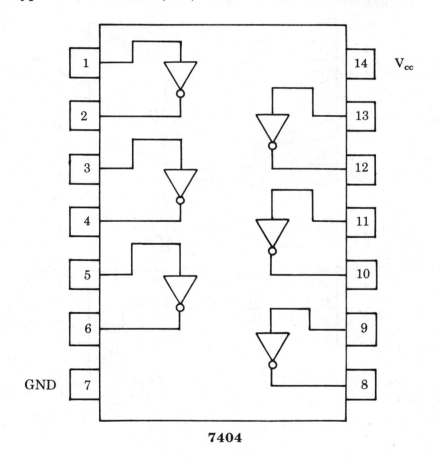

7404

7405 Hex Inverter (O.C.)

As logic elements are combined in series to perform logic functions, voltage levels tend to degrade. Thus, amplifiers are sometimes needed to restore voltages or currents to proper levels. Assuming no inversion is encountered, a true input will produce a true output, and a false input will produce a false output. When inversion occurs, an inversion is placed at the output, and the symbol is usually termed an inverter.

	74S	74H	74LS	74
Typ. Delay Time (ns)	5	8	16	22
Typ. Power Per Gate (mW)	17.5	22	2	10

7405

7406 Hex Inverter Buffer/Driver (O.C.)

As logic elements are combined in series to perform logic functions, voltage levels tend to degrade. Thus, amplifiers are sometimes needed to restore voltages or currents to proper levels. Assuming no inversion is encountered, a true input will produce a true output, and a false input will produce a false output. When inversion occurs, an inversion is placed at the output, and the symbol is usually termed an inverter.

	74
High-Level Output Voltage (V)	30
Low-Level Output Current (mA)	40
Typ. Delay Time (ns)	12.5
Typ. Power Per Gate (mW)	26

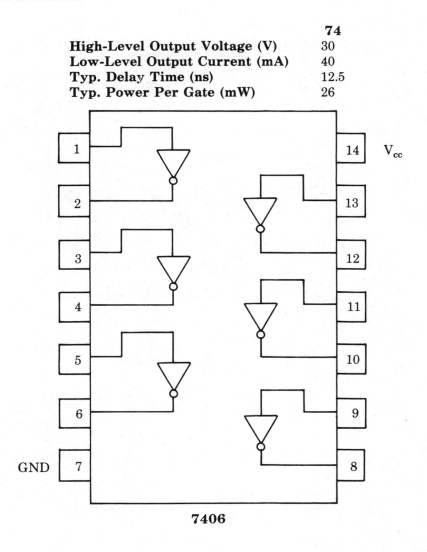

7406

7407 Hex Buffer/Driver (O.C.)

As logic elements are combined in series to perform logic functions, voltage levels tend to degrade. Thus, amplifiers are sometimes needed to restore voltages or currents to proper levels. Assuming no inversion is encountered, a true input will produce a true output, and a false input will produce a false output. When inversion occurs, an inversion is placed at the output, and the symbol is usually termed an inverter.

	74
High-Level Output Voltage (V)	30
Low-Level Output Current (mA)	40
Typ. Delay Time (ns)	13
Typ. Power Per Gate (mW)	21

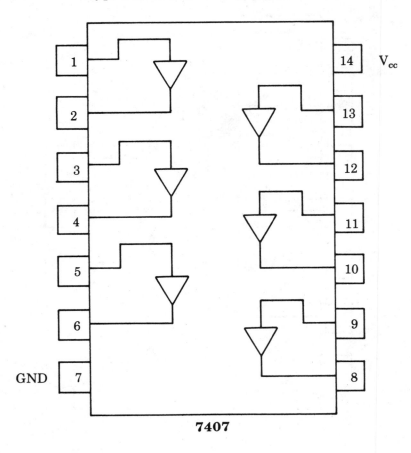

7407

7408 Quad 2-Input AND Gate

The symbol for the AND gate is shown below. By definition, for output C to be true, inputs A and B must be true; hence, the term AND gate.

	74LS	74
Typ. Delay Time (ns)	12	15
Typ. Power Per Gate (mW)	4.25	19

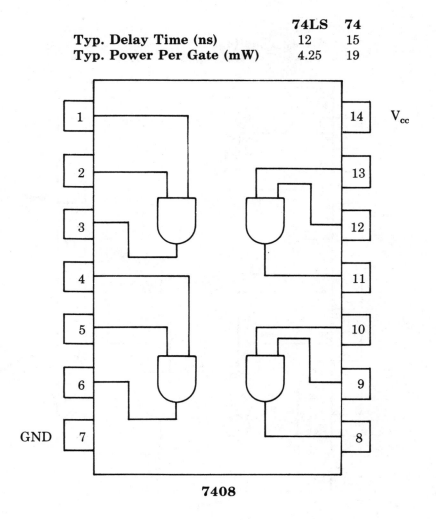

7408

7410 Triple 3-Input AND NAND Gate

The symbol for the AND gate is shown below. By definition, for output C to be true, inputs A and B must be true; hence, the term AND gate.

	74	74LS
Typ. Delay Time (ns)	18.5	20
Typ. Power Per Gate (mW)	19.4	4.25

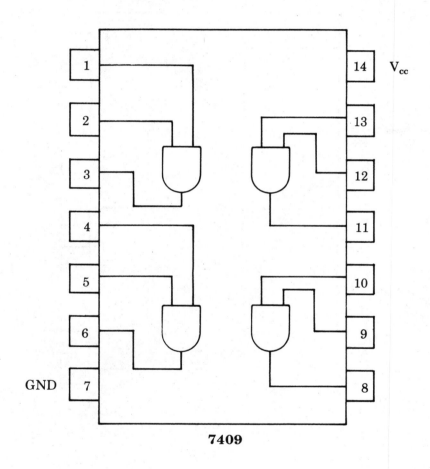

7409

7410 Triple 3-Input and NAND Gate

The NAND gate is a variation of the conventional AND gate, delivering an inverted (false) output when all inputs are true. The term *NAND* is a contraction of NOT AND. Note that the output is true when either or both of the inputs are false. Essentially, a NAND gate is the result of using an active inverting element in the gate circuitry. As with a conventional AND gate, the NAND gate can have any number of inputs.

	74S	74H	74LS	74	74L
Typ. Delay Time (ns)	3	6	9.5	10	33
Typ. Power Per Gate (mW)	19	22	2	10	1

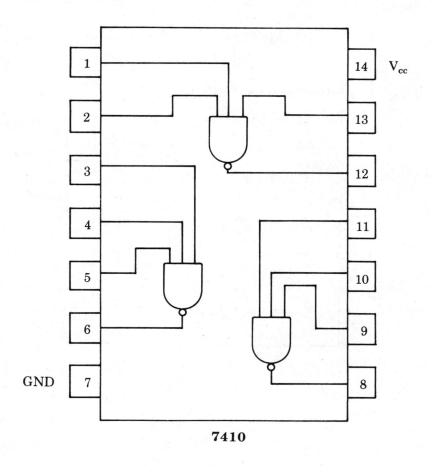

7410

7411 Triple 3-Input AND Gate

The symbol for the AND gate is shown here. By definition, for output C to be true, inputs A and B must be true; hence the term AND gate.

	74S	74H	74LS
Typ. Delay Time (ns)	4.75	8.2	12
Typ. Power Per Gate (mW)	31	40	4.25

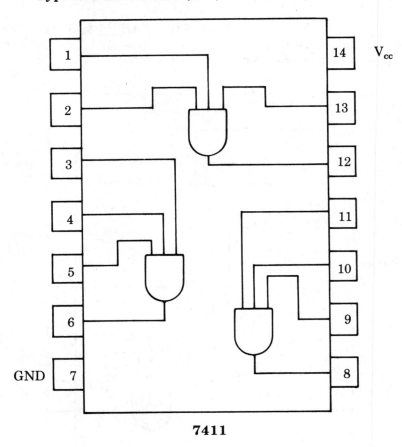

7411

7412 Triple 3-Input NAND Gate (O.C.)

The NAND gate is a variation of the conventional AND Gate, delivering an inverted (false) output when all inputs are true. The term *NAND* is a contraction of NOT AND. Note that the output is true when either or both of the inputs are false. Essentially, a NAND gate is the result of using an active inverting element in the gate circuitry. As with a conventional AND gate, the NAND gate can have any number of inputs.

	74LS
Typ. Delay Time (ns)	16
Typ. Power Per Gate (mW)	2

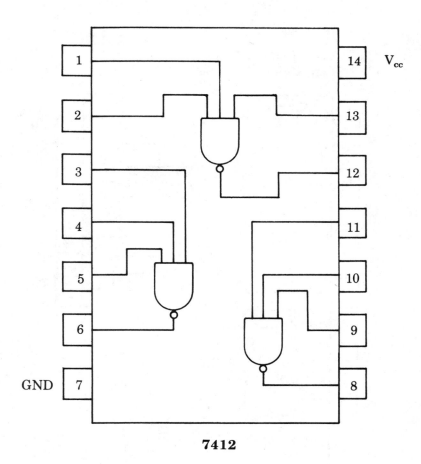

7412

7414 Hex Schmitt Trigger

The '14 contains six logic inverters that accept standard TTL input signals and provide standard TTL output levels. They are capable of transforming slowly changing input signals into sharply defined, jitter-free output signals. In addition, they have a greater noise margin than conventional inverters.

Each circuit contains a Schmitt trigger followed by a Darlington level shifter and a phase splitter driving a TTL totem-pole output. The Schmitt trigger uses positive feedback to effectively speed up slow input transition, and provide different input threshold voltages for positive-going and negative-going transitions. This hysteresis between the positive-going and negative-going input thresholds (typically 800 mV) is determined internally by resistor ratios and is essentially insensitive to temperature and supply voltage variations.

	74	74LS
Typ. Hysteresis (V)	0.8	0.8
Typ. Delay Time (ns)	15	15

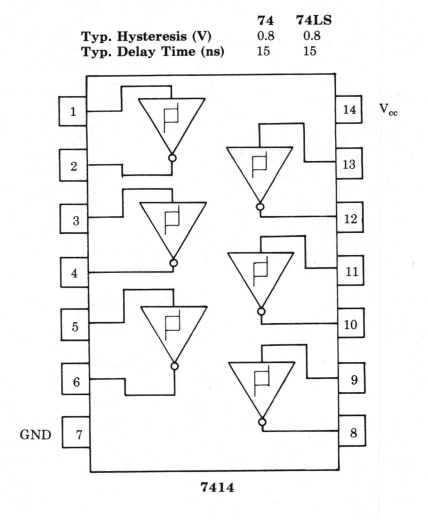

7414

7415 Triple 3-Input AND Gate (O.C.)

The symbol for the AND gate is shown here. By definition, for output C to be true, inputs A and C must be true; hence, the term AND gate.

	74S	74LS
Typ. Delay Time (ns)	6	20
Typ. Power Per Gate (mW)	28	4.25

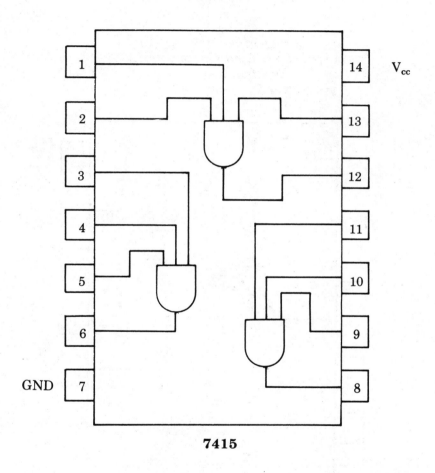

7415

7416 Hex Inverter Buffer/Driver (O.C.)

As logic elements are combined in series to perform logic functions, voltage levels tend to degrade. Thus, amplifiers are sometimes needed to restore voltages or currents to proper levels. Assuming no inversion is encountered, a true input will produce a true output, and a false input will produce a false output. When inversion occurs, an inversion is placed at the output, and the symbol is usually termed an inverter.

	74
High-Level Output Voltage (V)	15
Low-Level Output Current (mA)	40
Typ. Delay Time (ns)	12.5
Typ. Power Per Gate (mW)	26

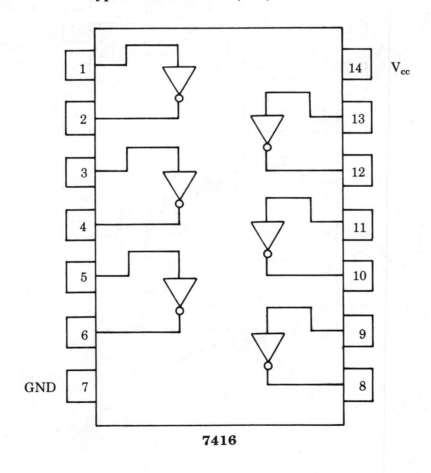

7416

7417 Hex Buffer/Driver (O.C.)

As logic elements are combined in series to perform logic functions, voltage levels tend to degrade. Thus, amplifiers are sometimes needed to restore voltages or currents to proper levels. Assuming no inversion is encountered, a true input will produce a true output, and a false input will produce a false output. When inversion occurs, an inversion is placed at the output, and the symbol is usually termed an inverter.

	74
High-Level Output Voltage (V)	15
Low-Level Output Current (mA)	40
Typ. Delay Time (ns)	13
Typ. Power Per Gate (mW)	21

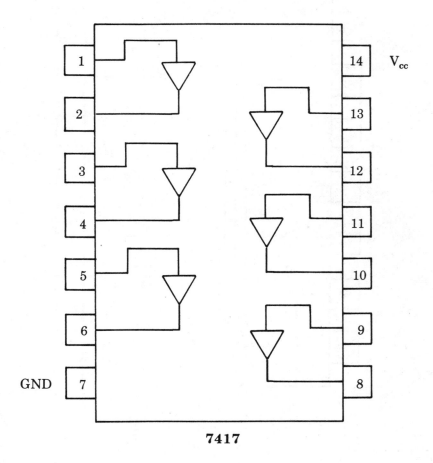

7417

23

7420 Dual 4-Input NAND Gate

The NAND gate is a variation of the conventional AND gate, delivering an inverted (false) output when all inputs are true. The term *NAND* is a contraction of NOT AND. Note that the output is true when either or both of the inputs are false. Essentially, a NAND gate is the result of using an active inverting element in the gate circuitry. As with a conventional AND gate, the NAND gate can have any number of inputs.

	74S	74H	74LS	74
Typ. Delay Time (ns)	3	6	9.5	10
Typ. Power Per Gate (mW)	19	22	2	10

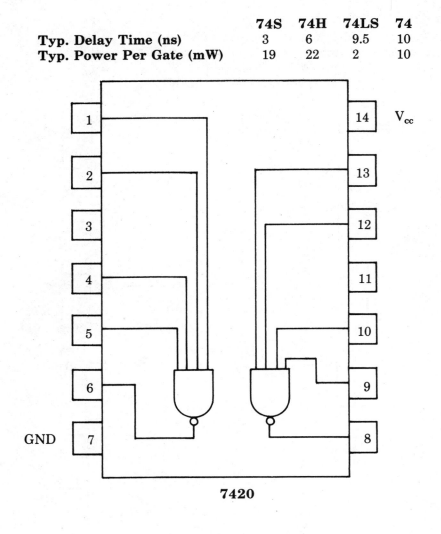

7420

7421 Dual 4-Input AND Gate

The symbol for the AND gate is shown below. By definition, for output E to be true, all inputs must be true; hence, the term *AND gate*.

	74H	74LS
Typ. Delay Time (ns)	8.2	12
Typ. Power Per Gate (mW)	40	4.25

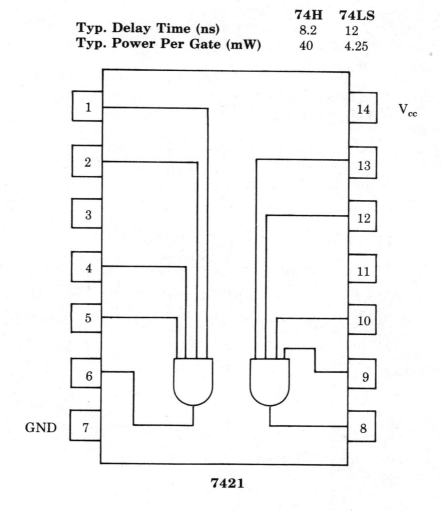

7421

7422 Dual 4-Input NAND Gate (O.C.)

The NAND gate is a variation of the conventional AND gate, delivering an inverted (false) output when all inputs are true. The term *NAND* is a contraction of NOT AND. Note that the output is true when any one or all of the inputs are false. Essentially, a NAND gate is the result of using an active inverting element in the gate circuitry. As with a conventional AND gate, the NAND gate can have any number of inputs.

	74S	74H	74LS
Typ. Delay Time (ns)	5	8	16
Typ. Power Per Gate (mW)	17.5	22	2

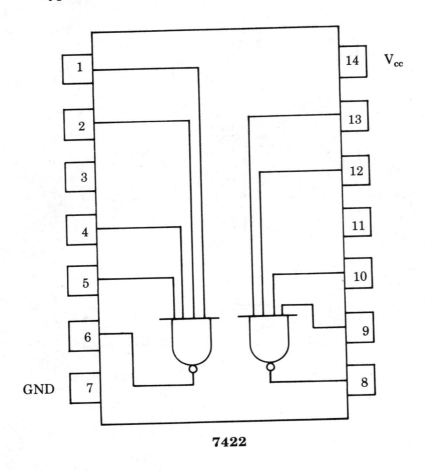

7422

7425 Dual 4-Input NOR Gate with Strobe

Similar to the NAND gate, the NOR gate is a variation of the conventional OR gate, delivering an inverted (false) output when any or all of its inputs are true. The term *NOR* is a contraction of NOT OR. Note that the output is true when all inputs are false. Like the NAND gate, the NOR gate used an active inverting element in the gate circuitry. The NOR gate also can have any number of inputs.

	74
Typ. Delay Time (ns)	10.5
Typ. Power Per Gate (nW)	23

7425

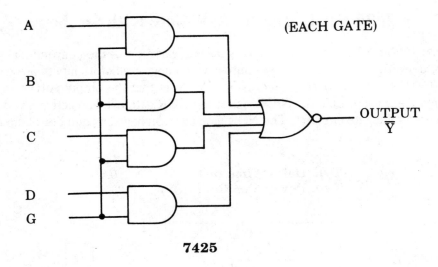

(EACH GATE)

OUTPUT
$\overline{Y}$

7425

7426 Quad 2-Input NAND Gate (O.C.)

The NAND gate is a variation of the conventional AND gate, delivering an inverted (false) output when all inputs are true. The term *NAND* is a contraction of NOT AND. Note that the output is true when either or both of the inputs are false. Essentially, a NAND gate is the result of using an active inverting element in the gate circuitry. As with a conventional AND gate, the NAND gate can have any number of inputs.

	74	74LS
High-Level Output Voltage (V)	15	15
Low-Level Output Current (mA)	16	8
Typ. Delay Time (ns)	13.5	16
Typ. Power Per Gate (mW)	10	2

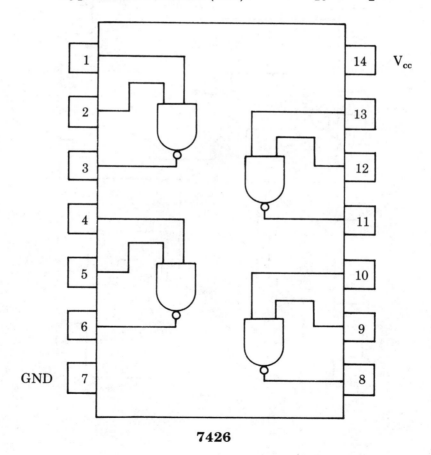

7426

29

7427 Triple 3-Input NOR Gate

Similar to the NAND gate, the NOR gate is a variation of the conventional OR gate, delivering an inverted (false) output when any or all of its inputs are true. The term *NOR* is a contraction of NOT OR. Note that the output is true when all inputs are false. Like the NAND gate, the NOR gate used an active inverting element in the gate circuitry. The NOR gate also can have any number of inputs.

	74	74LS
Typ. Delay Time (ns)	8.5	10
Typ. Power Per Gate (mW)	22	4.5

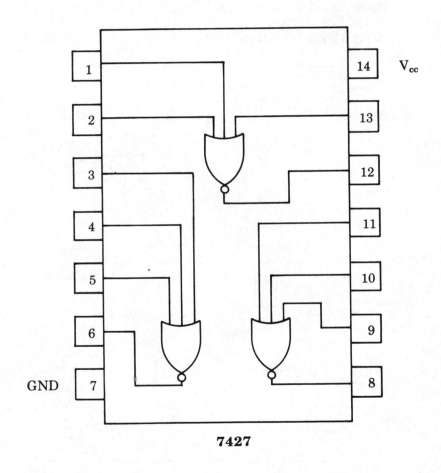

7427

7428 Quad 2-Input NOR Buffer

Similar to the NAND Gate, the NOR gate is a variation of the conventional OR gate, delivering an inverted (false) output when any or all of its inputs are true. The term *NOR* is a contraction of NOT OR. Note that the output is true when all inputs are false. Like the NAND gate, the NOR gate used an active inverting element in the gate circuitry. The NOR gate also can have any number of inputs.

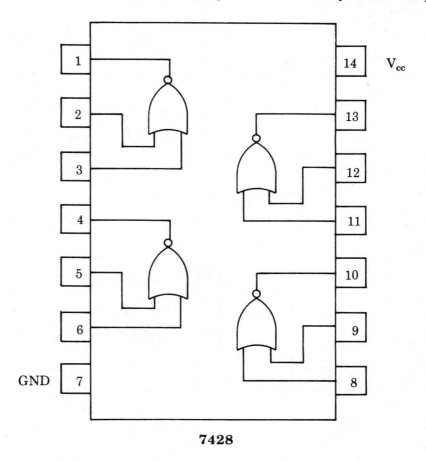

7428

7430 8-Input NAND Gate

The NAND gate is a variation of the conventional AND gate, delivering an inverted (false) output when all inputs are true. The term *NAND* is a contraction of NOT AND. Note that the output is true when any one or all of the inputs are false. Essentially, a NAND gate is the result of using an active inverting element in the gate circuitry. As with a conventional AND gate, the NAND gate can have any number of inputs.

	74S	74H	74	74LS	74L
Typ. Delay Time (ns)	3	6	10	17	33
Typ. Power Per Gate (mW)	19	22	10	2.4	1

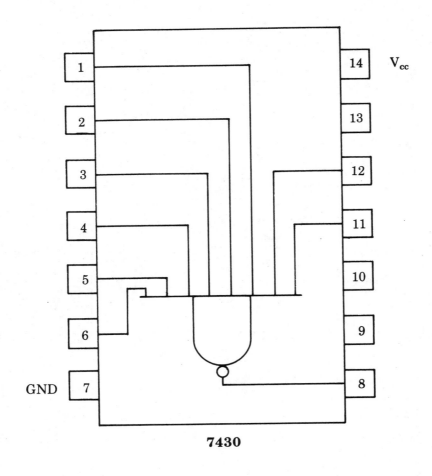

7430

7432 Quad 2-Input OR Gate

Note the symbol for the OR gate. By definition, for C to be true, either input A or input B must be true; hence, the name *OR gate*.

	74
Typ. Delay Time (ns)	12
Typ. Power Per Gate (mW)	24

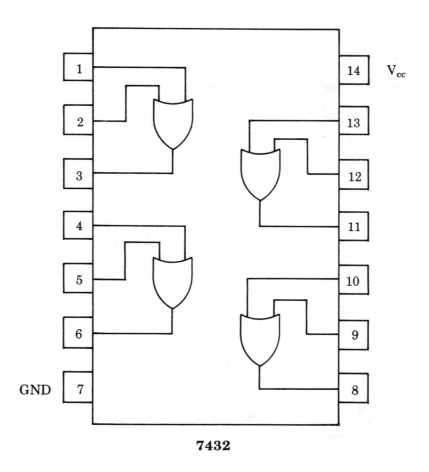

7432

7437 Quad 2-Input NAND Buffer

The NAND gate is a variation of the conventional AND gate, delivering an inverted (false) output when all inputs are true. The term *NAND* is a contraction of NOT AND. Note that the output is true when either or both of the inputs are false. Essentially, a NAND gate is the result of using an active inverting element in the gate circuitry. As with a conventional AND gate, the NAND gate can have any number of inputs.

	74
Low-Level Output Current (mA)	48
High-Level Output Current (mA)	−1.2
Typ. Delay Time (ns)	10.5
Typ. Power Per Gate (mW)	27

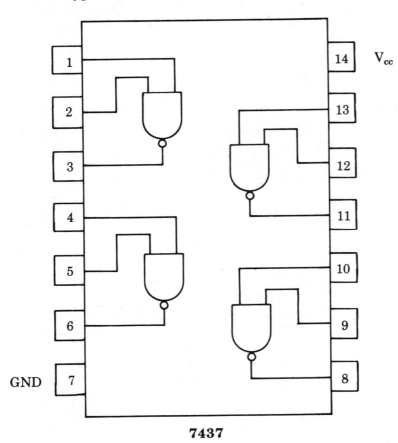

7437

7440 Dual 4-Input NAND Buffer

The NAND gate is a variation of the conventional AND gate, delivering an inverted (false) output when all inputs are true. The term NAND is a contraction of NOT AND. Note that the output is true when either or both of the inputs are false. Essentially, a NAND gate is the result of using an active inverting element in the gate circuitry. As with a conventional AND gate, the NAND gate can have any number of inputs.

	74S	74H	74	74LS
Low-Level Output Current (mA)	60	60	48	24
High-Level Output Current (mA)	−3	−1.5	−1.2	−1.2
Typ. Delay Time (ns)	4	7.5	10.5	12
Typ. Power Per Gate (mW)	44	44	26	4.3

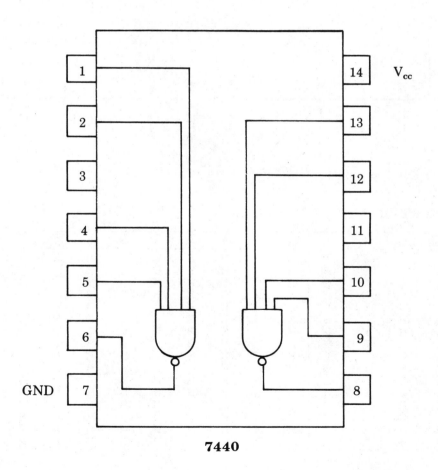

7440

7442 BCD-to-Decimal Decoder

The '42 decoder accepts four active high BCD inputs and provides 10 mutually exclusive active low outputs, as shown by logic symbol. The active low outputs facilitate addressing other MSI units with active low input enables.

The logic design of the '42 ensures that all outputs are high when binary codes greater than nine are applied to the inputs. The most significant input, A_3, produces a useful inhibit function when the '42 is used as a one-or-eight decoder. The A_3 input can also be used as the data input in an 8-output demultiplexer application.

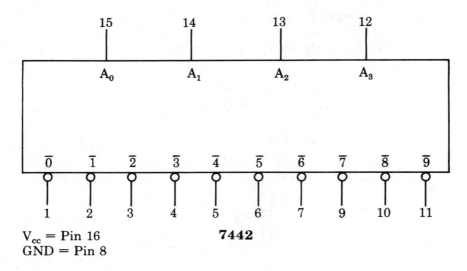

V_{cc} = Pin 16
GND = Pin 8

7442

Truth Table

A_3	A_2	A_1	A_0	$\bar{0}$	$\bar{1}$	$\bar{2}$	$\bar{3}$	$\bar{4}$	$\bar{5}$	$\bar{6}$	$\bar{7}$	$\bar{8}$	$\bar{9}$
L	L	L	L	L	H	H	H	H	H	H	H	H	H
L	L	L	H	H	L	H	H	H	H	H	H	H	H
L	L	H	L	H	H	L	H	H	H	H	H	H	H
L	L	H	H	H	H	H	L	H	H	H	H	H	H
L	H	L	L	H	H	H	H	L	H	H	H	H	H
L	H	L	H	H	H	H	H	H	L	H	H	H	H
L	H	H	L	H	H	H	H	H	H	L	H	H	H
L	H	H	H	H	H	H	H	H	H	H	L	H	H
H	L	L	L	H	H	H	H	H	H	H	H	L	H
H	L	L	H	H	H	H	H	H	H	H	H	H	L
H	L	H	L	H	H	H	H	H	H	H	H	H	H
H	L	H	H	H	H	H	H	H	H	H	H	H	H
H	H	L	L	H	H	H	H	H	H	H	H	H	H
H	H	L	H	H	H	H	H	H	H	H	H	H	H
H	H	H	L	H	H	H	H	H	H	H	H	H	H
H	H	H	H	H	H	H	H	H	H	H	H	H	H

7442

7445 BCD-to-Decimal Decoder/Driver (O.C.)

The '45 decoder accepts BCD on the A_0 to A_3 address lines and generates 10 mutually exclusive active low outputs. When an input code greater than nine is applied, all outputs are off. This device can therefore be used as a 1-of-8 decoder with A_3 used as an active low enable.

The '45 can sink 20 mA while maintaining the standardized guaranteed output low voltage (V_{OL}) of 0.4 V, but it can sink up to 80 mA with a guaranteed V_{OL} of less than 0.9 V. The '45 features an output breakdown voltage of 30 V and is ideally suited as a lamp and solenoid driver.

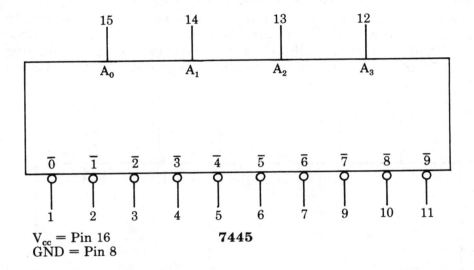

V_{cc} = Pin 16
GND = Pin 8

7445

Truth Table

A_3	A_2	A_1	A_0	$\overline{0}$	$\overline{1}$	$\overline{2}$	$\overline{3}$	$\overline{4}$	$\overline{5}$	$\overline{6}$	$\overline{7}$	$\overline{8}$	$\overline{9}$
L	L	L	L	L	H	H	H	H	H	H	H	H	H
L	L	L	H	H	L	H	H	H	H	H	H	H	H
L	L	H	L	H	H	L	H	H	H	H	H	H	H
L	L	H	H	H	H	H	L	H	H	H	H	H	H
L	H	L	L	H	H	H	H	L	H	H	H	H	H
L	H	L	H	H	H	H	H	H	L	H	H	H	H
L	H	H	L	H	H	H	H	H	H	L	H	H	H
L	H	H	H	H	H	H	H	H	H	H	L	H	H
H	L	L	L	H	H	H	H	H	H	H	H	L	H
H	L	L	H	H	H	H	H	H	H	H	H	H	L
H	L	H	L	H	H	H	H	H	H	H	H	H	H
H	L	H	H	H	H	H	H	H	H	H	H	H	H
H	H	L	L	H	H	H	H	H	H	H	H	H	H
H	H	L	H	H	H	H	H	H	H	H	H	H	H
H	H	H	L	H	H	H	H	H	H	H	H	H	H
H	H	H	H	H	H	H	H	H	H	H	H	H	H

7445

7446A, 7447A BCD-to-7-Segment Decoder/Driver

The '46A and '47A 7-segment decoders accept a 4-bit BCD code input and produce the appropriate outputs for selection of segments in a 7-segment matrix display used for representing the decimal numbers 0 through 9. The 7 outputs, ($\bar{a}$, $\bar{b}$, $\bar{c}$, $\bar{d}$, $\bar{e}$, $\bar{f}$, $\bar{g}$) of the decoder select the corresponding segments in the matrix as shown.

The '46A and '47A have provisions for automatic blanking of the leading and/or trailing edge zeroes in a multidigit decimal number, resulting in an easily readable decimal display conforming to normal writing practice. In an 8-digit mixed integer fraction decimal representation, using the automatic blanking capability, 0070.0500 would be displayed as 70.05. Leading-edge zero suppression is obtained by connecting the ripple blanking output ($\overline{BI/RBO}$) of a decoder to the ripple blanking input ($\overline{RBI}$) of the next lower stage device. The most significant decoder stage should have the $\overline{RBI}$ input grounded, and because sup-

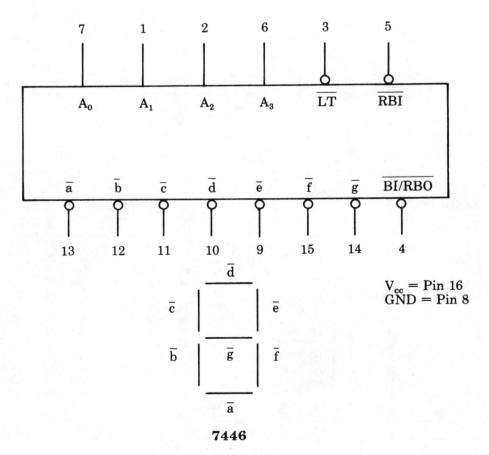

V_{cc} = Pin 16
GND = Pin 8

7446

pression of the least significant integer zero in a number is not usually desired, the $\overline{\text{RBI}}$ input of this decoder stage should be left open. A similar procedure for the fractional part of a display will provide automatic suppression of trailing-edge zeroes.

The decoder has an active low input lamp test which overrides all other input combinations and enables a check to be made on possible display malfunctions. The $\overline{\text{BI}}/\overline{\text{RBO}}$ terminal of the decoder can be OR-tied with a modulating signal via an isolating buffer to achieve pulse duration intensity modulation. A suitable signal can be generated for this purpose by forming a variable frequency multivibrator with a cross-coupled pair of open collector gates.

FUNCTION TABLE

DECIMAL OR FUNCTION	INPUTS							OUTPUTS						
	LT	RBI	A_3	A_2	A_1	A_0	$\overline{\text{BI}/\text{RBO}}^{(b)}$	$\overline{a}$	$\overline{b}$	$\overline{c}$	$\overline{d}$	$\overline{e}$	$\overline{f}$	$\overline{g}$
0	H	H	L	L	L	L	H	L	L	L	L	L	L	H
1	H	X	L	L	L	H	H	H	L	L	H	H	H	H
2	H	X	L	L	H	L	H	L	L	H	L	L	H	L
3	H	X	L	L	H	H	H	L	L	L	L	H	H	L
4	H	X	L	H	L	L	H	H	L	L	H	H	L	L
5	H	X	L	H	L	H	H	L	H	L	L	H	L	L
6	H	X	L	H	H	L	H	H	H	L	L	L	L	L
7	H	X	L	H	H	H	H	L	L	L	H	H	H	H
8	H	X	H	L	L	L	H	L	L	L	L	L	L	L
9	H	X	H	L	L	H	H	L	L	L	H	H	L	L
10	H	X	H	L	H	L	H	H	H	H	L	L	H	L
11	H	X	H	L	H	H	H	H	H	L	L	H	H	L
12	H	X	H	H	L	L	H	H	L	H	H	H	L	L
13	H	X	H	H	L	H	H	L	H	H	L	H	L	L
14	H	X	H	H	H	L	H	H	H	H	L	L	L	L
15	H	X	H	H	H	H	H	H	H	H	H	H	H	H
$\overline{\text{BI}}^{(b)}$	X	X	X	X	X	X	L	H	H	H	H	H	H	H
$\overline{\text{RBI}}^{(b)}$	H	L	L	L	L	L	L	H	H	H	H	H	H	H
$\overline{\text{LT}}$	L	X	X	X	X	X	H	L	L	L	L	L	L	L

H = High voltage level
L = Low voltage level
X = Don't care

7447

7448 BCD-to-7-Segment Decoder

The '48 7-segment decoder accepts a 4-bit BCD code input and produces the appropriate outputs for selection of segments in a 7-segment matrix display used for representing the decimal numbers 0 through 9. The seven outputs (a,b,c, d,e,f,g) of the decoder select the corresponding segments in the matrix.

The decoder has active high outputs so a buffer transistor may be used directly to provide the high currents required for multiplexed LED displays. If additional base drive current is required external resistors may be added from the supply voltage to the 7-segment outputs of the decoders. The value of this resistor is constrained by the 6.4-mA current sinking capability of the output transistors of the circuit.

The '48 has provision for automatic blanking of the leading and/or trailing-edge zeroes in a multidigit decimal number, resulting in an easily readable decimal display conforming to normal writing practice. In an eight-digit mixed integer fraction decimal representation, using the automatic blanking capability, 0060.0300 would be displayed as 60.03. Leading-edge zero suppression is obtained by connecting the ripple blanking output ($\overline{\text{BI}}/\overline{\text{RBO}}$) of a decoder to the ripple blanking input ($\overline{\text{RBI}}$) of the next lower stage device. The most significant decoder stage should have the $\overline{\text{RBI}}$ input grounded, and because suppression of the least significant integer zero in a number is not usually desired, the $\overline{\text{RBI}}$ input of this decoder stage should be left open. A similar procedure for the fractional part of a display will provide automatic suppression of trailing-edge zeroes.

The decoder has an active low input lamp test which overrides all other input combinations and enables a check to be made on possible display malfunctions. The $\overline{\text{BI}}/\overline{\text{RBO}}$ terminal of the decoder can be OR-tied with a modulating signal via an isolating buffer to achieve pulse duration intensity modulation. A suitable signal can be generated for this purpose by forming a variable frequency multivibrator with a cross-coupled pair of open collector gates.

7451 Dual 2-Wide 2-Input AND/OR/Invert Gate

The symbol for the AND gate is shown here. By definition, for output C to be true, inputs A and B must be true; hence, the term *AND gate* .

Note symbol for the OR gate. By definition, for C to be true either input A or input B must be true, hence the name *OR gate*.

As logic elements are combined in series to perform logic functions, voltage levels tend to degrade. Thus, amplifiers are sometimes needed to restore voltages or currents to proper levels. Assuming no inversion is encountered, a true input will produce a true output, and a false input will produce a false output. When inversion occurs, an inversion circle is placed at the output, and the symbol is usually termed an *inverter*.

	74S	74H	74	74LS	74L
Typ. Delay Time (ns)	3.5	6.5	10.5	12.5	43
Typ. Power Per Gate (mW)	28	29	14	2.75	1.5

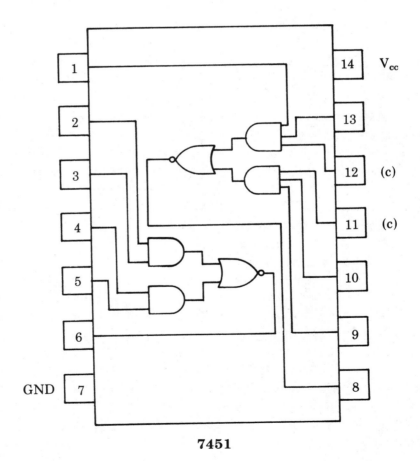

7451

7453 Expandable 4-Wide 2-Input AND/OR/Invert Gate

The symbol for the AND gate is shown here. By definition, for output C to be true, inputs A and B must be true; hence, the term *AND gate* .

Note symbol for the OR gate. By definition, for C to be true either input A or input B must be true, hence the name *OR gate*.

As logic elements are combined in series to perform logic functions, voltage levels tend to degrade. Thus, amplifiers are sometimes needed to restore voltages or currents to proper levels. Assuming no inversion is encountered, a true input will produce a true output, and a false input will produce a false output. When inversion occurs, an inversion circle is placed at the output, and the symbol is usually termed an *inverter*.

	74H	74
Typ. Delay Time (ns)	6.6	10.5
Typ. Power Per Gate (mW)	41	23

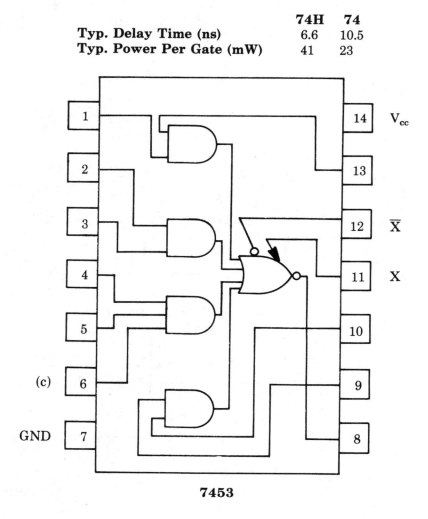

7453

42

7454 4-Wide 2- & 3-Input AND/OR/Invert Gate

The symbol for the AND gate is shown here. By definition, for the output (C) to be true, both inputs (A and B) must be true; hence, the term *AND gate*.

Note also the symbol for the OR gate. By definition, for the output (C) to be true, either input A or input B must be true; hence, the name *OR gate*.

The output of the OR gate is inverted (indicated by the small circle), so C becomes $\overline{C}$ (Not C); hence the term *invert gate*, or *inverter*.

As logic elements are combined in series to perform logic functions, voltage levels tend to degrade. Thus, amplifiers (or buffers) are sometimes needed to restore voltages or currents to their proper levels. Assuming no inversion is encountered, a true input will produce a true output, and a false input will produce a false output. When inversion occurs, an inversion circle is placed at the output, and the symbol is usually termed an *inverter*.

	74H	74	74LS	74L
Typ. Delay Time (ns)	6.5	10.5	12.5	43
Typ. Power Per Gate (mW)	41	23	4.5	1.5

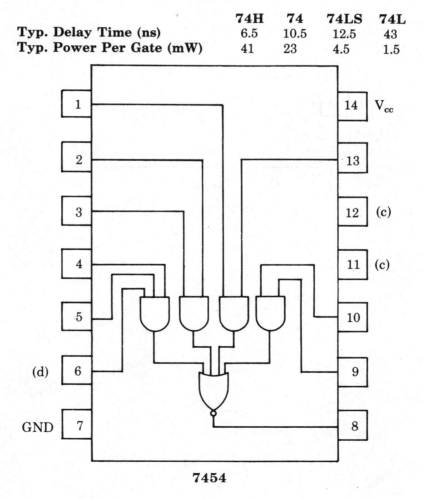

7454

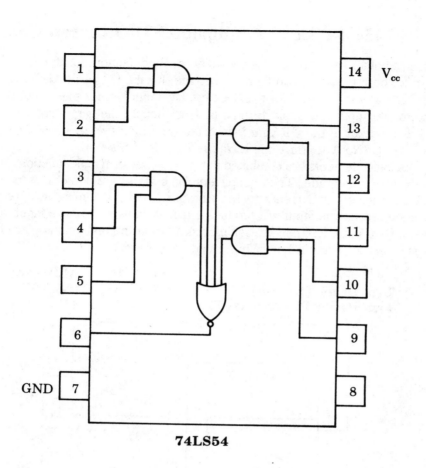

74LS54

7455 Expandable 2-Wide 4-Input AND/OR/Invert Gate

The symbol for the AND gate is shown here. By definition, for output C to be true, inputs A and B must be true; hence, the term *AND gate*.

Note symbol for the OR gate. By definition, for C to be true either input A or input B must be true, hence the name *OR gate*.

As logic elements are combined in series to perform logic functions, voltage levels tend to degrade. Thus, amplifiers are sometimes needed to restore voltages or currents to proper levels. Assuming no inversion is encountered, a true input will produce a true output, false input will produce a false output. When inversion occurs, an inversion circle is placed at the output, and the symbol is usually termed an *inverter*.

	74H	74LS (Not Expandable)
Typ. Delay Time (ns)	6.8	12.5
Typ. Power Per Gate (mW)	30	2.75

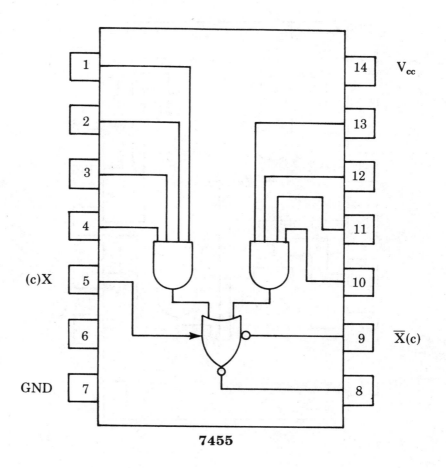

7455

7464 4-2-32-Input AND/OR/Invert Gate

The symbol for the AND gate is shown here. By definition, for output C to be true, inputs A and B must be true; hence, the term *AND gate*.

Note symbol for the OR gate. By definition, for C to be true either input A or input B must be true; hence, the name *OR gate*.

As logic elements are combined in series to perform logic functions, voltage levels tend to degrade. Thus, amplifiers are sometimes needed to restore voltages or currents to proper levels. Assuming no inversion is encountered, a true input will produce a true output, and a false input will produce a false output. When inversion occurs, an inversion circle is placed at the output, and the symbol is usually termed an *inverter*.

	74S	74H	74	74LS	74L
Typ. Delay Time (ns)	3.5	6.6	10.5	12.5	43
Typ. Power Per Gate (mW)	29	41	23	4.5	1.5

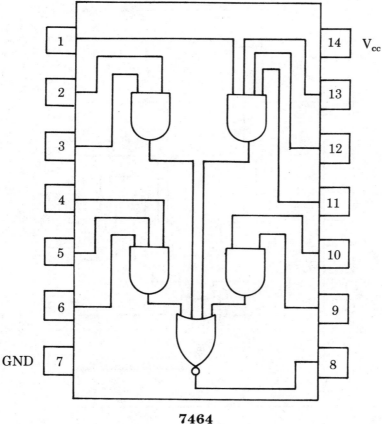

7464

7465 4-2-32 Input AND/OR/Invert Gate (O.C.)

	74S
Typ. Delay Time (ns)	5.5
Typ. Power Per Gate (mW)	36

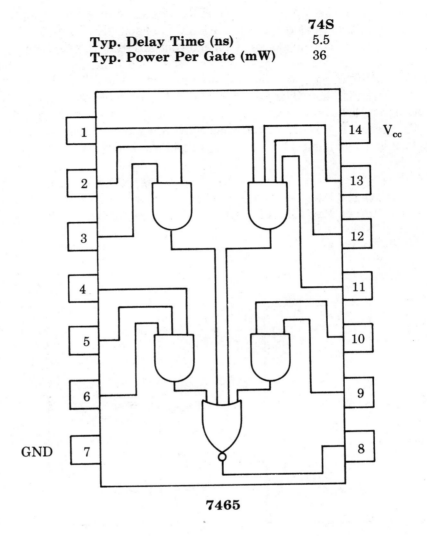

7465

7473 Dual JK Flip-Flop

The '73 is a dual flip-flop with individual JK, clock and direct reset inputs. The 7473 and 74H73 are positive pulse-triggered flip-flops. JK information is loaded into the master while the clock is high and transferred to the slave on the high-to-low clock transition. For these devices, the J and K inputs should be stable while the clock is high for conventional operation. The 74LS73 is a negative edge-triggered flip-flop. The J and K inputs must be stable one setup time prior to the high-to-low Clock transition for predictable operation.

The Reset ($\overline{R}_D$) is an asynchronous active low input. When low, it overrides the clock and data inputs, forcing the Q output low and the $\overline{Q}$ output high.

	74H	74	74L	74LS
Typ. Max. Clock Frequency (MHz)	30	20	6	45
Typ. Power Per Flip-Flop (mW)	80	50	3.8	10
Setup Time (ns)	0	0	0	20
Hold Time (ns)	0	0	0	0

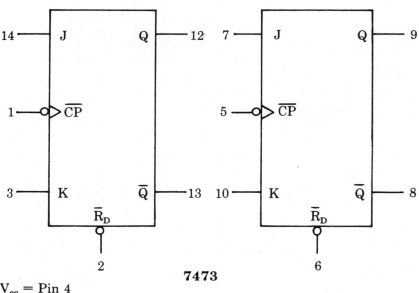

7473

V_{cc} = Pin 4
GND = Pin 11

Truth Table

OPERATING MODE	INPUTS				OUTPUTS	
	$\overline{R_D}$	$\overline{CP}$ (d)	J	K	Q	$\overline{Q}$
Asynchronous Reset (Clear)	L	X	X	X	L	H
Toggle	H	⊓	h	h	$\overline{q}$	q
Load "0" (Reset)	H	⊓	l	h	L	H
Load "1" (Set)	H	⊓	h	l	H	L
Hold "no change"	H	⊓	l	l	q	$\overline{q}$

H   High voltage level steady state
L   Low voltage level steady state
h   High voltage level one setup time prior to the high-to-low clock transition [c]
l   Low voltage level one setup time prior to the high-to-low clock transition [c]
X   Don't care
q   Lower case letters indicate the state of the referenced output prior to the high-to-low clock transition
⊓   Positive clock pulse

7474 Dual D-Type Flip-Flop

The '74 is a dual positive edge-triggered D-type flip-flop featuring individual data, clock, set and reset inputs, and complementary Q and $\overline{Q}$ outputs. Set ($\overline{S}_D$) and reset ($\overline{R}_D$) are asynchronous active low inputs and operate independently of the clock input. Information on the data (D) input is transferred to the Q output on the low-to-high transition of the clock pulse. The D inputs must be stable one setup time prior to the low-to-high clock transition for predictable operation. Although the clock input is level sensitive, the positive transition of the clock pulse between the 0.8 V and 2.0 V levels should be equal to or less than the clock to output delay time for reliable operation.

	74S	74H	74LS	74	74L
Typ. Max. Clock Frequency (MHz)	110	43	33	25	6
Typ. Power Per Flip-Flop (mW)	75	75	10	43	4
Setup Time (ns)	3	15	25	20	50
Hold Time (ns)	2	5	5	5	15

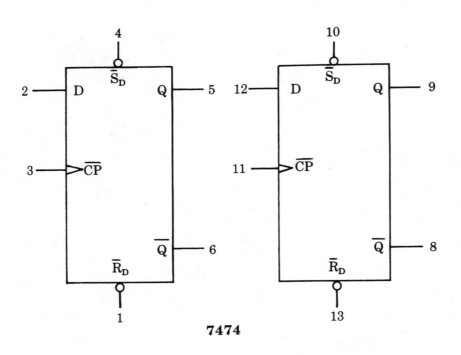

7474

Truth Table

OPERATING MODE	INPUTS				OUTPUTS	
	$\overline{S}_D$	$\overline{R}_D$	$\overline{CP}$	D	Q	$\overline{Q}$
Asynchronous Set	L	H	X	X	H	L
Asynchronous Reset (Clear)	H	L	X	X	L	H
Undetermined (c)	L	L	X	X	H	H
Load "1" (Set)	H	H	↑	h	H	L
Load "0" (Reset)	H	H	↑	l	L	H

H = High voltage level steady state
h = High voltage level one setup time prior to the low-to-high clock transition
L = Low voltage level steady state
l = Low voltage level one setup time prior to the low-to-high clock transition
X = Don't care

7475 Dual 2-Bit Transparent Latch

The '75 has two independent 2-bit transparent latches. Each 2-bit latch is controlled by an active high enable input (E). When E is high, the data enters the latch and appears at the Q output. The Q outputs follow the data inputs as long as E is high. The data (on the D) input one setup time before the high-to-low transition of the enable will be stored in the latch. The latched outputs remain stable as long as the enable is low.

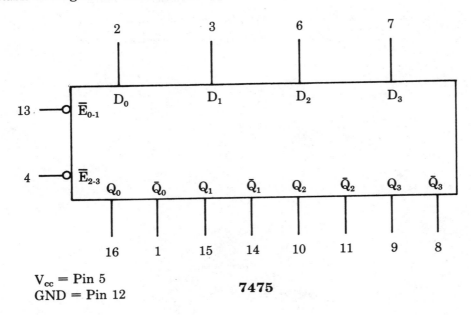

V_{cc} = Pin 5
GND = Pin 12

7475

MODE SELECT—FUNCTION TABLE

OPERATING MODE	INPUTS		OUTPUTS	
	$\overline{E}$	D	Q	$\overline{Q}$
Data Enabled	H	L	L	H
	H	H	H	L
Data Latched	L	X	q	$\overline{q}$

H = High voltage level
L = Low voltage level
X = Don't care
q = Lower case letters indicate the state of referenced output one setup time prior to the high-to-low enable transition.

7476 Dual JK Flip-Flop

The '76 is a dual JK flip-flop with individual J, K, clock, set, and reset inputs. The 7476 and 74H76 are positive pulse-triggered flip-flops. JK information is loaded into the master while the clock is high and transferred to the slave on the high-to-low clock transition. The J and K inputs must be stable while the clock is high for conventional operation.

The 74LS76 is a negative edge-triggered flip-flop. The J and K inputs must be stable only one setup time prior to the high-to-low clock transition. The set ($\overline{S}_D$) and reset ($\overline{R}_D$) are asynchronous active low inputs. When low, they override the clock and data inputs forcing the outputs to the steady state levels, as shown in the truth table.

	74H	74	74LS
Typ. Max. Clock Frequency (MHz)	30	20	45
Typ. Power Per Flip-Flop (mW)	80	50	10
Setup Time (ns)	0	0	20
Hold Time (ns)	0	0	0

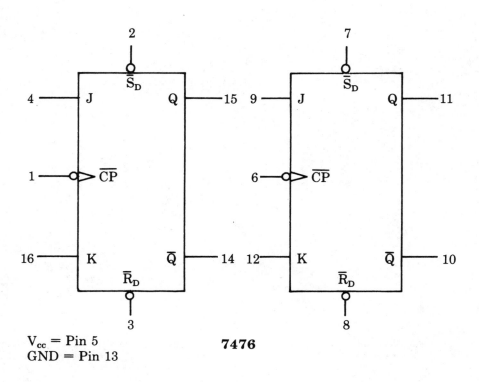

V_{cc} = Pin 5
GND = Pin 13

7476

Truth Table

OPERATING MODE	INPUTS					OUTPUTS	
	$\overline{S}_D$	$\overline{R}_D$	$\overline{CP}$ (d)	J	K	Q	$\overline{Q}$
Asynchronous Set	L	H	X	X	X	H	L
Asynchronous Reset (Clear)	H	L	X	X	X	L	H
Undetermined (c)	L	L	X	X	X	H	H
Toggle	H	H	⊓	h	h	$\overline{q}$	q
Load "0" (Reset)	H	H	⊓	l	h	L	H
Load "1" (Set)	H	H	⊓	h	l	H	L
Hold "no change"	H	H	⊓	l	l	q	$\overline{q}$

H   High voltage level steady state
L   Low voltage level steady state
h   High voltage level one setup time prior to the high-to-low clock transition [c]
l   Low voltage level one setup time prior to the high-to-low clock transition [c]
X   Don't care
q   Lower case letters indicate the state of the referenced output prior to the high-to-low clock transition
⊓   Positive clock pulse

7478 Dual JK Edge-Triggered Flip-Flop

The '78 is a dual JK negative edge-triggered flip-flop featuring individual J, K, set, common-clock, and common-reset inputs. The set ($\overline{S}_D$) and reset ($\overline{R}_D$) inputs, when low, set or reset the outputs as shown in the truth table, regardless of the levels at the other inputs. A high level on the clock ($\overline{CP}$) input enables the J and K inputs and data to be accepted. The logic levels at the J and K inputs can be allowed to change while the $\overline{CP}$ is high and the flip-flop will perform according to the truth table as long as minimum setup and hold times are observed. Output state changes are initiated by the high-to-low transition of $\overline{CP}$.

	74H	74L	74LS
Typ. Max. Clock Frequency (MHz)	30	6	45
Typ. Power Per Flip-Flop (mW)	80	3.8	10
Setup Time (ns)	0	0	20
Hold Time (ns)	0	0	0

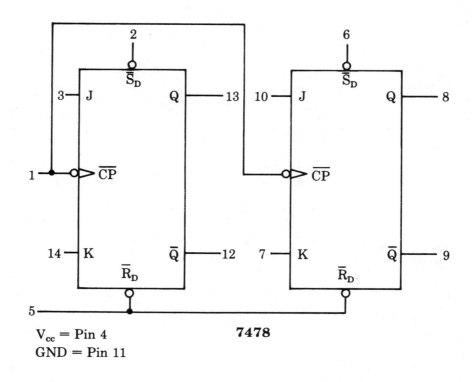

V_{cc} = Pin 4
GND = Pin 11

7478

Truth Table

OPERATING MODE	INPUTS					OUTPUTS	
	$\overline{S}_D$	$\overline{R}_D$	$\overline{CP}$	J	K	Q	$\overline{Q}$
Asynchronous Set	L	H	X	X	X	H	L
Asynchronous Reset (Clear)	H	L	X	X	X	L	H
Undetermined [c]	L	L	X	X	X	H	H
Toggle	H	H	.	h	h	$\overline{q}$	q
Load "0" (Reset)	H	H	.	l	h	L	H
Load "1" (Set)	H	H	.	h	l	H	L
Hold "no change"	H	H	.	l	l	q	$\overline{q}$

H   High voltage level steady state
h   High voltage level one setup time prior to the high-to-low clock transition
L   Low voltage level steady state
l   Low voltage level one setup time prior to the high-to-low clock transition
q   Lower case letters indicate the state of the referenced output prior to the high-to-low clock transition
X   Don't care

7483 4-Bit Full Adder

The '83 is a high-speed 4-bit binary full adder with internal carry lookahead. It accepts two 4-bit binary words (A_1 through A_4, B_1 through B_4) and a carry input (C_{IN}). The sum of the two 4-bit words is combined with the carry input and presented at the four sum outputs (Σ_1 through Σ_4) and the carry output (C_{OUT}). It operates with either high or low operands (positive or negative logic).

Because of the symmetry of the binary add function, the '83 can be used with either all active high operands (positive logic) or with all active low operands (negative logic). With active high inputs, C_{IN} cannot be left open; instead, it must be held low when no carry in is intended. Interchanging the inputs of equal weight does not affect the operation, so C_{IN}, A_1 and B_1 can arbitrarily be assigned to pins 10, 11, 13, etc.

	74LS	74
Typ. Carry Time (ns)	10	10
Typ. Add Time (ns)	15	16
Typ. Power Per Bit (mW)	24	76

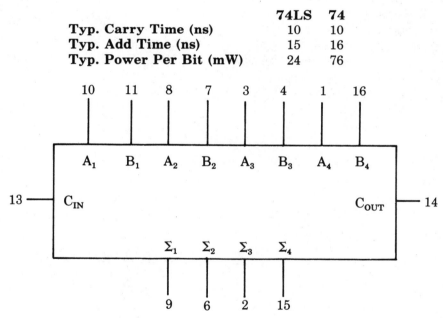

V_{cc} = Pin 5
GND = Pin 12

PINS	C_{IN}	A_1	A_2	A_3	A_4	B_1	B_2	B_3	B_4	Σ_1	Σ_2	Σ_3	Σ_4	C_{OUT}
Logic Levels	L	L	H	L	H	H	L	L	H	H	H	L	L	H
Active high	0	0	1	0	1	1	0	0	1	1	1	0	0	1
Active Low	1	1	0	1	0	0	1	1	0	0	0	1	1	0

(10+9=19)
(carry+5+6=12)

7483

7485 4-Bit Magnitude Comparator

The '85 is a 4-bit magnitude comparator that can be expanded to almost any length. It compares two 4-bit binary, BCD, or other monotonic codes and presents the three possible magnitude results at the outputs. The 4-bit inputs are weighted $(A_0 \rightarrow A_3)$ and $(B_0 \rightarrow B_3)$, where A_3 and B_3 are the most significant bits.

The operation of the '85 is described in the truth table showing all possible logic conditions. The upper part of the table describes the normal operation under all conditions that will occur in a single device or in a series expansion scheme. In the upper part of the table, the three outputs are mutually exclusive. In the lower part of the table, the outputs reflect the feed-forward conditions that exist in the parallel expansion scheme.

The expansion inputs $1_{A>B}$, $1_{A=B}$ and $1_{A<B}$ are the least significant bit positions. When used for series expansion, the $A>B$, $A=B$, and $A<B$ outputs of the least significant word are connected to the corresponding $1_{A>B}$, $1_{A=B}$ and $1_{A<B}$ inputs of the next higher stage. Stages can be added in this manner to any length, but a propagation delay penalty of about 15 ns is added with each additional stage. For proper operation, the expansion inputs of the least significant word should be tied as follows: $1_{A>B}$ = high, $1_{A=B}$ = low and $1_{A<B}$ = high.

	74	74L
Typ. Compare Time (ns)	21	70
Typ. Total Power (mW)	275	20

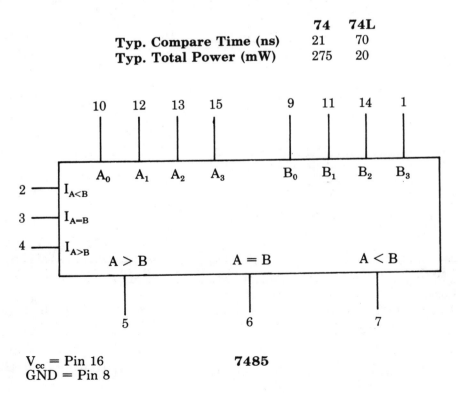

V_{cc} = Pin 16
GND = Pin 8

7485

The parallel expansion scheme demonstrates the most efficient general use of these comparators. In the parallel expansion scheme, the expansion inputs can be used as a fifth input bit position except on the least significant device which must be connected as in the serial scheme. The expansion inputs are used by labeling $1_{A>B}$ as an A input, $1_{A<B}$ as a B input and setting $1_{A=B}$ low. The '85 can be used as a 5-bit comparator only when the outputs are used to drive the (A_0 through A_3) and (B_0 through B_3) inputs of another '85 device. The parallel technique can be expanded to any number of bits as shown in the table.

Truth Table

COMPARING INPUTS				CASCADING INPUTS			OUTPUTS		
A_3,B_3	A_2,B_2	A_1,B_1	A_0,B_0	$I_{A>B}$	$I_{A<B}$	$I_{A=B}$	$A>B$	$A<B$	$A=B$
$A_3>B_3$	X	X	X	X	X	X	H	L	L
$A_3<B_3$	X	X	X	X	X	X	L	H	L
$A_3=B_3$	$A_2>B_2$	X	X	X	X	X	H	L	L
$A_3=B_3$	$A_2<B_2$	X	X	X	X	X	L	H	L
$A_3=B_3$	$A_2=B_2$	$A_1>B_1$	X	X	X	X	H	L	L
$A_3=B_3$	$A_2=B_2$	$A_1<B_1$	X	X	X	X	L	H	L
$A_3=B_3$	$A_2=B_2$	$A_1=B_1$	$A_0>B_0$	X	X	X	H	L	L
$A_3=B_3$	$A_2=B_2$	$A_1=B_1$	$A_0<B_0$	X	X	X	L	H	L
$A_3=B_3$	$A_2=B_2$	$A_1=B_1$	$A_0=B_0$	H	L	L	H	L	L
$A_3=B_3$	$A_2=B_2$	$A_1=B_1$	$A_0=B_0$	L	H	L	L	H	L
$A_3=B_3$	$A_2=B_2$	$A_1=B_1$	$A_0=B_0$	L	L	H	L	L	H
$A_3=B_3$	$A_2=B_2$	$A_1=B_1$	$A_0=B_0$	X	X	H	L	L	H
$A_3=B_3$	$A_2=B_2$	$A_1=B_1$	$A_0=B_0$	H	H	L	L	L	L
$A_3=B_3$	$A_2=B_2$	$A_1=B_1$	$A_0=B_0$	L	L	L	H	H	L

H = High voltage level
L = Low voltage level
X = Don't care

7485

7486 Quad 2-Input Exclusive-OR Gate

In an ordinary OR gate, the output (C) is high if either input (A or B) is high, *or* if both inputs (A and B) are high.

An exclusive-OR gate, such as the '86 is a variation on the basic OR gate. In the exclusive-OR gate, the output (C) is high if either input (A or B) is high, but the output (C) is low if both inputs are high, or if both inputs are low.

The exclusive-OR gate could be considered a *difference detector*, or a one-bit digital comparator.

	74S	74LS	74	74L
Typ. Delay Time (ns)	7	10	14	29
Typ. Total Power (mW)	250	30	150	15

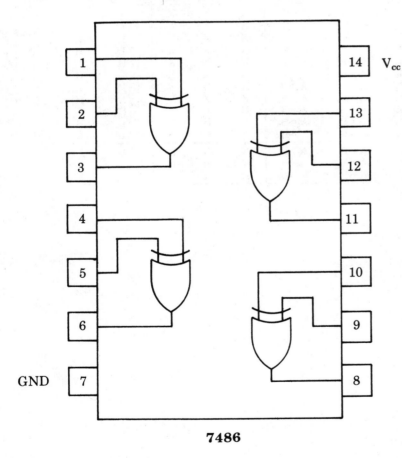

7486

Truth Table

INPUTS		OUTPUT
A	**B**	**Y**
L	L	L
L	H	H
H	L	H
H	H	L

L = Low voltage level
H = High voltage level

7489 64-Bit Random-Access Memory (O.C.)

The '89 is a high-speed array of 64 memory cells organized as 16 words of 4 bits each. A 1-of-16 address decoder selects a single word which is specified by the four address inputs (A_0 through A_3). A READ operation is initiated after the address lines are stable when the write-enable ($\overline{WE}$) input is high and the chip select-memory enable ($\overline{CS}$) input is low. Data is read at the outputs inverted from the data that were written into the memory.

A WRITE operation requires that the $\overline{WE}$ and $\overline{CS}$ inputs are low. The address inputs must be stable during the WRITE mode for predictable operation. When the write mode is selected, the outputs are the complement of the data inputs. The selected memory cells are transparent to changes in the data during the WRITE mode. Therefore, data must be stable one setup time before the low-to-high transition of $\overline{CE}$ or $\overline{WE}$.

	74
Read Time (ns)	33
Write Time (ns)	48
Current Per Package (mA)	75

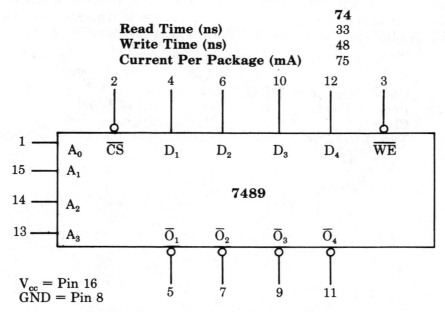

V_{cc} = Pin 16
GND = Pin 8

MODE SELECT — FUNCTION TABLE

OPERATING MODE	INPUTS		OUTPUTS	
	$\overline{CS}$	$\overline{WE}$	D_n	$\overline{O}_n$
Write	L	L	L	H
	L	L	H	L
Read	L	H	X	$\overline{Data}$
Inhibit Writing	H	L	L	H
	H	L	H	L
Store-Disable Outputs	H	H	X	H

7490 Decade Counter

The '90 is a 4-bit ripple-type decade counter. The device consists of four master-slave flip-flops internally connected to provide a divide-by-2 section and a divide-by-5 section. Each section has a separate clock input to initiate stage changes of the counter on the high-to-low clock transition. State changes of the Q outputs do not occur simultaneously because of internal ripple delays. Therefore, decoded output signals are subject to decoding spikes and should not be used for clocks or strobes. The Q_0 output is designed and specified to drive the rate fan-out plus the $\overline{CP}_1$ input of the device.

A gated AND asynchronous master reset ($MR_1 \bullet MR_2$) is provided, which overrides both clock and resets (clears) all the flip-flops. Also provided is a gated AND asynchronous master set ($MS_1 \bullet MS_2$) which overrides the clocks and the MR inputs, setting the outputs to nine (HLLH).

Because the output from the divide-by-two section is not internally connected to the succeeding stages, the device can be operated in various counting modes. In a BCD (8421) counter, the $\overline{CP}_1$ input must be externally connected to

	74LS	74	74L
Count Frequency (MHz)	32	32	6
Parallel Load	set to 9	set to 9	set to 9
Clear	High	High	High
Typ. Total Power (mW)	40	160	20

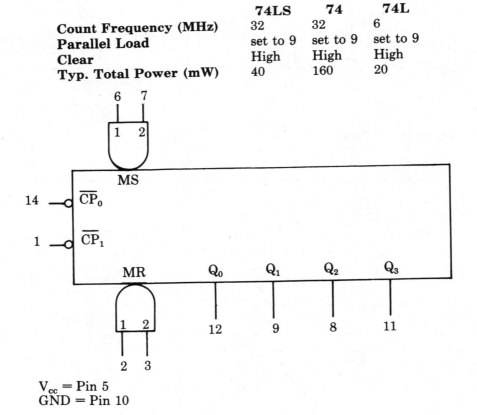

V_{cc} = Pin 5
GND = Pin 10

62

the Q_0 output. The CP_0 input receives the incoming count, producing a BCD count sequence. In a symmetrical BIquinary divide-by-10 counter, the Q_3 output must be connected externally to the $\overline{CP}_0$ input. The input count is then applied to the $\overline{CP}_1$ input, and a divide-by-10 square wave is obtained at output Q_0. To operate as a divide-by-2 and a divide-by-5 counter, no external interconnections are required. The first flip-flop is used as a binary element for the divide-by-2 function ($\overline{CP}_0$ as the input and Q_0 as the output). The $\overline{CP}_1$ input is used to obtain divide-by-5 operation at the Q_3 output.

Truth Table

COUNT	OUTPUT			
	Q_0	Q_1	Q_2	Q_3
0	L	L	L	L
1	H	L	L	L
2	L	H	L	L
3	H	H	L	L
4	L	L	H	L
5	H	L	H	L
6	L	H	H	L
7	H	H	H	L
8	L	L	L	H
9	H	L	L	H

NOTE: Output Q_0 connected to Input $\overline{CP}_1$

Truth Table

RESET/SET INPUTS				OUTPUTS			
MR_1	MR_2	MS_1	MS_2	Q_0	Q_1	Q_2	Q_3
H	H	L	X	L	L	L	L
H	H	X	L	L	L	L	L
X	X	H	H	H	L	L	H
L	X	L	X			Count	
X	L	X	L			Count	
L	X	X	L			Count	
X	L	L	X			Count	

H = High voltage level
L = Low voltage level
X = Don't care

7490

7492 Divide-by-12 Counter

The '92 is a 4-bit ripple-type divide-by-12 counter. The device consists of four master-slave flip-flops internally connected to provide a divide-by-2 section and a divide-by-6 section. Each section has a separate clock input to initiate state changes of the counter on the high-to-low clock transition. State changes of the Q outputs do not occur simultaneously because of internal ripple delays. Therefore, decoded output signals are subject to decoding spikes and should not be used for clocks or strobes. The Q_0 output is designed and specified to drive the rated fanout plus the $\overline{CP}_1$ input of the device. A gated AND asynchronous master reset ($MR_1 \cdot MR_2$) is provided which overrides both clocks and resets (clears) all the flip-flops.

Because the output from the divide-by-2 section is not internally connected to the succeeding stages, the device can be operated in various counting modes. In a modulo-12, divide-by-12 counter, the $\overline{CP}_1$ input must be externally connected to Q_0 output. The $\overline{CP}_0$ input receives the incoming count, and Q_3 produces a symmetrical divide-by-12 square-wave output. In a divide-by-6 counter, no external connections are required. The first flip-flop is used as a binary element for the divide-by-2 function. The $\overline{CP}_1$ input is used to obtain divide-by-3 operation at the Q_1 and Q_2 outputs and divide-by-6 operation at the Q_3 output.

	74LS	74
Count Frequency (MHz)	32	32
Parallel Lead	None	None
Clear	High	High
Typ. Total Power (mW)	39	160

V_{cc} = Pin 5
GND = Pin 10

7492

MODE SELECTION

RESET INPUTS		OUTPUTS			
MR$_1$	MR$_2$	Q$_0$	Q$_1$	Q$_2$	Q$_3$
H	H	L	L	L	L
L	H		Count		
H	L		Count		
L	L		Count		

H = High voltage level
L = Low voltage level
X = Don't care

Truth Table

COUNT	OUTPUT			
	Q$_0$	Q$_1$	Q$_2$	Q$_3$
0	L	L	L	L
1	H	L	L	L
2	L	H	L	L
3	H	H	L	L
4	L	L	H	L
5	H	L	H	L
6	L	L	L	H
7	H	L	L	H
8	L	H	L	H
9	H	H	L	H
10	L	L	H	H
11	H	L	H	H

NOTE: Output Q$_0$ connected to Input $\overline{\overline{CP}}_1$

7493 4-Bit Binary Ripple Counter

The '93 is a 4-bit ripple-type binary counter. The device consists of four master-slave flip-flops internally connected to provide a divide-by-2 section and a divide-by-8 section. Each section has a separate clock input to initiate state changes of the counter on the high-to-low clock transition. State changes of the Q outputs do not occur simultaneously because of internal ripple delays. Therefore, decoded output signals are subject to decoding spikes and should not be used for clocks or strobes. The Q_0 output is designed and specified to drive the rated fanout plus the $\overline{CP}_1$ input of the device. A gated AND asynchronous master reset ($MR_1 \cdot MR_2$) is provided, which overrides both clocks and resets (clears) all the flip-flops.

Since the output from the divide-by-2 section is not internally connected to the succeeding stages, the device can be operated in various counting modes. In a 4-bit ripple counter, the output Q_0 must be connected externally to input $\overline{CP}_1$. The input count pulses are applied to input $\overline{CP}_0$. Simultaneous divisions of 2, 4, 8, and 16 are performed at the Q_0, Q_1, Q_2, and Q_3 outputs, as shown in the truth table. As a 3-bit ripple counter, the input count pulses are applied to input $\overline{CP}_1$. Simultaneous frequency divisions of 2, 4, and 8 are available at the Q_1, Q_2, and Q_3 outputs. Independent use of the first flip-flop is available if the reset function coincides with the reset of the 3-bit ripple-through counter.

	74LS	74	74L
Count Frequency (MHz)	32	32	6
Parallel Load	None	None	None
Clear	High	High	High
Typ. Total Power (mW)	39	160	20

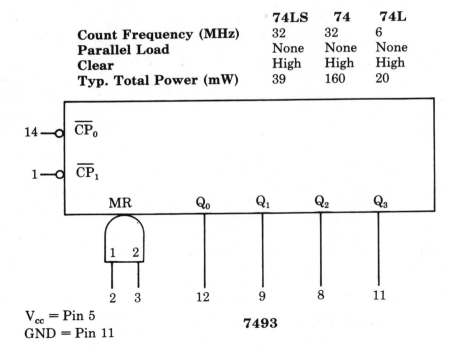

V_{cc} = Pin 5
GND = Pin 11

7493

MODE SELECTION

RESET INPUTS		OUTPUTS			
MR$_1$	MR$_2$	Q$_0$	Q$_1$	Q$_2$	Q$_3$
H	H	L	L	L	L
L	H		Count		
H	L		Count		
L	L		Count		

H = High voltage level
L = Low voltage level
X = Don't care

Truth Table

COUNT	OUTPUT			
	Q$_0$	Q$_1$	Q$_2$	Q$_3$
0	L	L	L	L
1	H	L	L	L
2	L	H	L	L
3	H	H	L	L
4	L	L	H	L
5	H	L	H	L
6	L	H	H	L
7	H	H	H	L
8	L	L	L	H
9	H	L	L	H
10	L	H	L	H
11	H	H	L	H
12	L	L	H	H
13	H	L	H	H
14	L	H	H	H
15	H	H	H	H

NOTE: Output Q$_0$ connected to Input $\overline{CP_1}$.

7495 4-Bit Shift Register

The '95 is a 4-bit shift register with serial and parallel synchronous operation modes. It has a serial data (D_S) and four parallel data (D_0 through D_3) inputs and four parallel outputs (Q_0 through Q_3). The serial or parallel mode of operation is controlled by a mode select input (S) and two clock inputs ($\overline{CP}_1$ and $\overline{CP}_2$). The serial (shift right) or parallel data transfers occur synchronously with the high-to-low transition of the selected clock input.

When the mode select input (S) is high, $\overline{CP}_2$ is enabled. A high-to-low transition on enabled $\overline{CP}_2$ loads parallel data from the D_0 through D_3 inputs into the register. When S is low, $\overline{CP}_1$ is enabled. A high-to-low transition on enabled $\overline{CP}_1$ shifts the data from serial input D_S to Q_0 and transfers the data in Q_0 to Q_1, Q_1 to Q_2, and Q_2 to Q_3, respectively (shift right). Shift left is accomplished by externally connecting Q_3 to D_2, Q_2 to D_1, Q_1 to D_0, and operating the '95 in the parallel mode (S = high).

In normal operations the mode select should change states only when both clock inputs are low. However, changing S from high-to-low while $\overline{CP}_2$ is low, or changing S from low-to-high while $\overline{CP}_1$ is low will not cause any changes on the register outputs.

	74	74LS	74L
Shift Frequency (MHz)	25	25	6
Serial Data Input	D	D	D
Asynchronous Clear	None	None	None
Shift-Right Mode	Yes	Yes	Yes
Shift-Left Mode	No	No	No
Lead Mode	Yes	Yes	Yes
Hold Mode	No	No	No
Typ. Total Power (mW)	195	65	24

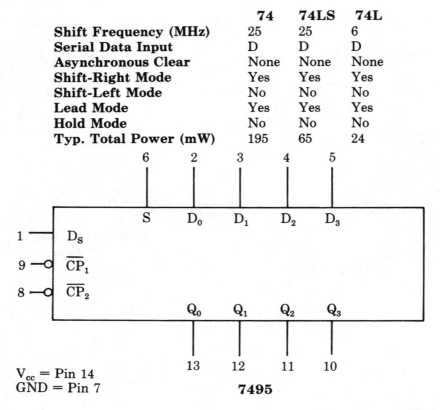

V_{cc} = Pin 14
GND = Pin 7

7495

MODE SELECT — FUNCTION TABLE

OPERATING MODE	INPUTS					OUTPUTS			
	S	$\overline{CP}_1$	$\overline{CP}_2$	D_s	D_n	Q_0	Q_1	Q_2	Q_3
Parallel Load	H	X	↓	X	l	L	L	L	L
	H	X	↓	X	h	H	H	H	H
Shift right	L	↓	X	l	X	L	q_0	q_1	q_2
	L	↓	X	h	X	H	q_0	q_1	q_2
Mode change	↑	L	X	X	X	no change			
	↑	H	X	X	X	undetermined			
	↓	X	L	X	X	no change			
	↓	X	H	X	X	undetermined			

H = High voltage level steady state.
L = Low voltage level steady state.
h = High voltage level one setup time prior to the high-to-low clock transition.
l = Low voltage level one setup time prior to the high-to-low clock transition.
X = Don't care.
q = Lower case letters indicate the state of the referenced output prior to the high-to-low clock transition.
↓ = High-to-low transition of clock or mode Select.
↑ = Low-to-high transition of mode Select.

74107 Dual JK Flip-Flop

The '107 is a dual flip-flop with individual JK, clock, and direct reset inputs. The 74107 is a positive pulse-triggered flip-flop. JK information is loaded into the master while the clock is high and transferred to the slave on the high-to-low clock transition. For these devices, the J and K inputs should be stable while the clock is high for conventional operation.

The 74LS107 is a negative edge-triggered flip-flop. The J and K inputs must be stable one setup time prior to the high-to-low clock transition for predictable operation. The reset ($\overline{R}_D$ is an asynchronous active low input. When low, it overrides the clock and data inputs, forcing the Q output low and the $\overline{Q}$ output high.

	74LS
Typ. Max. Clock Frequency (MHz)	45
Typ. Power Per Flip-Flop (mW)	10
Setup Time (ns)	20
Hold Time (ns)	0

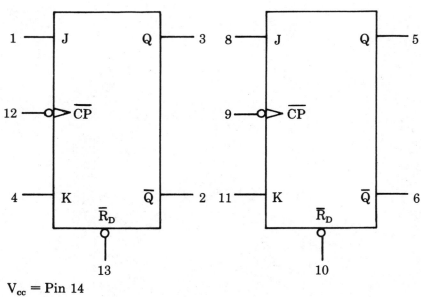

V_{cc} = Pin 14
GND = Pin 7

74107

MODE SELECT — TRUTH TABLE

OPERATING MODE	INPUTS				OUTPUTS	
	$\overline{R_D}$	$\overline{CP}$ (d)	J	K	Q	$\overline{Q}$
Asynchronous Reset (Clear)	L	X	X	X	L	H
Toggle	H	⊓	h	h	$\overline{q}$	q
Load "0" (Reset)	H	⊓	l	h	L	H
Load "1" (Set)	H	⊓	h	l	H	L
Hold "no change"	H	⊓	l	l	q	$\overline{q}$

H = High voltage level steady state.
L = Low voltage level steady state.
h = High voltage level one setup time prior to the high-to-low clock transition[c].
l = Low voltage level one setup time prior to the high-to-low clock transition[c].
X = Don't care.
q = Lower case letters indicate the state of the referenced output prior to high-to-low clock transition.
⊓ = Positive clock pulse.

74109 Dual JK̄ Positive Edge-Triggered Flip-Flop

The '109 is a dual positive edge-triggered JK̄-type flip-flop that features individual J, K, clock, set, and reset inputs and also complementary Q and Q̄ outputs. Set ($\overline{S}_D$) and reset ($\overline{R}_D$) are asynchronous active low inputs and operate independently of the clock input.

The J and K̄ are edge-triggered inputs that control the state changes of the flip-flops as described in the mode-select truth table. The J and K̄ inputs must be stable just one setup time prior to the low-to-high transition of the clock for predictable operation. The JK̄ design allows operation as a D flip-flop by tying the J and K̄ inputs together.

Although the clock input is level-sensitive, the positive transition of the clock pulse between the 0.8 V and 2.0 V levels should be equal to or less than the clock-to-output delay time for reliable operation.

	74LS	74
Typ. Max. Clock Frequency (MHz)	33	33
Typ. Power Per Flip-Flop (mW)	10	45
Setup Time (ns)	20	10
Hold Time (ns)	5	6

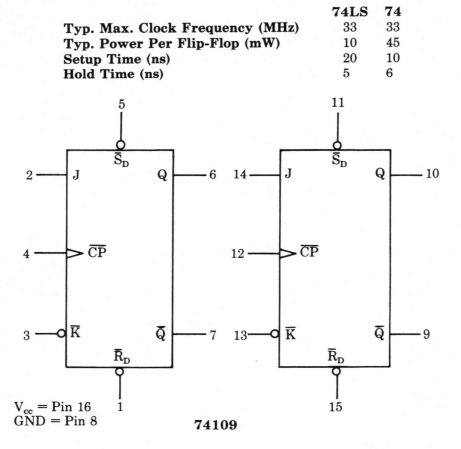

V_{cc} = Pin 16
GND = Pin 8

74109

MODE SELECT — TRUTH TABLE

OPERATING MODE	INPUTS					OUTPUTS	
	$\overline{S}_D$	$\overline{R}_D$	$\overline{CP}$	J	$\overline{K}$	Q	$\overline{Q}$
Asynchronous Set	L	H	X	X	X	H	L
Asynchronous Reset (Clear)	H	L	X	X	X	L	H
Undetermined[c]	L	L	X	X	X	H	H
Toggle	H	H	↑	h	l	$\overline{q}$	q
Load "0" (Reset)	H	H	↑	l	h	L	H
Load "1" (Set)	H	H	↑	h	l	H	L
Hold "no change"	H	H	↑	l	h	q	$\overline{q}$

H = High voltage level steady state

L = Low voltage level steady state

h = High voltage level one setup time prior to the low-to-high clock transition

l = Low voltage level one setup time prior to the low-to-high clock transition

X = Don't care

q = Lower case letters indicate the state of the referenced output prior to the low-to-high clock transition

↑ = Low-to-high clock transition

74112 Dual JK Edge-Triggered Flip-Flop

The '112 is a dual JK negative edge-triggered flip-flop featuring individual J, K, clock, set, and reset inputs. The set ($\overline{S_D}$) and reset ($\overline{R_D}$) inputs, when low, set or reset the outputs as shown in the truth table, regardless of the levels at the other inputs.

A high level on the clock ($\overline{CP}$) input enables the J and K inputs, and data will be accepted. The logic levels at the J and K inputs can be allowed to change while the $\overline{CP}$ is high and the flip-flop will perform according to the truth table as long as minimum setup and hold times are observed. Output state changes are initiated by the high-to-low transition of $\overline{CP}$.

	74S	74LS
Typ. Max. Clock Frequency (MHz)	125	45
Typ. Power Per Flip-Flop (mW)	75	10
Setup Time (ns)	6	20
Hold Time (ns)	0	0

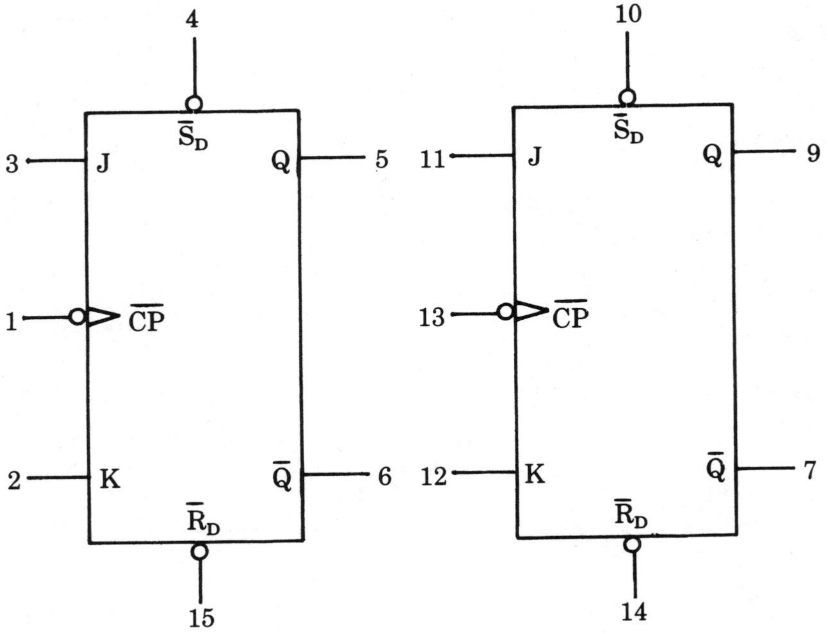

V_{cc} = Pin 16
GND = Pin 8

74112

MODE SELECT — TRUTH TABLE

OPERATING MODE	INPUTS					OUTPUTS	
	$\overline{S}_D$	$\overline{R}_D$	$\overline{CP}$	J	K	Q	$\overline{Q}$
Asynchronous Set	L	H	X	X	X	H	L
Asynchronous Reset (Clear)	H	L	X	X	X	L	H
Undetermined[(c)]	L	L	X	X	X	H	H
Toggle	H	H	↓	h	h	$\overline{q}$	q
Load "0" (Reset)	H	H	↓	l	h	L	H
Load "1" (Set)	H	H	↓	h	l	H	L
Hold "no change"	H	H	↓	l	l	q	$\overline{q}$

H = High voltage level steady state.
h = High voltage level one setup time prior to the high-to-low clock transition.
L = Low voltage level steady state.
l = Low voltage level one setup time prior to the high-to-low clock transition.
q = Lower case letters indicate the state of the referenced output one setup time prior to the high-to-low clock transition.
X = Don't care.

74113 Dual JK Edge-Triggered Flip-Flop

The '113 is a dual JK negative edge-triggered flip-flop featuring individual J, K, set, and clock inputs. The asynchronous set ($\overline{S_D}$) input, when low, forces the outputs to the steady-state levels as shown in the truth table, regardless of the levels at the other inputs.

A high level on the clock ($\overline{CP}$) input enables the J and K inputs, and data will be accepted. The logic levels at the J and K inputs can be allowed to change while the $\overline{CP}$ is high and the flip-flop will perform according to the truth table as long as minimum setup and hold times are observed. Output state changes are initiated by the high-to-low transition of $\overline{CP}$.

	74S	74LS
Typ. Max. Clock Frequency (MHz)	125	45
Typ. Power Per Flip-Flop (mW)	75	10
Setup Time (ns)	6	20
Hold Time (ns)	0	0

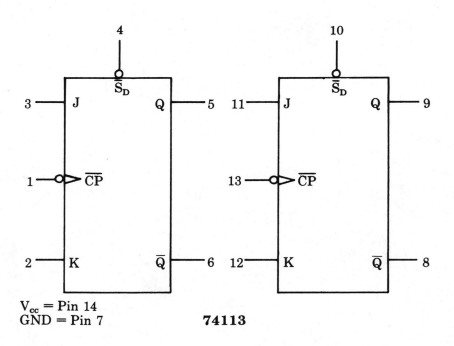

V_{cc} = Pin 14
GND = Pin 7

74113

MODE SELECT — TRUTH TABLE

OPERATING MODE	INPUTS				OUTPUTS	
	$\overline{S}_D$	$\overline{CP}$	J	K	Q	$\overline{Q}$
Asynchronous Set	L	X	X	X	H	L
Toggle	H	↓	h	h	$\overline{q}$	q
Load "0" (Reset)	H	↓	l	h	L	H
Load "1" (Set)	H	↓	h	l	H	L
Hold "no change"	H	↓	l	l	q	$\overline{q}$

H = High voltage level steady state.
h = High voltage level one setup time prior to the high-to-low clock transition.
L = Low voltage level steady state.
l = Low voltage level one setup time prior to the high-to-low clock transition.
q = Lower case letters indicate the state of the referenced output one setup time prior
    to the high-to-low clock transition.
X = Don't care.

74114 Dual JK Edge-Triggered Flip-Flop

The '114 is a dual JK negative edge-triggered flip-flop featuring individual J, K, and set inputs and common clock and reset inputs. The set $(\overline{S}_D)$ and reset $(\overline{R}_D)$ inputs, when low, set or reset the outputs, as shown in the truth table, regardless of the levels at the other inputs.

A high level on the clock $(\overline{CP})$ input enables the J and K inputs, and data will be accepted. The logic levels at the J and K inputs can be allowed to change while the $\overline{CP}$ is high, and the flip-flop will perform according to the truth table as long as minimum setup and hold times are observed. Output state changes are initiated by the high-to-low transition of $\overline{CP}$.

	74S	74LS
Typ. Max. Clock Frequency (MHz)	125	45
Typ. Power Per Flip-Flop (mW)	75	10
Setup Time (ns)	6	20
Hold Time (ns)	0	0

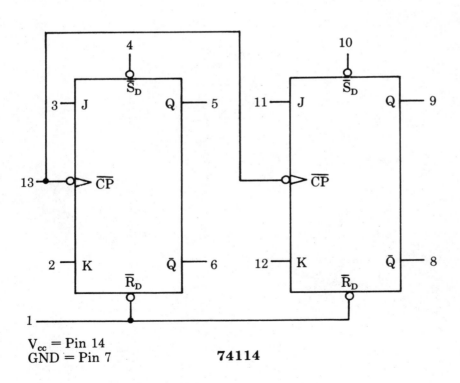

V_{cc} = Pin 14
GND = Pin 7

74114

MODE SELECT — TRUTH TABLE

OPERATING MODE	INPUTS					OUTPUTS	
	$\overline{S}_D$	$\overline{R}_D$	$\overline{CP}$	J	K	Q	$\overline{Q}$
Asynchronous Set	L	H	X	X	X	H	L
Asynchronous Reset (Clear)	H	L	X	X	X	L	H
Undetermined[c]	L	L	X	X	X	H	H
Toggle	H	H	↓	h	h	$\overline{q}$	q
Load "0" (Reset)	H	H	↓	l	h	L	H
Load "1" (Set)	H	H	↓	h	l	H	L
Hold "no change"	H	H	↓	l	l	q	$\overline{q}$

H = High voltage level steady state.
h = High voltage level one setup time prior to the high-to-low clock transition.
L = Low voltage level steady state.
l = Low voltage level one setup time prior to the high-to-low clock transition.
q = Lower case letters indicate the state of the referenced output one setup time prior to the high-to-low
    clock transition.
X = Don't care.

74121 Monostable Multivibrator

These multivibrators feature dual active low-going edge inputs and a single active high-going edge input, which can be used as an active high enable input. Complementary output pulses are provided.

Pulse triggering occurs at a particular voltage level and is not directly related to the transition time of the input pulse. Schmitt-trigger input circuitry (TTL hysteresis) for the B input allows jitter-free triggering from inputs with transition rates as slow as 1 volt/second, providing the circuit with an excellent noise immunity of typically 1.2 volts. A high immunity to V_{CC} noise of typically 1.5

	74
Positive Inputs	1
Negative Inputs	2
Output Pulse Range (ns to s)	40ns-28s
Typ. Total Power (mW)	90

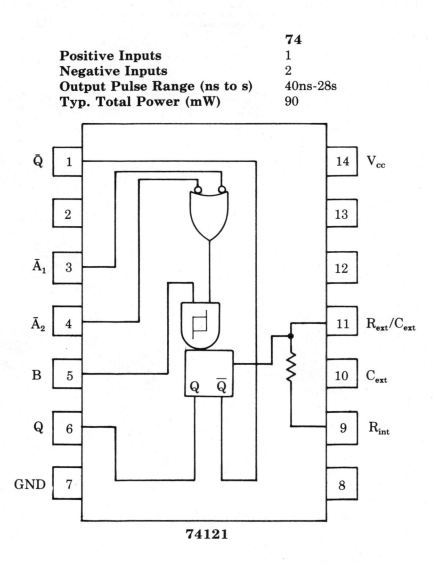

74121

FUNCTION TABLE

INPUTS			OUTPUTS	
$\overline{A_1}$	$\overline{A_2}$	B	Q	$\overline{Q}$
L	X	H	L	H
X	L	H	L	H
X	X	L	L	H
H	H	X	L	H
H	↓	H	⊓	⊔
↓	H	H	⊓	⊔
↓	↓	H	⊓	⊔
L	X	↑	⊓	⊔
X	L	↑	⊓	⊔

H = High voltage level
L = Low voltage level
X = Don't care
↑ = Low-to-high transition
↓ = High-to-low transition

volts is also provided by internal latching circuitry. Once fired, the outputs are independent of further transitions of the inputs and are a function only of the timing components. Input pulses can be of any duration relative to the output pulse. Output pulse length can be varied from 20 nanoseconds to 28 seconds by choosing appropriate timing components. With no external timing components (i.e., R_{int} connected to V_{CC}, C_{ext} and R_{ext}/C_{ext} open), an output pulse of typically 30 or 35 nanoseconds is achieved that can be used as a dc-triggered reset signal. Output rise and fall times are TTL compatible and independent of pulse length.

Pulse width stability is achieved through internal compensation and is virtually independent of V_{CC} and temperature. In most applications, pulse stability will only be limited by the accuracy of external timing components.

Jitter-free operation is maintained over the full temperature and V_{CC} ranges for more than six decades of timing capacitance (10 pF to 10 μF) and more than one decade of timing resistance (2 kΩ to 40 kΩ). In circuits where pulse cutoff is not critical, timing capacitance of up to 1000 μF and timing resistance of as low as 1.4 kΩ can be used.

74122 Retriggerable Monostable Multivibrator

The '122 is a retriggerable monostable multivibrator featuring output pulse width control by three methods. The basic pulse time is programmed by selection of external resistance and capacitance values. The '122 has an internal timing resistor that allows the circuit to be used with only an external capacitor, if so desired. Once triggered, the basic pulse width can be extended by retriggering the gated active low-going edge inputs ($\overline{A}_1$, $\overline{A}_2$) or the active high-going edge inputs ($\overline{B}_1$, $\overline{B}_2$), or be reduced by use of the overriding active low reset.

	74LS
Positive Inputs	2
Negative Inputs	2
Direct Clear	Yes
Output Pulse Range (ns)	45ns-00 (inf.)
Typ. Total Power (mW)	30

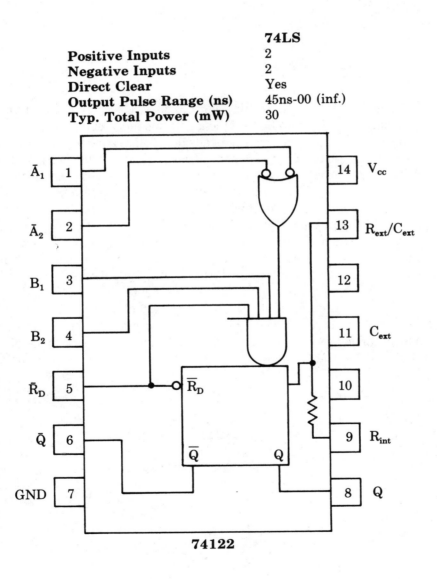

74122

FUNCTION TABLE

INPUTS					OUTPUTS	
$\overline{R}_D$	$\overline{A}_1$	$\overline{A}_2$	B_1	B_2	Q	$\overline{Q}$
L	X	X	X	X	L	H
X	H	H	X	X	L	H
X	X	X	L	X	L	H
X	X	X	X	L	L	H
H	L	X	↑	H	⊓	⊔
H	L	X	H	↑	⊓	⊔
H	X	L	↑	H	⊓	⊔
H	X	L	H	↑	⊓	⊔
H	H	↓	H	H	⊓	⊔
H	↓	↓	H	H	⊓	⊔
H	↓	H	H	H	⊓	⊔
↑	L	X	H	H	⊓	⊔
↑	X	L	H	H	⊓	⊔

H = High voltage level
L = Low voltage level
X = Don't care
↑ = Low-to-high input transition
↓ = High-to-low input transition
⊓ = Active high pulse
⊔ = Active low pulse

    To use the internal timing resistor of the '122, connect R_{int} to V_{CC}. For improved pulse width accuracy and repeatability, connect an external resistor between R_{ext}/C_{ext} and V_{CC} with R_{int} left open. To obtain variable pulse widths, connect an external variable resistance between R_{int} or R_{ext}/C_{ext} and V_{CC}.

74123 Dual Retriggerable Monostable Multivibrator

This retriggerable monostable multivibrator features dc triggering from gated active low inputs ($\overline{A}$) and active high inputs (B), and also provides overriding direct-reset inputs. Complementary outputs are provided. The retrigger capability simplifies the generation of output pulses of extremely long duration. By trig-

	74	74L	74LS
Positive Inputs	1	1	1
Negative Inputs	1	1	1
Direct Clear	Yes	Yes	Yes
Output Pulse Range (ns)	45ns-00 (inf.)	90ns-00 (inf.)	45ns-00 (inf.)
Typ. Total Power (mW)	230	25	60

74123

FUNCTION TABLE

INPUTS			OUTPUTS	
$\overline{R_D}$	$\overline{A}$	B	Q	$\overline{Q}$
L	X	X	L	H
X	H	X	L	H
X	X	L	L	H
H	L	↑	⊓	⊔
H	↓	H	⊓	⊔
↑	L	H	⊓	⊔

H = High voltage level
L = Low voltage level
X = Don't care
↑ = Low-to-high transition
↓ = High-to-low transition

gering the input before the output pulse is terminated, the output pulse can be extended. The overriding reset capability permits any output pulse to be terminated at a predetermined time that is independent of the timing components, R and C.

74125 Quad 3-State Buffer

The output of each section of the '125 is the same state as the digital input (A) if the control input (C) is low. If, however, the control input (C) is made high, the buffer's output will go into the high-impedance third state. The state of the data input (A) will be irrelevant in this case.

	74
Typ. Delay Time (ns)	10
Typ. Power Per Gate (mW)	40

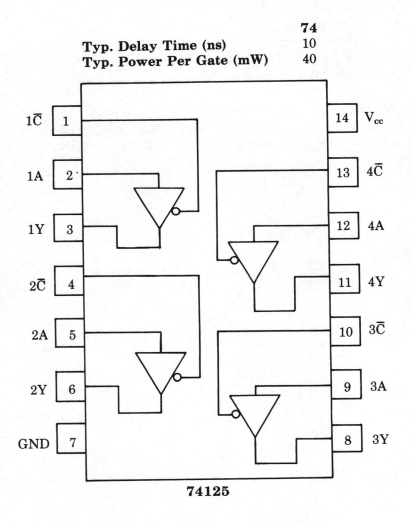

74125

Truth Table

INPUTS		OUTPUT
$\overline{C}$	A	Y
L	L	L
L	H	H
H	X	(Z)

L = Low voltage level
H = High voltage level
X = Don't care
(Z) = High impedance (off)

74126 Quad 3-State Buffer

The output of each section of the '126 is the same state as the digital input (A) if the control input (C) is high. If, however, the control input (C) is made low, the buffer's output will go into the high-impedance third state. The state of the data input (A) will be irrelevant in this case.

Notice that in the '126 the control input functions in the exact opposite manner as in the '125.

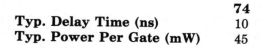

	74
Typ. Delay Time (ns)	10
Typ. Power Per Gate (mW)	45

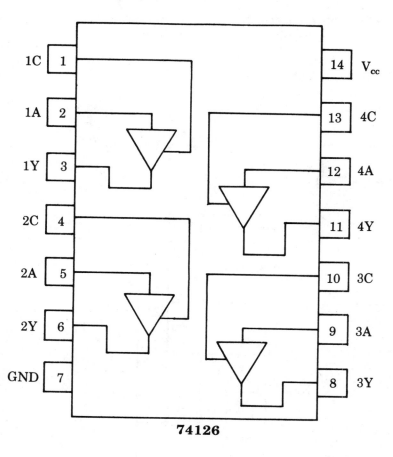

74126

Truth Table

INPUTS		OUTPUT
C	**A**	**Y**
H	L	L
H	H	H
L	X	(Z)

L = Low voltage level
H = High voltage level
X = Don't care
(Z) = High impedance (off)

74132 Quad 2-Input NAND Schmitt Trigger

The '132 contains four 2-input NAND gates that accept standard TTL input signals and provide standard TTL output levels. They are capable of transforming slowly changing input signals into sharply defined jitter-free output signals. In addition, they have greater noise margins than conventional NAND gates.

Each circuit contains a 2-input Schmitt trigger followed by a Darlington level shifter and a phase splitter driving a TTL totem-pole output. The Schmitt trigger uses positive feedback to effectively speedup slow-input transition and provide different input threshold voltages for positive-going and negative-going transitions. This hysteresis between the positive-going and negative-going input threshold (typically 800 mW) is determined internally by resistor ratios and is essentially insensitive to temperature and supply-voltage variations. As long as one input remains at a more positive voltage than V_T + (Max), the gate will respond to the transitions of the other input, as shown in the figure.

	74	74LS
Typ. Hysteresis (V)	0.8	0.8
Typ. Delay Time (ns)	15	15

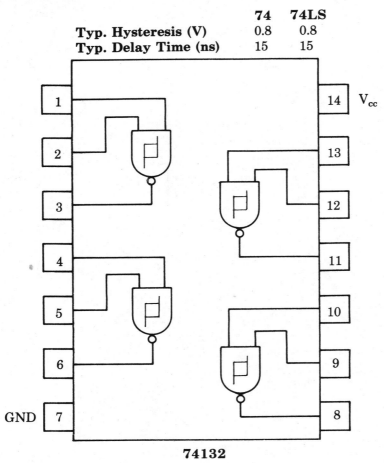

74132

74133 13-Input NAND Gate

The output of the '133 (pin #9) is high as long as at least one (or more) of the 13 inputs is low. The output is low if, and only if, all 13 inputs are in the high state. This chip is just an expansion of the basic NAND gate.

If less than 13 data inputs are required in a given application, just tie the unused inputs to a constant high voltage. This action will preserve the NAND function for the remaining inputs.

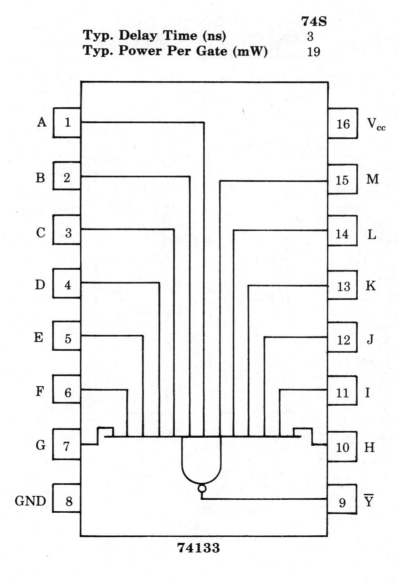

	74S
Typ. Delay Time (ns)	3
Typ. Power Per Gate (mW)	19

74133

74134 12-Input NAND Gate (3-State)

The 74134 is very similar to the 74133. The only difference is that in the '133 there are only 12 (instead of 13) data inputs. The remaining input (OE—pin #15) is a control input to force the chip's output into the high-impedance third state when the control input is high. The data at the other 12 inputs are irrelevant in this case.

	74S
Typ. Delay Time (ns)	4.5
Typ. Power Per Gate (mW)	45

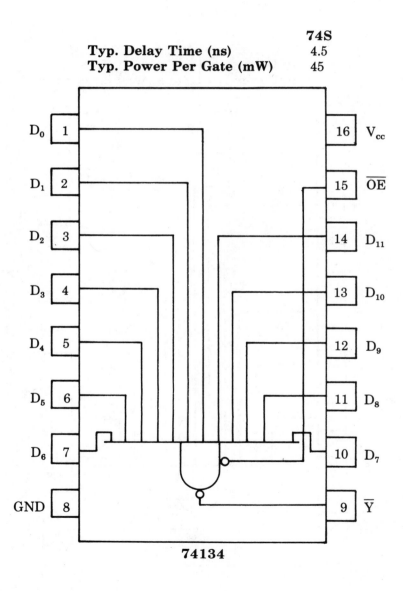

74134

Truth Table

INPUTS		OUTPUT
D_0 - - - - D_{11}	$\overline{OE}$	$\overline{Y}$
H - - - - - H	L	L
one input = L	L	H
X - - - - - X	H	(Z)

H = High voltage level
L = Low voltage level
X = Don't care
(Z)= High impedance "off" state

When the control input (OE) is held low, the output of the '134 (pin #9) is high as long as at least one (or more) of the 13 inputs is low. The output is low if, and only if, all 13 inputs are in the high state.

74135 Quad Exclusive-OR/NOR Gate

In the '135, exclusive-OR gates are combined in pairs to produce an exclusive-OR/NOR function, as defined in the truth table. Notice that one C INPUT is shared for each of two pairs of outputs. The two joined sections therefore are not completely independent.

	74S
Max. Supply Current (mA)	99
Typ. Propagation Delay (ns)	12

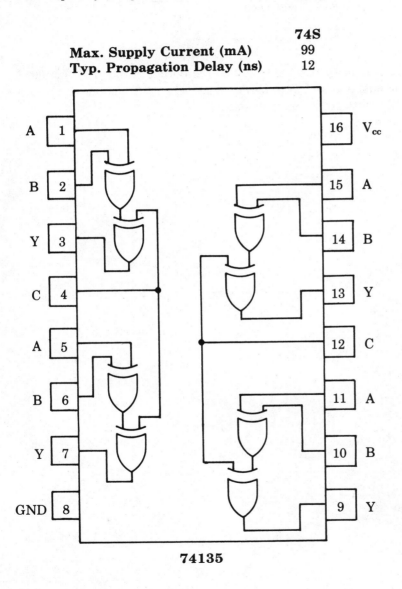

74135

Truth Table

INPUTS			OUTPUT
A	**B**	**C**	**Y**
L	L	L	L
L	H	L	H
H	L	L	H
H	H	L	L
L	L	H	H
L	H	H	L
H	L	H	L
H	H	H	H

H = High voltage level
L = Low voltage level

92

74136 Quad 2-Input Exclusive-OR Gate (O.C.)

The basic functioning of the 74136 is quite similar to the 7486, described earlier in this section.

	74LS
Max. Supply Current (mA)	10
Max. Propagation Delay (ns)	30

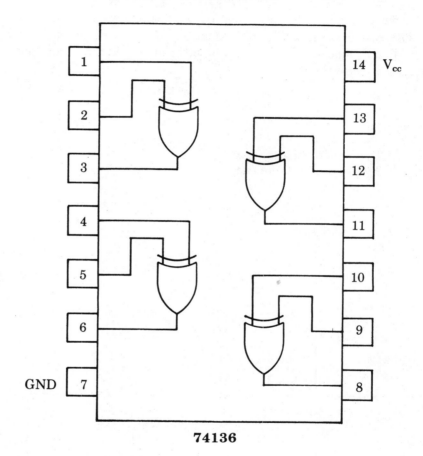

74136

Truth Table

INPUTS		OUTPUT
A	B	Y
L	L	L
L	H	H
H	L	H
H	H	L

L = Low voltage level
H = High voltage level

93

74138 1-of-8 Decoder/Demultiplexer

The '138 decoder accepts three binary weighted inputs (A_0, A_1, and A_2) and when enabled, provides eight mutually exclusive active low outputs ($\overline{0}$, $\overline{7}$). The device features three enable inputs: two active low ($\overline{E}_1$, $\overline{E}_2$) and one active high (E_3). Every output will be high unless $\overline{E}_1$ and $\overline{E}_2$ are low and E_3 is high. This multiple enable function allows easy parallel expansion of the device to a 1-of-32 (5 lines to 32 lines) decoder with just four 138's and one inverter.

The device can be used as an eight-output demultiplexer by using one of the active low enable inputs as the data input and the remaining enable inputs as strobes. Enable inputs not used must be permanently tied to their appropriate active-high or active-low state.

Type of Output	74S Totem Pole	74LS Totem Pole
Typ. Select Time (ns)	8	22
Typ. Enable Time (ns)	7	21
Typ. Total Power (mW)	225	31

V_{cc} = Pin 16
GND = Pin 8

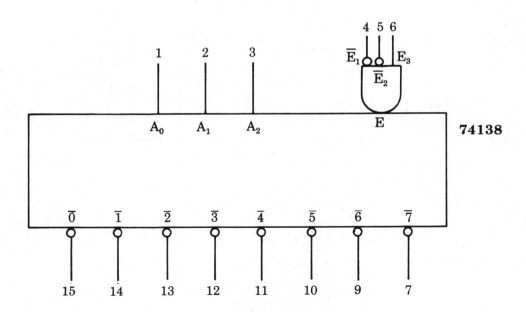

Truth Table

INPUTS						OUTPUTS							
$\overline{E}_1$	$\overline{E}_2$	E_3	A_0	A_1	A_2	$\overline{0}$	$\overline{1}$	$\overline{2}$	$\overline{3}$	$\overline{4}$	$\overline{5}$	$\overline{6}$	$\overline{7}$
H	X	X	X	X	X	H	H	H	H	H	H	H	H
X	H	X	X	X	X	H	H	H	H	H	H	H	H
X	X	L	X	X	X	H	H	H	H	H	H	H	H
L	L	H	L	L	L	L	H	H	H	H	H	H	H
L	L	H	H	L	L	H	L	H	H	H	H	H	H
L	L	H	L	H	L	H	H	L	H	H	H	H	H
L	L	H	H	H	L	H	H	H	L	H	H	H	H
L	L	H	L	L	H	H	H	H	H	L	H	H	H
L	L	H	H	L	H	H	H	H	H	H	L	H	H
L	L	H	L	H	H	H	H	H	H	H	H	L	H
L	L	H	H	H	H	H	H	H	H	H	H	H	L

NOTES
H = High voltage level
L = Low voltage level
X = Don't care

74139 Dual 1-of-4 Decoder/Demultiplexer

The '139 is a high-speed dual 1-of-4 decoder/demultiplexer. This device has two independent decoders, each accepting two binary weighted inputs (A_0 and A_1) and providing four mutually exclusive active low outputs ($\overline{0}$ through $\overline{3}$). Each decoder has an active low enable ($\overline{E}$). When $\overline{E}$ is high, every output is forced high. The enable can be used as the data input for a 1-of-4 demultiplexer application.

Type of Output	74S Totem Pole	74LS Totem Pole
Typ. Select Time (ns)	7.5	22
Typ. Enable Time (ns)	6	19
Typ. Total Power (mW)	300	34

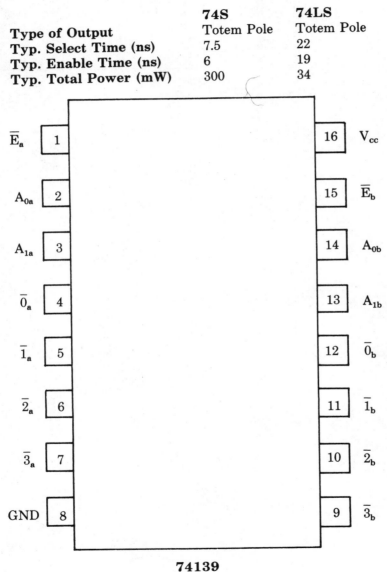

74139

74145 BCD-to-Decimal Decoder/Driver (O.C.)

The '145 is a 1-of-10 decoder with open collector outputs. This decoder accepts BCD inputs on the A_0 to A_3 address lines and generates 10 mutually exclusive active low outputs. When an input code greater than nine is applied, all outputs are high. This device can therefore be used as a 1-of-8 decoder with A_3 used as an active low enable. The 145 features an output breakdown voltage of 15 V. This device is ideal as a lamp or solenoid driver.

	74
Output Sink Current (mA)	80
Off-State Output Voltage (V)	15
Typ. Total Power (mW)	215
Blanking	Invalid Codes

V_{cc} = Pin 16
GND = Pin 8

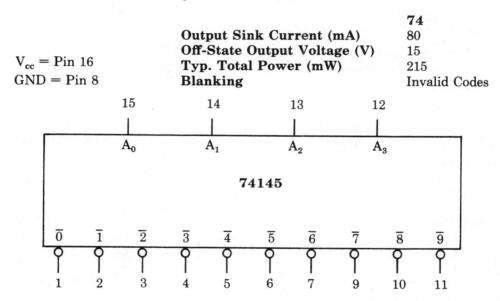

Truth Table

A_3	A_2	A_1	A_0	$\overline{0}$	$\overline{1}$	$\overline{2}$	$\overline{3}$	$\overline{4}$	$\overline{5}$	$\overline{6}$	$\overline{7}$	$\overline{8}$	$\overline{9}$
L	L	L	L	L	H	H	H	H	H	H	H	H	H
L	L	L	H	H	L	H	H	H	H	H	H	H	H
L	L	H	L	H	H	L	H	H	H	H	H	H	H
L	L	H	H	H	H	H	L	H	H	H	H	H	H
L	H	L	L	H	H	H	H	L	H	H	H	H	H
L	H	L	H	H	H	H	H	H	L	H	H	H	H
L	H	H	L	H	H	H	H	H	H	L	H	H	H
L	H	H	H	H	H	H	H	H	H	H	L	H	H
H	L	L	L	H	H	H	H	H	H	H	H	L	H
H	L	L	H	H	H	H	H	H	H	H	H	H	L
H	L	H	L	H	H	H	H	H	H	H	H	H	H
H	L	H	H	H	H	H	H	H	H	H	H	H	H
H	H	L	L	H	H	H	H	H	H	H	H	H	H
H	H	L	H	H	H	H	H	H	H	H	H	H	H
H	H	H	L	H	H	H	H	H	H	H	H	H	H
H	H	H	H	H	H	H	H	H	H	H	H	H	H

H = High voltage levels
L = Low voltage levels

74147 10-Line-to-4-Line Priority Encoder

The '147 nine-input priority encoder accepts data from nine active low inputs ($\bar{I}_1$ through $\bar{I}_9$) and provides a binary representation on the four active low outputs (A_0 through A_3). A priority is assigned to each input so that when two or more inputs are simultaneously active, the input with the highest priority is represented on the output, with input line $\bar{I}_9$ having the highest priority.

The device provides the 10-line-to-4-line priority encoding function by use of the implied decimal zero. The zero is encoded when all nine data inputs are high, forcing all four outputs high.

	74
Typ. Delay Time (ns)	10
Typ. Total Power (mW)	225

V_{cc} = Pin 16
GND = Pin 8

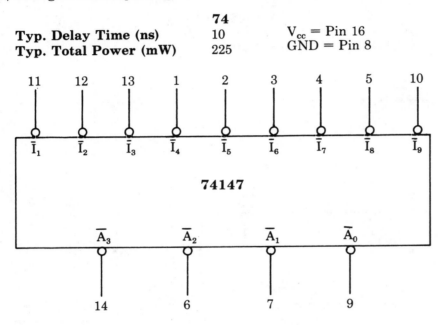

Truth Table

INPUTS										OUTPUTS			
$\bar{I}_1$	$\bar{I}_2$	$\bar{I}_3$	$\bar{I}_4$	$\bar{I}_5$	$\bar{I}_6$	$\bar{I}_7$	$\bar{I}_8$	$\bar{I}_9$	$\bar{A}_3$	$\bar{A}_2$	$\bar{A}_1$	$\bar{A}_0$
H	H	H	H	H	H	H	H	H	H	H	H	H
X	X	X	X	X	X	X	X	L	L	H	H	L
X	X	X	X	X	X	X	L	H	L	H	H	H
X	X	X	X	X	X	L	H	H	H	L	L	L
X	X	X	X	X	L	H	H	H	H	L	L	H
X	X	X	X	L	H	H	H	H	H	L	H	L
X	X	X	L	H	H	H	H	H	H	L	H	H
X	X	L	H	H	H	H	H	H	H	H	L	L
X	L	H	H	H	H	H	H	H	H	H	L	H
L	H	H	H	H	H	H	H	H	H	H	H	L

H = High voltage level
L = Low voltage level
X = Don't care

74148 8-Input Priority Encoder

The '148 eight-input priority encoder accepts data from eight active low inputs and provides a binary representation on the three active low outputs. A priority is assigned to each input so that when two or more inputs are simultaneously active, the input with the highest priority is represented on the output, with input line $\overline{I_7}$ having the highest priority. A high on the input enable ($\overline{EI}$) will force all outputs to the inactive (high) state and allow new data to settle without producing erroneous information at the outputs.

A group signal output ($\overline{GS}$) an an enable output ($\overline{EO}$) are provided with the three data outputs. The $\overline{GS}$ is active level low when any input is low. This indicates when any input is active. The $\overline{EO}$ is active level low when all inputs are high. Using the output enable along with the input enable allows priority coding of N input signals. Both $\overline{EO}$ and $\overline{GS}$ are active high when the input enable is high.

		74
V_{CC} = Pin 24	**Typ. Delay Time (ns)**	12
GND = Pin 12	**Typ. Total Power (mW)**	130

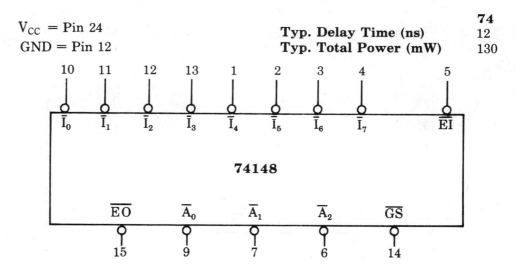

Truth Table

INPUTS									OUTPUTS				
$\overline{EI}$	$\overline{I_0}$	$\overline{I_1}$	$\overline{I_2}$	$\overline{I_3}$	$\overline{I_4}$	$\overline{I_5}$	$\overline{I_6}$	$\overline{I_7}$	$\overline{GS}$	$\overline{A_0}$	$\overline{A_1}$	$\overline{A_2}$	$\overline{EO}$
H	X	X	X	X	X	X	X	X	H	H	H	H	H
L	H	H	H	H	H	H	H	H	H	H	H	H	L
L	X	X	X	X	X	X	X	L	L	L	L	L	H
L	X	X	X	X	X	X	L	H	L	H	L	L	H
L	X	X	X	X	X	L	H	H	L	L	H	L	H
L	X	X	X	X	L	H	H	H	L	H	H	L	H
L	X	X	X	L	H	H	H	H	L	L	L	H	H
L	X	X	L	H	H	H	H	H	L	H	L	H	H
L	X	L	H	H	H	H	H	H	L	L	H	H	H
L	L	H	H	H	H	H	H	H	L	H	H	H	H

H = High voltage level
L = Low voltage level
X = Don't care

74150 16-Input Multiplexer

The '150 is a logical implementation of a single pole, 16-position switch with the switch position controlled by the state of four select inputs: S_0, S_1, S_2 and S_3. The multiplexer output ($\overline{Y}$) inverts the selected data. The enable input ($\overline{D}$) is active low. When $\overline{E}$ is high, the $\overline{Y}$ output is high, regardless of all other inputs. In one package, the 150 provides the ability to select from 16 sources of data or control information.

	74
Type of Output	Standard
Typ. Delay, Data to Inverting Output (ns)	Standard
Typ. Delay Time, From Enable (ns)	18
Typ. Total Power (mW)	200

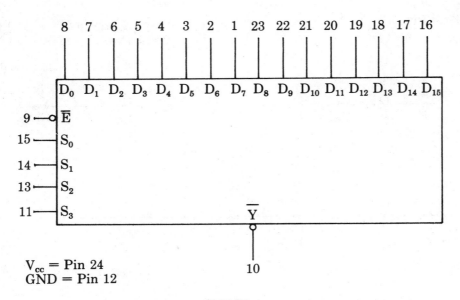

V_{cc} = Pin 24
GND = Pin 12

74150

Truth Table

S_3	S_2	S_1	S_0	$\overline{E}$	D_0	D_1	D_2	D_3	D_4	D_5	D_6	D_7	D_8	D_9	D_{10}	D_{11}	D_{12}	D_{13}	D_{14}	D_{15}	$\overline{Y}$
X	X	X	X	H	X	X	X	X	X	X	X	X	X	X	X	X	X	X	X	X	H
L	L	L	L	L	L	X	X	X	X	X	X	X	X	X	X	X	X	X	X	X	H
L	L	L	L	L	H	X	X	X	X	X	X	X	X	X	X	X	X	X	X	X	L
L	L	L	H	L	X	L	X	X	X	X	X	X	X	X	X	X	X	X	X	X	H
L	L	L	H	L	X	H	X	X	X	X	X	X	X	X	X	X	X	X	X	X	L
L	L	H	L	L	X	X	L	X	X	X	X	X	X	X	X	X	X	X	X	X	H
L	L	H	L	L	X	X	H	X	X	X	X	X	X	X	X	X	X	X	X	X	L
L	L	H	H	L	X	X	X	L	X	X	X	X	X	X	X	X	X	X	X	X	H
L	L	H	H	L	X	X	X	H	X	X	X	X	X	X	X	X	X	X	X	X	L
L	H	L	L	L	X	X	X	X	L	X	X	X	X	X	X	X	X	X	X	X	H
L	H	L	L	L	X	X	X	X	H	X	X	X	X	X	X	X	X	X	X	X	L
L	H	L	H	L	X	X	X	X	X	L	X	X	X	X	X	X	X	X	X	X	H
L	H	L	H	L	X	X	X	X	X	H	X	X	X	X	X	X	X	X	X	X	L
L	H	H	L	L	X	X	X	X	X	X	L	X	X	X	X	X	X	X	X	X	H
L	H	H	L	L	X	X	X	X	X	X	H	X	X	X	X	X	X	X	X	X	L
L	H	H	H	L	X	X	X	X	X	X	X	L	X	X	X	X	X	X	X	X	H
L	H	H	H	L	X	X	X	X	X	X	X	H	X	X	X	X	X	X	X	X	L
H	L	L	L	L	X	X	X	X	X	X	X	X	L	X	X	X	X	X	X	X	H
H	L	L	L	L	X	X	X	X	X	X	X	X	H	X	X	X	X	X	X	X	L
H	L	L	H	L	X	X	X	X	X	X	X	X	X	L	X	X	X	X	X	X	H
H	L	L	H	L	X	X	X	X	X	X	X	X	X	H	X	X	X	X	X	X	L
H	L	H	L	L	X	X	X	X	X	X	X	X	X	X	L	X	X	X	X	X	H
H	L	H	L	L	X	X	X	X	X	X	X	X	X	X	H	X	X	X	X	X	L
H	L	H	H	L	X	X	X	X	X	X	X	X	X	X	X	L	X	X	X	X	H
H	L	H	H	L	X	X	X	X	X	X	X	X	X	X	X	H	X	X	X	X	L
H	H	L	L	L	X	X	X	X	X	X	X	X	X	X	X	X	L	X	X	X	H
H	H	L	L	L	X	X	X	X	X	X	X	X	X	X	X	X	H	X	X	X	L
H	H	L	H	L	X	X	X	X	X	X	X	X	X	X	X	X	X	L	X	X	H
H	H	L	H	L	X	X	X	X	X	X	X	X	X	X	X	X	X	H	X	X	L
H	H	H	L	L	X	X	X	X	X	X	X	X	X	X	X	X	X	X	L	X	H
H	H	H	L	L	X	X	X	X	X	X	X	X	X	X	X	X	X	X	H	X	H
H	H	H	H	L	X	X	X	X	X	X	X	X	X	X	X	X	X	X	X	L	H
H	H	H	H	L	X	X	X	X	X	X	X	X	X	X	X	X	X	X	X	H	L

H = High voltage level
L = Low voltage level
X = Don't care

74151 8-Input Multiplexer

The '151 is a logical implementation of a single-pole, eight-position switch with the switch position controlled by the state of three select inputs: S_0, S_1, and S_2. True (Y) and complement ($\overline{Y}$) outputs are both provided. The enable input ($\overline{E}$) is active low when E is high and Y output is low, regardless of all other inputs.

In one package, the 151 provides the ability to select from eight sources of data or control information. The device can provide any logic function of four variables and its negation with correct manipulation.

	74S	74	74LS
Type of Output	Standard	Standard	Standard
Typ. Delay, Data to Inverting Output (ns)	4.5	8	11
Typ. Delay, Data to Noninverting Output (ns)	8	16	18
Typ. Delay Time, From Enable (ns)	9	22	27
Typ. Total Power (mW)	225	145	30

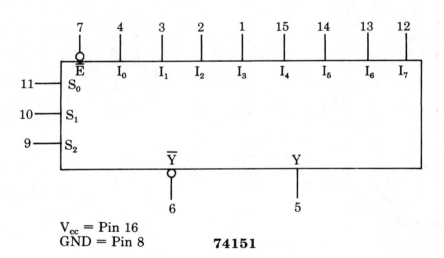

V_{cc} = Pin 16
GND = Pin 8

74151

Truth Table

	INPUTS											OUTPUTS	
$\overline{E}$	S_2	S_1	S_0	I_0	I_1	I_2	I_3	I_4	I_5	I_6	I_7	$\overline{Y}$	Y
H	X	X	X	X	X	X	X	X	X	X	X	H	L
L	L	L	L	L	X	X	X	X	X	X	X	H	L
L	L	L	L	H	X	X	X	X	X	X	X	L	H
L	L	L	H	X	L	X	X	X	X	X	X	H	L
L	L	L	H	X	H	X	X	X	X	X	X	L	H
L	L	H	L	X	X	L	X	X	X	X	X	H	L
L	L	H	L	X	X	H	X	X	X	X	X	L	H
L	L	H	H	X	X	X	L	X	X	X	X	H	L
L	L	H	H	X	X	X	H	X	X	X	X	L	H
L	H	L	L	X	X	X	X	L	X	X	X	H	L
L	H	L	L	X	X	X	X	H	X	X	X	L	H
L	H	L	H	X	X	X	X	X	L	X	X	H	L
L	H	L	H	X	X	X	X	X	H	X	X	L	H
L	H	H	L	X	X	X	X	X	X	L	X	H	L
L	H	H	L	X	X	X	X	X	X	H	X	L	H
L	H	H	H	X	X	X	X	X	X	X	L	H	L
L	H	H	H	X	X	X	X	X	X	X	H	L	H

H = High voltage level
L = Low voltage level
X = Don't care

74153 Dual 4-Line to 1-Line Multiplexer

The '153 is a dual 4-input multiplexer that can select two bits of data from up to four sources under control of the common select inputs (S_0 and S_1). The two 4-input multiplexer circuits have individual active low enables ($\overline{E}_a$, $\overline{E}_b$) that can be used to strobe the outputs independently. Outputs (Y_a and Y_b) are forced low when the corresponding enables (E_a and E_b) are high.

The device is the logical implementation of a 2-pole, 4-position switch, where the position of the switch is determined by the logic levels supplied to the two select inputs. The '153 can be used to move data to a common output bus from a group of registers. The state of the select inputs would determine the particular register from which the data came. An alternative application is as a function generator. The device can generate two functions of three variables, which is useful for implementing highly irregular random logic.

Type of Output	74S Standard	74 Standard	74LS Standard
Typ. Delay, Data to Noninverting Output (ns)	6	14	14
Typ. Delay Time, From Enable (ns)	9.5	17	17
Typ. Total Power (mW)	225	180	31

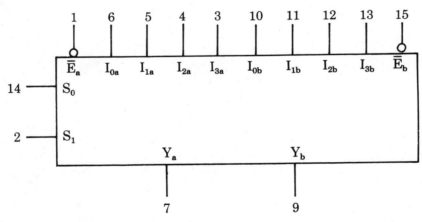

74153

V_{cc} = Pin 16
GND = Pin 8

Truth Table

SELECT INPUTS		INPUTS (a or b)					OUTPUT
S_0	S_1	$\overline{E}$	I_0	I_1	I_2	I_3	Y
X	X	H	X	X	X	X	L
L	L	L	L	X	X	X	L
L	L	L	H	X	X	X	H
H	L	L	X	L	X	X	L
H	L	L	X	H	X	X	H
L	H	L	X	X	L	X	L
L	H	L	X	X	H	X	H
H	H	L	X	X	X	L	L
H	H	L	X	X	X	H	H

H = High voltage level
L = Low voltage level
X = Don't care

74154 1-of-16 Decoder/Demultiplexer

The '154 accepts four active high binary address inputs and provides 16 mutually exclusive active low outputs. The two-input enable gate can be used to strobe the decoder to eliminate the normal decoding glitches on the outputs, or it can be used to expand the decoder. The enable gate has two ANDed inputs that must be low to enable the outputs.

The '154 can be used as a 1-of-16 demultiplexer by using one of the enable inputs as the multiplexed data input. When the other enable is low, the addressed output will follow the state of the applied data.

	74	74LS	74L
Type of Output	Totem Pole	Totem Pole	Totem Pole
Typ. Select Time (ns)	19.5	23	55
Typ. Enable Time (ns)	17.5	19	45
Typ. Total Power (mW)	170	45	24

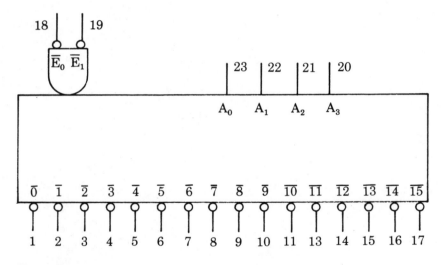

V_{cc} = Pin 24
GND = Pin 12

74154

Truth Table

INPUTS						OUTPUTS															
$\overline{E_0}$	$\overline{E_1}$	A_3	A_2	A_1	A_0	$\overline{0}$	$\overline{1}$	$\overline{2}$	$\overline{3}$	$\overline{4}$	$\overline{5}$	$\overline{6}$	$\overline{7}$	$\overline{8}$	$\overline{9}$	$\overline{10}$	$\overline{11}$	$\overline{12}$	$\overline{13}$	$\overline{14}$	$\overline{15}$
L	H	X	X	X	X	H	H	H	H	H	H	H	H	H	H	H	H	H	H	H	H
H	L	X	X	X	X	H	H	H	H	H	H	H	H	H	H	H	H	H	H	H	H
H	H	X	X	X	X	H	H	H	H	H	H	H	H	H	H	H	H	H	H	H	H
L	L	L	L	L	L	L	H	H	H	H	H	H	H	H	H	H	H	H	H	H	H
L	L	L	L	L	H	H	L	H	H	H	H	H	H	H	H	H	H	H	H	H	H
L	L	L	L	H	L	H	H	L	H	H	H	H	H	H	H	H	H	H	H	H	H
L	L	L	L	H	H	H	H	H	L	H	H	H	H	H	H	H	H	H	H	H	H
L	L	L	H	L	L	H	H	H	H	L	H	H	H	H	H	H	H	H	H	H	H
L	L	L	H	L	H	H	H	H	H	H	L	H	H	H	H	H	H	H	H	H	H
L	L	L	H	H	L	H	H	H	H	H	H	L	H	H	H	H	H	H	H	H	H
L	L	L	H	H	H	H	H	H	H	H	H	H	L	H	H	H	H	H	H	H	H
L	L	H	L	L	L	H	H	H	H	H	H	H	H	L	H	H	H	H	H	H	H
L	L	H	L	L	H	H	H	H	H	H	H	H	H	H	L	H	H	H	H	H	H
L	L	H	L	H	L	H	H	H	H	H	H	H	H	H	H	L	H	H	H	H	H
L	L	H	L	H	H	H	H	H	H	H	H	H	H	H	H	H	L	H	H	H	H
L	L	H	H	L	L	H	H	H	H	H	H	H	H	H	H	H	H	L	H	H	H
L	L	H	H	L	H	H	H	H	H	H	H	H	H	H	H	H	H	H	L	H	H
L	L	H	H	H	L	H	H	H	H	H	H	H	H	H	H	H	H	H	H	L	H
L	L	H	H	H	H	H	H	H	H	H	H	H	H	H	H	H	H	H	H	H	L

74155 Dual 2-Line to 4-Line Decoder/Demultiplexer

The '155 is a dual of 1-of-4 decoder/demultiplexer with common-address inputs and separate gated enable inputs. Each decoder section, when enabled, will accept the binary weighted address input (A_0 and A_1) and provide four mutually exclusive active low outputs (0 through 3). When the enable requirements of each decoder are not met, all outputs of that decoder are high.

Both decoder sections have a two-input enable gate. For decoder a, the enable gate requires one active high input and one active low input ($E_a \cdot \overline{E}_a$). Decoder a can accept either true or complemented data in demultiplexing applications, by using the $\overline{E}_a$ or E_a inputs respectively. The decoder b enable gate requires two active low inputs ($E_b \cdot \overline{E}_b$). The device can be used as a 1-of-8 decoder/demultiplexer by tying E_a or $\overline{E}_b$ and relabeling the common connection address as A_2, forming the common enable by connecting the remaining $\overline{E}_b$ and $\overline{E}_a$.

Type of Output	74LS Totem Pole	74 Totem Pole
Typ. Select Time (ns)	18	21
Typ. Enable Time (ns)	15	16
Type. Total Power (mW)	30	250

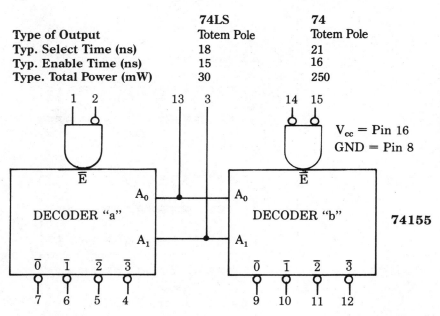

V_{cc} = Pin 16
GND = Pin 8

74155

Truth Table

ADDRESS		ENABLE "a"		OUTPUT "a"				ENABLE "b"		OUTPUT "b"			
A_0	A_1	E_a	$\overline{E}_a$	$\overline{0}$	$\overline{1}$	$\overline{2}$	$\overline{3}$	$\overline{E}_b$	$\overline{E}_b$	$\overline{0}$	$\overline{1}$	$\overline{2}$	$\overline{3}$
X	X	L	X	H	H	H	H	H	X	H	H	H	H
X	X	X	H	H	H	H	H	X	H	H	H	H	H
L	L	H	L	L	H	H	H	L	L	L	H	H	H
H	L	H	L	H	L	H	H	L	L	H	L	H	H
L	H	H	L	H	H	L	H	L	L	H	H	L	H
H	H	H	L	H	H	H	L	L	L	H	H	H	L

H = High voltage level
L = Low voltage level
X = Don't care

74156 Dual 2-Line to 4-Line Decoder/Demultiplexer (O.C.)

The '156 is a dual 1-of-4 decoder/demultiplexer with common address inputs and gated enable inputs. Each decoder section, when enabled, will accept the binary weighted address inputs (A_0 and A_1) and provide four mutually exclusive action low outputs ($\overline{0}$ through $\overline{3}$). When the enable requirements of each decoder are not met, all outputs of that decoder are high.

Both decoder sections have a two-input enable gate. For decoder a, the enable gate requires one active high input and one active low input ($E_a \cdot \overline{E}_a$). Decoder a can accept either true or complemented data in demultiplexing applications by using the $\overline{E}_a$ or E_a inputs, respectively. The decoder b enable gate requires two active low inputs ($\overline{E}_b \cdot \overline{E}_b$). The device can be used as a 1-of-8 decoder/demultiplexer by tying E_a to $\overline{E}_b$ and relabeling the common connection address as A_2, forming the common enable by connecting the remaining $\overline{E}_b$ and $\overline{E}_a$.

The '156 can be used to generate all four minterms of two variables. The four minterms are useful to replace multiple gate functions in some applications.

Typ. of Output	74	74LS
	Open Collector	Open Collector
Typ. Select Time (ns)	23	33
Typ. Enable Time (ns)	18	26
Typ. Total Power (mW)	250	31

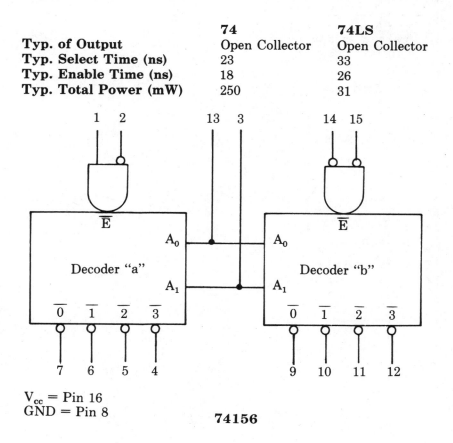

V_{cc} = Pin 16
GND = Pin 8

74156

109

Truth Table

ADDRESS		ENABLE "a"		OUTPUT "a"				ENABLE "b"		OUTPUT "b"			
A_0	A_1	E_a	$\overline{E}_a$	$\overline{0}$	$\overline{1}$	$\overline{2}$	$\overline{3}$	$\overline{E}_b$	$\overline{E}_b$	$\overline{0}$	$\overline{1}$	$\overline{2}$	$\overline{3}$
X	X	L	X	H	H	H	H	H	X	H	H	H	H
X	X	X	H	H	H	H	H	X	H	H	H	H	H
L	L	H	L	L	H	H	H	L	L	L	H	H	H
H	L	H	L	H	L	H	H	L	L	H	L	H	H
L	H	H	L	H	H	L	H	L	L	H	H	L	H
H	H	H	L	H	H	H	L	L	L	H	H	H	L

H = High voltage level
L = Low voltage level
X = Don't care

74157 Quad 2-Input Data
Selector/Multiplexer (Noninverted)

The '157 is a quad two-input multiplexer that selects four bits of data from two sources under the control of a common select input (S). The enable input ($\overline{E}$) is active low. When $\overline{E}$ is high, all of the outputs (Y) are forced low, regardless of all other input conditions.

Moving data from two groups of registers to four common output busses is a common use of the '157. The state of the select input determines the particular register from which the data comes. It can also be used as a function generator. The device is useful for implementing highly irregular logic by generating any four of the 16 different functions of two variables with one variable common. The device is the logic implementation of a four-pole, two-position switch where the position of the switch is determined by the logic levels supplied to the select input.

	74S Standard	74LS Standard	74 Standard	74L Standard
Type of Output				
Type Delay, Data to Noninverting Output (ns)	5	9	9	40
Typ. Delay, from Enable (ns)	8	14	4	60
Typ. Total Power (mW)	250	49	150	15

V_{cc} = Pin 16
GND = Pin 8

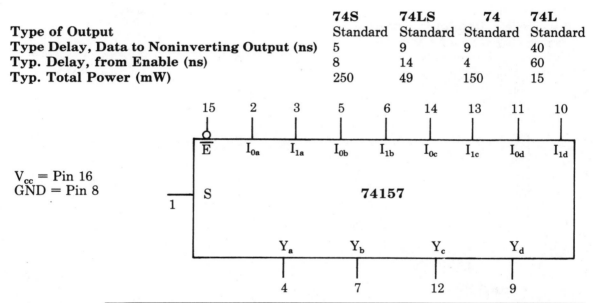

Truth Table

ENABLE	SELECT INPUT	DATA INPUTS		OUTPUT
$\overline{E}$	S	I_0	I_1	Y
H	X	X	X	L
L	H	X	L	L
L	H	X	H	H
L	L	L	X	L
L	L	H	X	H

H = High voltage level
L = Low voltage level
X = Don't care

74158 Quad 2-Input Data Selector/Multiplexer (Inverted)

The '158 is a quad two-input multiplexer that selects four bits of data from two sources under the control of a common select input (S), presenting the data in inverted form at the four outputs ($\overline{Y}$). The enable input ($\overline{E}$) is active low. When $\overline{E}$ is high, all of the outputs ($\overline{Y}$) are forced high, regardless of all other input conditions.

Moving data from two groups of registers to four common output busses is a common use of the 74158. The state of the select input determines the particular register from which the data comes. It can also be used as a function generator. The device is useful for implementing gating functions by generating any four functions of two variables with one variable common. The device is the logic implementation of a four-pole, two-position switch where the position of the switch is determined by the logic levels supplied to the select input.

		74S	**74LS**
Type of Output		Standard	Standard
Typ. Delay, Data to Inverting Output (ns)		4	7
Typ. Delay, From Enable (ns)		7	12
Typ. Total Power (mW)		195	24

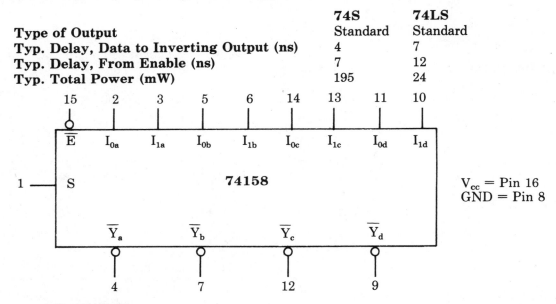

V_{cc} = Pin 16
GND = Pin 8

Truth Table

ENABLE	SELECT INPUT	DATA INPUTS		OUTPUTS
$\overline{E}$	S	I_0	I_1	$\overline{Y}$
H	X	X	X	H
L	L	L	X	H
L	L	H	X	L
L	H	X	L	H
L	H	X	H	L

H = High voltage level
L = Low voltage level
X = Don't care

74160 DEC Decade Counter

The '160 is a high-speed BCD decade counter. The counters are positive edge-triggered, synchronously presettable, and are easily cascaded to n-bit synchronous applications without additional gating. A terminal count output is provided, which detects a count of HLLH. The master reset asynchronously clears all flip-flops.

The '160 is a synchronous presettable BCD decade counter featuring an internal carry lookahead for applications in high-speed counting designs. Synchronous operation is provided by having all flip-flops clocked simultaneously so that the outputs change coincident with each other when so instructed by the count-enable inputs and internal gating. This mode of operation eliminates the output counting that is normally associated with asynchronous (ripple clock) counters. A buffered clock input triggers the four flip-flops on the positive-going edge of the clock. The clock input on the LS 160 features about 400 mV of hysteresis to reduce false triggering caused by noise on the clock line or by slowly rising clock edges.

The counter is fully programmable; that is, the outputs can be preset to either level. Presetting is synchronous with the clock, and takes place regardless of the levels of the count-enable inputs. A low level on the parallel-enable ($\overline{PE}$) input disables the counter and causes the data at the D_n inputs to be loaded into the counter on the next low-to-high transition of the clock. The reset (clear) function for the '160 is asynchronous. A low level on the master reset ($\overline{MR}$) input sets all four of the flip-flop outputs low, regardless of the levels of the CP, $\overline{PE}$, CET, and CEP inputs.

The carry lookahead circuitry provides for cascading counters for n-bit synchronous applications without additional gating. Instrumental in accomplishing this function are two count-enable inputs (CET • CEP) and a terminal count (TC) output. Both count-enable inputs must be high to count. The CET input is fed forward to enable the TC output. The TC output thus enabled will produce a high output pulse with a duration approximately equal to the high level portion of the Q_0 output. This high-level TC pulse is used to enable successive cascaded stages. The fast synchronous multistage counting connections are shown here.

All changes of the Q outputs (except due to the asynchronous master reset) occur as a result of, and synchronous with, the low-to-high transition of the clock input (CP). As long as the setup time requirements are met, there are no special timing or activity constraints on any of the mode control or data inputs. However, for conventional operation of the 74160 the following transitions should be avoided:

- High-to-low transition on the CEP or CET input if the clock is low.
- Low-to-high transition on the parallel enable input when the CP is low, if the count enables are high at or before the transition.

	74LS	**74**
Count Frequency (MHz)	25	25
Parallel Load	Synchronous	Synchronous
Clear	Asynchronous-Low	Asynchronous-Low
Typ. Total Power (mW)	93	305

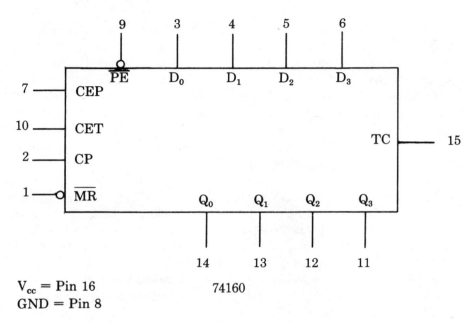

V_{cc} = Pin 16
GND = Pin 8

74160

MODE SELECT-FUNCTION TABLE

OPERATING MODE	INPUTS						OUTPUTS	
	$\overline{MR}$	CP	CEP	CET	$\overline{PE}$	D_n	Q_n	TC
Reset (Clear)	L	X	X	X	X	X	L	L
Parallel Load	H	↑	X	X	l	l	L	L
	H	↑	X	X	l	h	H	(b)
Count	H	↑	h	h	h(d)	X	count	(b)
Hold (do nothing)	H	X	l(c)	X	h(d)	X	q_n	(b)
	H	X	X	l(c)	h(d)	X	q_n	L

H = High voltage level steady state.
L = Low voltage level steady state.
h = High voltage level one setup time prior to the low-to-high clock transition.
l = Low voltage level one setup time prior to the low-to-high clock transition.
x = Don't care.
q = Lower case letters indicate the state of the referenced output prior to the low-to-high clock transition.
↑ = Low-to-high clock transition.

NOTES
(b) The TC output is high when CET is high and the counter is at Terminal Count (HLLH for "160").
(c) The high-to-low transition of CEP or CET on the 54/74160 should only occur while CP is high for conventional operation.
(d) The low-to-high transition of $\overline{PE}$ on the 54/74160 should only occur while CP is high for conventional operation.

114

Synchronous Multistage Counting Scheme

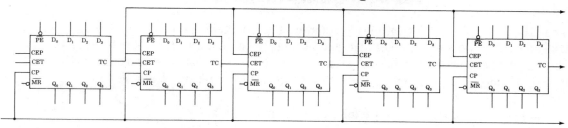

For some applications, the designer might want to change those inputs while the clock is low. In this case, the 74160 will behave in a predictable manner. For example, if $\overline{PE}$ goes high while the clock is low, and the count enable is not active during the remaining clock low period (i.e., CEP or CET are low), the subsequent low-to-high clock transition will change Q_0 through Q_3 to the D_0 through D_3 data that existed at the setup time before the rising edge of $\overline{PE}$. If $\overline{PE}$ goes high while the clock is low, and the count enable is active (CEP and CET are high) during some portion of the remaining clock low period, the 74160 will perform a mixture of counting and loading. On the low-to-high clock transition, outputs Q_0 through Q_3 will change as the count sequence or the loading requires. Only the outputs that would not change in the count sequence and that are also reloaded with their present value stay constant.

If the count enable is active (i.e., CEP and CET are high) during some portion of the clock low period, and $\overline{PE}$ is high (inactive) during the entire clock low period, the subsequent low-to-high clock transition will change Q_0 through Q_3 to the next count value.

74161 4-Bit Binary Counter

The '161 is a high-speed 4-bit binary counter. The counters are positive edge-triggered, synchronously presettable and are easily cascaded to n-bit synchronous applications without additional gating. A terminal count that detects a count of HHHH output is provided. The master reset asynchronously clears all flip-flops.

Refer to 74160 for a further explanation of binary counters.

	74LS	**74**
Count Frequency (MHz)	25	25
Parallel Load	Synchronous	Synchronous
Clear	Asynchronous-Low	Asynchronous-Low
Typ. Total Power (mW)	93	305

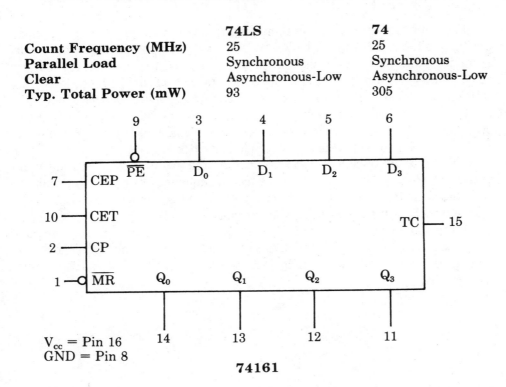

V_{cc} = Pin 16
GND = Pin 8

74161

MODE SELECT-FUNCTION TABLE

OPERATING MODE	INPUTS						OUTPUTS	
	$\overline{MR}$	CP	CEP	CET	$\overline{PE}$	D_n	Q_n	TC
Reset (Clear)	L	X	X	X	X	X	L	L
Parallel Load	H	↑	X	X	l	l	L	L
	H	↑	X	X	l	h	H	(b)
Count	H	↑	h	h	h(d)	X	count	(b)
Hold (do nothing)	H	X	l(c)	X	h(d)	X	q_n	(b)
	H	X	X	l(c)	h(d)	X	q_n	L

H = High voltage level steady state.
L = Low voltage level steady state.
h = High voltage level one setup time prior to the low-to-high clock transition.
l = Low voltage level one setup time prior to the low-to-high clock transition.
X = Don't care.
q = Lower case letters indicate the state of the referenced output prior to the low-to-high clock transition.
↑ = Low-to-high clock transition.

NOTES
(b) The TC output is high when CET is high and the counter is at Terminal Count (HHHH for "161").
(c) The high-to-low transition of CEP or CET on the 54/74161 should only occur while CP is high for conventional operation.
(d) The low-to-high transition of PE on the 54/74161 should only occur while CP is high for conventional operation.

117

74162 BCD Decade Counter

The '162 is a high-speed BCD decade counter. The counters are positive edge-triggered, synchronously presettable and are easily cascaded to n-bit synchronous applications without additional gating. A terminal count output that detects a count of HLLH is provided. The synchronous reset is edge-triggered. It overrides all control inputs, but is active only during the rising clock edge.

Refer to 74160 for a further explanation of binary counters.

	74LS	74
Count Frequency (MHz)	25	25
Parallel Load	Synchronous	Synchronous
Clear	Synchronous-Low	Synchronous-Low
Typ. Total Power (mW)	93	305

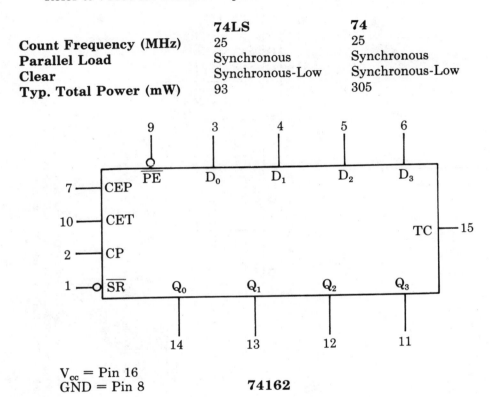

V_{cc} = Pin 16
GND = Pin 8

74162

MODE SELECT-FUNCTION TABLE

OPERATING MODE	INPUTS						OUTPUTS	
	$\overline{SR}$	CP	CEP	CET	$\overline{PE}$	D_n	Q_n	TC
Reset (Clear)	l	↑	X	X	X	X	L	L
Parallel Load	h(d)	↑	X	X	l	l	L	L
	h(d)	↑	X	X	l	h	H	(b)
Count	h(d)	↑	h	h	h(d)	X	count	(b)
Hold (do nothing)	h(d)	X	l(c)	X	h(d)	X	q_n	(b)
	h(d)	X	X	l(c)	h(d)	X	q_n	L

H = High voltage level steady state.
L = Low voltage level steady state.
h = High voltage level one setup time prior to the low-to-high clock transition.
l = Low voltage level one setup time prior to the low-to-high clock transition.
X = Don't care.
q = Lower case letters indicate the state of the referenced output prior to the low-to-high clock transition.
↑ = Low-to-high clock transition.

NOTES
(b) The TC output is high when CET is high and the counter is at Terminal Count (HLLH for "162").
(c) The high-to-low transition of CEP or CET on the 54/74162 should only occur while CP is high for conventional operation.
(d) The low-to-high transition of $\overline{PE}$ or $\overline{SR}$ on the 54/74162 should only occur while CP is high for conventional operation.

74163 4-Bit Binary Counter

The '163 is a high-speed 4-bit binary counter. The counters are positive edge-triggered, synchronously presettable and are easily cascaded to n-bit synchronous applications without additional gating. A terminal count output that detects a count of HHHH is provided. The synchronous reset is edge-triggered. It overrides all other control inputs, but is active only during the rising clock edge.

Refer to 74160 for a further explanation of binary counters.

	74LS	**74**
Count Frequency (MHz)	25	25
Parallel Load	Synchronous	Synchronous
Clear	Synchronous-Low	Synchronous-Low
Typ. Total Power (mW)	93	305

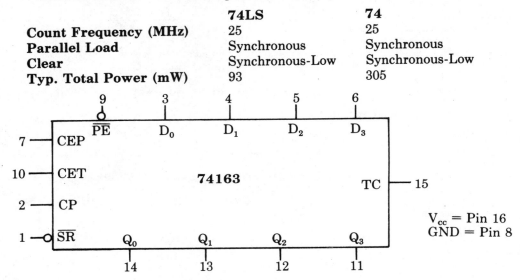

V_{cc} = Pin 16
GND = Pin 8

MODE SELECT-FUNCTION TABLE

OPERATING MODE	INPUTS						OUTPUTS	
	$\overline{SR}$	CP	CEP	CET	$\overline{PE}$	D_n	Q_n	TC
Reset (Clear)	1	↑	X	X	X	X	L	L
Parallel Load	h(d)	↑	X	X	l	l	L	L
	h(d)	↑	X	X	l	h	H	(b)
Count	h(d)	↑	h	h	h(d)	X	count	(b)
Hold (do nothing)	h(d)	X	l(c)	X	h(d)	X	q_n	(b)
	h(d)	X	X	l(c)	h(d)	X	q_n	L

H = High voltage level steady state.
L = Low voltage level steady state.
h = High voltage level one setup time prior to the low-to-high clock transition.
l = Low voltage level one setup time prior to the low-to-high clock transition.
X = Don't care.
q = Lower case letters indicate the state of the referenced output prior to the low-to-high clock transition.
↑ = Low-to-high clock transition.

NOTES
(b) The TC output is high when CET is high and the counter is at Terminal Count (HHHH for "163").
(c) The high-to-low transition of CEP or CET on the 54/74163 should only occur while CP is high for conventional operation.
(d) The low-to-high transition of $\overline{PE}$ or $\overline{SR}$ on the 54/74163 should only occur while CP is high for conventional operation.

74164 8-Bit Serial-In Parallel-Out Shift Register

The '164 is an 8-bit edge-triggered shift register with serial data entry and an output from each of the eight stages. Data are entered serially through one of two inputs (D_{sa} or D_{sb}). Either input can be used as an active high enable for data entry through the other input. Both inputs must be connected together or an unused input must be tied high.

Data shift one place to the right on each low-to-high transition of the clock (CP) input, and enter into Q_0 the logical AND of the two data inputs ($D_{sa} \cdot D_{sb}$) that existed one setup time before the rising clock edge. A low level on the master reset ($\overline{MR}$) input overrides all other inputs and clears the register asynchronously, forcing all outputs low.

	74LS	74	74L
Shift Frequency (MHz)	25	25	6
Serial Data Input	Gated D	Gated D	Gated D
Asynchronous Clear	Low	Low	Low
Shift-Right Mode	Yes	Yes	Yes
Shift-Left Mode	No	No	No
Load	No	No	No
Hold	No	No	No
Typ. Total Power (mW)	80	175	30

V_{cc} = Pin 14
GND = Pin 7

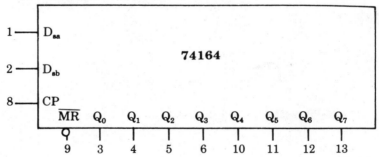

Truth Table

OPERATING MODE	INPUTS				OUTPUTS			
	$\overline{MR}$	CP	D_{sa}	D_{sb}	Q_0	Q_1	—	Q_7
Reset (Clear)	L	X	X	X	L	L	—	L
Shift	H	↑	l	l	L	q_0	—	q_6
	H	↑	l	h	L	q_0	—	q_6
	H	↑	h	l	L	q_0	—	q_6
	H	↑	h	h	H	q_0	—	q_6

H = High voltage level
h = High voltage level one setup time prior to the low-to-high clock transition
L = Low voltage level
l = Low voltage level one setup time prior to the low-to-high clock transition
q = Lower case letters indicate the state of the referenced input (or output) one setup time prior to the low-to-high clock transition
X = Don't care
↑ = Low-to-high clock transition

121

74165 8-Bit Serial/Parallel-In Serial-Out Shift Register

The '165 is an 8-bit parallel load or serial-in shift register with complementary serial outputs (Q_7 and $\overline{Q_7}$) available from the last stage. When the parallel load ($\overline{PL}$) input is low, parallel data from the D_0 through D_7 inputs are loaded into the register asynchronously. When the $\overline{PL}$ input is high, data enter the register serially at the D_s input and shift one place to the right ($Q_0 \rightarrow Q_1 \rightarrow Q_2$, etc.) with each positive-going clock transition. This feature allows parallel to serial converter expansion by tying the Q_7 output to the D_s input of the succeeding stage.

The clock input is a gated OR structure that allows one input to be used as an active low clock enable ($\overline{CE}$) input. The pin assignment for the CP and $\overline{CE}$ inputs is arbitrary and can be reversed for layout convenience. The low-to-high transition of the $\overline{CE}$ input should only take place while the CP is high for predictable operation. Also, the CP and $\overline{CE}$ inputs should be low before the low-to-high transition of $\overline{PL}$ to prevent shifting the data when $\overline{PL}$ is released.

	74
Shift Frequency (MHz)	25
Serial Data Input	D
Asynchronous Clear	None
Shift-Right Mode	Yes
Shift-Left Mode	No
Load	Yes
Hold	Yes
Typ. Total Power (mW)	200

MODE SELECT-FUNCTION TABLE

OPERATING MODES	INPUTS					Q_n REGISTER		OUTPUTS	
	$\overline{PL}$	$\overline{CE}$	CP	D_s	D_0 - D_7	Q_0	Q_1 - Q_6	Q_7	$\overline{Q_7}$
Parallel Load	L	X	X	X	L	L	L - L	L	H
	L	X	X	X	H	H	H - H	H	L
Serial Shift	H	L	↑	l	X	L	q_0 - q_5	q_6	$\overline{q_6}$
	H	L	↑	h	X	H	q_0 - q_5	q_6	$\overline{q_6}$
Hold "Do Nothing"	H	H	X	X	X	q_0	q_1 - q_6	q_7	$\overline{q_7}$

H = High voltage level.
h = High voltage level one setup time prior to the low-to-high clock transition.
L = Low voltage level.
l = Low voltage level one setup time prior to the low-to-high clock transition.
q_n = Lower case letters indicate the state of the referenced output one setup time prior to the low-to-high clock transition.
X = Don't care.
↑ = Low-to-high clock transition.

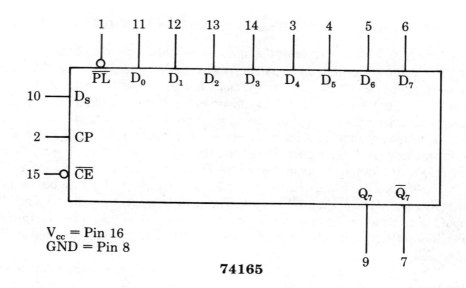

V_{cc} = Pin 16
GND = Pin 8

74165

74166 8-Bit Serial/Parallel-In Serial-Out Shift Register

The '166 is an 8-bit shift register that has fully synchronous serial or parallel data entry selected by an active low parallel enable ($\overline{PE}$) input. When the $\overline{PE}$ is low one setup time before the low-to-high clock transition, parallel data are entered into the register. When $\overline{PE}$ is high, data are entered into the register. When $\overline{PE}$ is high, data are entered into internal bit position Q_0 from serial data input (D_s), and the remaining bits are shifted one place to the right ($Q_0 \rightarrow Q_1 \rightarrow Q_2$) with each positive-going clock transition. To expand the register in parallel to serial converters, the Q_7 output is connected to the D_s input of the succeeding stage.

The clock input is a gated OR structure that allows one input to be used as an active low clock enable ($\overline{CE}$) input. The pin assignment for the CP and $\overline{CE}$ inputs is arbitrary and can be reversed for layout convenience. The low-to-high transition of $\overline{CE}$ input should only occur while the CP is high for predictable operation.

A low on the master reset ($\overline{MR}$) input overrides all other inputs and clears the register asynchronously, forcing all bit positions to a low state.

	74
Shift Frequency (MHz)	20
Serial Data Input	D
Asynchronous Clear	Low
Shift-Right Mode	Yes
Shift-Left Mode	No
Load	Yes
Hold	Yes
Typ. Total Power (mW)	360

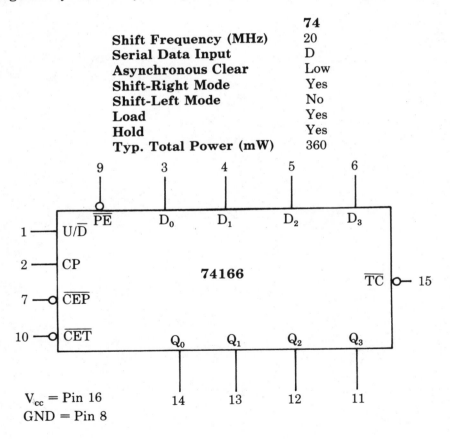

V_{cc} = Pin 16
GND = Pin 8

MODE SELECT-FUNCTION TABLE

OPERATING MODE	INPUTS						OUTPUTS	
	CP	U/$\overline{\text{D}}$	$\overline{\text{CEP}}$	$\overline{\text{CET}}$	$\overline{\text{PE}}$	D_n	Q_n	$\overline{\text{TC}}$
Parallel Load	↑	X	X	X	l	l	L	(b)
	↑	X	X	X	l	h	H	(b)
Count Up	↑	h	l	l	h	X	Count Up	(b)
Count Down	↑	l	l	l	h	X	Count Down	(b)
Hold (do nothing)	↑	X	h	X	h	X	q_n	(b)
	↑	X	X	h	h	X	q_n	H

H = High voltage level steady state.
L = Low voltage level steady state.
h = High voltage level one setup time prior to the low-to-high clock transition.
l = Low voltage level one setup time prior to the low-to-high clock transition.
X = Don't care.
q = Lower case letters indicate the state of the referenced output prior to the low-to-high clock transition.
↑ = Low-to-high clock transition.

NOTE
(b) The $\overline{\text{TC}}$ is low when $\overline{\text{CET}}$ is low and the counter is at Terminal Count. Terminal Count Up is (HLLH), and Terminal Count Down is (LLLL).

74168 4-Bit Up/Down Synchronous Counter

The '168 is a synchronous presettable BCD decade up/down counter featuring an internal carry lookahead for applications in high-speed counting designs. Synchronous operation is provided by having all flip-flops clocked simultaneously so that the outputs change coincident with each other when so instructed by the count-enable inputs and internal gating. This mode of operation eliminates the output spikes which are normally associated with asynchronous (ripple clock) counters. A buffered clock input triggers the flip-flops on the low-to-high transition of the clock.

The counter is fully programmable; that is, the outputs can be present to either level. Presetting is synchronous with the clock and occurs regardless of the levels of the count-enable inputs. A low level on the parallel enable ($\overline{PE}$) input disables the counter and causes the data at the D_n inputs to be loaded into the counter on the next low-to-high transition of the clock. The direction of counting is controlled by the up/down ($U/\overline{D}$) input; a high will cause the count to increase, and a low will cause the count to decrease.

	74LS
Count Frequency (MHz)	25
Parallel Load	Synchronous
Clear	None
Typ. Total Power (mW)	100

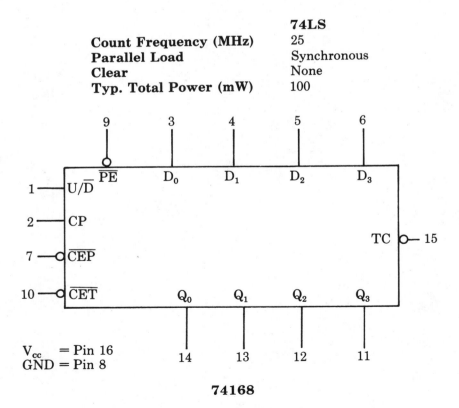

V_{cc} = Pin 16
GND = Pin 8

74168

MODE SELECT-FUNCTION TABLE

OPERATING MODE	INPUTS					OUTPUTS	
	CP	U/$\overline{\text{D}}$	$\overline{\text{CEP}}$	$\overline{\text{CET}}$	$\overline{\text{PE}}$	D_n	Q_n	$\overline{\text{TC}}$
Parallel Load	↑	X	X	X	l	l	L	(b)
	↑	X	X	X	l	h	H	(b)
Count Up	↑	h	l	l	h	X	Count Up	(b)
Count Down	↑	l	l	l	h	X	Count Down	(b)
Hold (do nothing)	↑	X	h	X	h	X	q_n	(b)
	↑	X	X	h	h	X	q_n	H

H = High voltage level steady state.
L = Low voltage level steady state.
h = High voltage level one setup time prior to the low-to-high clock transition.
l = Low voltage level one setup time prior to the low-to-high clock transition.
X = Don't care.
q = Lower case letters indicate the state of the referenced output prior to the low-to-high clock transition.
↑ = Low-to-high clock transition.

NOTE
(b) The $\overline{\text{TC}}$ is low when $\overline{\text{CET}}$ is low and the counter is at Terminal Count. Terminal Count Up is (HLLH), and Terminal Count Down is (LLLL).

this function are two count-enable inputs ($\overline{\text{CET}} \cdot \overline{\text{CEP}}$) and a terminal count ($\overline{\text{TC}}$) output. Both count-enable inputs must be low to count. The $\overline{\text{CET}}$ input is fed forward to enable the $\overline{\text{TC}}$ output. The $\overline{\text{TC}}$ output, thus enabled, will produce a low output pulse with a duration approximately equal to the high-level portion of the Q_0 output. This low-level $\overline{\text{TC}}$ pulse is used to enable successive cascaded stages. The fast synchronous multistage counting connections are shown here.

74169 4-Bit Up/Down Synchronous Counter

The '169 is a synchronous presettable modulo 16 binary up/down counter featuring an internal carry lookahead for applications in high-speed counting designs. Synchronous operation is provided by having all flip-flops clocked simultaneously so that the outputs change coincident with each other when so instructed by the count-enable inputs and internal gating. This mode of operation eliminates the output spikes that are normally associated with asynchronous (ripple clock) counters. A buffered clock input triggers the flip-flops on the low-to-high transition of the clock.

The counter is fully programmable; that is, the outputs can be preset to either level. Presetting is synchronous with the clock and occurs regardless of the levels of the count enable inputs. A low level on the parallel enable ($\overline{PE}$) input disables the counter and causes the data at the D_n inputs to be loaded into the counter on the next low-to-high transition of the clock. The direction of counting is controlled by the up/down ($U/\overline{D}$) input. A high will cause the count to increase, and a low will cause the count to decrease.

	74LS
Count Frequency (MHz)	25
Parallel Load	Synchronous
Clear	None
Typ. Total Power (mW)	100

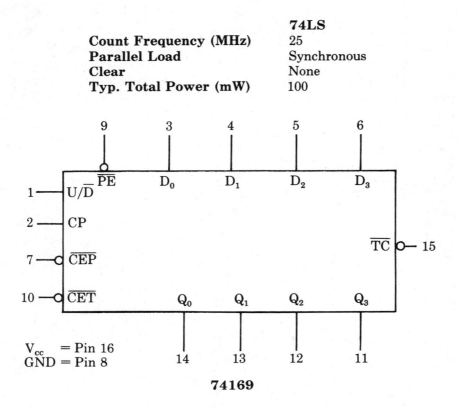

74169

V_{cc} = Pin 16
GND = Pin 8

MODE SELECT — FUNCTION TABLE

OPERATING MODE	INPUTS						OUTPUTS	
	CP	U/$\overline{\text{D}}$	$\overline{\text{CEP}}$	$\overline{\text{CET}}$	$\overline{\text{PE}}$	D_n	Q_n	$\overline{\text{TC}}$
Parallel Load	↑	X	X	X	l	l	L	(b)
	↑	X	X	X	l	h	H	(b)
Count Up	↑	h	l	l	h	X	Count Up	(b)
Count Down	↑	l	l	l	h	X	Count Down	(b)
Hold (do nothing)	↑	X	h	X	h	X	q_n	(b)
	↑	X	X	h	h	X	q_n	H

H = High voltage level steady state.
L = Low voltage level steady state.
h = High voltage level one setup time prior to the low-to-high clock transition.
l = Low voltage level one setup time prior to the low-to-high clock transition.
X = Don't care.
q = Lower case letters indicate the state of the referenced output prior to the low-to-high clock transition.
↑ = Low-to-high clock transition.

NOTE
(b) The $\overline{\text{TC}}$ is low when $\overline{\text{CET}}$ is low and the counter is at Terminal Count. Terminal Count up is (HHHH) and Terminal Count Down is (LLLL).

The carry lookahead circuitry provides for cascading counters for n-bit synchronous applications without additional gating. Instrumental in accomplishing this function are two count-enable inputs ($\overline{\text{CEP}} \cdot \overline{\text{CEP}}$) and a terminal count ($\overline{\text{TC}}$) output. Both count-enable inputs must be low to count. The $\overline{\text{CET}}$ input is fed forward to enable the $\overline{\text{TC}}$ output. The $\overline{\text{TC}}$ output, thus enabled, will produce a low output pulse with a duration approximately equal to the high-level portion of the Q_0 output. This low-level $\overline{\text{TC}}$ pulse is used to enable successive cascaded stages. See 74168 for the fast synchronous multistage counting connections.

74173 Quad D-Type Flip-Flop with 3-State Outputs

The '173 is a 4-bit parallel load register with clock enable control, 3-state buffered outputs and master reset. When the two clock-enable ($\overline{E}_1$ and $\overline{E}_2$) inputs are low, data on the D inputs are loaded into the register synchronously with the low-to-high clock (CP) transition. When one or both $\overline{E}$ inputs are high one setup time before the low-to-high clock transition, the register will retain the previous data. The data inputs and clock-enable inputs are fully edge-triggered and must be stable only one setup time before the low-to-high clock transition. The master reset (MR) is an active high asynchronous input. When the MR is high, all four flip-flops are reset (cleared) independently of any other input condition.

The 3-state output buffers are controlled by a 2-input NOR gate. When both output enable ($\overline{OE}_1$ and $\overline{OE}_2$) inputs are low, the data in the register is presented at the Q outputs. When one or both $\overline{OE}$ inputs is high, the outputs are forced to a high-impedance off state. The 3-state output buffers are completely independent of the register operation. The OE transitions do not affect the clock and reset operations.

	74
Frequency (MHz)	25
Asynchronous Clear	High
Typ. Total Power (mW)	250

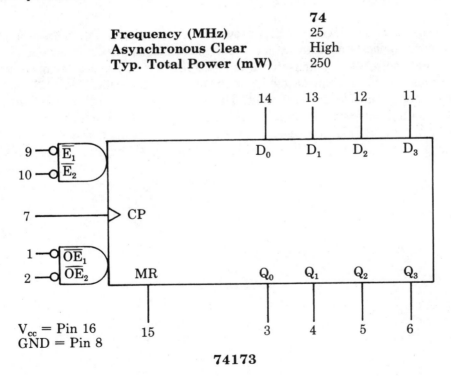

V_{cc} = Pin 16
GND = Pin 8

74173

MODE SELECT — FUNCTION TABLE

REGISTER OPERATING MODES	INPUTS					OUTPUTS
	MR	CP	$\overline{E}_1$	$\overline{E}_2$	D_n	Q_n (Register)
Reset (clear)	H	X	X	X	X	L
Parallel Load	L	↑	l	l	l	L
	L	↑	l	l	h	H
Hold (No change)	L	X	h	X	X	q_n
	L	X	X	h	X	q_n

3-STATE BUFFER OPERATING MODES	INPUTS			OUTPUTS
	Q_n (Register)	$\overline{OE}_1$	$\overline{OE}_2$	Q_0, Q_1, Q_2, Q_3
Read	L	L	L	L
	H	L	L	H
Disabled	X	H	X	(Z)
	X	X	H	(Z)

NOTES

H = High voltage level
h = High voltage level one setup time prior to the low-to-high clock transition
L = Low voltage level
l = Low voltage level one setup time prior to the low-to-high clock transition
q_n = Lower case letters indicate the state of the referenced input (or output) one setup time prior to the low-to-high clock transition
X = Don't care
(Z) = High impedance "off" state
↑   = Low-to-high transition

74174 Hex D Flip-Flop

The '174 has six edge-triggered D-type flip-flops with individual D inputs and Q outputs. The common buffered clock (CP) and master reset ($\overline{\text{MR}}$) inputs load and reset (clear) all flip-flops simultaneously. The register is fully edge-triggered. The state of each D input, one setup time before the low-to-high clock transition, is transferred to the corresponding Q output of the flip-flop.

All outputs will be forced low independently of clock or data inputs by a low voltage level on the $\overline{\text{MR}}$ input. The device is useful for applications where the true output only is required and the clock and master reset are common to all storage elements.

	74S	**74LS**	**74**
Frequency (MHz)	75	30	25
Asynchronous Clear	Low	Low	Low
Typ. Total Power (mW)	450	80	225

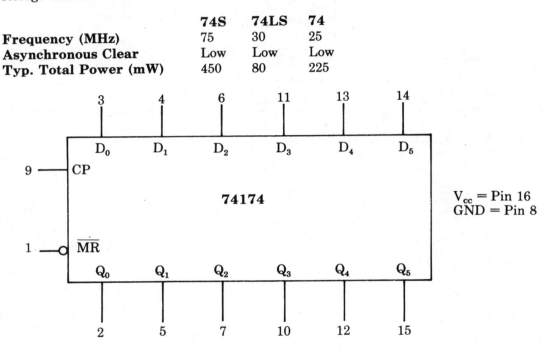

V_{cc} = Pin 16
GND = Pin 8

MODE SELECT-FUNCTION TABLE

OPERATING MODE	INPUTS			OUTPUTS
	$\overline{\text{MR}}$	CP	D_n	Q_n
Reset (clear)	L	X	X	L
Load "1"	H	↑	h	H
Load "0"	H	↑	l	L

H = High voltage level steady state
h = High voltage level one setup time prior to the low-to-high clock transition
L = Low voltage level steady state
l = Low voltage level one setup time prior to the low-to-high clock transition
X = Don't care
↑ = Low-to-high clock transition

74175 Quad D Flip-Flop

The '175 is a quad edge-triggered D-type flip-flop with individual D inputs and both Q and $\overline{Q}$ outputs. The common buffered clock (CP) and master reset ($\overline{MR}$) inputs load and reset (clear) all flip-flops simultaneously.

The register is fully edge-triggered. The state of each D input, one setup time before the low-to-high clock transition, is transferred to the corresponding Q output of the flip-flop.

All Q outputs will be forced low independently of clock or data inputs by a low voltage level on the $\overline{MR}$ input. The device is useful for applications where both true and complement outputs are required, and the clock and master reset are common to all storage elements.

	74S	74LS	74
Frequency (MHz)	75	30	25
Asynchronous Clear	Low	Low	Low
Typ. Total Power (mW)	300	55	150

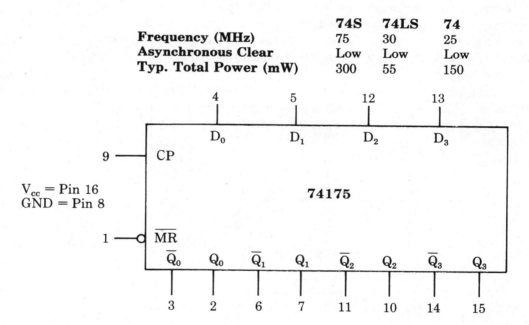

V_{cc} = Pin 16
GND = Pin 8

MODE SELECT — FUNCTION TABLE

OPERATING MODE	INPUTS			OUTPUTS	
	$\overline{MR}$	CP	D_n	Q_n	$\overline{Q}_n$
Reset (clear)	L	X	X	L	H
Load "1"	H	↑	h	H	L
Load "0"	H	↑	l	L	H

H = High voltage level steady state.
h = High voltage level one setup time prior to the low-to-high clock transition.
L = Low voltage level steady state.
l = Low voltage level one setup time prior to the low-to-high clock transition.
X = Don't care.
↑ = Low-to-high clock transition.

133

74180 9-Bit Odd/Even Parity Generator/Checker

The '180 is a 9-bit parity generator or checker commonly used to detect errors in high-speed data transmissions or data-retrieval systems. Both even and odd parity enable inputs and parity outputs are available for generating or checking parity on 9-bits.

True active high or true active low parity can be generated at both the even and odd outputs. True active high parity is established with even parity enable input (P_E) set high and the odd parity enable input (P_O) set low. True active low parity is established when P_E is low and P_O is high. When both enable inputs are at the same logic level, both outputs will be forced to the opposite logic level.

Parity checking of a 9-bit word (8-bit plus parity) is possible by using the two enable inputs plus an inverter as the ninth data input. To check for true active high parity, the ninth data input is tied to the P_O input and an inverter is connected between the P_O and P_E inputs. To check for true active low parity, the ninth data input is tied to the P_E input and an inverter is connected between the P_E and P_O inputs.

Expansion to larger word sizes is accomplished by serially cascading the '180 in 8-bit increments. The even and odd parity outputs of the first stage are connected to the corresponding P_E and P_O inputs, respectively, of the succeeding stage.

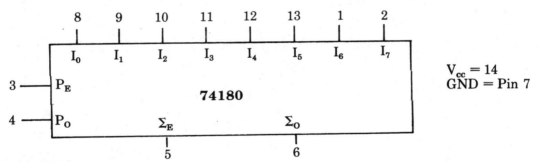

$V_{cc} = 14$
$GND = $ Pin 7

Truth Table

INPUTS			OUTPUTS	
Number of HIGH Data Inputs (I_0-I_7)	P_E	P_O	Σ_E	Σ_O
Even	H	L	H	L
Odd	H	L	L	H
Even	L	H	L	H
Odd	L	H	H	L
X	H	H	L	L
X	L	L	H	H

H = High voltage level
L = Low voltage level
X = Don't care

	74
Typ. Delay Time (ns)	35
Typ. Total Power (mW)	170

74181 4-Bit Arithmetic Logic Unit

The '181 is a 4-bit high-speed parallel arithmetic logic unit (ALU). Controlled by the four function select inputs ($S_0 \ldots S_3$) and the mode control input (M), it can perform all the 16 possible logic operations or 16 different arithmetic operations on active high or active low operands. The function table lists these operations.

When the mode control input (M) is high, all internal carries are inhibited and the device performs logic operations on the individual bits as listed. When the mode control input is low, the carries are enabled and the device performs arithmetic operations on the two 4-bit words. The device incorporates full internal carry look ahead and provides for either ripple carry between devices using the C_{n+4} output, or for carry look ahead between packages using the signals $\overline{P}$ (carry propagate) and $\overline{G}$ (Carry Generate). $\overline{P}$ and $\overline{G}$ are not affected by carry in. When speed requirements are not stringent, it can be used in a simple ripple-carry mode by connecting the carry output (C_{n+4}) signal to the carry input (C_n) of the next unit. For high-speed operation, the device is used in conjunction with

	74
Typ. Carry Time (ns)	12.5
Typ. Add Time (ns)	24
Typ. Total Power (mW)	455

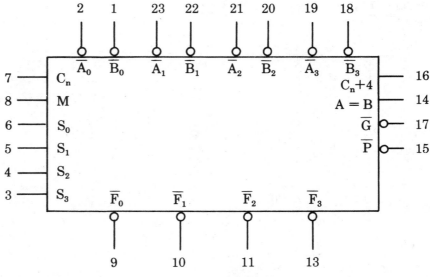

V_{cc} = Pin 24
GND = Pin 12

74181

MODE SELECT - FUNCTION TABLE

MODE SELECT INPUTS				ACTIVE HIGH INPUTS & OUTPUTS	
S_3	S_2	S_1	S_0	LOGIC (M = H)	ARITHMETIC** (M = L) (C_n = H)
L	L	L	L	$\overline{A}$	A
L	L	L	H	$\overline{A + B}$	A + $\overline{B}$
L	L	H	L	$\overline{A}B$	A + $\overline{B}$
L	L	H	H	Logical 0	minus 1
L	H	L	L	$\overline{AB}$	A plus A$\overline{B}$
L	H	L	H	$\overline{B}$	(A + B) plus A$\overline{B}$
L	H	H	L	A$\oplus$B	A minus B minus 1
L	H	H	H	A$\overline{B}$	AB minus 1
H	L	L	L	$\overline{A} + B$	A plus AB
H	L	L	H	$\overline{A\oplus B}$	A plus B
H	L	H	L	B	(A + $\overline{B}$) plus AB
H	L	H	H	AB	AB minus 1
H	H	L	L	Logical 1	A plus A*
H	H	L	H	A + $\overline{B}$	(A + B) plus A
H	H	H	L	A + B	(A + $\overline{B}$) plus A
H	H	H	H	A	A minus 1

*Each bit is shifted to the next more significant position
**Arithmetic operations expressed in 2s complement notation

L = Low voltage level
H = High voltage level

MODE SELECT INPUTS				ACTIVE LOW INPUTS & OUTPUTS	
S_3	S_2	S_1	S_0	LOGIC (M = H)	ARITHMETIC** (M = L) (C_n = L)
L	L	L	L	$\overline{A}$	A minus 1
L	L	L	H	$\overline{AB}$	A$\overline{B}$ minus 1
L	L	H	L	$\overline{A} + B$	AB minus 1
L	L	H	H	Logical 1	minus 1
L	H	L	L	$\overline{A + B}$	A plus (A + $\overline{B}$)
L	H	L	H	$\overline{B}$	AB plus (A + $\overline{B}$)
L	H	H	L	$\overline{A\oplus B}$	A minus B minus 1
L	H	H	H	A + $\overline{B}$	A + $\overline{B}$
H	L	L	L	A$\overline{B}$	A plus (A + B)
H	L	L	H	A$\oplus$B	A plus B
H	L	H	L	B	A$\overline{B}$ plus (A + B)
H	L	H	H	A + B	A + B
H	H	L	L	Logical 0	A plus A*
H	H	L	H	A$\overline{B}$	A$\overline{B}$ plus A
H	H	H	L	AB	AB plus A
H	H	H	H	A	A

*Each bit is shifted to the next more significant position
**Arithmetic operations expressed in 2s complement notation

L = Low voltage level
H = High voltage level

the '182 carry-look-ahead circuit. One carry-look-ahead package is required for each group of four '181 devices. Carry look ahead can be provided at various levels and offers high-speed capability over extremely long word lengths.

The $A = B$ output from the device goes high when all four $\overline{F}$ outputs are high and can be used to indicate logic equivalence over four bits when the unit is in the subtract mode. The $A = B$ output is an open collector and can be wired-AND with other $A = B$ outputs to give a comparison for more than four bits. The $A = B$ signal can be used with the C_{n+4} signal to indicate $A > B$ and $A < B$.

The function table lists the arithmetic operations that are performed without a carry-in. An incoming carry adds a one to each operation. Thus, select code LHHL generates A minus B minus 1 (2s complement notation) without a carry-in and generates A minus B when a carry is applied. Because subtraction is actually performed by complementary addition (1s complement), a carry-out means borrow; thus, a carry is generated when there is no underflow and no carry is generated when there is underflow.

This device can be used with either active low inputs producing active low outputs or with active high inputs producing active high outputs. For either case, the table lists the operations that are performed to the operands labeled inside the logic symbol.

74182 Carry-Look-Ahead Generator

The '182 carry-look-ahead generator accepts up to four pairs of active low carry propogate ($\overline{P}_0$, $\overline{P}_1$, $\overline{P}_2$, and $\overline{P}_3$) and carry generate ($\overline{G}_0$, $\overline{G}_1$, $\overline{G}_2$, ad $\overline{G}_3$) signals and an active high carry input (C_n) and provides anticipated active high carries (C_{n+x} $C_n + y$ C_{n+z}) across four groups of binary adders. The '182 also has active low carry propagate ($\overline{P}$) and carry-generate ($\overline{G}$) outputs that can be used for further levels of look ahead.

Also, the '182 can also be used with binary. ALUs in an active low or active high input operand mode. The connections to and from the ALU to the carry-look-ahead generator are identical in both cases.

	74S	74
Typ. Carry Time (ns)	7	13
Typ. Total Power (mW)	260	180

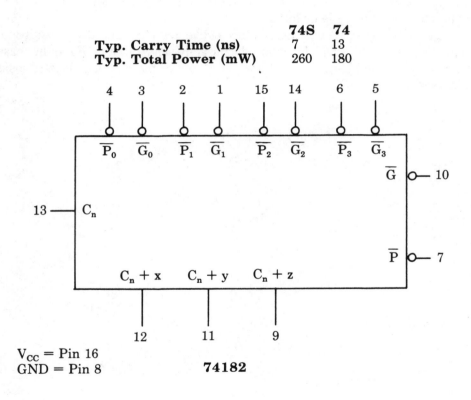

V_{CC} = Pin 16
GND = Pin 8

74182

Truth Table

INPUTS									OUTPUTS				
C_n	$\overline{G}_0$	$\overline{P}_0$	$\overline{G}_1$	$\overline{P}_1$	$\overline{G}_2$	$\overline{P}_2$	$\overline{G}_3$	$\overline{P}_3$	C_{n+x}	C_{n+y}	C_{n+z}	$\overline{G}$	$\overline{P}$
X	H	H							L				
L	H	X							L				
X	L	X							H				
H	X	L							H				
X	X	X	H	H						L			
X	H	H	H	X						L			
L	H	X	H	X						L			
X	X	X	L	X						H			
X	L	X	X	L						H			
H	X	L	X	L						H			
X	X	X	X	X	H	H					L		
X	X	X	H	H	H	X					L		
X	H	H	H	X	H	X					L		
L	H	X	H	X	H	X					L		
X	X	X	X	X	L	X					H		
X	X	X	L	X	X	L					H		
X	L	X	X	L	X	L					H		
H	X	L	X	L	X	L					H		
	X		X	X	X	X	H	H				H	
	X		X	X	H	H	H	X				H	
	X		H	H	H	X	H	X				H	
	H		H	X	H	X	H	X				H	
	X		X	X	X	X	L	X				L	
	X		X	X	L	X	X	L				L	
	X		L	X	X	L	X	L				L	
	L		X	L	X	L	X	L				L	
		H		X		X		X					H
		X		H		X		X					H
		X		X		H		X					H
		X		X		X		H					H
		L		L		L		L					L

H = High voltage level
L = Low voltage level
X = Don't care

74190 Presettable BCD/Decade Up/Down Counter

The '190 is an asynchronously presettable up/down BCD decade counter. It contains four master-slave flip-flops with internal gating and steering logic to provide asynchronous preset and synchronous countup and countdown operations.

Asynchronous parallel load capability permits the counter to be preset to any desired number. Information present on the parallel-data inputs (D_0 through D_3) is loaded into the counter and appears on the outputs when the parallel-load ($\overline{PL}$) input is low. As indicated in the mode-select table, this operation overrides the counting function.

Counting is inhibited by a high level on the count-enable ($\overline{CE}$) input. When $\overline{CE}$ is low, internal state changes are initiated synchronously by the low-to-high transition of the clock input. The up/down ($\overline{U}/D$) input signal determines the direction of counting as indicated in the mode-select table. The $\overline{CE}$ input can go low when the clock is in either state; however, the low-to-high $\overline{CE}$ transition must occur only while the clock is high. Also, the $\overline{U}/D$ input should be changed only when either $\overline{CE}$ or CP is high.

	74LS	74
Count Frequency (MHz)	20	20
Parallel Load	Asynchronous	Asynchronous
Clear	None	None
Typ. Total Power (mW)	100	325

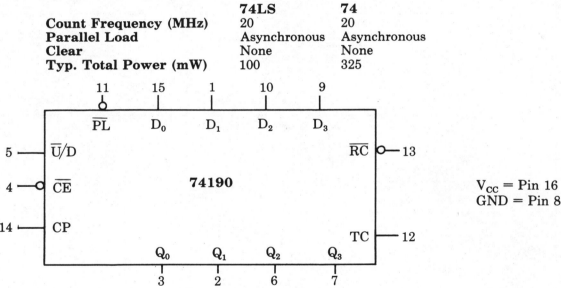

V_{CC} = Pin 16
GND = Pin 8

MODE SELECT-FUNCTION TABLE

OPERATING MODE	INPUTS					OUTPUTS
	$\overline{PL}$	$\overline{U}/D$	$\overline{CE}$	CP	D_n	Q_n
Parallel load	L	X	X	X	L	L
	L	X	X	X	H	H
Count up	H	L	l	↑	X	count up
Count down	H	H	l	↑	X	count down
Hold "do nothing"	H	X	H	X	X	no change

TC AND $\overline{\text{RC}}$ TRUTH TABLE

INPUTS			TERMINAL COUNT STATE				OUTPUTS	
$\overline{\text{U}}/\text{D}$	$\overline{\text{CE}}$	CP	Q_0	Q_1	Q_2	Q_3	TC	$\overline{\text{RC}}$
H	X	X	H	X	X	H	L	H
L	H	X	H	X	X	H	H	H
L	L	⎍	H	X	X	H	H	⎍
L	X	X	L	L	L	L	L	H
H	H	X	L	L	L	L	H	H
H	L	⎍	L	L	L	L	H	⎍

H = High voltage level steady state.
L = Low voltage level steady state.
l = Low voltage level one setup time prior to the low-to-high clock transition.
X = Don't care.
↑ = Low-to-high clock transition.
⎍ = Low pulse.

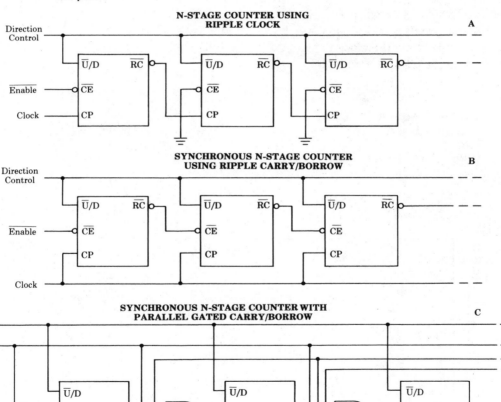

N-STAGE COUNTER USING RIPPLE CLOCK A

SYNCHRONOUS N-STAGE COUNTER USING RIPPLE CARRY/BORROW B

SYNCHRONOUS N-STAGE COUNTER WITH PARALLEL GATED CARRY/BORROW C

74191 Presettable 4-Bit Binary Up/Down Counter

The '191 is an asynchronously presettable up/down 4-bit binary counter. It contains four master-slave flip-flops with internal gating and steering logic to provide asynchronous preset and synchronous countup and countdown operation.

Asynchronous parallel load capability permits the counter to be preset to any desired number. Information present on the parallel data inputs (D_0 through D_3) is loaded into the counter and appears on the outputs when the parallel-load ($\overline{PL}$) input is low. As indicated in the mode-select table, this operation overrides the counting function.

Counting is inhibited by a high level on the count-enable ($\overline{CE}$) input. When $\overline{CE}$ is low, internal state changes are initiated synchronously by the low-to-high transition of the clock input. The up/down ($\overline{U}/D$) input signal determines the direction of counting as indicated in the mode-select table. The $\overline{CE}$ input can go low when the clock is in either state; however, the low-to-high $\overline{CE}$ transition must occur only while the clock is high. Also, the $\overline{U}/D$ input should be changed only when either $\overline{CE}$ or CP is high.

	74LS	74
Count Frequency (MHz)	20	20
Parallel Load	Asynchronous	Asynchronous
Clear	None	None
Typ. Total Power (mW)	90	325

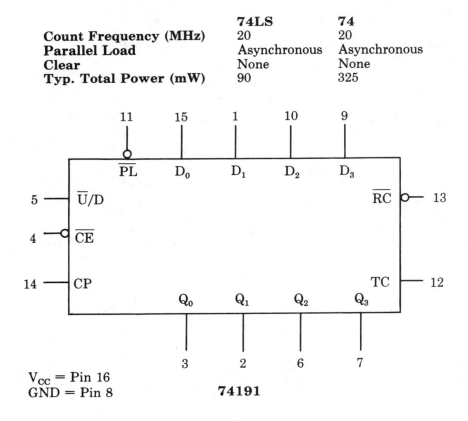

V_{CC} = Pin 16
GND = Pin 8

74191

MODE SELECT-FUNCTION TABLE

OPERATING MODE	INPUTS					OUTPUTS
	$\overline{PL}$	$\overline{U}/D$	$\overline{CE}$	CP	D_n	Q_n
Parallel load	L	X	X	X	L	L
	L	X	X	X	H	H
Count up	H	L	l	↑	X	count up
Count down	H	H	l	↑	X	count down
Hold "do nothing"	H	X	H	X	X	no change

TC AND $\overline{RC}$ TRUTH TABLE

INPUTS			TERMINAL COUNT STATE				OUTPUTS	
$\overline{U}/D$	$\overline{CE}$	CP	Q_0	Q_1	Q_2	Q_3	TC	$\overline{RC}$
H	X	X	H	H	H	H	L	H
L	H	X	H	H	H	H	H	H
L	L	⊔	H	H	H	H	H	⊔
L	X	X	L	L	L	L	L	H
H	H	X	L	L	L	L	H	H
H	L	⊔	L	L	L	L	H	⊔

H = High voltage level steady state.
L = Low voltage level steady state.
l = Low voltage level one setup time prior to the low-to-high clock transition.
X = Don't care.
↑ = Low-to-high clock transition.
⊔ = Low pulse.

74192 Presettable BCD Decade Up/Down Counter

The '192 is an asynchronously presettable up/down (reversible) internal gating and steering logic to provide asynchronous master reset (clear), parallel load, and synchronous countup and countdown operations.

Each flip-flop contains JK feedback from slave to master such that a low-to-high transition on the clock inputs causes the Q outputs to change state synchronously. A low-to-high transition on the countdown-clock-pulse (CP_D) input will decrease the count by one, while a similar transition on the countup-clock-pulse (CP_U) input will advance the count by one. One clock should be held high while counting with the other, because the circuit will either count by twos or not at all, depending on the state of the first flip-flop, which cannot toggle as long as either clock input is low. Applications requiring reversible operation must make the reversing decision while the activating clock is high to avoid erroneous counts.

The terminal countup ($\overline{TC_U}$) and terminal countdown ($\overline{TC_D}$) outputs are normally high. When the circuit has reached the maximum count state of nine, the next high-to-low transition of CP_U will cause $\overline{TC_U}$ to go low. $\overline{TC_U}$ will stay low until CP_U goes high again, duplicating the countup clock, although delayed by two gate delays. Likewise, the $\overline{TC_D}$ output will go low when the circuit is in the zero state and the CP_D goes low. The $\overline{TC}$ outputs can be used as the clock-input signals to the next higher order circuit in a multistage counter, because they duplicate the clock waveforms. Multistage counters will not be fully synchronous, because there is a two-gate delay time difference added for each stage that is added.

The counter can be preset by the asynchronous parallel load capability of the circuit. Information present on the parallel-data inputs (D_0 through D_3) is loaded into the counter and appears on the outputs, regardless of the conditions of the clock inputs when the parallel-load ($\overline{PL}$) input is low. A high level on the master-reset (MR) input will disable the parallel-load gates, override both clock inputs and set all Q outputs low. If one of the clock inputs is low during and after a reset or load operation, the next low-to-high transition of that clock will be interpreted as a legitimate signal and will be counted.

	74LS	74	74L
Count Frequency (MHz)	25	20	6
Parallel Load	Asynchronous	Asynchronous	Asynchronous
Clear	Asynchronous-High	Asynchronous-High	Asynchronous-High
Typ. Total Power (mW)	85	325	40

LOGIC EQUATIONS FOR TERMINAL COUNT

$$\overline{TC}_U = Q_0 \cdot Q_3 \cdot CP_U$$
$$\overline{TC}_D = Q_0 \cdot Q_1 \cdot Q_2 \cdot Q_3 \cdot CP_D$$

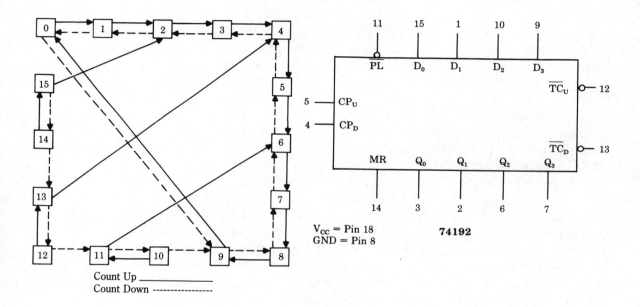

Count Up _____
Count Down ------------------

V_{CC} = Pin 18
GND = Pin 8

74192

MODE SELECT-FUNCTION TABLE

OPERATING MODE	INPUTS					OUTPUTS		
	MR	$\overline{PL}$	CP_U	CP_D	$D_0, \ D_1, \ D_2, \ D_3$	$Q_0, \ Q_1, \ Q_2, \ Q_3$	$\overline{TC}_U$	$\overline{TC}_D$
Reset (clear)	H	X	X	L	X X X X	L L L L	H	L
	H	X	X	H	X X X X	L L L L	H	H
Parallel load	L	L	X	L	L L L L	L L L L	H	L
	L	L	X	H	L L L L	L L L L	H	H
	L	L	L	X	H X X H	$Q_n = D_n$	L	H
	L	L	H	X	H X X H	$Q_n = D_n$	H	H
Count up	L	H	↑	H	X X X X	Count up	H[b]	H
Count down	L	H	H	↑	X X X X	Count down	H	H[c]

H = High voltage level
L = Low voltage level
X = Don't care
↑ = Low-to-high clock transition

NOTES
(b) $\overline{TC}_U = CP_U$ at terminal count up (HLLH)
(c) $\overline{TC}_D = CP_D$ at terminal count down (LLLL)

74193 Presettable 4-Bit Binary Up/Down Counter

The '193 is an asynchronously presettable, up/down (reversible) 4-bit binary counter. It contains four master-slave flip-flops with internal gating and steering logic to provide asynchronous master reset (clear) and parallel load, and synchronous countup and countdown operations.

Each flip-flop contains JK feedback from slave to master such that a low-to-high transition on the clock inputs causes the Q outputs to change state synchronously. A low-to-high transition on the countdown-clock-pulse (CP_D) input will decrease the count by one, while similar transition on the countup-clock-pulse (CP_U) input will advance the count by one. One clock should be held high while counting with the other, because the circuit will either count by twos or not at all, depending on the state of the first flip-flop, which cannot toggle as long as either clock input is low. Applications requiring reversible operation must make the reversing decision while the activating clock is high to avoid erroneous counts.

The terminal countup ($\overline{TC_U}$) and terminal countdown ($\overline{TC_D}$) outputs are normally high. When the circuit has reached the maximum count state of 15, the next high-to-low transition of CP_U will cause $\overline{TC_U}$ to go low. $\overline{TC_U}$ will stay low until CP_U goes high again, duplicating the countup clock, although delayed by two gate delays. Likewise, the $\overline{TC_D}$ output will go low when the circuit is in the zero state and the CP_D goes low. The $\overline{TC}$ outputs can be used as the clock-input signals to the next higher order circuit in a multistage counter, because they duplicate the clock waveforms. Multistage counters will not be fully synchronous for there is a two-gate delay time difference added for each stage that is added.

The counter can be preset by the asynchronous parallel load capability of the circuit. Information present on the parallel-data inputs (D_0 through D_3) is loaded into the counter and appears on the outputs, regardless of the conditions of the clock inputs when the parallel-load ($\overline{PL}$) input is low. A high level on the master-reset (MR) input will disable the parallel-load gates, override both clock inputs and set all Q outputs low. If one of the clock inputs is low during and after a reset or load operation, the next low-to-high transition of that clock will be interpreted as a legitimate signal and will be counted.

	74LS	74	74L
Count Frequency (MHz)	25	20	6
Parallel Load	Asynchronous	Asynchronous	Asynchronous
Clear	Asynchronous-High	Asynchronous-High	Asynchronous-High
Typ. Total Power (mW)	85	325	40

LOGIC EQUATIONS FOR TERMINAL COUNT

$$\overline{TC}_U = Q_0 \cdot Q_1 \cdot Q_2 \cdot Q_3 \cdot CP_U$$
$$\overline{TC}_D = Q_0 \cdot Q_1 \cdot Q_2 \cdot Q_3 \cdot CP_D$$

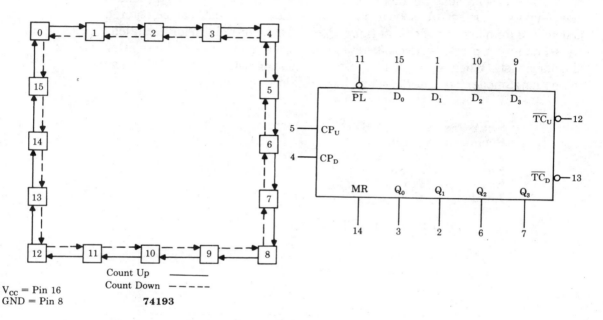

Count Up ———
Count Down – – – – –

V_{CC} = Pin 16
GND = Pin 8

74193

MODE SELECT-FUNCTION TABLE

OPERATING MODE	INPUTS								OUTPUTS					
	MR	$\overline{PL}$	CP_U	CP_D	D_0,	D_1,	D_2,	D_3	Q_0,	Q_1,	Q_2,	Q_3	$\overline{TC}_U$	$\overline{TC}_D$
Reset (clear)	H	X	X	L	X	X	X	X	L	L	L	L	H	L
	H	X	X	H	X	X	X	X	L	L	L	L	H	H
Parallel load	L	L	X	L	L	L	L	L	L	L	L	L	H	L
	L	L	X	H	L	L	L	L	L	L	L	L	H	H
	L	L	L	X	H	H	H	H	H	H	H	H	L	H
	L	L	H	X	H	H	H	H	H	H	H	H	H	H
Count up	L	H	↑	H	X	X	X	X	Count up				H[b]	H
Count down	L	H	H	↑	X	X	X	X	Count down				H	H[c]

H = High voltage level
L = Low voltage level
X = Don't care
↑ = Low-to-high clock transition

NOTES
(b) $\overline{TC}_U = CP_U$ at terminal count up (HHHH)
(c) $\overline{TC}_D = CP_D$ at terminal count down (LLLL)

74194 4-Bit Directional Universal Shift Register

The functional characteristics of the '194 4-bit bidirectional shift register are indicated in the logic diagram and truth table. The register is full-synchronous, with all operations taking place in less than 20 nanoseconds (typical) for the 74 and 74LS, and 12 ns (typical) for 74S, making the device especially useful for implementing very high-speed CPUs, or for memory-buffer registers.

The '194 design has special logic features that increase the application range. The synchronous operation of the device is determined by two mode-select inputs, S_0 and S_1. As shown in the mode-select table, data can be entered and shifted from left to right (shift right, $Q_0 \rightarrow Q_1$, etc.) or right to left (shift left, $Q_3 \rightarrow Q_2$, etc.) or parallel data can be entered, loading all four bits of the register simultaneously. When both S_0 and S_1 are low, existing data is retained in a hold (do nothing) mode. The interfering with parallel-load operation.

	74S	74LS	74
Shift Frequency (MHz)	70	25	25
Serial Data Input	D	D	D
Asynchronous Clear	Low	Low	Low
Shift-Right Mode	Yes	Yes	Yes
Shift-Left Mode	Yes	Yes	Yes
Load	Yes	Yes	Yes
Hold	Yes	Yes	Yes
Typ. Total Power (mW)	450	75	195

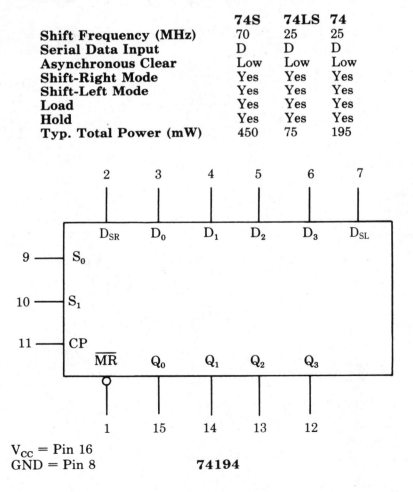

V_{CC} = Pin 16
GND = Pin 8

74194

MODE SELECT-FUNCTION TABLE

OPERATING MODE	INPUTS							OUTPUTS			
	CP	$\overline{MR}$	S_1	S_0	D_{SR}	D_{SL}	D_n	Q_0	Q_1	Q_2	Q_3
Reset (clear)	X	L	X	X	X	X	X	L	L	L	L
Hold (do nothing)	X	H	l(b)	l(b)	X	X	X	q_0	q_1	q_2	q_3
Shift Left	↑	H	h	l(b)	X	l	X	q_1	q_2	q_3	L
	↑	H	h	l(b)	X	h	X	q_1	q_2	q_3	H
Shift Right	↑	H	l(b)	h	l	X	X	L	q_0	q_1	q_2
	↑	H	l(b)	h	h	X	X	H	q_0	q_1	q_2
Parallel Load	↑	H	h	h	X	X	d_n	d_0	d_1	d_2	d_3

H = High voltage level
h = High voltage level one setup time prior to the low-to-high clock transition
L = Low voltage level
l = Low voltage level one setup time prior to the low-to-high clock transition
d_n (q_n) = Lower case letters indicate the state of the referenced input (or output) one setup time prior to the low-to-high clock transition
X = Don't care
↑ = Low-to-high clock transition

NOTES
(b) The high-to-low transition of the S_0 and S_1 inputs on the 54/74194 should only take place while CP is high for conventional operation.

Mode-select and data inputs on the 74S194 and 74LS194A are edge-triggered, responding only to the low-to-high transition of the clock (CP). Therefore, the only timing restriction is that the mode-control and selected data inputs must be stable one setup time prior to the positive transition of the clock pulse. The mode select inputs of the 74194 are gated with the clock and should be changed from high-to-low only while the clock input is high.

The four parallel data inputs (D_0 through D_3) are D-type inputs. Data appearing on D_0 through D_3 inputs when S_0 and S_1 are high are transferred to the Q_0 through Q_3 outputs respectively, following the next low-to-high transition of the clock. When low, the asynchronous master reset ($\overline{MR}$) overrides all other input conditions and forces the Q outputs low.

74195 4-Bit Parallel Access Shift Register

The functional characteristics of the '195 four-bit parallel-access shift register are indicated in the logic diagram and function table. The device is useful in a wide variety of shifting, counting and storage applications. It performs serial, parallel, serial-to-parallel, or parallel-to-serial data transfers at very high speeds.

The '195 operates on two primary modes: shift right ($Q_0 \rightarrow Q_1$) and parallel load, which are both controlled by the state of the parallel enable ($\overline{PE}$) input. Serial data enters the first flip-flop (Q_0) via the J and $\overline{K}$ inputs when the $\overline{PE}$ input is high, and is shifted one bit in the direction $Q_0 \rightarrow Q_1 \rightarrow Q_2 \rightarrow Q_3$ following each low-to-high clock transition. The J and $\overline{K}$ inputs provide the flexibility of the JK-type input for special applications and, by tying the two pins together, the simple D-type input for general applications. The device appears as four common clocked D flip-flops when the $\overline{PE}$ input is low. After the low-to-high clock transi-

	74S	74	74LS
Shift Frequency (MHz)	70	30	30
Serial Data Input	J-$\overline{K}$	J-$\overline{K}$	J-$\overline{K}$
Asynchronous Clear	Low	Low	Low
Shift-Right Mode	Yes	Yes	Yes
Shift-Left Mode	No	No	No
Load	Yes	Yes	Yes
Hold	No	No	No
Typ. Total Power (mW)	375	195	70

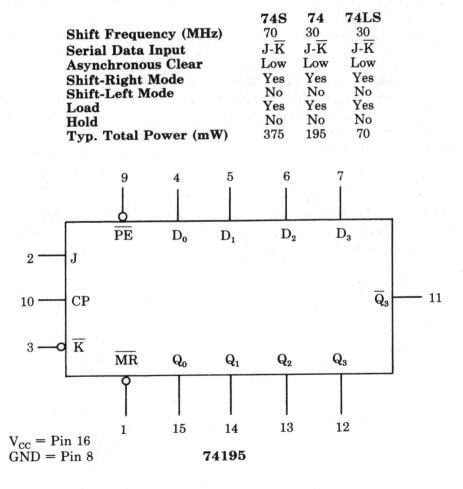

V_{CC} = Pin 16
GND = Pin 8

74195

150

MODE SELECT-FUNCTION TABLE

OPERATING MODES	INPUTS						OUTPUTS				
	$\overline{MR}$	CP	$\overline{PE}$	J	$\overline{K}$	D_n	Q_0	Q_1	Q_2	Q_3	$\overline{Q_3}$
Asynchronous Reset	L	X	X	X	X	X	L	L	L	L	H
Shift, Set First Stage	H	↑	h	h	h	X	H	q_0	q_1	q_2	$\overline{q_2}$
Shift, Reset First Stage	H	↑	h	l	l	X	L	q_0	q_1	q_2	$\overline{q_2}$
Shift, Toggle First Stage	H	↑	h	h	l	X	$\overline{q_0}$	q_0	q_1	q_2	$\overline{q_2}$
Shift, Retain First Stage	H	↑	h	l	h	X	q_0	q_0	q_1	q_2	$\overline{q_2}$
Parallel Load	H	↑	l	X	X	d_n	d_0	d_1	d_2	d_3	$\overline{d_3}$

H = High voltage level.
L = Low voltage level.
X = Don't care.
l = Low voltage level one setup time prior to the low-to-high clock transition.
h = High voltage level one setup time prior to the low-to-high clock transition.
d_n (q_n) = Lower case letters indicate the state of the referenced input (or output) one setup time prior to the low-to-high clock transition.
↑ = Low-to-high clock transition.

tion, data on the parallel inputs (D_0 through D_3) is transferred to the respective Q_0 through Q_3 outputs. Shift left operation ($Q_3 \rightarrow Q_2$) can be achieved by tying the Q_n outputs to the D_{n-1} inputs and holding the $\overline{PE}$ input low.

All parallel and serial data transfers are synchronous, occurring after each low-to-high clock transition. The '195 utilizes edge-triggering; therefore, there is no restriction on the activity of the J, $\overline{K}$, D_n, and $\overline{PE}$ inputs for logic operation, other than the setup and release time requirements.

A low on the asynchronous master reset ($\overline{MR}$) input sets all Q outputs low, independent of any other input condition. The $\overline{MR}$ on the 54/74195 is gated with the clock. Therefore, the low-to-high $\overline{MR}$ transition should only occur while the clock is low to avoid false clocking of the 74195.

74196 Presettable Decade Ripple Counter

The '196 is an asynchronously presettable decade ripple counter that is partitioned into divide-by-2 and divide-by-5 sections with each section having a separate clock input. State changes are initiated in the counting modes by the high-to-low transition of the clock inputs; however, state changes of the Q outputs do not occur simultaneously because of the internal ripple delays. Designers should keep in mind when using external logic to decode the Q outputs that the unequal delays can lead to spikes, and thus a decoded signal should not be used as a strobe or clock.

The Q_0 flip-flop is triggered by the $\overline{CP}_0$ input, while the $\overline{CP}_1$ input triggers the divide-by-five section. The Q_0 output is designed and specified to drive the rated fanout plus the $\overline{CP}_1$ input.

As indicated in the count-sequence tables, the '196 can be connected to operate in two different count sequences. The circuit counts in the BCD (8,4,2,1) sequence with the input connected to $\overline{CP}_0$ and with Q_0 driving $\overline{CP}_1$. Q_0 becomes the low-frequency output and has a 50-percent duty cycle waveform with the input connected to $\overline{CP}_1$ and Q_3 driving $\overline{CP}_0$. The maximum-counting rate is reduced in the biquinary configuration because of the interstage gating delay within the divide-by-five section.

	74	74LS
Count Frequency (MHz)	50	30
Parallel Load	Yes	Yes
Clear	Low	Low
Typ. Total Power (mW)	240	60

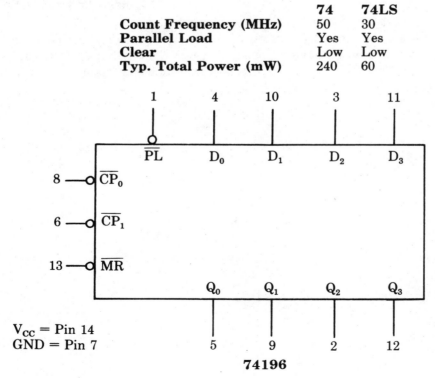

V_{CC} = Pin 14
GND = Pin 7

74196

MODE SELECT-FUNCTION TABLE

OPERATING MODE	INPUTS				OUTPUTS
	$\overline{MR}$	$\overline{PL}$	$\overline{CP}$	D_n	Q_n
Reset (Clear)	L	X	X	X	L
Parallel Load	H	L	X	L	L
	H	L	X	H	H
Count	H	H	↓	X	count

H = High voltage level
L = Low voltage level
X = Don't care
↓ = High-to-low clock transition

COUNT SEQUENCES

BCD DECADE[b]					BIQUINARY[c]				
COUNT	Q_3	Q_2	Q_1	Q_0	COUNT	Q_0	Q_3	Q_2	Q_1
0	L	L	L	L	0	L	L	L	L
1	L	L	L	H	1	L	L	L	H
2	L	L	H	L	2	L	L	H	L
3	L	L	H	H	3	L	L	H	H
4	L	H	L	L	4	L	H	L	L
5	L	H	L	H	5	H	L	L	L
6	L	H	H	L	6	H	L	L	H
7	L	H	H	H	7	H	L	H	L
8	H	L	L	L	8	H	L	H	H
9	H	L	L	H	9	H	H	L	L

NOTES

(b) Input applied to CP_0; Q_0 connected to CP_1
(c) Input applied to CP_1; Q_3 connected to CP_0

The device has an asynchronous active low master-reset input ($\overline{MR}$) which overrides all other inputs and forces all outputs low. The counter is also asynchronously presettable. A low on the parallel-load input ($\overline{PL}$) overrides the clock inputs and loads the data from parallel-data (D_0 through D_3) inputs into the flip-flops. The counter acts as a transparent latch while the $\overline{PL}$ is low, and any change in the D_n inputs will be reflected in the outputs.

74197 Presettable 4-Bit Binary Ripple Counter

The '197 is an asynchronously presettable binary ripple counter that is partitioned into divide-by-2 and divide-by-8 sections, with each section having a separate clock input. State changes are initiated in the counting modes by the high-to-low transition of the clock inputs; however, stage changes of the Q outputs do not occur simultaneously because of the internal ripple delays. Designers should remember, when using external logic to decode the Q outputs, that the unequal delays can lead to decoding spikes, and thus a decoded signal should not be used as a strobe or clock. The Q_0 output is designed and specified to drive the rated fanout plus the CP_1 input.

The device has an asynchronous active low master-reset input ($\overline{MR}$) that overrides all other inputs and forces all outputs low. The counter is also asynchronously presettable. A low on the parallel-load input ($\overline{PL}$) overrides the clock inputs and loads the data from parallel-data (D_0 through D_3) inputs into the flip-flops. The counter acts as a transparent latch while the $\overline{PL}$ is low, and any change in the D_n inputs will be reflected in the outputs.

LOGIC SYMBOL

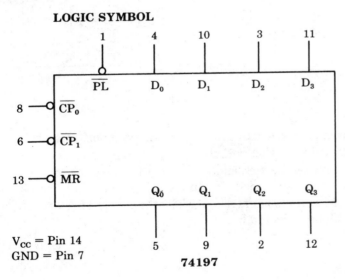

V_{CC} = Pin 14
GND = Pin 7

74197

	74	74LS
Count Frequency (MHz)	50	30
Parallel Load	Yes	Yes
Clear	Low	Low
Typ. Total Power (mW)	240	60

COUNT SEQUENCE

COUNT	4-Bit Binary[b]			
	Q_3	Q_2	Q_1	Q_0
0	L	L	L	L
1	L	L	L	H
2	L	L	H	L
3	L	L	H	H
4	L	H	L	L
5	L	H	L	H
6	L	H	H	L
7	L	H	H	H
8	H	L	L	L
9	H	L	L	H
10	H	L	H	L
11	H	L	H	H
12	H	H	L	L
13	H	H	L	H
14	H	H	H	L
15	H	H	H	H

NOTE
(b) Q_0 connected to $\overline{CP_1}$; input applied to $\overline{CP_0}$

MODE SELECT-FUNCTION TABLE

OPERATING MODE	INPUTS				OUTPUTS
	$\overline{MR}$	$\overline{PL}$	$\overline{CP}$	D_n	Q_n
Reset (Clear)	L	X	X	X	L
Parallel Load	H	L	X	L	L
	H	L	X	H	H
Count	H	H	↓	X	count

H = High voltage level
L = Low voltage level
X = Don't care
↓ = High-to-low clock transition

154

74221 Dual Monostable Multivibrator

The '221 is a dual monostable multivibrator with performance characteristics virtually identical to those of the '121. Each multivibrator features an active low-going edge input ($\overline{A}$) and an active high-going edge input ($\overline{B}$), either of which can be used as an enable input.

Pulse triggering occurs at a particular voltage level and is not directly related to the transition time of the input pulse. Schmitt-trigger input circuitry (TTL hysteresis) for the B input allows jitter-free triggering from inputs with transition rates as low as 1 volt per second, providing the circuit with excellent noise immunity of typically 1.2 volts. A high immunity to V_{CC} noise of typically 1.5 volts is also provided by internal-latching circuitry.

Once fired, the outputs are independent of further transitions of the $\overline{A}$ and B inputs and are a function of the timing components. The output pulses can be terminated by the overriding active low Reset ($\overline{R_D}$). Input pulses can be of any duration relative to the output pulse. Output-pulse length can be varied from 35 nanoseconds to the maximums shown here by choosing appropriate timing components. With $R_{ext} = 2$ kΩ and $C_{ext} = 0$, an output pulse of typically 30 nanoseconds is achieved which can be used as a dc-triggered reset signal. Output rise and fall times are TTL compatible and independent of pulse length.

Pulse width stability is achieved through internal compensation and is virtually independent of V_{CC} and temperature. In most applications, pulse stability will only be limited by the accuracy of external timing components.

Jitter free operation is maintained over the full temperature and V_{CC} ranges for more than six decades of timing capacitance (10 pF to 10 μF) and more than one decade of timing resistance (2 K to 40 kΩ for the 74221 and 2 K to 100 K for the 74LS221). Throughout these ranges, pulse width is defined by the following relationship:

$$t_w \text{ (out)} = C_{ext} \, R_{ext} \, I_n 2$$
$$t_w \text{ (out)} = 0.7 C_{ext} \, R_{ext}$$

In circuits where pulse cutoff is not critical, timing capacitance of up to 1000 μF and timing resistance of as low as 1.4 kΩ can be used. Pin assignments for these devices are identical to those of the '123 so that the '221 can be substituted for those products in systems not using the retrigger by merely changing the value of R_{ext} and/or C_{ext}.

	74LS
Positive Inputs	1
Negative Inputs	1
Output Pulse Range (ns to s)	20ns — 70s
Typ. Total Power (mW)	23

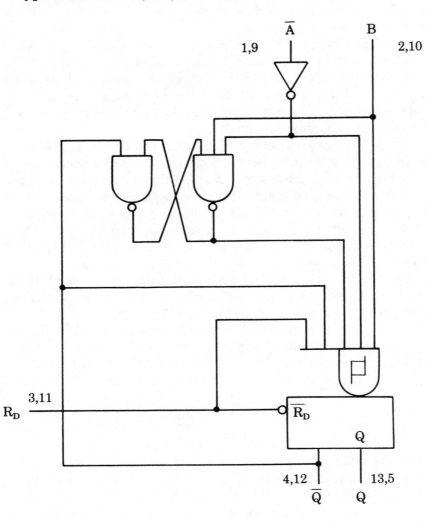

V_{CC} = Pin 16 C_{ext} = Pins 14,6
GND = Pin 8 C_{ext}/R_{ext} = Pins 15,7

74221

74251 8-Input Multiplexer (3-State)

The '251 is a logical implementation of a single-pole, 8-position switch with the state of the three select inputs (S_0, S_1, and S_2) controlling the switch position. Assertion (Y) and negation ($\overline{Y}$) outputs are both provided. The output enable input ($\overline{OE}$) is active low. The logic function provided at the output, when activated is:

$$Y = \overline{OE}\,(I_0 \bullet \overline{S}_0 \bullet \overline{S}_2 + I_1 \bullet S_0 \bullet S_1 \bullet \overline{S}_2 + I_2 \bullet \overline{S}_0 \bullet S_1 \bullet \overline{S}_2 + I_3 \bullet S_0 \bullet S_1 \bullet \overline{S}_2 + I_4 \bullet \overline{S}_0 \bullet \overline{S}_1 \bullet S_2 + I_5 \bullet S_0 \bullet \overline{S}_1 \bullet S_2 + I_6 \bullet \overline{S}_0 \bullet S_1 \bullet S_2 + I_7 \bullet S_0 \bullet S_1 \bullet S_2).$$

Both outputs are in the high-impedance (high-Z) state when the output enable is high, allowing multiplexer expansion by tying the outputs of up to 128 devices together. All but one device must be in the high-impedance state to avoid high currents that would exceed the maximum ratings when the outputs of the 3-state devices are tied together. Design of the output enable signals must ensure there is no overlap in the active low portion of the enable voltages.

Type of Output	74S 3-State	74 3-State	74LS 3-State
Typ. Delay, Data to Inverting Output (ns)	4.5	11	17
Typ. Delay, Data to Noninverting Output (ns)	8	18	21
Typ. Delay, From Enable (ns)	14	17	21
Typ. Total Power (mW)	275	155	35

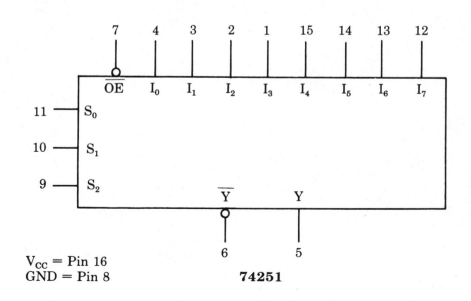

V_{CC} = Pin 16
GND = Pin 8

74251

Truth Table

INPUTS												OUTPUTS	
$\overline{OE}$	S_2	S_1	S_0	I_0	I_1	I_2	I_3	I_4	I_5	I_6	I_7	Y	$\overline{Y}$
H	X	X	X	X	X	X	X	X	X	X	X	(Z)	(Z)
L	L	L	L	L	X	X	X	X	X	X	X	H	L
L	L	L	L	H	X	X	X	X	X	X	X	L	H
L	L	L	H	X	L	X	X	X	X	X	X	H	L
L	L	L	H	X	H	X	X	X	X	X	X	L	H
L	L	H	L	X	X	L	X	X	X	X	X	H	L
L	L	H	L	X	X	H	X	X	X	X	X	L	H
L	L	H	H	X	X	X	L	X	X	X	X	H	L
L	L	H	H	X	X	X	H	X	X	X	X	L	H
L	H	L	L	X	X	X	X	L	X	X	X	H	L
L	H	L	L	X	X	X	X	H	X	X	X	L	H
L	H	L	H	X	X	X	X	X	L	X	X	H	L
L	H	L	H	X	X	X	X	X	H	X	X	L	H
L	H	H	L	X	X	X	X	X	X	L	X	H	L
L	H	H	L	X	X	X	X	X	X	H	X	L	H
L	H	H	H	X	X	X	X	X	X	X	L	H	L
L	H	H	H	X	X	X	X	X	X	X	H	L	H

H = High voltage level
L = Low voltage level
X = Don't care
(Z) = High impedance (off)

74253 Dual 4-Input Multiplexer (3-State)

The '253 has two identical 4-input multiplexers with 3-state outputs which select two bits from four sources selected by common select inputs ($S_0 S_1$). When the individual output enable ($\overline{E}_{0a}$, $\overline{E}_{0b}$) inputs of the 4-input multiplexers are high, the outputs are forced to a high-impedance (high-Z) state.

The '253 is the logic implementation of a 2-pole, 4-position switch; the position of the switch is determined by the logic levels supplied to the two select inputs. Logic equations for the outputs are:

$$Y_a = \overline{OE}_a \bullet (I_{0a} \bullet \overline{S}_1 \bullet \overline{S}_0 + I_{1a} \bullet \overline{S}_1 \bullet S_0 + I_{2a} \bullet S_1 \bullet \overline{S}_0 + I_{3a} \bullet S_1 \bullet S_0)$$

$$Y_b = \overline{OE}_b \bullet (I_{0b} \bullet \overline{S}_1 \bullet \overline{S}_0 + I_{1b} \bullet \overline{S}_1 \bullet S_0 + I_{2b} \bullet S_1 \bullet \overline{S}_0 + I_{3b} \bullet S_1 \bullet S_0)$$

All but one device must be in the high-impedance state to avoid high currents exceeding the maximum ratings, if the outputs of 3-state devices are tied together. The output enable signal design must ensure that there is no overlap.

Type of Output	74LS
	3-State
Typ. Delay, Data to Noninverting Output (ns)	12
Typ. Delay, From Enable (ns)	16
Typ. Total Power (mW)	35

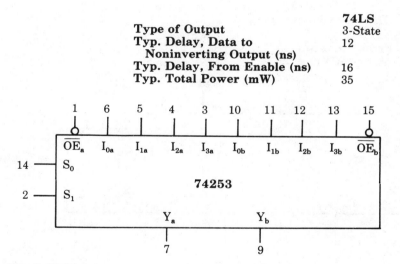

Truth Table

SELECT INPUTS		DATA INPUTS				OUTPUT ENABLE	OUTPUT
S_0	S_1	I_0	I_1	I_2	I_3	$\overline{OE}$	Y
X	X	X	X	X	X	H	(Z)
L	L	L	X	X	X	L	L
L	L	H	X	X	X	L	H
H	L	X	L	X	X	L	L
H	L	X	H	X	X	L	H
L	H	X	X	L	X	L	L
L	H	X	X	H	X	L	H
H	H	X	X	X	L	L	L
H	H	X	X	X	H	L	H

V_{CC} = Pin 16
GND = Pin 8

H = High voltage level
L = Low voltage level
X = Don't care
(Z) = High-impedance (off) state

74257 Quad 2-Line-to-1-Line Data Selector/Multiplexer (3-State)

The '257 has four identical 2-input multiplexers with 3-state outputs that select four bits of data from two sources under control of a common-data select input (S). The I_0 inputs are selected when the select input is low, and the I_1 inputs are selected when the select input is high. Data appears at the outputs in true (non-inverted) form from the selected inputs.

The '257 is the logic implementation of a 4-pole, 2-position switch where the position of the switch is determined by the logic levels supplied to the select input. Outputs are forced to a high-impedance off-state when the output enable input ($\overline{OE}$) is high. All but one device must be in the high-impedance state to avoid currents exceeding the maximum ratings if outputs are tied together. Design of the output enable signals must ensure that there is no overlap when outputs of 3-state devices are tied together.

	74S	74LS
Type of Output	3-State	3-State
Typ. Delay, Data to Inverting Output (ns)	–	–
Typ. Delay, Data to Noninverting Output (ns)	5	12
Typ. Delay, From Enable (ns)	14	20
Typ. Total Power (mW)	320	50

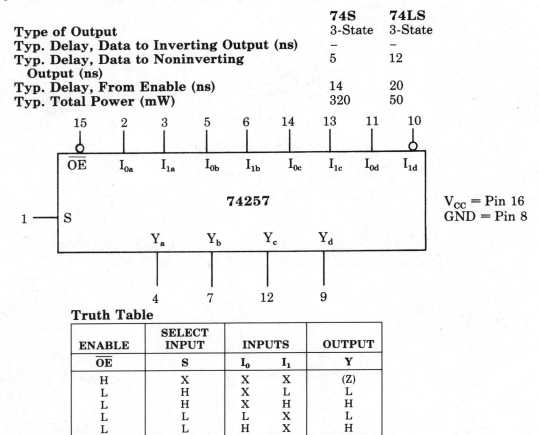

V_{CC} = Pin 16
GND = Pin 8

Truth Table

ENABLE	SELECT INPUT	INPUTS		OUTPUT
$\overline{OE}$	S	I_0	I_1	Y
H	X	X	X	(Z)
L	H	X	L	L
L	H	X	H	H
L	L	L	X	L
L	L	H	X	H

H = High voltage level   X = Don't care
L = Low voltage level   (Z) = High-impedance (off) state

160

74258 Quad 2-Line-to-1-Line Data Selector/Multiplexer (3-State)

The '258 has four identical 2-input multiplexers with 3-state outputs that select four bits of data from two sources under control of a common-data select input (S). The I_0 inputs are selected when the select input is low, and the I_1 inputs are selected when the select input is high. Data appear at the outputs in inverted (complementary) form.

The '258 is the logic implementation of a 4-pole, 2-position switch where the position of the switch is determined by the logic levels supplied to the select input. Outputs are forced to a high-impedance off-state when the output enable input ($\overline{OE}$) is high. All but one device must be in the high-impedance state to avoid currents exceeding the maximum ratings if outputs of the 3-state devices are tied together. Design of the output enable signals must ensure that there is no overlap when outputs of 3-state devices are tied together.

	74S	74LS
Type of Output	3-State	3-State
Typ. Delay, Data to Inverting Output (ns)	4	12
Typ. Delay, Data to Noninverting Output (ns)	–	–
Typ. Delay, From Enable (ns)	4	20
Typ. Total Power (mW)	280	35

V_{CC} = Pin 16
GND = Pin 8

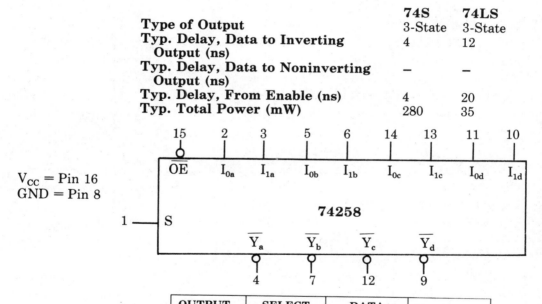

Truth Table

OUTPUT ENABLE	SELECT INPUT	DATA INPUTS		OUTPUTS
$\overline{OE}$	S	I_0	I_1	$\overline{Y}$
H	X	X	X	(Z)
L	H	X	L	H
L	H	X	H	L
L	L	L	X	H
L	L	H	X	L

H = High voltage level
L = Low voltage level
X = Don't care
(Z) = High-impedance (off) state

74259 8-Bit Addressable Latch

The '259 addressable latch has four distinct modes of operation that are selectable by controlling the clear and enable inputs. In the addressable latch mode, data at the data (D) inputs are written into the addressable latches. The addressed latches will follow the data input with all unaddressed latches remaining in their previous states. In the memory mode, all latches remain in their previous states and are unaffected by the data or address inputs. To eliminate the possibility of entering erroneous data in the latches, the enable should be held high (inactive) while the address lines are changing. In the one-of-eight decoding or demultiplexing mode, ($\overline{CLR} = \overline{E}$ = low) addressed outputs will follow the level of the D inputs with all other outputs low. In the clear mode, all outputs are low and unaffected by the address and data inputs.

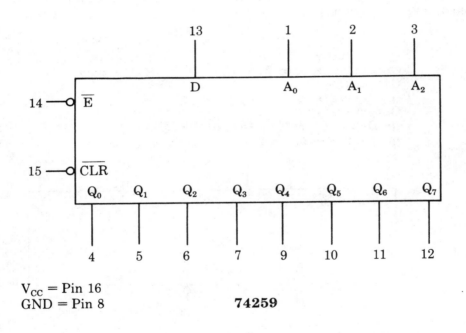

V_{CC} = Pin 16
GND = Pin 8

74259

MODE SELECT-FUNCTION TABLE

OPERATING MODE	INPUTS						OUTPUTS							
	$\overline{CLR}$	$\overline{E}$	D	A_0	A_1	A_2	Q_0	Q_1	Q_2	Q_3	Q_4	Q_5	Q_6	Q_7
Clear	L	H	X	X	X	X	L	L	L	L	L	L	L	L
Demultiplex (active High decoder when D = H)	L	L	d	L	L	L	Q = d	L	L	L	L	L	L	L
	L	L	d	H	L	L	L	Q = d	L	L	L	L	L	L
	L	L	d	L	H	L	L	L	Q = d	L	L	L	L	L
	•	•	•	•	•	•	•	•	•	•	•	•	•	•
	•	•	•	•	•	•	•	•	•	•	•	•	•	•
	•	•	•	•	•	•	•	•	•	•	•	•	•	•
	L	L	d	H	H	H	L	L	L	L	L	L	L	Q = d
Store (do nothing)	H	H	X	X	X	X	q_0	q_1	q_2	q_3	q_4	q_5	q_6	q_7
Addressable latch	H	L	d	L	L	L	Q = d	q_1	q_2	q_3	q_4	q_5	q_6	q_7
	H	L	d	H	L	L	q_0	Q = d	q_2	q_3	q_4	q_5	q_6	q_7
	H	L	d	L	H	L	q_0	q_1	Q = d	q_3	q_4	q_5	q_6	q_7
	•	•	•	•	•	•	•	•	•	•	•	•	•	•
	•	•	•	•	•	•	•	•	•	•	•	•	•	•
	•	•	•	•	•	•	•	•	•	•	•	•	•	•
	H	L	d	H	H	H	q_0	q_1	q_2	q_3	q_4	q_5	q_6	Q = d

H = High voltage level steady state
L = Low voltage level steady state
X = Don't care
d = High or low data one setup time prior to low-to-high enable transition
q = Lower case letters indicate the state of the referenced output established during the last cycle in which it was addressed or cleared.

74266 Quad 2-Input Exclusive-NOR
Gate with Open Collector Outputs

The exclusive-NOR gate is rather uncommon, but it is essentially just the opposite of an exclusive-OR gate (refer to the description of the 7486).

In an exclusive-OR gate, the output is high if one, but not both, of the inputs is high. To create an exclusive-NOR gate, the output of an exclusive-OR gate is inverted. Therefore, in an exclusive-NOR gate, the output is high if both outputs are low, or if both outputs are high.

Either an exclusive-OR gate or an exclusive-NOR gate can be considered a one-bit digital comparator. An exclusive-OR functions as a "difference detector," but an exclusive-NOR gate operates as an "equality detector."

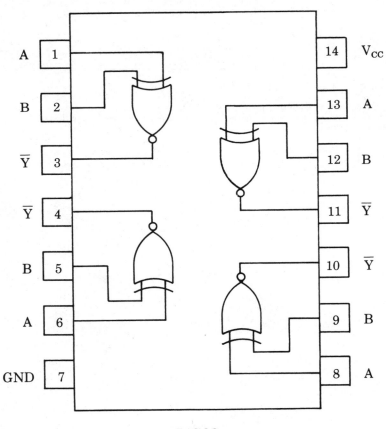

74266

74273 Octal D Flip-Flop

The '273 has eight edge-triggered D-type flip-flops with individual D inputs and Q outputs. The common-buffered clock (CP) and master-reset ($\overline{\text{MR}}$) inputs load and reset (clear) all flip-flops simultaneously.

The register is fully edge-triggered. The state of each D input, one setup time before the low-to-high clock transition, is transferred to the corresponding flip-flop Q output.

All outputs will be forced low independently of clock or data inputs by a low voltage level on the $\overline{\text{MR}}$ input. The device is useful for applications where the true output only is required and the clock and master reset are common to all storage elements.

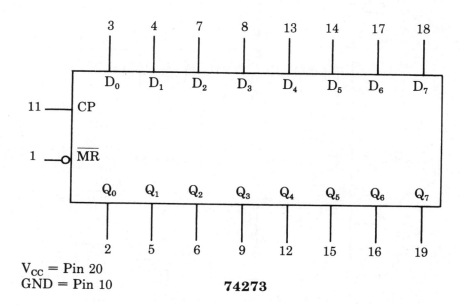

V_{CC} = Pin 20
GND = Pin 10

74273

MODE SELECT-FUNCTION TABLE

OPERATING MODE	INPUTS			OUTPUTS
	$\overline{\text{MR}}$	CP	D_n	Q_n
Reset (clear)	L	X	X	L
Load "1"	H	↑	h	H
Load "0"	H	↑	l	L

H = High voltage level steady state.
h = High voltage level one setup time prior to the low-to-high clock transition.
L = Low voltage level steady state.
l = Low voltage level one setup time prior to the low-to-high clock transition.
X = Don't care.
↑ = Low-to-high clock transition.

165

74279A Quad SR Latch

A latch is basically a simplified flip-flop. It is used to hold a digital value (a 1 or a 0), even after the original signal is removed.

The $\overline{S}$ inputs set the latch, and the $\overline{R}$ input resets it. Both the $\overline{S}$ and $\overline{R}$ inputs are inverted in the 279A.

Notice that two of the four latches in the 279A have two $\overline{S}$ inputs and two have only one. All four latches have just a single $\overline{R}$ input.

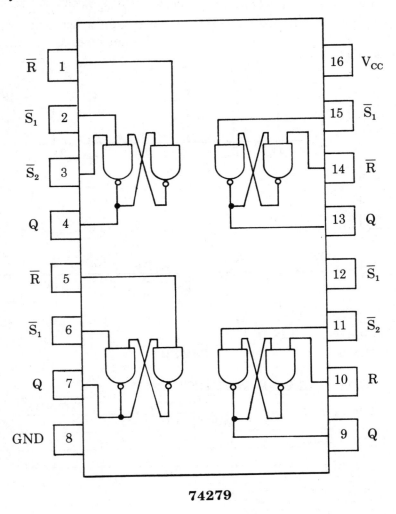

74279

166

74280 9-Bit Odd/Even Parity Generator/Checker

The '280 is a 9-bit parity generator or checker commonly used to detect errors in high-speed data transmission or data retrieval systems. Both even and odd parity outputs are available for generating or checking even or odd parity on up to nine bits.

The even parity output (Σ E) is high when an even number of data inputs (I_0 through I_8) is high. The odd parity output (Σ_0) is high when an odd number of data inputs is high.

Expansion to larger word sizes is accomplished by tying the even outputs (Σ E) of up to nine parallel devices to the data inputs of the final stage.

	74S
Typ. Delay Time (ns)	13
Typ. Total Power (mW)	335

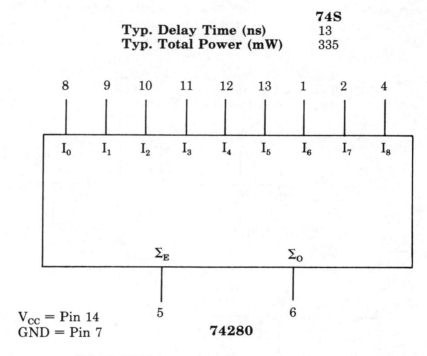

V_{CC} = Pin 14
GND = Pin 7

74280

Truth Table

INPUTS	OUTPUTS	
Number of HIGH data inputs ($I_0 - I_8$)	Σ_E	Σ_O
Even	H	L
Odd	L	H

74283 4-Bit Full Adder with Fast Carry

The '283 adds two 4-bit binary words (A_n plus B_n) plus the incoming carry. The binary sum appears on the sum outputs [Σ_1-Σ_4 and the outgoing carry (C_{out})] according to the equation:

$$C_{IN} + (A_1 + B_1) + 2(A_2 + B_2) + 4(A_3 + B_3) + 8(A_4 + B_4) = \Sigma_1 + 2\,\Sigma_2 + 4\,\Sigma_3 + 8\,\Sigma_4 + 16 C_{OUT},$$

Where $(+)$ = plus.

Due in the symmetry of the binary add function, the '283 can be used with either all active high operands (positive logic) or with all active low operands (negative logic). With active high inputs, C_{IN} cannot be left open; it must be held low when no carry in is intended. Interchanging inputs of equal weight does not affect the operation; thus, C_{IN}, A_1, and B_1 can arbitrarily be assigned to pins 5, 6, 7, etc.

	74LS
Typ. Carry Time (ns)	10
Typ. Add Time (ns)	15
Typ. Power Per Bit (mW)	24

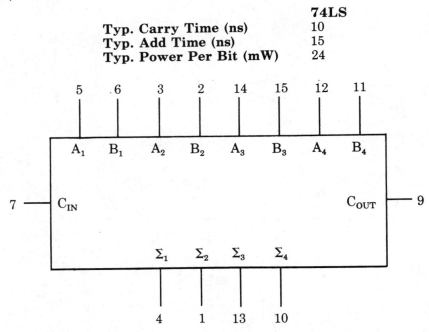

V_{CC} = Pin 16
GND = Pin 8

74283

PINS	C_{IN}	A_1	A_2	A_3	A_4	B_1	B_2	B_3	B_4	Σ_1	Σ_2	Σ_3	Σ_4	C_{OUT}
Logic Levels	L	L	H	L	H	H	L	L	H	H	H	L	L	H
Active high	0	0	1	0	1	1	0	0	1	1	1	0	0	1
Active low	1	1	0	1	0	0	1	1	0	0	0	1	1	0

74289 65-Bit Random-Access Memory (O.C.)

The '289 is a high-speed array of 64 memory cells organized as 16 words of four bits each. A one-of-sixteen address decoder selects a single word that is specified by the four address inputs (A_0 through A_3). A READ operation is initiated

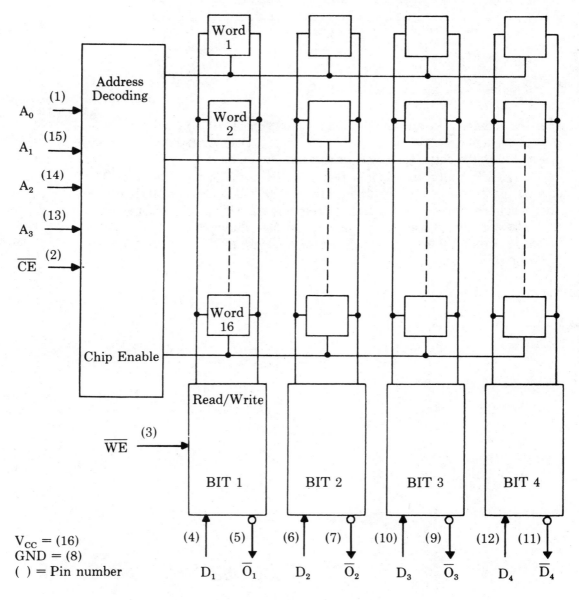

$V_{CC} = (16)$
$GND = (8)$
( ) = Pin number

74289

MODE SELECT-FUNCTION TABLE

OPERATING MODE	INPUTS			OUTPUTS
	$\overline{CS}$	$\overline{WE}$	D_n	$\overline{O}_n$
Write—Disable Outputs	L L	L L	L H	H H
Read	L	H	X	$\overline{Data}$
Store-Disable Outputs	H	X	X	H

H = High voltage level
L = Low voltage level
X = Don't care
$\overline{Data}$ = Read complement of data from addressed word location

after the address lines are stable when the write enable ($\overline{WE}$) input is high and the chip select-memory enable ($\overline{CS}$) input is low. Data is read at the outputs inverted from the data, which was written into the memory.

A WRITE operation requires that the $\overline{WE}$ and $\overline{CS}$ inputs be low. The address inputs must be stable during the WRITE mode for predictable operation. When the write mode is selected, the outputs are high. The selected memory cells are transparent to changes in the data during the WRITE mode; therefore, data must be stable one setup time before the low-to-high transition of $\overline{CE}$ or $\overline{WE}$.

74290 Decade Counter

The '290 is a 4-bit ripple-type decade counter. The device consists of four master-slave flip-flops internally connected to provide a divide-by-2 section and a divide-by-5 section. Each section has a separate clock input to initiate state changes of the counter on the high-to-low clock transition. State changes of the Q outputs do not occur simultaneously because of internal ripple delays. Therefore, decoded output signals are subject to decoding spikes and should not be used for clocks or strobes. The Q_0 output is designed and specified to drive the rate fanout plus the $\overline{CP_1}$ input of the device.

A gated AND asynchronous master reset ($MR_1 \cdot MR_2$) is provided, which overrides both clocks and resets (clears) all the flip-flops. Also provided is a gated AND asynchronous master set ($MS_1 \cdot MS_2$), which overrides the clocks and the MR inputs, setting the outputs to nine (HLLH).

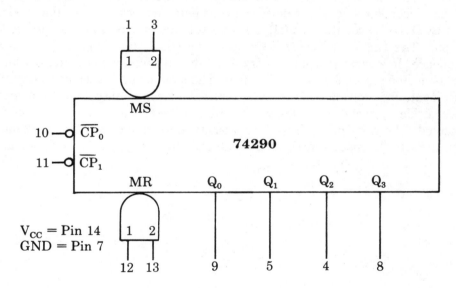

MODE SELECTION-TRUTH TABLE

RESET/SET INPUTS				OUTPUTS			
MR_1	MR_2	MS_1	MS_2	Q_0	Q_1	Q_2	Q_3
H	H	L	X	L	L	L	L
H	H	X	L	L	L	L	L
X	X	H	H	H	L	L	H
L	X	L	X		Count		
X	L	X	L		Count		
L	X	X	L		Count		
X	L	L	X		Count		

H = High voltage level
L = Low voltage level
X = Don't care

171

BCD COUNT SEQUENCE—TRUTH TABLE

COUNT	OUTPUT			
	Q_0	Q_1	Q_2	Q_3
0	L	L	L	L
1	H	L	L	L
2	L	H	L	L
3	H	H	L	L
4	L	L	H	L
5	H	L	H	L
6	L	H	H	L
7	H	H	H	L
8	L	L	L	H
9	H	L	L	H

NOTE: Output Q_0 connected to input $\overline{CP_1}$

Because the output from the divide-by-2 section is not internally connected to the succeeding stages, the device can be operated in various counting modes. In a BCD (8421) counter, the $\overline{CP_1}$ input must be externally connected to the Q_0 output. The $\overline{CP_0}$ input receives the incoming count, producing a BCD count sequence. In a symmetrical biquinary divide-by-10 counter, the Q_3 output must be connected externally to the $\overline{CP_0}$ input. The input count is then applied to the $\overline{CP_1}$ input, and a divide-by-10 square wave is obtained at output Q_0. To operate as a divide-by-2 and a divide-by-5 counter, no external interconnections are required. The first flip-flop is used as a binary element for the divide-by-2 function ($\overline{CP_0}$ as the input and Q_0 as the output). The $\overline{CP_1}$ input is used to obtain divide-by-5 operation at the Q_3 output.

74293 4-Bit Binary Ripple Counter

The '293 is a 4-bit ripple-type binary counter. The device consists of four master-slave flip-flops internally connected to provide a divide-by-2 section and a divide-by-8 section. Each section has a separate clock input to initiate state changes of the counter on the high-to-low clock transition. State changes of the Q outputs do not occur simultaneously because of internal ripple delays. Therefore, decoded output signals are subject to decoding spikes and should not be used for clocks or strobes. The Q_0 output is designed and specified to drive the rated fanout plus the $\overline{CP}_1$ input of the device. A gate AND asynchronous master reset ($MR_1 \bullet MR_2$) is provided, which overrides both clocks and resets (clears) all the flip-flops.

Because the output from the divide-by-2 section is not internally connected to the succeeding stages, the device can be operated in various counting modes. In a 4-bit ripple counter, output Q_0 must be connected externally to input $\overline{CP}_1$. The input count pulses are applied to input $\overline{CP}_0$. Simultaneous divisions of 2, 4, 8, and 16 are performed at the Q_0, Q_1, Q_2, and Q_3 outputs, as shown in the truth table. As a 3-bit ripple counter, the input count pulses are applied to input $\overline{CP}_1$. Simultaneous frequency divisions of 2, 4, and 8 are available at the Q_1, Q_2, and Q_3 outputs. Independent use of the first flip-flop is available if the reset function coincides with reset of the 3-bit ripple-through counter.

MODE SELECTION

RESET INPUTS		OUTPUTS			
MR_1	MR_2	Q_0	Q_1	Q_2	Q_3
H	H	L	L	L	L
L	H		Count		
H	L		Count		
L	L		Count		

H = High voltage level
L = Low voltage level
X = Don't care

Truth Table

COUNT	OUTPUT			
	Q_0	Q_1	Q_2	Q_3
0	L	L	L	L
1	H	L	L	L
2	L	H	L	L
3	H	H	L	L
4	L	L	H	L
5	H	L	H	L
6	L	H	H	L
7	H	H	H	L
8	L	L	L	H
9	H	L	L	H
10	L	H	L	H
11	H	H	L	H
12	L	L	H	H
13	H	L	H	H
14	L	H	H	H
15	H	H	H	H

NOTE: Output Q_0 connected to input $\overline{CP}_1$

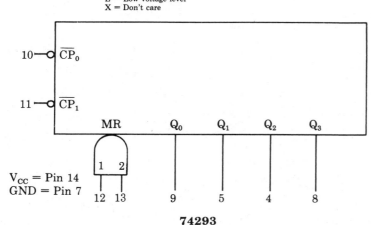

V_{CC} = Pin 14
GND = Pin 7

74293

74299 8-Bit Universal Shift/Storage Register

The '229 is an 8-bit general purpose shift-storage register useful in a wide variety of shifting and 3-state bus interface applications. The register has four synchronous operating modes controlled by the two select inputs, as shown in the mode-select function table. The mode select (S_0 and S_1) inputs, the serial-data (D_{S0} and D_{S7}) inputs and the parallel-data (I/O_0 through I/O_7) inputs are edge-triggered, responding only to the low-to-high transition of the clock ($\overline{CP}$) input. Therefore, the only timing restriction is that the S_0, S_1, and selected data inputs must be stable one setup time prior to the positive transition of the clock pulse. The master reset ($\overline{MR}$) is an asynchronous active low input. When low, the $\overline{MR}$ overrides the clock and all other inputs and clears the register.

Serial mode expansion of the register is accomplished by tying the Q_0 serial output to the D_{S7} input of the preceding register, and tying the Q_7 serial output to the D_{S0} input of the following register. Recirculating the (n × 8) bit words is accomplished by tying the Q_7 output of the last stage to the D_{S0} input of the first stage.

The 3-state bidirectional input output port has three modes of operation. When the two output-enable ($\overline{OE}_1$ and $\overline{OE}_2$) inputs are low, and one or both of the select inputs are low, data in the register are presented at the eight outputs. When both select inputs are high, the 3-state outputs are forced to the high-impedance off state and the register is prepared to load data from the 3-state bus coincident with the next low-to-high clock transition. In this parallel load mode, the select inputs disable the outputs even if $\overline{OE}_1$ and $\overline{OE}_2$ are both low. A high level on one of the output-enable inputs will force the outputs to the high-impedance off-state. When disabled, the 3-state I/O ports present one unit load to the bus, because an input is tied to the I/O node. The enabled 3-state output is designed to drive heavy capacitive loads or heavily loaded 3-state buses.

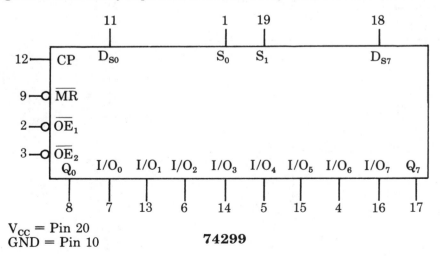

V_{CC} = Pin 20
GND = Pin 10

74299

174

MODE SELECT-FUNCTION TABLES

REGISTER OPERATING MODES	INPUTS							REGISTER OUTPUTS		
	$\overline{MR}$	CP	S_0	S_1	D_{S0}	D_{S7}	I/O_n	Q_0	Q_1---Q_6	Q_7
Reset (clear)	L	X	X	X	X	X	X	L	L---L	L
Shift right	H	↑	h	l	l	X	X	L	q_0---q_5	q_6
	H	↑	h	l	h	X	X	H	q_0---q_5	Q_6
Shift left	H	↑	l	h	X	l	X	q_1	q_2---q_7	L
	H	↑	l	h	X	h	X	q_1	q_2---q_7	H
Hold (do nothing)	H	↑	l	l	X	X	X	q_0	q_1---q_6	q_7
Parallel load	H	↑	h	h	X	X	l	L	L---L	L
	H	↑	h	h	X	X	h	H	H---H	H

3-STATE I/O PORT OPERATING MODE	INPUTS					INPUTS/OUTPUTS
	$\overline{OE_1}$	$\overline{OE_2}$	S_0	S_1	Q_n (Register)	I/O_0----I/O_7
Read register	L	L	L	X	L	L
	L	L	L	X	H	H
	L	L	X	L	L	L
	L	L	X	L	H	H
Load register	X	X	H	H	$Q_n = I/O_n$	I/O_n = inputs
Disable I/O	H	X	X	X	X	(Z)
	X	H	X	X	X	(Z)

H = High voltage level
h = High voltage level one setup time prior to low-to-high clock transition
L = Low voltage level
l = Low voltage level one setup time prior to the low-to-high clock transition
q_n = Lower case letters indicate the state of the referenced output one setup prior to the low-to-high clock transition
X = Don't care
(Z) = High-impedance "off" state
↑ = Low-to-high clock transition.

74323 8-Bit Universal Shift/Storage Register

The '323 is an 8-bit general purpose shift-storage register useful in a wide variety of shifting and 3-state bus interface applications. The register has five synchronous operating modes controlled by the two select inputs and the synchronous reset as shown in the mode-select function table. The mode-select (S_0 and S_1) inputs, the synchronous reset ($\overline{SR}$) input, the serial-data (D_{S0} and D_{S7}) inputs and the parallel data I/O_0 through I/O_1 inputs are edge-triggered, responding only to the low-to-high transition of the clock (CP) input. Therefore, the only timing restriction is that the $\overline{SR}$, S_0, S_1, and selected data inputs must be stable one setup time prior to the positive transition of the clock pulse. The $\overline{SR}$ input overrides the select and data inputs when low and clears the register coincident with the next positive clock transition.

Serial-mode expansion of the register is accomplished by tying the Q_0 serial output to the D_{S7} input of the preceding register, and tying the Q_7 serial output to the D_{S0} input of the following register. Recirculating the (n × 8) bit words is accomplished by tying the Q_7 output of the last stage to the D_{S0} input of the first stage.

The 3-state bidirectional Input/Output port has three modes of operation. When the two output-enable (OE_1 and OE_2) inputs are low, and one or both of the selected inputs are low, the data in the register is presented at the eight outputs. When both select inputs are high, the 3-state outputs are forced to the high-impedance off-state, and the register is prepared to load data from the 3-state bus coincident with the next low-to-high clock transition. In this parallel-load mode, the select inputs disable the outputs even if $\overline{OE}_1$ and $\overline{OE}_2$ are both

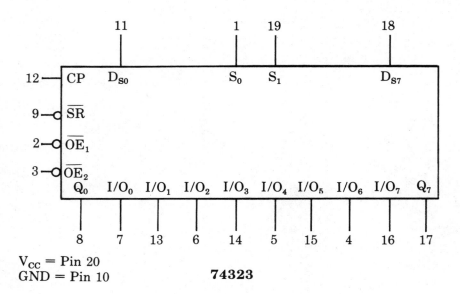

V_{CC} = Pin 20
GND = Pin 10

74323

176

MODE SELECT-FUNCTION TABLES

REGISTER OPERATING MODES	INPUTS							REGISTER OUTPUTS		
	$\overline{SR}$	CP	S_0	S_1	D_{S0}	D_{S7}	I/O_n	Q_0	Q_1---Q_6	Q_7
Reset (clear)	l	↑	X	X	X	X	X	L	L---L	L
Shift right	h	↑	h	l	l	X	X	L	q_0---q_5	q_6
	h	↑	h	l	h	X	X	H	q_0---q_5	Q_6
Shift left	h	↑	l	h	X	l	X	q_1	q_2---q_7	L
	h	↑	l	h	X	h	X	q_1	q_2---q_7	H
Hold (do nothing)	h	↑	l	l	X	X	X	q_0	q_1---q_6	q_7
Parallel load	h	↑	h	h	X	X	l	L	L---L	L
	h	↑	h	h	X	X	h	H	H---H	H

3-STATE I/O PORT OPERATING MODE	INPUTS					INPUTS/OUTPUTS
	$\overline{OE_1}$	$\overline{OE_2}$	S_0	S_1	Q_n (REGISTER)	I/O_0----I/O_7
Read register	L	L	L	X	L	L
	L	L	L	X	H	H
	L	L	X	L	L	L
	L	L	X	L	H	H
Load register	X	X	H	H	$Q_n = I/O_n$	I/O_n = inputs
Disable I/O	H	X	X	X	X	(Z)
	X	H	X	X	X	(Z)

H = High voltage level
h = High voltage level one setup time prior to low-to-high clock transition
L = Low voltage level
l = Low voltage level one setup time prior to the low-to-high clock transition
q_n = Lower case letters indicate the state of the referenced output one setup prior to the low-to-high clock transition
X = Don't care
(Z) = High-impedance "off" state
↑ = Low-to-high clock transition.

low. A high level on one of the output enable inputs will force the outputs to the high-impedance of state. When disabled, the 3-state I/O ports present one unit load to the bus, because an input is tied to the I/O mode. The enabled 3-state output is designed to drive heavy capacitive loads or heavily loaded 3-state buses.

74350 4-Bit Shifter with 3-State Outputs

The '350 is a combination logic circuit that shifts a 4-bit word from one to three places. No clocking is required as with shift registers.

The '350 can be used to shift any number of bits to any number of places, up or down by suitable interconnection. Shifting can be:

- *Logical*: the logic zeros fill in at either end of the shifting field.
- *Arithmetic*: the sign bit is extended during a shift down.
- *End around*: the data word forms a continuous loop.

The 3-state outputs are useful for bus-interface applications or expansion to a large number of shift positions in end-around shifting. The active low output enable ($\overline{OE}$) input controls the state of the outputs. The outputs are in the high-impedance off-state when $\overline{OE}$ is high, and they are active when $\overline{OE}$ is low.

Truth Table

$\overline{OE}$	S_1	S_0	I_3	I_2	I_1	I_0	I_{-1}	I_{-2}	I_{-3}	Y_3	Y_2	Y_1	Y_0
H	X	X	X	X	X	X	X	X	X	Z	Z	Z	Z
L	L	L	D_3	D_2	D_1	D_0	X	X	X	D_3	D_2	D_1	D_0
L	L	H	X	D_2	D_1	D_0	D_{-1}	X	X	D_2	D_1	D_0	D_{-1}
L	H	L	X	X	D_1	D_0	D_{-1}	D_{-2}	X	D_1	D_0	D_{-1}	D_{-2}
L	H	H	X	X	X	D_0	D_{-1}	D_{-2}	D_{-3}	D_0	D_{-1}	D_{-2}	D_{-3}

H = High voltage level
L = Low voltage level
X = Don't care
(Z) = High-impedance (off) state
D_n = High or low state of the referenced I_n input

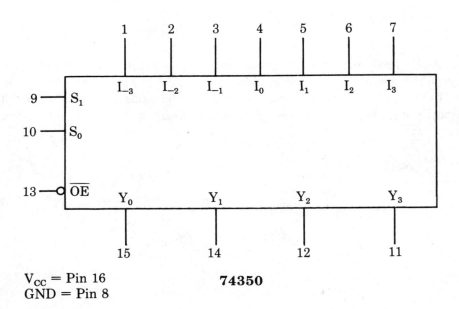

V_{CC} = Pin 16
GND = Pin 8

74350

74365 Hex Buffer/Driver (3-State)

Ordinarily, each of the six buffers in the '365 operates in the usual way—the output state is the same as the input state. But this chip also features two control, or *output-enable* inputs (OE1 and OE2). When a high signal is placed on either or both of the output enable pins, all six buffers are disabled. All outputs go to the third, high impedance (Z) state. Both output enable pins must be held low for the buffers to recognize the signals at their inputs.

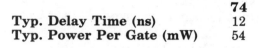

	74
Typ. Delay Time (ns)	12
Typ. Power Per Gate (mW)	54

Truth Table

INPUTS			OUTPUTS
$\overline{OE}_1$	$\overline{OE}_2$	I	Y
L	L	L	L
L	L	H	H
X	H	X	(Z)
H	X	X	(Z)

L = Low voltage level.
H = High voltage level.
X = Don't care.
(Z) = High-impedance (off) state.

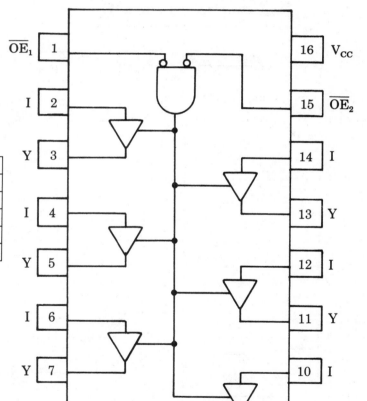

74365

74366 Hex Inverter Buffer (3-State)

The 74366 is very similar to the 74365 discussed previously, except six inverters are used, instead of the six buffers in the '365.

Ordinarily, each of the six inverters in the '366 operates in the usual way—the output state is the opposite of the input state. That is, when the input is low, the output is high, and vice versa. However, this chip features two control, or *output-enable* inputs (OE1 and OE2). When a high signal is placed on either or both of the output-enable pins, all six inverters are disabled. All outputs go to the third high-impedance (Z) state. Both output-enable pins must be held low for the inverters to recognize the signals at their inputs.

	74
Typ. Delay Time (ns)	11
Typ. Power Per Gate (mW)	49

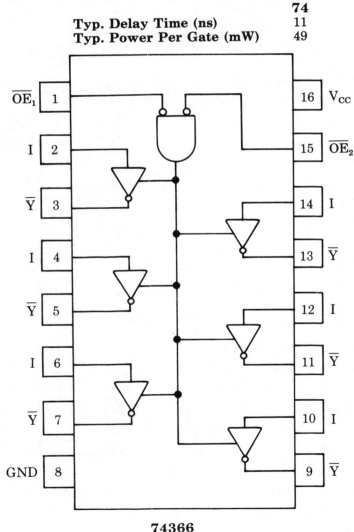

74366

Truth Table

INPUTS			OUTPUTS
$\overline{OE_1}$	$\overline{OE_2}$	I	$\overline{Y}$
L	L	L	H
L	L	H	L
X	H	X	(Z)
H	X	X	(Z)

L = Low voltage level.
H = High voltage level.
X = Don't care.
(Z) = High-impedance (off) state.

74367 Hex Buffer/Driver (3-State)

The 74367 is quite similar to the 74365 described earlier in this section. The big difference here is that the six buffers are divided into two groups. Each group is controlled by its own output-enable input. Pin #1 is the output-enable control for four of the internal buffers. The remaining two buffer stages are controlled by a second output-enable input at pin #15.

When a high signal is placed on one of the output-enable pins, the appropriate buffers are disabled. The outputs of the controlled buffers go to the third high-impedance (Z) state. The appropriate output-enable pin must be held low for the buffers in its group to recognize the signals at their inputs. As long as the signal at the appropriate output-enable pin is low, each buffer's output signal will be identical to its input signal.

		74
Typ. Delay Time (ns)		12
Typ. Power Per Gate (mW)		54

Truth Table

INPUTS		OUTPUTS
$\overline{OE}$	I	Y
L	L	L
L	H	H
H	X	(Z)

L = Low voltage level
H = High voltage level
X = Don't care
(Z) = High-impedance (off) state

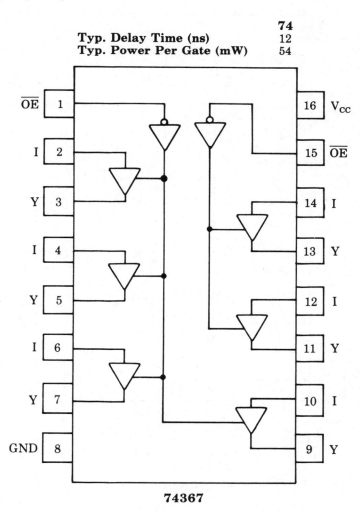

74367

181

74368 Hex Inverter Buffer (3-State)

The '368 is identical to the '367 just described, except this chip contains six inverters instead of six buffers.

A high output-enable signal disables the inverters in its group. The affected inverter outputs go to the high-impedance (Z) state and their inputs are ignored. When the appropriate output-enable pin is held low, the inverters function in the normal manner. The output signal is always at the opposite state as the input signal.

	74
Typ. Delay Time (ns)	11
Typ. Power Per Gate (mW)	49

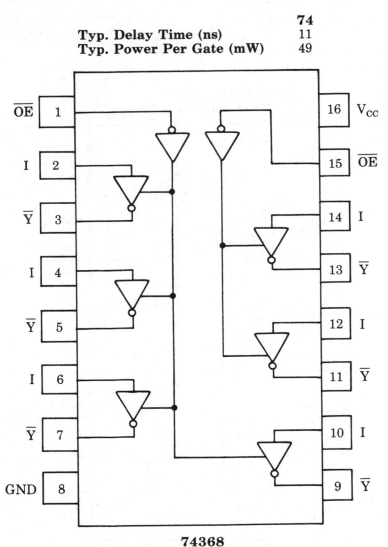

74368

Truth Table

INPUTS		OUTPUTS
$\overline{OE}$	I	$\overline{Y}$
L	L	H
L	H	L
H	X	(Z)

L = Low voltage level.
H = High voltage level.
X = Don't care.
(Z) = High-impedance (off) state.

74373 Octal Transparent Latch with 3-State Outputs

The '373 is an octal transparent latch coupled to eight 3-state output buffers. The two sections of the device are controlled independently by latch-enable (E) and output-enable ($\overline{OE}$) control gates.

Data on the D inputs are transferred to the latch outputs when the latch-enable (E) input is high. The latch remains transparent to the data inputs while E is high, and stores the data present one setup time before the high-to-low enable transition. The enable gate has about 400 mV of hysteresis built in to help minimize problems that signal and ground noise can cause in the latching operation.

The 3-state output buffers are designed to drive heavily loaded 3-state buses, MOS memories, or MOS microprocessors. The active low output-enable ($\overline{OE}$) controls all eight 3-state buffers independent of the latch operation. When $\overline{OE}$ is low, latched or transparent data appear at the outputs. When $\overline{OE}$ is high, the outputs are in the high-impedance off-state, which means they will neither drive nor load the bus.

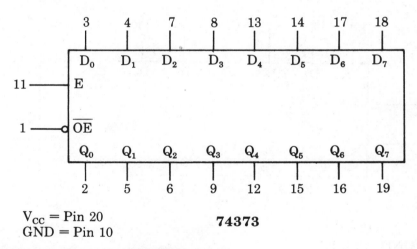

V_{CC} = Pin 20
GND = Pin 10

74373

MODE SELECT-FUNCTION TABLE

OPERATING MODES	INPUTS			INTERNAL REGISTER	OUTPUTS
	$\overline{OE}$	E	D_n		$Q_0 - Q_7$
Enable & read register	L	H	L	L	L
	L	H	H	H	H
Latch & read register	L	L	l	L	L
	L	L	h	H	H
Latch register & disable outputs	H	L	l	L	(Z)
	H	L	h	H	(Z)

H = High voltage level
h = High voltage level one setup time prior to the high-to-low enable transition
L = Low voltage level
l = Low voltage level one setup time prior to the high-to-low enable transition
(Z) = High impedance "off" state

74374 Octal D Flip-Flop with 3-State Outputs

The '374 is an 8-bit edge-triggered register coupled to eight 3-state output buffers. The two sections of the device are controlled independently by the clock (CP) and output-enable ($\overline{OE}$) control gates.

The register is fully edge-triggered. The state of each D input, one setup time before the low-to-high clock transition, is transferred to the corresponding Q output of the flip-flop. The clock buffer has about 400 mV of hysteresis built in to help minimize problems that signal and ground noise can cause in the clocking operation.

The 3-state output buffers are designed to drive heavily loaded 3-state buses, MOS memories, or MOS microprocessors. The active low output-enable ($\overline{OE}$) controls all eight 3-state buffers independent of the register operation. When $\overline{OE}$ is low, the data in the register appears at the outputs. When $\overline{OE}$ is high, the outputs are in the high-impedance off-state, which means they will neither drive nor load the bus.

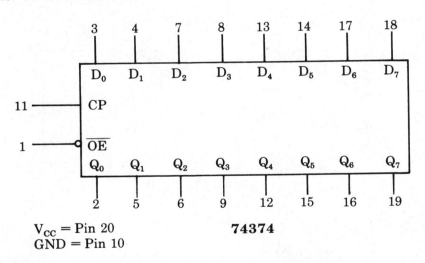

V_{CC} = Pin 20
GND = Pin 10

74374

MODE SELECT-FUNCTION TABLE

| OPERATING MODES | INPUTS | | | INTERNAL REGISTER | OUTPUTS |
	$\overline{OE}$	CP	D_n		$Q_0 - Q_7$
Load & read register	L	↑	l	L	L
	L	↑	h	H	H
Load register & disable outputs	H	↑	l	L	(Z)
	H	↑	h	H	(Z)

H = High voltage level
h = High voltage level one setup time prior to the low-to-high clock transition
L = Low voltage level
l = Low voltage level one setup time prior to the low-to-high clock transition
(Z) = High impedance "off" state
↑ = Low-to-high clock transition

184

74375 Dual 2-Bit Transparent Latch

The '275 has two independent 2-bit transparent latches. Each 2-bit latch is controlled by an active high enable input (E). When E is high, data enters the latch and appears at the Q output. The Q outputs follow the data inputs as long as E is high. Data on the D inputs one setup time before the high-to-low transition of the enable will be stored in the latch. The latched outputs remain stable as long as the enable is low.

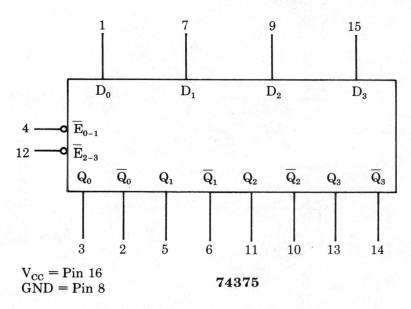

V_{CC} = Pin 16
GND = Pin 8

74375

MODE SELECT-FUNCTION TABLE

OPERATING MODE	INPUTS			OUTPUTS
	$\overline{E}$	D	Q	$\overline{Q}$
Data Enabled	H	L	L	H
	H	H	H	L
Data Latched	L	X	q	$\overline{q}$

H = High voltage level
L = Low voltage level
X = Don't care
q = Lower case letters indicate the state of referenced output one setup time prior to the high-to-low enable transition.

185

74377 Octal D Flip-Flop with Clock Enable

The '377 has eight edge-triggered D-type flip-flops with individual D inputs and Q outputs. The common buffered clock (CP) input loads all flip-flops simultaneously when the clock enable ($\overline{CE}$) is low.

The register is fully edge-triggered. The state of each D input, one setup time before the low-to-high clock transition, is transferred to the corresponding Q output of the flip-flop. The $\overline{CE}$ input is also edge-triggered, and must be stable only one setup time prior to the low-to-high clock transition for predictable operation.

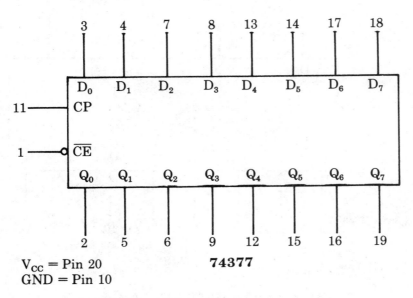

V_{CC} = Pin 20
GND = Pin 10

74377

MODE SELECT-FUNCTION TABLE

OPERATING MODE	INPUTS			OUTPUTS
	CP	$\overline{CE}$	D_n	Q_n
Load "1"	↑	l	h	H
Load "0"	↑	l	l	L
Hold (do nothing)	↑ X	h H	X X	no change no change

H = High voltage level steady state.
h = High voltage level one setup time prior to the low-to-high clock transition.
L = Low voltage level steady state.
l = Low voltage level one setup time prior to the low-to-high clock transition.
X = Don't care.
↑ = Low-to-high clock transition.

74378 Hex D Flip-Flop with Clock Enable

The '378 has six edge-triggered D-type flip-flops with individual D inputs and Q outputs. The common buffered clock (CP) input loads all flip-flops simultaneously when the clock enable ($\overline{\text{CE}}$) is low.

The register is fully edge-triggered. The state of each D input, one setup time before the low-to-high clock transition, is transferred to the corresponding Q output of the flip-flop. The $\overline{\text{CE}}$ input is also edge-triggered, and must be stable only one setup time prior to the low-to-high clock transition for predictable operation.

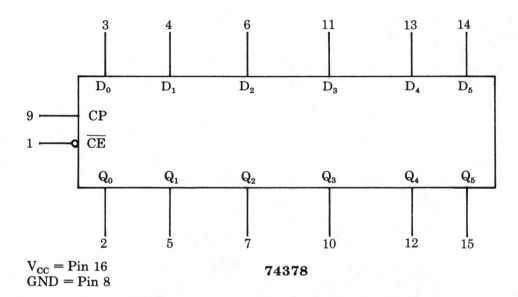

V_{CC} = Pin 16
GND = Pin 8

74378

MODE SELECT-FUNCTION TABLE

OPERATING MODE	INPUTS			OUTPUTS
	CP	$\overline{\text{CE}}$	D_n	Q_n
Load "1"	↑	l	h	H
Load "0"	↑	l	l	L
Hold (do nothing)	↑	h	X	no change
	X	H	X	no change

H = High voltage level steady state.
h = High voltage level one setup time prior to the low-to-high clock transition.
L = Low voltage level steady state.
l = Low voltage level one setup time prior to the low-to-high clock transition.
X = Don't care.
↑ = Low-to-high clock transition.

74379 Quad D Flip-Flop with Ciock Enable

The '379 is a quad edge-triggered D-type flip-flop with individual D inputs and both Q and $\overline{Q}$ outputs. The common buffered clock (CP) input loads all flip-flops simultaneously when the clock enable ($\overline{CE}$) is low.

The register is fully edge-triggered. The state of each D input, one setup time before the low-to-high clock transition, is transferred to the corresponding Q output of the flip-flop. The $\overline{CE}$ input is also edge-triggered and must be stable only one setup time prior to the low-to-high clock transition for predictable operation.

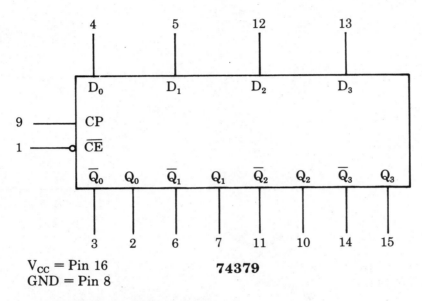

V_{CC} = Pin 16
GND = Pin 8

74379

MODE SELECT-FUNCTION TABLE

OPERATING MODE	INPUTS			OUTPUTS	
	CP	$\overline{CE}$	D_n	Q_n	$\overline{Q}_n$
Load "1"	↑	l	h	H	L
Load "0"	↑	l	l	L	H
Hold (do nothing)	↑ X	h H	X X	no change no change	

H = High voltage level steady state.
h = High voltage level one setup time prior to the low-to-high clock transition.
L = Low voltage level steady state.
l = Low voltage level one setup time prior to the low-to-high clock transition.
X = Don't care.
↑ = Low-to-high clock transition.

74390 Dual Decade Ripple Counter

The '390 is a dual 4-bit decade ripple counter that is divided into four separately clocked sections. The counter has two divide-by-2 sections and two divide-by-5 sections. The sections are normally used in a BCD decade or a biquinary configuration, because they share a common master reset input. If the two master resets can be used to simultaneously clear all 8 bits of the counter, a number of counting configurations are possible within one package. The separate clocks of each section allow ripple counter or frequency division applications of divide by 2, 4, 5, 10, 20, 25, 50, or 100.

Each section is triggered by the high-to-low transition of the clock ($\overline{CP}$) inputs. For BCD decade operation, the Q_0 output is connected to the $\overline{CP}_1$ input of the divide-by-5 section. For biquinary decade operation (50 percent duty-cycle output), the Q_3 output is connected to the $\overline{CP}_0$ input, and Q_0 becomes the decade output.

The master resets (MR_a and MR_b) are active high asynchronous inputs to each decade counter. These inputs operate on the portion of the counter identified by the a and b suffixes in the pin configuration. A high level on the MR input overrides the clocks and sets the four outputs low.

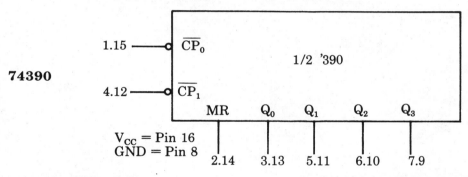

BCD COUNT SEQUENCE
For 1/2 the '390

COUNT	OUTPUT			
	Q_0	Q_1	Q_2	Q_3
0	L	L	L	L
1	H	L	L	L
2	L	H	L	L
3	H	H	L	L
4	L	L	H	L
5	H	L	H	L
6	L	H	H	L
7	H	H	H	L
8	L	L	L	H
9	H	L	L	H

NOTE: Output Q_0 is connected to Input $\overline{CP}_1$ with counter input on $\overline{CP}_0$.

BIQUINARY COUNT SEQUENCE
For 1/2 the '390

COUNT	OUTPUT			
	Q_0	Q_1	Q_2	Q_3
0	L	L	L	L
1	L	H	L	L
2	L	L	H	L
3	L	H	H	L
4	L	L	L	H
5	H	L	L	L
6	H	H	L	L
7	H	L	H	L
8	H	H	H	L
9	H	L	L	H

NOTE: Output Q_3 is connected to input $\overline{CP}_0$ with counter input on $\overline{CP}_1$.

74393 Dual 4-Bit Binary Ripple Counter

The '393 is a dual 4-bit binary ripple counter with separate clock and master-reset inputs to each counter. The operation of each half of the '393 is the same as the '93, except no external clock connections are required. The counters are triggered by a high-to-low transition of the clock ($\overline{CP}_a$ and $\overline{CP}_b$) inputs. The counter outputs are internally connected to provide clock inputs to succeeding stages. The outputs are designed to drive the internal flip-flops, plus the rated fanout of the device. The outputs of the ripple counter do not change synchronously and should not be used for high-speed address decoding.

The master resets (MR_a and MR_b) are active high asynchronous inputs to each 4-bit counter identified by the a and b suffixes in the pin configuration. A high level on the MR input overrides the clock and sets the outputs low.

COUNT SEQUENCE
For 1/2 the '393

COUNT	OUTPUT			
	Q_0	Q_1	Q_2	Q_3
0	L	L	L	L
1	H	L	L	L
2	L	H	L	L
3	H	H	L	L
4	L	L	H	L
5	H	L	H	L
6	L	H	H	L
7	H	H	H	L
8	L	L	L	H
9	H	L	L	H
10	L	H	L	H
11	H	H	L	H
12	L	L	H	H
13	H	L	H	H
14	L	H	H	H
15	H	H	H	H

74393

74399 Quad 2-Port Register

The '399 is a high-speed quad 2-port register. It selects four bits of data from two sources (ports) under the control of a common select input (S). The selected data is loaded into 4-bit output register synchronous with the low-to-high transition of the clock input (CP).

The operation of the device is fully synchronous. The data inputs (I_0 and I_1) and the select input (S) must be stable only one setup time prior to the low-to-high clock transition for predictable operation.

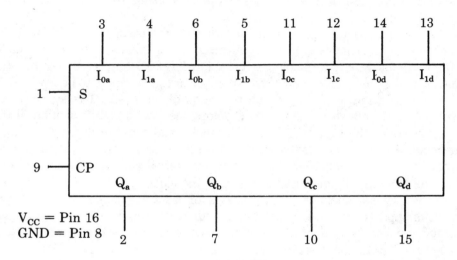

74399

MODE SELECT-FUNCTION TABLE

OPERATING MODE	INPUTS				OUTPUTS
	CP	S	I_0	I_1	Q_n
Load Source "0"	↑	l	l	X	L
	↑	l	h	X	H
Load Source "1"	↑	h	X	l	L
	↑	h	X	h	H

H = High voltage level
h = High voltage level one setup time prior to the low-to-high clock transition
L = Low voltage level
l = Low voltage level one setup time prior to the low-to-high clock transition
X = Don't care
↑ = Low-to-high clock transition

74568 BCD Decade Up/Down
Synchronous Counter (3-State)

The '568 is a synchronous presettable BCD decade up/down counter featuring an internal carry look ahead for applications in high-speed counting designs. Synchronous operation is provided by having all flip-flops clocked simultaneously so that the outputs change coincident with each other when so instructed by the count-enable inputs and internal gating. This mode of operation eliminates the output spikes that are normally associated with asynchronous (ripple clock) counters. A buffered clock input triggers the flip-flops on the low-to-high transition of the clock.

The counter is fully programmable; that is, the outputs can be preset to either level. Presetting is synchronous with the clock and takes place regardless of the levels of the count-enable inputs. A low level on the parallel-enable ($\overline{PE}$) inputs disables the counter and causes the data at the D_n inputs to be loaded into the counter on the next low-to-high transition of the clock. The synchronous reset ($\overline{SR}$), when low one setup time before the low-to-high transition of the clock, overrides the $\overline{CEP}$, $\overline{CET}$, and $\overline{PE}$ inputs, and causes the flip-flops to go low coincident with the positive clock transition. The master reset ($\overline{MR}$) is an asynchronous overriding clear function which forces all stages to a low state while the $\overline{MR}$ input is low without regard to the clock.

The carry look ahead circuitry provides for cascading counters for n-bit synchronous applications without additional gating. Instrumental in accomplishing this function are two count-enable inputs ($\overline{CET} \cdot \overline{CEP}$) and a terminal count ($\overline{TC}$) output. Both count-enable inputs must be low to count. The $\overline{CET}$ input is fed forward to enable the $\overline{TC}$ output. The $\overline{TC}$ output, thus enabled, will produce a low output pulse with a duration approximately equal to the high level portion of the Q_0 output. This low level $\overline{TC}$ pulse is used to enable successive cascaded stages. See the '168 data for the fast synchronous multistage counting connections.

The gated-clock output (GC) is a terminal-count output that provides a high-low-high pulse for a duration equal to the low time of the clock pulse when $\overline{TC}$ is low. The GC output can be used as a clock input for the next stage in a simple ripple-expansion scheme.

The direction of counting is controlled by the up/down ($U/\overline{D}$) input; a high will cause the count to increase, and a low will cause the count to decrease.

The active low output enable ($\overline{OE}$) input controls the 3-state buffer outputs independent of the counter operation. When $\overline{OE}$ is low, the count appears at the buffer outputs. When $\overline{OE}$ is high, the outputs are in the high-impedance off-state, which means they will neither drive nor load the bus.

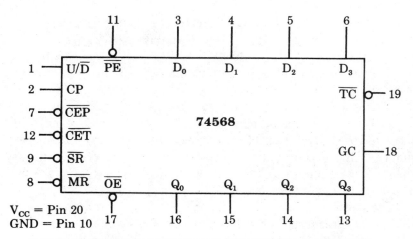

V_{CC} = Pin 20
GND = Pin 10

3-STATE BUFFER OPERATING MODES	INPUTS		OUTPUTS
	$\overline{OE}$	Q_n-Counter	Q_0, Q_1, Q_2, Q_3
Read counter	L	L	L
	L	H	H
Disable outputs	H	L	(Z)
	H	H	(Z)

MODE SELECT-FUNCTION TABLE

COUNTER OPERATING MODES	INPUTS								COUNTER STATES			
	$\overline{MR}$	CP	$\overline{SR}$	U/$\overline{D}$	$\overline{PE}$	$\overline{CEP}$	$\overline{CET}$	D_n	Q_0	Q_1	Q_2	Q_3
Asynchronous Reset	L	X	X	X	X	X	X	X	L	L	L	L
Synchronous Reset	H	↑	l	X	X	L	L	X	L	L	L	L
Parallel load	H	↑	h	X	l	X	X	l	L	L	L	L
	H	↑	h	X	l	X	X	h	H	H	H	H
Count up	H	↑	h	h	h	l	l	X	count up			
Count down	H	↑	h	l	h	l	l	X	count down			
Hold (do nothing)	H	↑	h	X	h	h	X	X	no change			
	H	↑	h	X	h	X	h	X	no change			

TERMINAL COUNT TRUTH TABLE

INPUTS				COUNTER STATES				OUTPUTS	
CP	U/$\overline{D}$	$\overline{CEP}$	$\overline{CET}$	Q_0	Q_1	Q_2	Q_3	$\overline{TC}$	GC
H	L	L	L	L	L	L	L	L	H
L	L	L	L	L	L	L	L	L	L
X	L	H	L	L	L	L	L	L	H
X	L	X	H	L	L	L	L	H	H
H	H	L	L	H	X	X	H	L	H
L	H	L	L	H	X	X	H	L	L
X	H	H	L	H	X	X	H	L	H
X	H	X	H	H	X	X	H	H	H

H = High voltage level
h = High voltage level one setup time prior to the low-to-high clock transition
L = Low voltage level
l = Low voltage level one setup time prior to the low-to-high clock transition
X = Don't care
(Z) = High-impedance "off" state
↑ = Low-to-high clock transition

74569 4-Bit Binary Up/Down Synchronous Counter (3-State)

The '569 is a synchronous presettable modulo 16 binary up/down counter featuring an internal carry look ahead for applications in high-speed counting designs. Synchronous operation is provided by having all flip-flops clocked simultaneously so that the outputs change coincident with each other when so instructed by the count-enable inputs and internal gating. This mode of operation eliminates the output spikes that are normally associated with asynchronous (ripple clock) counters. A buffered clock input triggers the flip-flops on the low-to-high transition of the clock.

The counter is fully programmable; that is, the outputs may be preset to either level. Presetting is synchronous with the clock and takes place regardless of the levels of the count enable inputs. A low level on the parallel-enable ($\overline{PE}$) input disables the counter and causes the data at the D_n inputs to be loaded into the counter on the next low-to-high transition of the clock. The synchronous reset ($\overline{SR}$), when low one setup time before the low-to-high transition of the clock, overrides the $\overline{CEP}$, $\overline{CET}$, and $\overline{PE}$ inputs, and cause the flip-flops to go low coincident with the positive clock transition. The master reset ($\overline{MR}$) is an asynchronous overriding clear function, which forces all stages to a low state while the $\overline{MR}$ input is low without regard to the clock.

The carry look ahead circuitry provides for cascading counters for n-bit synchronous applications without additional gating. Instrumental in accomplishing this function are two count enable inputs ($\overline{CET} \bullet \overline{CEP}$) and a terminal count

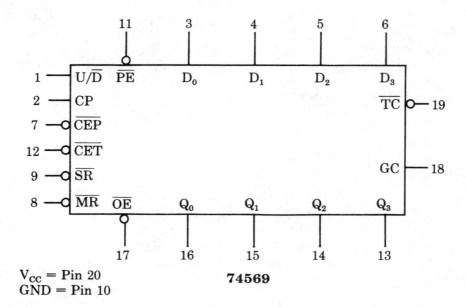

V_{CC} = Pin 20
GND = Pin 10

74569

($\overline{TC}$) output. Both count-enable inputs must be low to count. The $\overline{CET}$ input is fed forward to enable the $\overline{TC}$ outputs. The $\overline{TC}$ output, thus enabled, will produce a low output pulse with a duration approximately equal to the high level portion of the Q_0 output. This low level $\overline{TC}$ pulse is used to enable successive cascaded stages. See the '169 data for the fast synchronous multistage counting connections.

The gated-clock output (GC) is a terminal-count output that provides a high-low-high pulse for a duration equal to the low time of the clock pulse when $\overline{TC}$ is low. The GC output can be used as a clock input for the next stage in a simple ripple-expansion scheme. The direction of counting is controlled by the up/down (U/$\overline{D}$) input; a high will cause the count to increase, and a low will cause the count to decrease.

The active low output enable ($\overline{OE}$) input controls the 3-state buffer outputs independent of the counter operation. When $\overline{OE}$ is low, the count appears at the buffer outputs. When $\overline{OE}$ is high, the outputs are in the high-impedance off-state, which means they will neither drive nor load the bus.

74670 4 × 4 Register File (3-State)

The '670 is a 16-bit 3-state register file organized as 4 words of 4 bits each. Separate read and write address and enable inputs are available permitting simultaneous writing into one word location and reading from another location. The 4-bit word to be stored is presented to four data inputs. The write-address inputs (W_a and W_b) determine the location of the stored word. When the write-enable ($\overline{WE}$) input is low, the data is entered into the addressed location. The addressed location remains transparent to the data while the $\overline{WE}$ is low. Data supplied at the inputs will be read out in true (noninverting) form from the 3-state outputs. Data and write-address inputs are inhibited when $\overline{WE}$ is high.

Direct acquisition of data stored in any of the four registers is made possible by individual read address inputs (R_a and R_b). The addressed word appears at the four outputs when the read enable ($\overline{RE}$) is low. Data outputs are in the high-impedance off-state when the read-enable input is high. This permits outputs to be tied together to increase the word capacity to very large numbers.

Up to 128 devices can be stacked to increase the word size to 512 locations by tying the 3-state outputs together. Because the limiting factor for expansion is the output high current, further stacking is possible by tying pullup resistors to the outputs to increase the I_{OH} current available. Design of the read enable signals that the stacked devices must ensure there is no overlap in the low levels, which would cause more than one output to be active at the same time. Parallel expansion to generate n-bit words is accomplished by driving the enable and address inputs of each device in parallel.

	74LS
Typ. Address Time (ns)	24
Typ. Read Enable Time (ns)	19
Data Input Rate (MHz)	20
Typ. Total Power (mW)	135

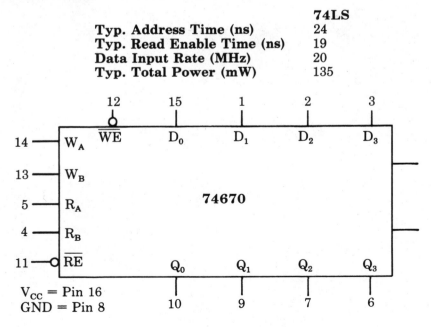

V_{CC} = Pin 16
GND = Pin 8

196

WRITE MODE SELECT TABLE

OPERATING MODE	INPUTS		INTERNAL LATCHES[b]
	$\overline{\text{WE}}$	D_n	
Write Data	L L	L H	L H
Data Latched	H	X	no change

NOTE
(b) The Write Address (W_A & W_B) to the "internal latches" must be stable while $\overline{\text{WE}}$ is low for conventional operation.

READ MODE SELECT TABLE

OPERATING MODE	INPUTS		OUTPUTS
	$\overline{\text{RE}}$	INTERNAL LATCHES[c]	Q_n
Read	L L	L H	L H
Disabled	H	X	(Z)

NOTE
(c) The Read Address (R_A & R_B) changes to select the "internal latches" are not constrained by $\overline{\text{WE}}$ or $\overline{\text{RE}}$ operation.

H = High voltage level
L = Low voltage level
X = Don't care
(Z) = High-impedance "off" state

2
SECTION

CMOS

Included in this chapter are the 4000 and 74C series of
complementary MOS, or CMOS, digital ICs. Throughout, you'll find logic diagrams, which are block diagrams using logic symbols, power-dissipation information, and truth tables. Also, data for quiescent current, TTL-driving capability load, and supply-voltage
range are given.

CMOS Chip Listing

4000 Dual 3-Input NOR Gate Plus Inverter

The 4000 is a monolithic complementary-MOS (CMOS) dual 3-input NOR gate plus an inverter. N-channel and P-channel enhancement mode transistors provide a symmetrical circuit with output swings essentially equal to the supply voltage. This results in high noise immunity over a wide supply-voltage range. No dc power other than that caused by leakage current is consumed during static conditions. All inputs are protected against static discharge and latching conditions.

Supply Voltage Range	3 to 15 V
Power	10 nW typ.
Noise Immunity	0.45 V_{DD} typ.

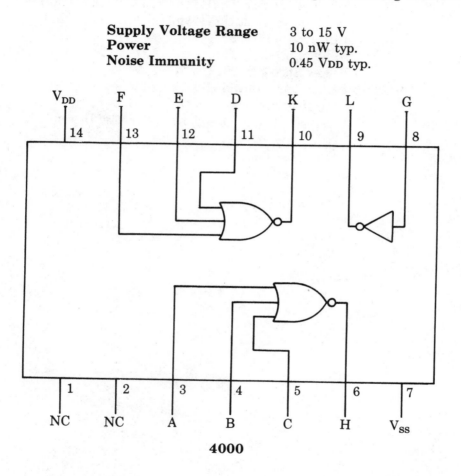

4000

4001 Quad 2-Input NOR Gate

The 4001 is a monolithic complementary-MOS (CMOS) quadruple 2-input NOR gate integrated circuit. N-channel and P-channel enhancement mode transistors provide a symmetrical circuit with output swings essentially equal to the supply voltage. This results in high noise immunity over a wide supply-voltage range. No dc power other than that caused by leakage current is consumed during static conditions. All inputs are protected against static discharge and latching conditions.

Supply Voltage Range	3 to 15 V
Power	10 nW (typ.)
Noise Immunity	0.45 V_{DD} (typ.)

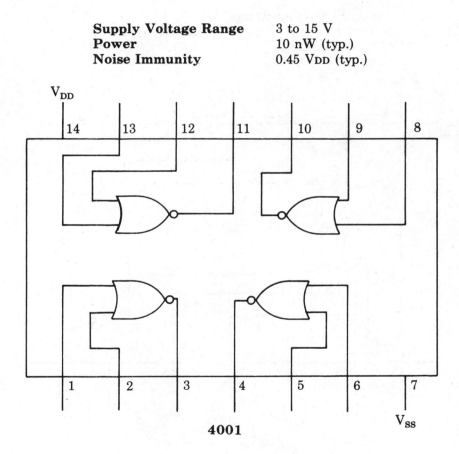

4001

4002 Dual 4-Input NOR Gate

The 4002 NOR gate is a monolithic complementary-MOS (CMOS) integrated circuit. The N-channel and P-channel enhancement-mode transistors provide a symmetrical circuit with output swings essentially equal to the supply voltage. This results in high noise immunity over a wide supply-voltage range. No dc power other than that caused by leakage current is consumed during static conditions. All inputs are protected against discharge and latching conditions.

Supply Voltage Range	3 to 15 V
Power	10 nW (typical)
Noise Immunity	0.45 V_{DD} (typical)

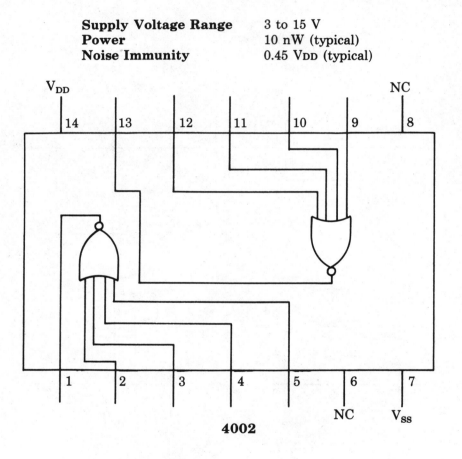

4002

4006 18-Stage Static-Shift Register

The 4006 18-stage static-shift register is comprised of four separate shift-register sections, two sections of four stages and two sections of five stages. Each section has an independent data input. Outputs are available at the fourth stage and the fifth stage of each section. A common-clock signal is used for all stages. Data is shifted to the next stage on the negative-going transition of the clock. Through appropriate connections of inputs and outputs, multiple register sections of 4, 5, 8, and 9 stages or single register sections of 10, 12, 13, 14, 16, 17, and 18 stages can be implemented using one package.

Supply Voltage Range   3 to 15 V
Noise Immunity   0.45 V_{DD} typ.
Clock Input Capacitance   6 pF typ.
Speed of Operation   10 MHz typ.
               with V_{DD} = 10 V

Truth Table

X = Don't care
Δ = Level change
NC = No change

D	CL$^\Delta$	D+1
0	⌐_	0
1	_⌐_	1
X	_⌐	NC

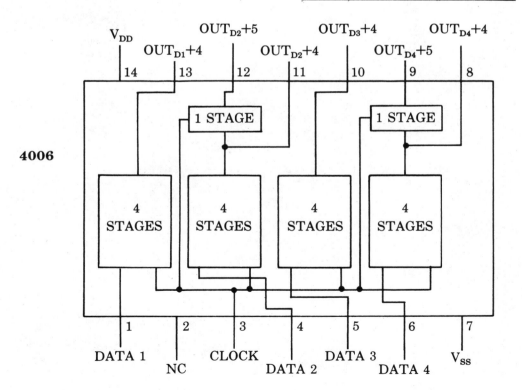

4007 Dual Complementary Pair Plus Inverter

The 4007 consists of three complementary pairs of N-channel and P-channel enhancement-mode MOS transistors suitable for series/shunt applications. All inputs are protected from static discharge by diode clamps to V_{DD} and V_{SS}.

For proper operation, the voltages at all pins must be constrained to be between $V_{SS} - 0.3$ V and $V_{DD} + 0.3$ V at all times.

Supply Voltage Range	3 to 15 V
Noise Immunity	0.45 Vcc typ.

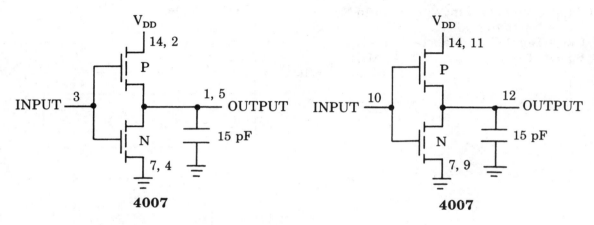

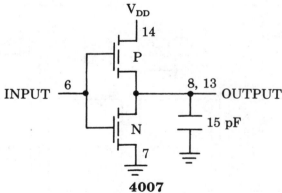

4008 4-Bit Full Adder

The 4008 consists of four full-adder stages with fast look ahead carry provision from stage to stage. Circuitry is included to provide a fast parallel carry out bit to permit high-speed operation in arithmetic sections using several 4008Bs. 4008B inputs include the four sets of bits to be added, A1 to A4 and B1 to B4, in addition to the carry in bit from a previous section. 4008B outputs include the four sum bits, S1 and S4, in addition to the high-speed parallel carry-out which can be utilized at a succeeding CD4008B section. All inputs are protected from damage as a result of static discharge by diode clamps to V_{DD} and GND.

			Truth Table	
A_i	B_i	C_i	CO	SUM
0	0	0	0	0
1	0	0	0	1
0	1	0	0	1
1	1	0	1	0
0	0	1	0	1
1	0	1	1	0
0	1	1	1	0
1	1	1	1	1

Supply Voltage Range   3 to 15 V
Noise Immunity   0.45 V_{DD} typ.
TTL Compatibility   Fanout of 2 driving 74L
      or 1 driving 74LS
Quiescent Current   15V
Maximum Input Leakage   1μA at 15V

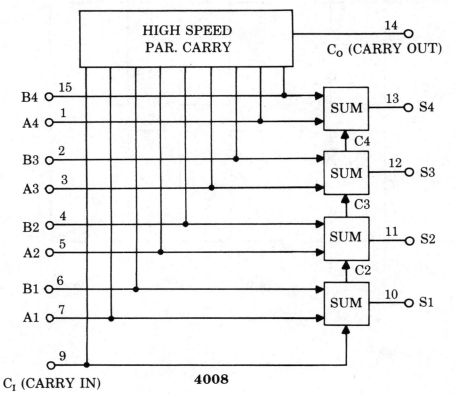

4008

4009 Hex Buffer (Inverting)

These hex buffers are monolithic complementary-MOS (CMOS) integrated circuits. The N-channel and P-channel enhancement-mode transistors provide a symmetrical circuit with output swings essentially equal to the supply voltage. This results in high noise immunity over a wide supply-voltage range. No dc power other than that caused by leakage current is consumed during static conditions. All inputs are protected against static discharge. These gates can be used as hex buffers, CMOS to DTL or TTL interfaces, or as CMOS current drivers. Conversion ranges are from 3 to 15 volts, providing $V_{CC} \leq V_{DD}$.

Supply Voltage Range	3 to 15 V
Power	100 nW (typical)
Noise Immunity	0.45 V_{DD} (typical)
Current Sinking	
Capability	8 mA (min) at $V_O = 0.5V$ and $V_{DD} = 10V$

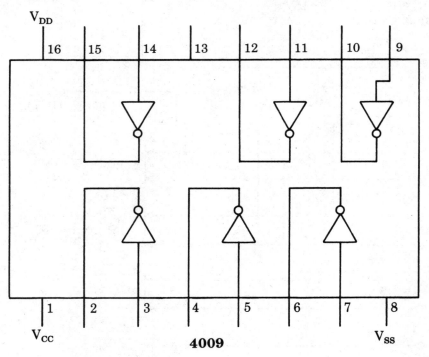

4009

208

4010 Hex Buffer (Noninverting)

These hex buffers are monolithic complementary-MOS (CMOS) integrated circuits. The N-channel and P-channel enhancement-mode transistors provide a symmetrical circuit with output swings essentially equal to the supply voltage. This results in high noise immunity over a wide supply-voltage range. No dc power other than that caused by leakage current is consumed during static conditions. All inputs are protected against static discharge. These gates can be used as hex buffers, CMOS to DTL or TTL interface, or as CMOS current drivers. Conversion ranges are from 3 to 15 volts providing that $V_{CC} \leq V_{DD}$.

Supply Voltage Range   3 to 15 V
Power   10 nW (typical)
Noise Immunity $0.45 V_{DD}$ (typical)
Current Sinking Capability   8 mA (min) at Vo = 0.5V and $V_{DD} = 10V$

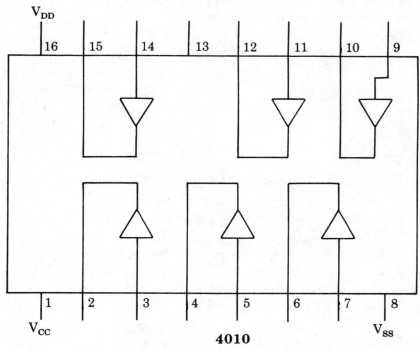

4010

4011 Quad 2-Input NAND Gate

These NAND gates are monolithic complementary-MOS (CMOS) integrated circuits. The N-channel and P-channel enhancement-mode transistors provide a symmetrical circuit with output swings essentially equal to the supply voltage. This results in high noise immunity over a wide supply-voltage range. No dc power other than that caused by leakage current is consumed during static conditions. All inputs are protected against static discharge and latching conditions.

Supply Voltage Range	3 to 15 V
Power	10 nW (typical)
Noise Immunity	0.45 V_{DD} (typical)

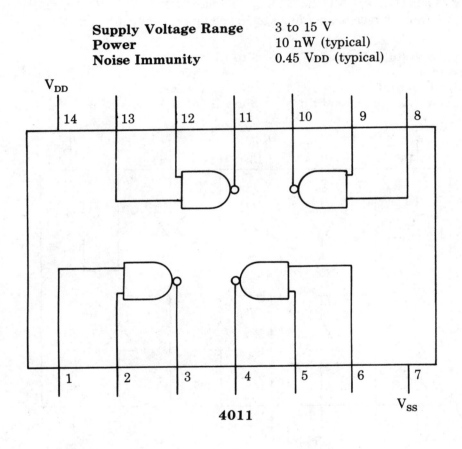

4011

4012 Dual 4-Input NAND Gate

These NAND gates are monolithic complementary-MOS (CMOS) integrated circuits. The N-channel and P-channel enhancement-mode transistors provide a symmetrical circuit with output swings essentially equal to the supply voltage. This results in high noise immunity over a wide supply-voltage range. No dc power other than that caused by leakage current is consumed during static conditions. All inputs are protected against static discharge and latching conditions.

Supply Voltage Range	3 to 15 V
Power	10 nW (typical)
Noise Immunity	0.45 V_{DD} (typical)

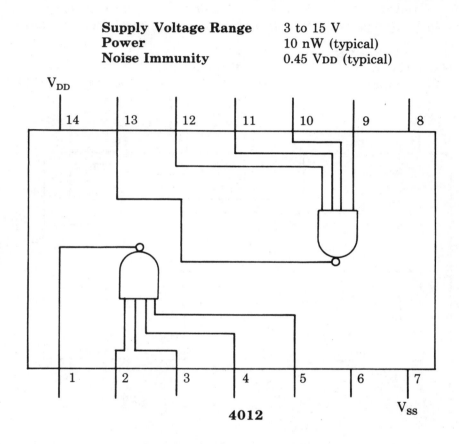

4012

4013 BM Dual-D Flip-Flop

The 4013 dual-D flip-flop is a monolithic complementary-MOS (CMOS) integrated circuit constructed with N-channel and P-channel enhancement transistors. Each flip-flop has independent data, set, reset, and clock inputs and Q and $\overline{Q}$ outputs. These devices can be used for shift register applications, and by connecting $\overline{Q}$ output to the data input, for counter and toggle applications. The logic level present at the D input is transferred to the Q output during the positive-going transition of the clock pulse. Setting or resetting is independent of the clock and is accomplished by a high level on the set or reset line, respectively.

Supply Voltage Range   3 to 15 V
Noise Immunity   0.45 V_{DD} typ.
TTL Compatibility   Fanout of 2 driving 74L or 1 driving 74LS

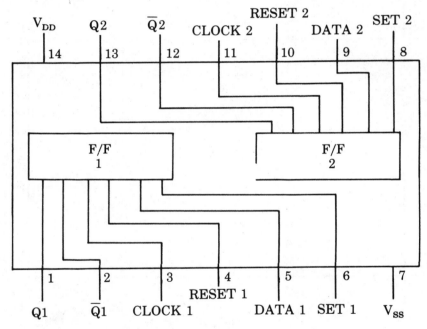

Truth Table

4013

CL†	D	R	S	Q	$\overline{Q}$
⟋	0	0	0	0	1
⟋	1	0	0	1	0
⟍	x	0	0	Q	$\overline{Q}$
x	x	1	0	0	1
x	x	0	1	1	0
x	x	1	1	1	1

No change
† = Level change
x = Don't care case

4014 8-Stage Static-Shift Register

The 4014 is an 8-stage parallel input/serial output shift register. A parallel/serial control input enables individual jam inputs to each of the eight stages. Q outputs are available from the sixth, seventh, and eighth stages.

When the parallel/serial control input is in the logic 0 state, data is serially shifted into the register synchronously with the positive transition of the clock. When the parallel/serial control input is in the logical 1 state, data is jammed into each stage of the register synchronously with the positive transition of the clock.

Supply Voltage Range   3 to 15 V
Noise Immunity   0.45 Vcc to typ.
Speed of Operation   5 MHz typ.

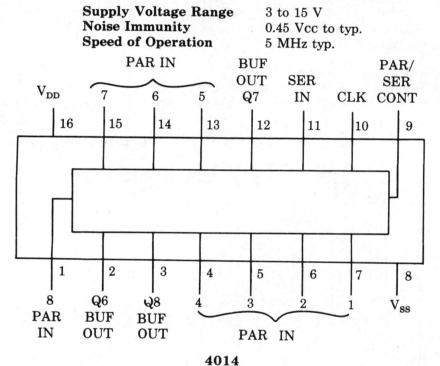

4014

Truth Table

CL$^\Delta$	SERIAL INPUT	PARALLEL/ SERIAL CONTROL	Pl 1	Pl n	Q1 (INTERNAL)	Q_n	
⤴	X	1	0	0	0	0	
⤴	X	1	1	0	1	0	
⤴	X	1	0	1	0	1	
⤴	X	1	1	1	1	1	
⤴	0	0	X	X	0	Q_n 1	
⤴	1	0	X	X	1	Q_n 1	
⤵	X	X	X	X	Q1	Q_n	No Change

Δ = Level change
x = Don't care case

4015 Dual 4-Bit Static Register

The 4015 consists of two identical, independent, 4-stage serial-input/parallel-output registers. Each register has independent clock and reset inputs, as well as a single serial-data input. Q outputs are available from each of the four stages on both registers. All register stages are D-type, master-slave flip-flops. The logic level present at the data input is transferred into the first register stage and shifted over one stage at each positive-going clock transition. Resetting of all stages is accomplished by a high level on the reset line. Register expansion to eight stages using one 4015 package, or to more than eight stages using additional 4015 is possible. All inputs are protected from static discharge by diode clamps to V_{DD} and V_{SS}.

Supply Voltage Range 3 to 15 V
Noise Immunity 0.45 Vcc typ.
Speed of Operation 9 MHz (typ.) clock rate at $V_{DD} - V_{SS} = 10$ V

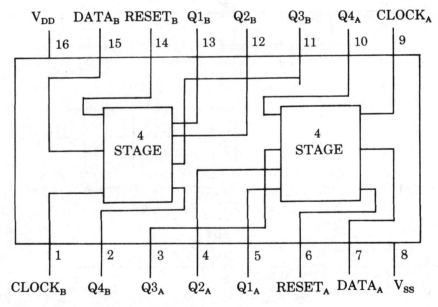

Truth Table

4015

$CL^{\triangle}$	D	R	Q1	Qn
⤴	0	0	0	$Q_n 1$
⤴	1	0	1	$Q_n 1$
⤵	X	0	Q1	Q_n
X	X	1	0	0

(No change)
$\triangle$ Level change.
X Don't care case.

4016 Quad Bilateral Switch

The 4016 is a quad bilateral switch that utilizes P-channel and N-channel complementary-MOS (CMOS) circuits to provide an extremely high off-resistance and low on-resistance switch. The switch will pass signals in either direction and is extremely useful in digital switching.

Supply Voltage Range	3 to 15 V
Noise Immunity	0.45 Vcc typ.
Digital and Analog Levels	$\pm$ 7.5 V_{peak}
On Resistance	300Ω typ.
	$V_{DD} - V_{DD} = 15$ V
Switch Characteristics	Δ $R_{ON} = 40\Omega$ typ.
On/Off Output	65 dB typ.
Voltage Ratio	@ fis = 10 kHz R_L = 10 kΩ
Linearity	.5% distortion typ.
	@ fis = 1 kHz
Leakage	V_{is} = 5 $V_{p\text{-}p}$
	$V_{DD} - V_{SS} = 10$ V
	R_L = 10 kΩ

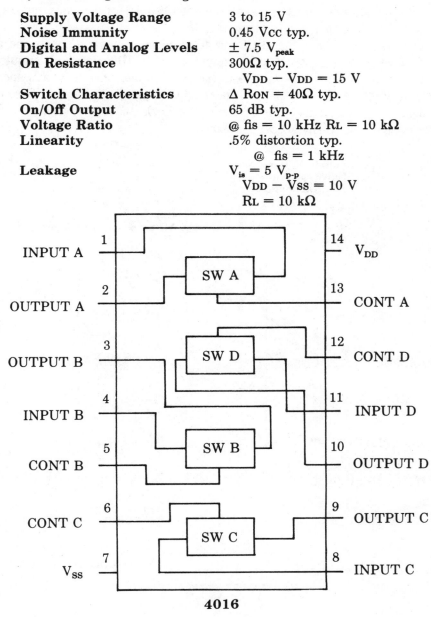

4016

215

4017 Decade Counter/Divider with 10 Decoded Outputs

The 4017 is a 5-stage divide-by-10 Johnson counter with 10 decoded outputs and a carry-out bit. The 4022 is a 4-stage divide-by-8 Johnson counter with eight decoded outputs and a carry-out bit.

These counters are cleared to their zero count by a logical 1 on their reset line. These counters are advanced on the positive edge of the clock signal when the clock-enable signal is in the logic 0 state.

The configuration of the 4017 and 4022 permits medium-speed operation and ensures a hazard-free counting sequence. The 10/8 decoded outputs are normally in the logic 0 state and go to the logic 1 state only at their respective time slot. Each decoded output remains high for one full clock cycle. The carry-out signal completes a full cycle for every 10/8 clock input cycles and is used as a ripple-carry signal to any succeeding stages.

Supply Voltage Range   3 to 15 V
Noise Immunity   0.45 V_{DD} typ.
TTL Compatibility   Fanout of 2 driving 74L or 1 driving 74LS
Speed of Operation   5.0 MHz typ. with 10 V V_{DD}
Power 10μ W typ.

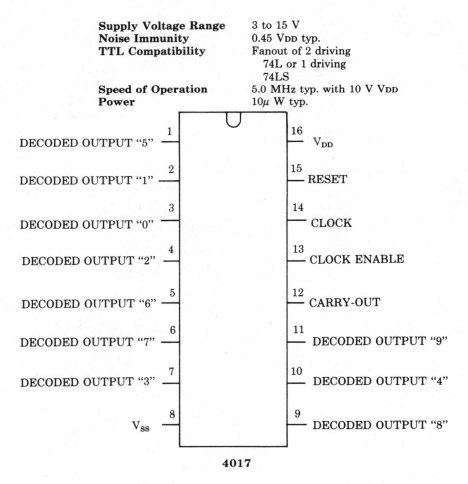

4017

216

4018 Presettable Divide-by-N Counter

The 4018B consists of five Johnson counter stages. A buffered $\overline{Q}$ output from each stage, clock, reset, data, preset enable, and five individual jam inputs are provided. The counter is advanced one count at the positive clock signal transition. A high reset signal clears the counters to an all-zero condition. A high preset-enable signal allows information on the jam inputs to preset the counter. Antilock gating is provided to assure the proper counting sequence.

Supply Voltage Range	3 to 15 V
Noise Immunity	0.45 V_{DD} typ.
TTL Compatibility	Fanout of 2 driving 74L
	or 1 driving 74LS

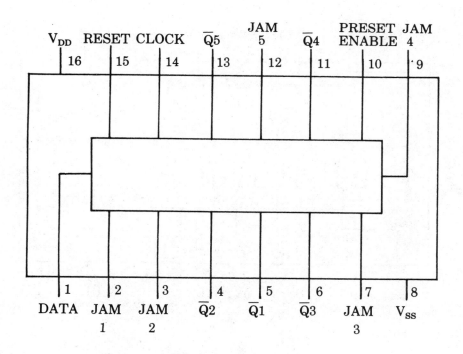

4018

4019 Quad AND/OR Select Gate

The 4019 is a complementary-MOS quad AND-OR select gate. Low power and a high noise margin is possible over a wide voltage range through implementation of N-channel and P-channel enhancement-mode transistors. These complementary-MOS (CMOS) transistors provide the building blocks for the 4 AND-OR select gate configurations, each consisting of two 2-input AND gates driving a single 2-input OR gate. Selection is accomplished by control bits, K_A and K_B. All inputs are protected against static-discharge damage.

Supply Voltage Range	3 to 15 V
Noise Immunity	0.45 V_{DD} typ.
TTL Compatibility	Driving 74L or 1 driving 74LS

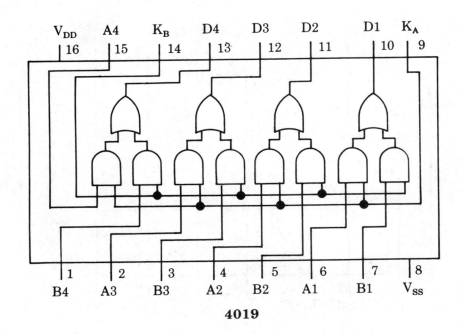

4019

4020 14-Stage Ripple-Carry Binary Counter

The 4020 and 4060 are 14-stage ripple-carry binary counters, and the 4040BM/ 4040BC is a 12-stage ripple-carry binary counter. The counters are advanced one count on the negative transition of each clock pulse. The counters are reset to the zero state by a logic 1 at the reset input independent of clock.

Supply Voltage Range	1 to 15 V
Noise Immunity	0.45 V_{DD} typ.
TTL Compatibility	Fanout of 2 driving 74L or 1 driving 74LS
Speed of Operation	8 MHz typ. at V_{DD} = 10 V

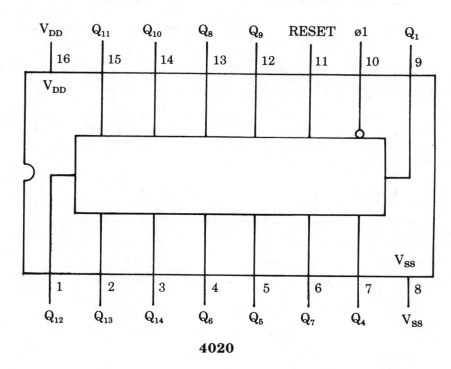

4020

4021 8-Stage Static-Shift Register

The 4021 is an 8-stage parallel input/serial output shift register. A parallel/serial control input enables individual jam inputs to each of eight stages. Q outputs are available from the sixth, seventh, and eighth stages.

When the parallel/serial control input is in the logic 0 state, data is serially shifted into the register synchronously with the positive transition of the clock. When the parallel/serial control is in the logic 1 state, data is jammed into each stage of the register asynchronously with the clock.

Supply Voltage Range	3 to 15 V
Noise Immunity	0.45 Vcc typ.
Speed of Operation	5 MHz typ.

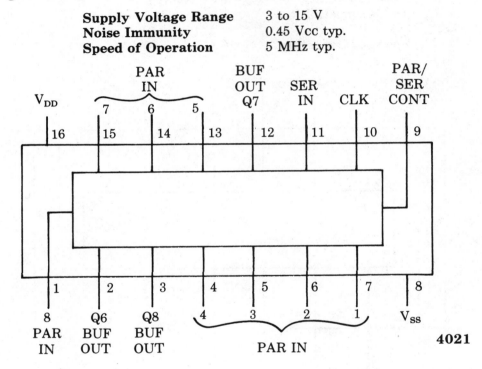

4021

Truth Table

CL$^\triangle$	SERIAL INPUT	PARALLEL/ SERIAL CONTROL	Pl 1	Pl n	Q1 (INTERNAL)	Q_n
X	X	1	Q	0	0	0
X	X	1	0	1	0	1
X	X	1	1	0	1	0
X	X	1	1	1	1	1
⟋	0	0	X	X	0	Q_n 1
⟋	1	0	X	X	1	Q_n 1
⟍	X	0	X	X	Q1	Q_n

No Change

$^\triangle$ Level change

X Don't care case

4022 Divide-by-8 Counter/Divider
with 8 Decoded Outputs

The 4017 is a 5-stage divide-by-10 Johnson counter with 10 decoded outputs and a carry-out bit. The 4022 is a 4-stage divide-by-8 Johnson counter with eight decoded outputs and a carry-out bit.

These counters are cleared to their zero count by a logic 1 on their reset line. These counters are advanced on the positive edge of the clock signal when the clock-enable signal is in the logic 0 state.

The configuration of the 4017 and 4022 permits medium-speed operation and ensures a hazard-free counting sequence. The 10/8 decoded outputs are normally in the logic 0 state and go to the logic 1 state only at their respective time slot. Each decoded output remains high for one full clock cycle. The carry-out signal completes a full cycle for every 10/8 clock input cycles and is used as a ripple-carry signal to any succeeding stages.

Supply Voltage Range	3 to 15 V
Noise Immunity	0.45 V_{DD} typ.
TTL Compatibility	Fanout of 2 driving 74L or 1 driving 74LS
Speed of Operation	5.0 MHz typ. with 10 V V_{DD}
Power	10μ W typ.

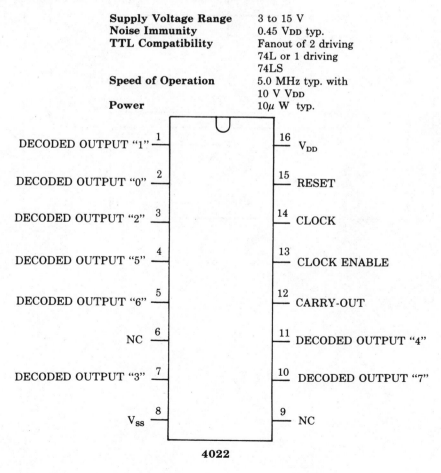

4022

4023 Triple 3-Input NAND Gate

These NAND gates are monolithic complementary-MOS (CMOS) integrated circuits. The N-channel and P-channel enhancement-mode transistors provide a symmetrical circuit with output swings essentially equal to the supply voltage. This results in high noise immunity over a wide supply-voltage range. No dc power other than that caused by leakage current is consumed during static conditions. All inputs are protected against static discharge and latching conditions.

Supply Voltage Range	3 to 15 V
Power	10 nW (typical)
Noise Immunity	0.45 V_{DD} (typical)

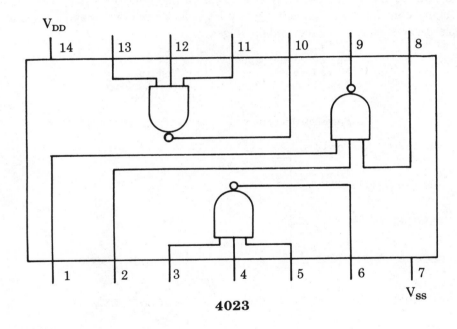

4023

4024 7-Stage Ripple-Carry Binary Counter

The 4024 is a 7-stage ripple-carry binary counter. Buffered outputs are externally available from stages 1 through 7. The counter is reset to its logic 0 state by a logic 1 on the reset input. The counter is advanced one count on the negative transition of each clock pulse.

Supply Voltage Range	3 to 15 V
Noise Immunity	0.45 V_{DD} typ.
TTL Compatibility	Fanout of 2 driving 74L
	or 1 driving 74LS
Speed	12 MHz (typ.)
	input pulse rate
	$V_{DD} - V_{SS} = 10$ V

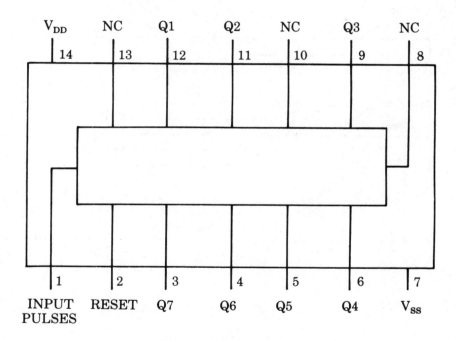

4024

4025 Triple 3-Input NOR Gate

These triple gates are monolithic complementary-MOS (CMOS) integrated circuits constructed with N-channel and P-channel enhancement-mode transistors. They have equal source-and sink-current capabilities and conform to standard B-series output drive. The devices also have buffered outputs that improve transfer characteristics by providing very high gain. All inputs are protected against static discharge with diodes to V_{DD} and V_{SS}.

Supply Voltage Range	3 to 15 V
Noise Immunity	0.45 V_{DD} typ.
TTL Compatibility	Fanout of 2 driving 74L
	or 1 driving 74LS
Maximum Input Leakage	1 μA at 15 V

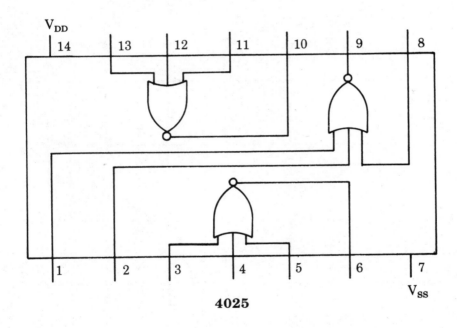

4025

4027 Dual JK Master/Slave Flip-Flop

These dual JK flip-flops are monolithic complementary-MOS (CMOS) integrated circuits constructed with N-channel and P-channel enhancement-mode transistors. Each flip-flop has independent J, K, set, reset and clock inputs, and buffered Q and $\overline{Q}$ outputs. These flip-flops are edge-sensitive to the clock input and change state on the positive-going transition of the clock pulses. Set or reset is independent of the clock and is accomplished by a high level on the respective input. All inputs are protected against damage as a result of static discharge by diode clamps to V_{DD} and V_{SS}.

Supply Voltage Range	3 to 15 V
Noise Immunity	0.45 V_{DD} typ.
TTL Compatibility	Fanout of 2 driving 74L or 1 driving 74LS
Power	50 nW typ.
Speed of Operation	12 MHz typ. with 10 V supply

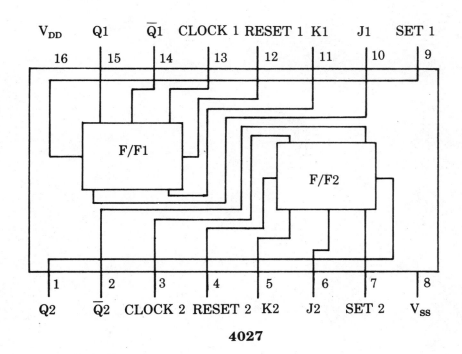

4027

Truth Table

		t_{n-1} INPUTS					t_n OUTPUTS	
CL▲	J	K	S	R	Q	Q	$\overline{Q}$
⌐	1	X	0	0	0	1	0
⌐	X	0	0	0	1	1	0
⌐	0	X	0	0	0	0	1
⌐	X	1	0	0	1	0	1
⌐	X	X	0	0	X	(No change)	
X	X	X	1	0	X	1	0
X	X	X	0	1	X	0	1
X	X	X	1	1	X	1	1

1 = High Level
0 = Low Level
▲ = Level Change
X = Don't Care
• = t_{n-1} refers to the time interval prior to the positive clock pulse transition
♦ = t_n refers to the time intervals after the positive clock pulse transition

4028 BCD-to-Decimal Decoder

The 4028 is a BCD-to-decimal or binary-to-octal decoder consisting of four inputs, decoding logic gates and 10 output buffers. A BCD code applied to the four inputs, A, B, C, and D, results in a high level at the selected one-of-10 decimal decoded outputs. Similarly, a 3-bit binary code applied to inputs A, B, and C is decoded in octal at outputs 0 through 7. A high-level signal at the D input inhibits octal decoding and causes outputs 0 through 7 to go low. All inputs are protected against static-discharge damage by diode clamps to V_{DD} and V_{SS}.

Supply Voltage Range	3 to 15 V
Noise Immunity	0.45 V_{DD} typ.
TTL Compatibility	Fanout of 2 driving 74L
Power	or 1 driving 74LS

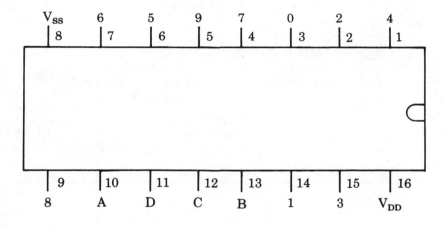

4028

Truth Table

D	C	B	A	0	1	2	3	4	5	6	7	8	9
0	0	0	0	1	0	0	0	0	0	0	0	0	0
0	0	0	1	0	1	0	0	0	0	0	0	0	0
0	0	1	0	0	0	1	0	0	0	0	0	0	0
0	0	1	1	0	0	0	1	0	0	0	0	0	0
0	1	0	0	0	0	0	0	1	0	0	0	0	0
0	1	0	1	0	0	0	0	0	1	0	0	0	0
0	1	1	0	0	0	0	0	0	0	1	0	0	0
0	1	1	1	0	0	0	0	0	0	0	1	0	0
1	0	0	0	0	0	0	0	0	0	0	0	1	0
1	0	0	1	0	0	0	0	0	0	0	0	0	1

4029 Presettable Binary/Decade Up/Down Counter

The 4029 is a presettable up/down counter that counts in either binary or decade mode depending on the voltage level applied at binary/decade input. When binary/decade is at logic 1, the counter counts in binary; otherwise, it counts in decade. Similarly, the counter counts up when the up/down input is at logic 1 and vice versa.

At logic 1 preset enable signal allows information at the jam inputs to preset the counter to any state asynchronously with the clock. The counter is advanced one count at the positive-going edge of the clock if the carry in and preset enable inputs are at logic 0. Advancement is inhibited when either or both of these two inputs are at logic 1. The carry-out signal is normally at the logic 1 state and goes to the logic 0 state when the counter reaches its maximum count in the up mode or the minimum count in the down mode, provided the carry input is at logic 0 state. All inputs are protected against static discharge by diode clamps to both V_{DD} and V_{SS}.

Supply Voltage Range	3 to 15 V
Noise Immunity	0.45 V_{DD} typ.
TTL Compatibility	Fanout of 2 driving 74L or 1 driving 74LS

4029

4030 Quad Exclusive-OR Gate

These exclusive-OR gates are monolithic complementary-MOS (CMOS) integrated circuits constructed with N-channel and P-channel enhancement-mode transistors. All inputs are protected against static discharge with diodes on V_{DD} and V_{SS}.

Supply Voltage Range	3 to 15 V
Power	100 nW (typ.)
Speed of Operation	40 ns (typ.)
Noise Immunity	0.45 Vcc (typ.)

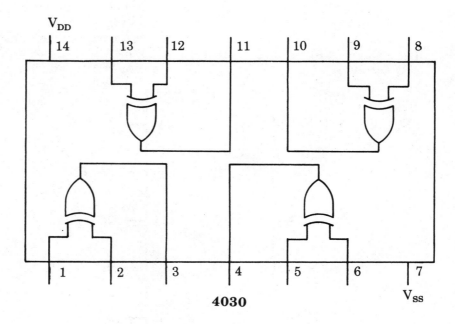

4030

Truth Table

A	B	J
0	0	0
1	0	1
0	1	1
1	1	0

Where: "1" = High Level
"0" = Low Level

4031 64-Stage Static-Shift Register

The 4031 is an integrated, complementary-MOS (CMOS), 64-stage, fully static-shift register. Two data inputs, data in and recirculate in, and a mode-control input are provided. Data at the data input (when mode control is low) or data at the recirculate input (when mode control is high), which meets the setup and

Supply Voltage Range	3 to 15 V
Noise Immunity	0.45 V_{DD} typ.
TTL Compatibility	Fanout of 2 driving 74L or 1 driving 74LS
Range of Operation	Dc to 8 MHz (typical @ V_{DD} = 10 V)
Clock Input	5 pF (typ.) Input Capacitance
High Current Sinking Capability, Q Output	1.6 mA @ V_{DD} = 5 V and 25°C

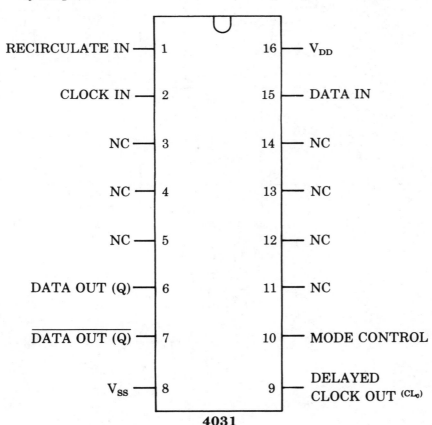

RECIRCULATE IN	1	16	V_{DD}
CLOCK IN	2	15	DATA IN
NC	3	14	NC
NC	4	13	NC
NC	5	12	NC
DATA OUT (Q)	6	11	NC
$\overline{\text{DATA OUT (Q)}}$	7	10	MODE CONTROL
V_{SS}	8	9	DELAYED CLOCK OUT $^{(CL_0)}$

4031

MODE CONTROL (data selection)

MODE CONTROL	DATA IN	RECIRCULATE IN	DATA INTO FIRST STAGE
0	0	X	0
0	1	X	1
1	X	0	0
1	X	1	1

EACH STAGE

D_n	CL	Q_n
0	⌐ /	0
1	⌐ /	1
X	⌐ \\	NC

X = irrelevant
NC = no change
⌐/ = Low to High level transition
⌐\\ = High to Low level transition

hold time requirements, are entered into the first stage of the register and are shifted one stage at each positive transition of the clock.

Data output is available in both true and complement forms from the 64th stage. Both the data-out (Q) and $\overline{\text{data-out}}$ ($\overline{\text{Q}}$) outputs are fully buffered.

The clock input of the 4031BM/4031BC is fully buffered and presents only a standard input load capacitance. However, a delayed clock output (CL_D) allows reduced clock drive-fanout and transition time requirements when cascading packages.

4034 8-Stage 3-State Bidirectional
Parallel/Serial Input/Output Bus Register

The 4034 is an 8-bit CMOS static-shift register with two parallel bidirectional data ports (A and B) which, when combined with serial-shifting operations, can be used to bidirectionally transfer parallel data between two buses, convert serial data to parallel form and direct them to either of two buses, store (recirculate) parallel data, or accept parallel data from either of two buses and convert them to serial form. These operations are controlled by five control inputs:

- **A enable (AE)** A data port is enabled only when AE is at logic 1. This action allows the use of a common bus for multiple packages.
- **A-bus-to-B-bus/B-bus-to-A-bus (A/B)** This input controls the direction of data flow. When at logic 1, data flows from port A to B (A is input and B is output). When at logic 0, the data-flow direction is reversed.
- **Asynchronous/synchronous (A/S)** When A/S is at logic 0, data transfer occurs at positive transition of the clock. When A/S is at logic 1, data transfer is independent of the clock for parallel operation. In the

Supply Voltage Range	3 to 18 V
Noise Immunity	0.45 V_{DD} typ.
TTL Compatibility	Fanout of 2 driving 74L
	or 1 driving 74LS

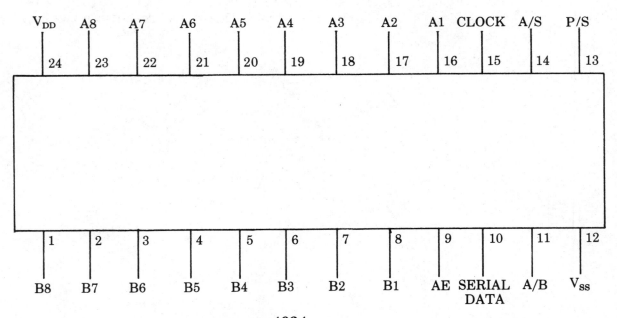

4034

serial mode, A/S input is internally disabled such that the operation is always synchronous. Asynchronous serial operation is not possible.

- **Parallel/serial (P/S)**   A logic 1 P/S input allows data transfer into the registers via A or B port (synchronous if A/S = logic 0 and asynchronous if A/S = logic 1). A logic 0 P/S allows serial data to transfer into the register synchronously with the positive transition of the clock, independent of the A/S input.
- **Clock**   Single phase, enabled only in synchronous mode. Either P/S = logic 1 and A/S = logic 0 or P/S = logic 0.

All register stages are D-type master-slave flip-flops with separate master and slave clock inputs, generated internally to allow synchronous or asynchronous data transfer from master to slave. All inputs are protected against damage as a result of static discharge by diode clamps to V_{DD} and V_{SS}.

4035 4-Bit Parallel-In/Parallel-Out Shift Register

The 4035 4-bit parallel-in/parallel-out shift register is a monolithic complementary-MOS (CMOS) integrated circuit constructed with P-channel and N-channel enhancement-mode transistors. This shift register is a 4-stage clocked serial register that has provisions for synchronous parallel inputs to each stage and serial inputs to the first stage via $\overline{JK}$ logic. Register stages 2, 3, and 4 are coup-

Supply Voltage Range	3 to 15 V
Noise Immunity	0.45 V_{DD} typ.
TTL Compatibility	Fanout of 2 driving 74L or 1 driving 74LS
Power Dissipation	5 μW typ. (ceramic)
Speed	To 5 MHz

4035

Truth Table

C_L	J	$\overline{K}$	R	Q_n-1	Q_n
_/	0	X	0	0	0
_/	1	X	0	0	1
_/	X	0	0	1	0
_/	1	0	0	Q_{n-1}	$\overline{Q}_{n-1}$ TOGGLE MODE
_/	X	1	0	1	1
_	X	X	0	Q_{n-1}	Q_{n-1}
X	X	X	1	X	0

led in a serial D flip-flop configuration when the register is in the serial mode (parallel/serial control low).

Parallel entry via the D line of each register stage is permitted only when the parallel/serial control is high. In the parallel or serial mode, information is transferred on positive clock transitions.

When the true/complement control is high, the true contents of the register are available at the output terminals. When the true/complement control is low, the outputs are the complements of the data in the register. The true/complement control functions asynchronously with respect to the clock signal.

$\overline{JK}$ input logic is provided on the first-stage serial input to minimize logic requirements, particularly in counting and sequence-generation applications. With $\overline{JK}$ inputs connected together, the first stage becomes a D flip-flop. An asynchronous common reset is also provided.

4040 14-Stage Ripple-Carry Binary Counter

The 4020 and 4060 are 14-stage ripple-carry binary counters, and the 4040BM/4040BC is a 12-stage ripple-carry binary counter. The counters are advanced one count on the negative transition of each clock pulse. The counters are reset to the zero state by a logic 1 at the reset input that is independent of clock.

Supply Voltage Range	1 to 15V
Noise Immunity	$0.45V_{DD}$ typ.
TTL Compatibility	Fanout of 2 driving 74L or
	1 driving 74LS
Speed of Operation	8 MHz typ. at $V_{DD} = 10$ V

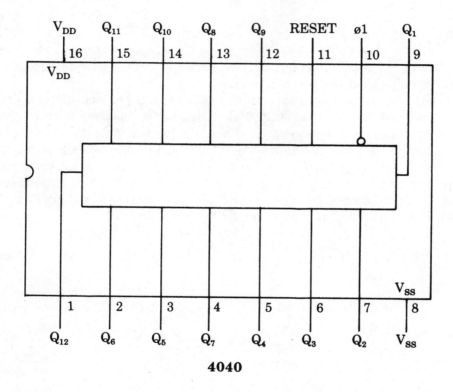

4040

4041 Quad True/Complement Buffer

The 4041 is a quad true/complement buffer consisting of N-channel and P-channel enhancement-mode transistors that have low-channel resistance and high-current (sourcing and sinking) capability. The 4041 is intended for use as a buffer, line driver, or CMOS-to-TTL driver. All inputs are protected from static discharge by diode clamps to V_{DD} and V_{SS}.

Supply Voltage Range	3 to 15 V
Noise Immunity	40% V_{DD} typ.
True Output:	
High Current Source and Sink Capability	8 mA (typ.) @ $V_O = 9.5$ V, $V_{DD} = 10$ V
	3.2 mA (typ.) @ $V_O = 0.4$ V, $V_{DD} = 5$ V (two TTL loads)
Complement Output:	Medium current source and sink capability
	3.6 mA (typ.) @ $V_O = 9.5$ V, $V_{DD} = 10V$
	1.6 mA (typ.) @ $V_O = 0.4$ V, $V_{DD} = 5$ V

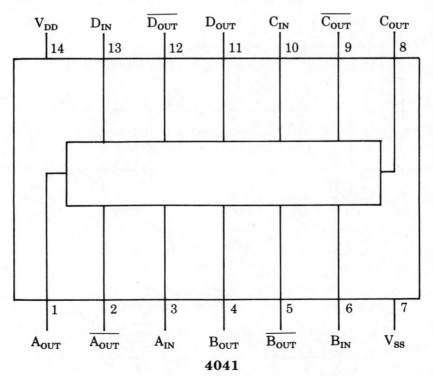

4041

4042 Quad Clocked D Latch

The 4042 quad clocked D latch is a monolithic complementary-MOS (CMOS) integrated circuit constructed with P-channel and N-channel enhancement-mode transistors. Outputs Q and $\overline{Q}$ either latch or follow the data input, depending on the clock level that is programmed by the polarity input. For polarity equal to 0, the information present at the data input is transferred to Q and $\overline{Q}$ during the 0 clock level. For polarity equal to 1, the transfer occurs during the 1 clock level. When a clock transition occurs (positive for polarity equal to 0 and negative for polarity equal to 1), the information present at the input during the clock transition is retained at the outputs until an opposite clock transition occurs.

Supply Voltage Range	3 to 15 V
Noise Immunity	0.45 V_{DD} typ.
TTL Compatibility	Fanout of 2 driving 74L or 1 driving 74LS

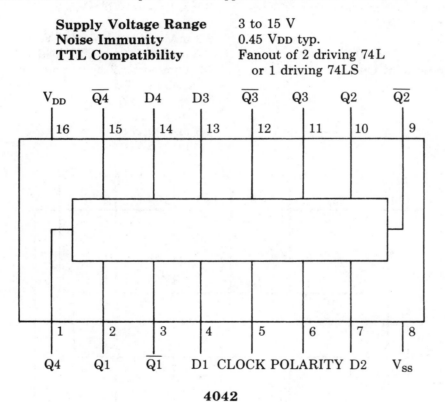

4042

Truth Table

CLOCK	POLARITY	Q
0	0	D
⌐	0	Latch
1	1	D
⌐_	1	Latch

238

4043 Quad 3-State NOR R/S Latches

The 4043 is a quad cross-coupled 3-state CMOS NOR latch, and CD4044 is a quad cross-coupled 3-state CMOS NAND latch. Each latch has a separate Q output and individual set and reset inputs. It has a common 3-state enable input for all four latches. A logic 1 on the enable input connects the latch states to the Q outputs. A logic 0 on the enable input disconnects the latch states from the Q outputs, resulting in an open circuit condition on the Q outputs. The 3-state feature allows common bussing of the outputs.

Supply Voltage Range	3 to 15 V	
Power	100 nW typ.	
Noise Immunity	0.45 V_{DD} typ.	

Truth Table

S	R	E	Q
X	X	0	OC
0	0	1	NC
1	0	1	1
0	1	1	0
1	1	1	Δ

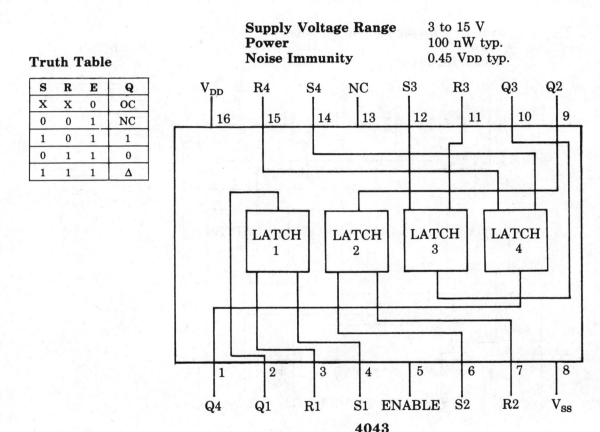

4043

4044 Quad 3-State NAND R/S Latches

The 4043 is a quad cross-coupled 3-state CMOS NOR latch, and CD4044 is a quad cross-coupled 3-state CMOS NAND latch. Each latch has a separate Q output and individual set and reset inputs. It has a common 3-state enable input for all four latches. A logic 1 on the enable input connects the latch states to the Q outputs. A logic 0 on the enable input disconnects the latch states from the Q outputs, resulting in an open circuit condition on the Q outputs. The 3-state feature allows common bussing of the outputs.

Supply Voltage Range   3 to 15 V
Power   100 nW typ.
Noise Immunity   0.45 V_{DD} typ.

Truth Table

S	R	E	Q
X	X	0	OC
1	1	1	NC
0	1	1	1
1	0	1	0
0	0	1	$\Delta\Delta$

OC — TRI-STATE
NC — No change
X — Don't care
Δ — Dominated by
     S=1 input
$\Delta\Delta$ — Dominated by
     R=0 input

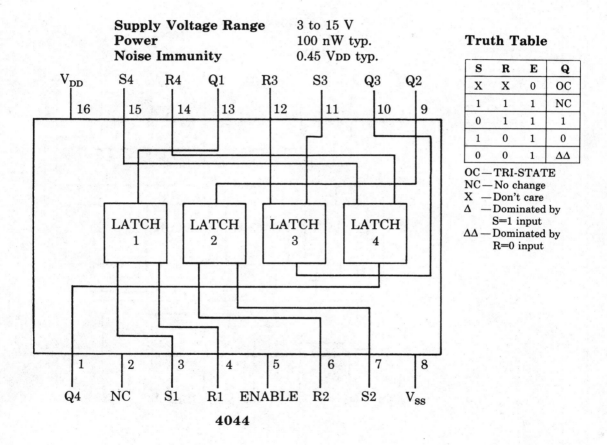

4044

4046 Micropower Phase-Locked Loop

The 4046 micropower phase-locked loop (PLL) consists of a low-power, linear, voltage-controlled oscillator (VCO), a source follower, a zener diode, and two phase comparators. The two phase comparators have a common signal input and a common comparator input. The signal input can be directly coupled for a large voltage signal, or capacitively coupled to the self-biasing amplifier at the signal input for a small voltage signal.

Supply Voltage Range	3 to 18 V
Dynamic Power Consumption	70μ W (typ.) at fo = 10 kHz, V_{DD} = 5 V
VCO Frequency	1.3 MHz (typ.) at V_{DD} = 10 V
Frequency Drift	0.06%/°C at V_{DD} = 10 V
VCO Linearity	1% (typ.)

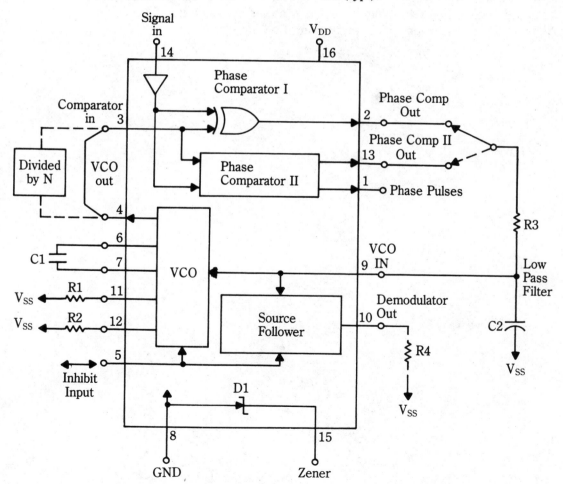

Phase comparator 1, an exclusive OR gate, provides a digital error signal (phase comparator 1 out) and maintains 90-degree shifts at the VCO center frequency. Between the signal input and the comparator input (both at 50-percent duty cycle), it can lock onto the signal input frequencies that are close to harmonics of the VCO center frequency.

Phase comparator 11 is an edge-controlled digital memory network. It provides a digital error signal (phase comparator 11 out) and lock-in signal (phase pulses) to indicate a locked condition and maintains a 0-degree phase shift between signal input and comparator input. The linear voltage-controlled oscillator (VCO) produces an output signal (VCO$_{out}$) whose frequency is determined by the voltage at the VCO$_{IN}$ input and the capacitor and resistors connected to pin C1$_A$, C1$_B$, R1, and R2.

The source-follower output of the VCO$_{IN}$ (demodulator out) is used with an external register of 10 kΩ or more. The inhibit input, when high, disables the VCO and source follower to minimize standby power consumption. The zener diode is provided for power-supply regulation, if necessary.

4047 Low-Power Monostable/Astable Multivibrator

The 4047 is capable of operating in either the monostable or astable mode. It requires an external capacitor between pins 1 and 3 and an external resistor between pins 2 and 3 to determine the output pulse width in the monostable mode, and the output frequency in the astable mode.

Astable operation is enabled by a high level on the astable input or low level on the $\overline{\text{astable}}$ input. The output frequency (at 50-percent duty cycle) at the Q and $\overline{Q}$ outputs is determined by the timing components. A frequency twice that of Q is available at the oscillator output. A 50-percent duty cycle is not guaranteed.

Monostable operation is obtained when the device is triggered by low-to-high transition at + trigger input or high-to-low transition at − trigger input. The device can be retriggered by applying a simultaneous low-to-high transition to both the + trigger and retrigger inputs. A high level on reset input resets the outputs Q to low and $\overline{Q}$ to high.

Supply Voltage Range	3 to 15 V
Noise Immunity	0.45 V$_{DD}$ typ.
TTL Compatibility	Fanout of 2 driving 74L or driving 74LS

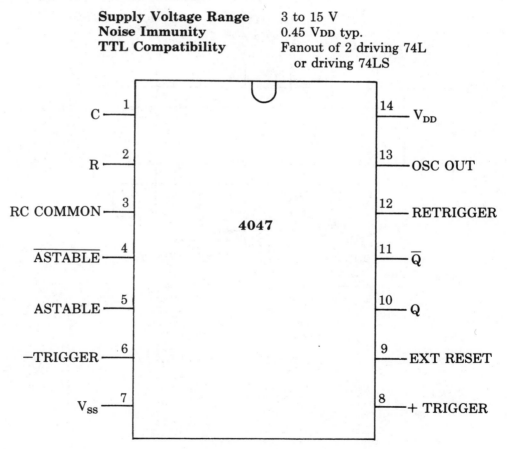

4048 3-State Expandable 8-Function 8-Input Gate

The 4048 is a programmable 8-input gate. Three binary control lines, K_a, K_b, and K_c, determine the eight different logic functions of the gate. These functions are OR, NOR, AND, NAND, OR/AND, OR/NAND, AND/OR, and AND/NOR. A fourth input, K_d, is a 3-state control. When K_d is high, the output is enabled; when k_d is low, the output is high impedance. This feature enables the user to connect the device to a common bus line. The expand input permits the user to increase the number of gate inputs. For example, two 8-input 4048's can be cascaded into a 16-input multifunction gate. When the expand input is not used, it should be connected to V_{SS}. All inputs are buffered and protected against electrostatic effects.

Supply Voltage Range   3 to 15 V
Noise Immunity   0.45 V_{DD} typ.
TTL Compatibility   Drives 1 standard
         TTL load at $V_{CC} = 5$ V, over full
         temperature range.

Truth Table

OUTPUT FUNCTION	BOOLEAN EXPRESSION	CONTROL INPUTS				UNUSED INPUTS
		K_a	K_b	K_c	K_d	
NOR	$J = \overline{A+B+C+D+E+F+G+H}$	0	0	0	1	V_{SS}
OR	$J = A+B+C+D+E+F+G+H$	0	0	1	1	V_{SS}
OR/AND	$J = \overline{(A+B+C+D) \bullet (E+F+G+H)}$	0	1	0	1	V_{SS}
OR/NAND	$J = (A+B+C+D) \bullet (E+F+G+H)$	0	1	1	1	V_{SS}
AND	$J = A \bullet B \bullet C \bullet D \bullet E \bullet F \bullet G \bullet H$	1	0	0	1	V_{DD}
NAND	$J = \overline{A \bullet B \bullet C \bullet D \bullet E \bullet F \bullet G \bullet H}$	1	0	1	1	V_{DD}
AND/NOR	$J = \overline{(A \bullet B \bullet C \bullet D) + (E \bullet F \bullet G \bullet H)}$	1	1	0	1	V_{DD}
AND/NOR	$J = (A \bullet B \bullet C \bullet D) + (E \bullet F \bullet G \bullet H)$	1	1	1	1	V_{DD}
H_1-Z		X	X	X	0	X

Positive logic 0 = low level, 1 = high level, X = irrelevant, EXPAND input tied to V_{SS}.

4049 Hex Inverting Buffer

These hex buffers are monolithic complementary-MOS (CMOS) integrated circuits constructed with N-channel and P-channel enhancement-mode transistors. These devices feature logic-level conversion using only one supply voltage (V_{DD}). The input-signal high level (V_{IH}) can exceed the V_{DD} supply voltage when these devices are used for logic-level conversions. These devices are intended for use as hex buffers, CMOS to DTL/TTL converters, or as CMOS current drivers. At V_{DD} = 5 V, they can drive directly two DTL/TTL loads over the full operating temperature range.

Supply Voltage Range   3 to 15 V
TTL Compatibility   Direct drive to 2
TTL loads at
5 V over full
temperature range.

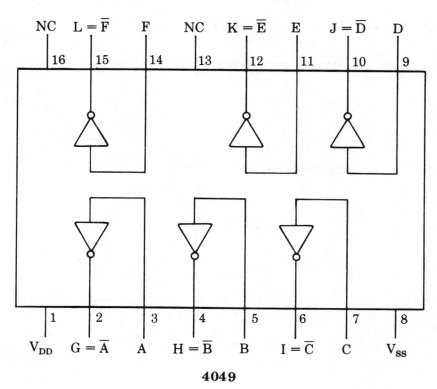

4049

4050 Hex Noninverting Buffer

These hex buffers are monolithic complementary-MOS (CMOS) integrated circuits constructed with N-channel and P-channel enhancement-mode transistors. These devices feature logic-level conversion using only one supply voltage (V_{DD}). The input-signal high level (V_{IH}) can exceed the V_{DD} supply voltage when these devices are used for logic-level conversions. These devices are intended for use as hex buffers, CMOS to DTL/TTL converters, or as CMOS current drivers. At V_{DD} = 5 V, they can drive directly two DTL/TTL loads over the full operating temperature range.

Supply Voltage Range   3 to 15 V
TTL Compatibility   Direct drive to 2 TTL loads at 5 V over full temperature range.

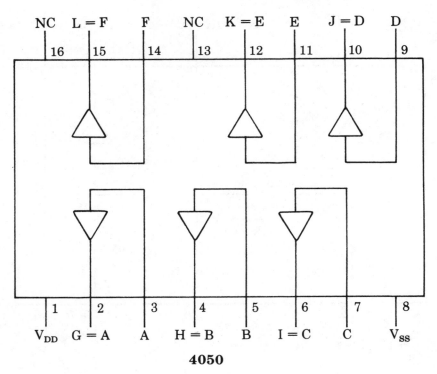

4050

4051 Single 8-Channel Analog Multiplexer/Demultiplexer

These analog multiplexers/demultiplexers are digitally controlled switches with low impedance and very low off leakage currents. Control of analog signals up to 15 V_{p-p} can be achieved by digital signal amplitudes of 3 to 15 V. For example, if $V_{DD} = 5$ V, $V_{SS} = 0$ V, and $V_{EE} = -5$ V, analog signals from -5 to $+5$ V can be controlled by digital inputs of 0 to 5 V. The multiplexer circuits dissipate extremely low quiescent power over the full V_{DD} to V_{SS} and V_{DD} to V_{EE} supply-voltage ranges, independent of the logic state of the control signals. When a logic 1 is present at the inhibit input terminal, all channels are off.

- 4051 is a single 8-channel multiplexer having three binary control inputs, A, B, and C, and an inhibit input. The three binary signals select one of eight channels to be turned on and connect the input to the output.
- 4052 is a differential 4-channel multiplexer having two binary control inputs, A and B, and an inhibit input. The two binary input signals select one of four pairs of channels to be turned on, and connect the differential analog inputs to the differential outputs.
- 4053 is a triple 2-channel multiplexer having three separate digital control inputs, A, B, and C, and an inhibit input. Each control input selects one of a pair of channels that are connected in a single-pole double-throw configuration.

Range of digital and analog signal levels: Digital 3 to 15 V, analog to 15 V p-p.

On resistance: 80 Ω (typ.) over entire 15 Vpp signal-input range for $V_{DD} - V_{EE} = 15$ V.

Off resistance: Channel leakage of ±10 pA (typ.) at $V_{DD} - V_{EE} = 10$ V.

Logic level conversion for digital addressing signals of 3 to 15 V ($V_{DD} - V_{SS} = 3$ to 15 V) to switch analog signals to 15 Vp-p ($V_{DD} - V_{EE} = 15$V).

Logic level conversion for digital addressing signals of $3 - 15$ V ($V_{DD} - V_{SS} = 3$ to 15 V) to switch analog signals to 15 Vp-p ($V_{DD} - V_{EE} = 15$ V).

Matched switch characteristics: $\Delta R_{ON} = 5$ Ω (Typ.) for $V_{DD} - V_{EE} = 15$V.

Quiescent power dissipation under all digital control input and supply conditions: 1 μ W (typ.) at $V_{DD} - V_{SS} = V_{DD} - V_{EE} = 10$ V.

Binary address decoding on chip.

CD4051BM/CD4051BC

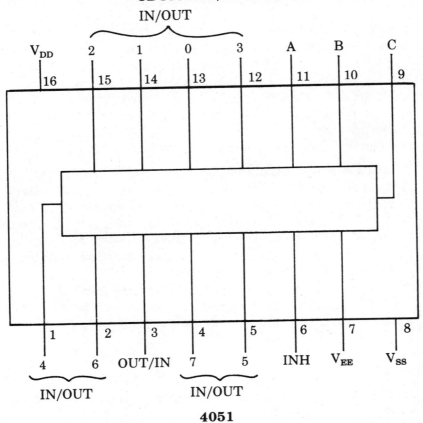

4051

Truth Table 4051, 4052, 4053

INPUT STATES				"ON" CHANNELS		
INHIBIT	C	B	A	CD4051B	CD4052B	CD4053B
0	0	0	0	0	0X, 0Y	cx, bx, ax
0	0	0	1	1	1X, 1Y	cx, bx, ay
0	0	1	0	2	2X, 2Y	cx, by, ax
0	0	1	1	3	3X, 3Y	cx, by, ay
0	1	0	0	4		cy, bx, ax
0	1	0	1	5		cy, bx, ay
0	1	1	0	6		cy, by, ax
0	1	1	1	7		cy, by, ay
1	*	*	*	NONE	NONE	NONE

*Don't Care Condition

248

4052 Dual 4-Channel Multiplexer/Demultiplexer

These analog multiplexers/demultiplexers are digitally controlled analog switches having low on impedance and very low off leakage currents. Control of analog signals up to 15 V_{p-p} can be achieved by digital signal amplitudes of 3 to 15 V. For example, if $V_{DD} = 5$ V, $V_{SS} = 0$ V and $V_{EE} = -5$ V, analog signals from -5 to $+5$ V can be controlled by digital inputs of 0 to 5 V. The multiplexer circuits dissipate extremely low quiescent power over the full V_{DD} to V_{SS} and V_{DD} to V_{EE} supply voltage ranges, independent of the logic state of the control signals. When a logic 1 is present at the inhibit input terminal, all channels are off.

- 4052 is a differential 4-channel multiplexer having two binary control inputs, A and B, and an inhibit input. The two binary input signals select one of four pairs of channels to be turned on, and connect the differential analog inputs to the differential outputs.
- 4053 is a triple 2-channel multiplexer having three separate digital control inputs, A, B, and C, and an inhibit input. Each control input selects one of a pair of channels that is connected in a single-pole double-throw configuration.

CD4052BM/CD4052BC

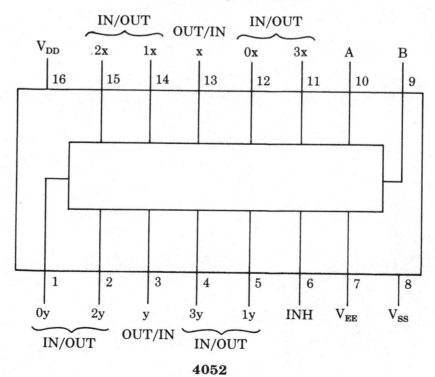

4052

249

4053 Triple 2-Channel Analog Multiplexer/Demultiplexer

These analog multiplexers/demultiplexers are digitally controlled analog switches having low on impedance and very low off leakage currents. Control of analog signals up to 15 V_{p-p} can be achieved by digital signal amplitudes of 3 to 15 V. For example, if V_{DD} = 5 V, V_{SS} = 0 V and V_{EE} = 5 V, analog signals from −5 to +5 V can be controlled by digital inputs of 0 to 5 V. The multiplexer circuits dissipate extremely low quiescent power over the full V_{DD} to V_{SS} and V_{DD} to V_{EE} supply-voltage ranges, independent of the logic state of the control signals. When a logic 1 is present at the inhibit input terminal, all channels are off.

- 4053 is a triple 2-channel multiplexer having three separate digital control inputs, A, B, and C, and an inhibit input. Each control input selects one of a pair of channels that are connected in a single-pole double-throw configuration.

CD4053BM/CD4053BC

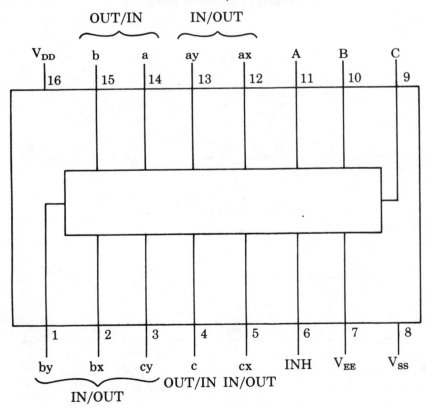

4053

4060 14-Stage Ripple-Carry Binary Counter

The 4020 and 4060 are 14-stage ripple-carry binary counters, and the 4040BM/4040BC is a 12-stage ripple-carry binary counter. The counters are advanced one count on the negative transition of each clock pulse. The counters are reset to the zero state by a logic 1 at the reset input independent of clock.

Supply Voltage Range	1 to 15 V
Noise Immunity	0.45 V_{DD} typ.
TTL Compatibility	Fanout of 2 driving 74L or 1 driving 74LS
Speed of Operation	8 MHz typ. at $V_{DD} = 10$ V

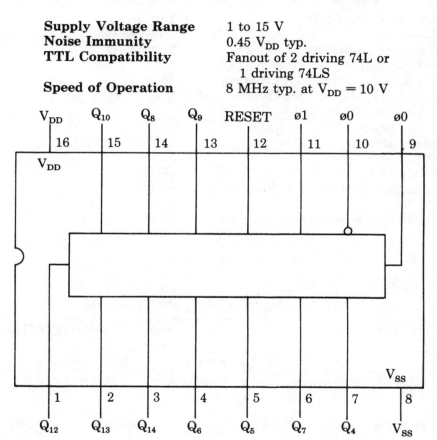

4060

4066 Quad Bilateral Switch

The 4066 is a quad bilateral switch intended for the transmitting or multiplexing of analog or digital signals. It is pin-for-pin compatible with 4016, but has a much lower on-resistance, and on-resistance is relatively constant over the input-signal range.

Supply Voltage Range	3 to 15 V
Noise Immunity	0.45 V_{DD} typ.
Range of Digital and Analog Switching	$\pm$7.5 V_{PEAK}
On Resistance for 15 V Operation	80 Ωtyp.
Matched on Resistance Over 15 V Signal Input	Δ RON = 5 Ω typ.
On/off Output Voltage Ratio	65 dB typ.
Linearity	0.4% distortion typ.
Off Switch Leakage	0.1 nA typ.
Control Input Impedance	10^{12} Ω typ.
Crosstalk Between Switches	−50 dB typ.
	@ fis = 0.9 MHz, R_L = 1 KΩ
Frequency Response, Switch On	40 MHz typ.

4070 Quad 2-Input Exclusive-OR Gate

Employing complementary-MOS (CMOS) transistors to achieve wide power-supply operating range, low power consumption, and high noise margin, this gate provides basic functions used in the implementation of digital integrated-circuit systems. The N-channel and P-channel enhancement-mode transistors provide a symmetrical circuit with output swing essentially equal to the supply voltage. No dc power other than that caused by leakage current is consumed during static condition. All inputs are protected from damage as a result of static discharge by diode clamps to V_{DD} and V_{SS}.

Truth Table

INPUTS		OUTPUTS
A	**B**	**Y**
L	L	L
L	H	H
H	L	H
H	H	L

Supply Voltage Range   3 to 15 V
Noise Immunity   0.45 V_{DD} typ.
TTL Compatibility   Fanout of 2 driving 74L
                      or 1 driving 74LS

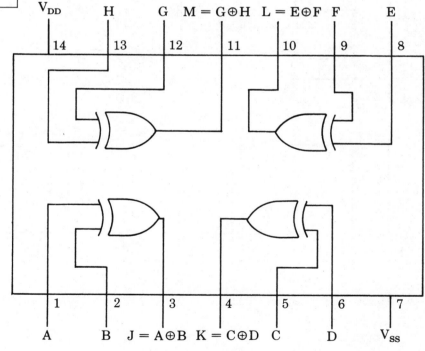

4070

4071 Quad 2-Input OR Buffered B Series Gate

These quad gates are monolithic complementary-MOS (CMOS) integrated circuits constructed with N-channel and P-channel enhancement-mode transistors. They have equal source and sink current capabilities and conform to standard B-series output drive. The devices also have buffered outputs that improve transfer characteristics by providing very high gain. All inputs are protected against static discharge with diodes to V_{DD} and V_{SS}.

TTL Compatibility   Fanout of 2 driving 74L
                               or 1 driving 74LS

Parametric Ratings $5 - 10 - 15$ V
Maximum Input Leakage $1\ \mu A$ at 15 V

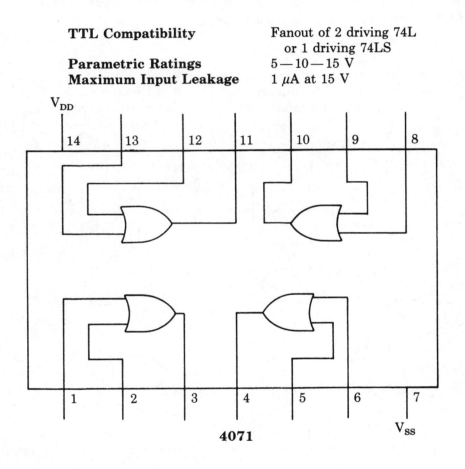

4071

4072 Dual 4-Input OR Gate

Each of the two OR gates in the 4072 are expanded versions of the basic 2-input OR gate. As long as at least one (or more) of the inputs is high, the output will be high. The output of the gate is low if, and only if, all four inputs are in the low state.

The truth table for this device is:

Truth Table

INPUTS				OUTPUT
A	B	C	D	
0	0	0	0	0
0	0	0	1	1
0	0	1	0	1
0	0	1	1	1
0	1	0	0	1
0	1	0	1	1
0	1	1	0	1
0	1	1	1	1
1	0	0	0	1
1	0	0	1	1
1	0	1	0	1
1	0	1	1	1
1	1	0	0	1
1	1	0	1	1
1	1	1	1	1

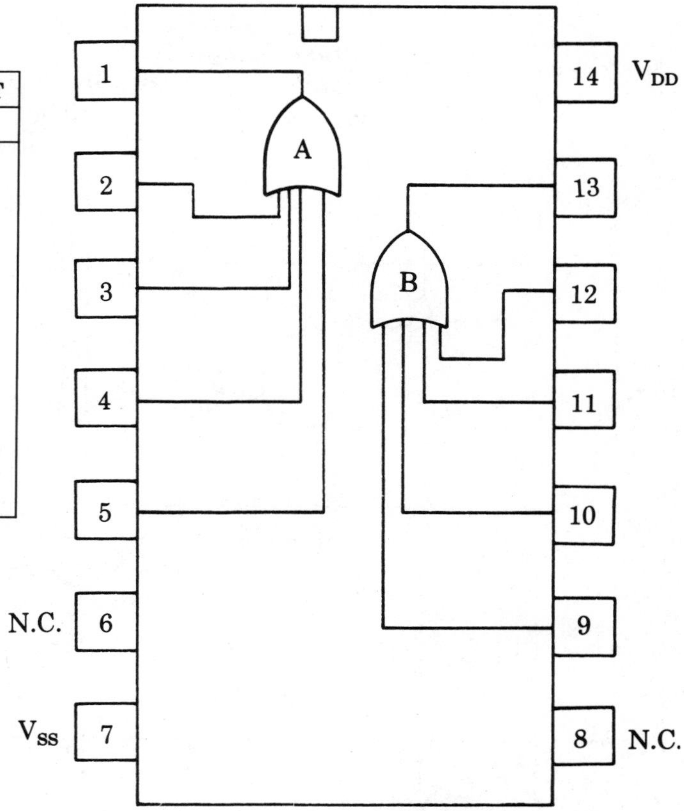

CD4072BM/CD4072BC

4073 Double-Buffered Triple 3-Input NAND Gate

These triple gates are monolithic complementary-MOS (CMOS) integrated circuits constructed with N-channel and P-channel enhancement-mode transistors. They have equal source and sink-current capabilities and conform to standard B-series output drive. The devices also have buffered outputs that improve transfer characteristics by providing very high gain. All inputs are protected against static discharge with diodes to V_{DD} and V_{SS}.

Supply Voltage Range	3 to 15V
Noise Immunity	0.45 VDD typ.
TTL Compatibility	2 driving 74L
	or 1 driving 74LS

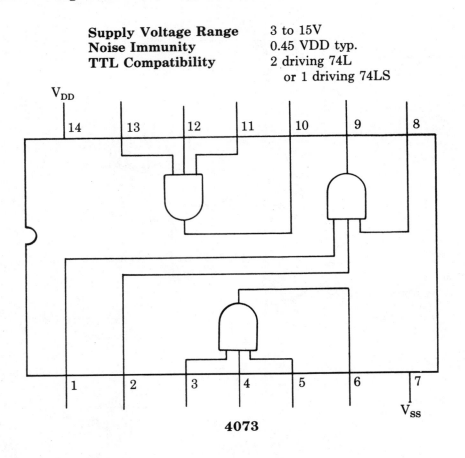

4073

4075 Double-Buffered Triple 3-Input NOR Gate

These triple gates are monolithic complementary-MOS (CMOS) integrated circuits constructed with N-channel and P-channel enhancement-mode transistors. They have equal source and sink-current capabilities and conform to standard B-series output drive. The devices also have buffered outputs that improve transfer characteristics by providing very high gain. All inputs are protected against static discharge with diodes to V_{DD} and V_{SS}.

Supply Voltage Range	3 to 15V
Noise Immunity	0.45 V_{DD} typ.
TTL Compatibility	2 driving 74L
	or 1 driving 74LS

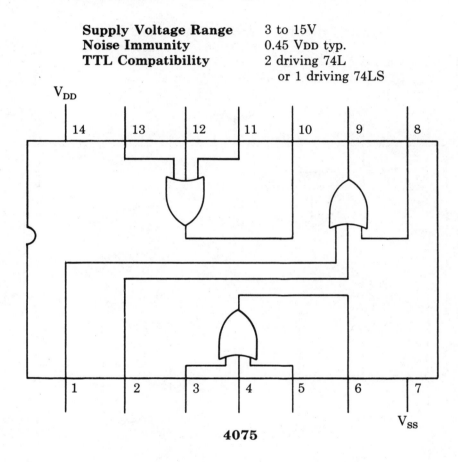

4075

4081 Quad 2-Input AND Buffered B-Series Gate

These quad gates are monolithic complementary-MOS (CMOS) integrated circuits constructed with N-channel and P-channel enhancement-mode transistors. They have equal source and sink-current capabilities and conform to standard B-series output drive. The devices also have buffered outputs that improve transfer characteristics by providing very high gain. All inputs are protected against static discharge with diodes to V_{DD} and V_{SS}.

TTL Compatibility	Fanout of 2 driving 74L or 1 driving 74LS
Parametric Ratings	5 — 10 — 15 V
Maximum Input Leakage	1 μA at 15 V

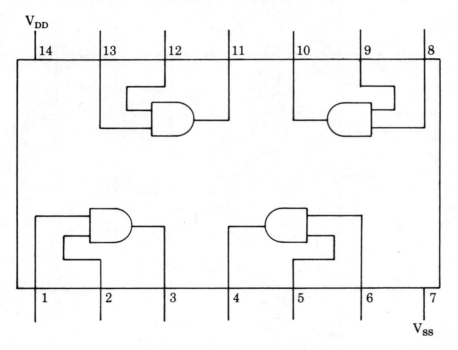

4082 Dual 4-Input AND Gate

Each of the two AND gates in the 4082 are expanded versions of the basic 2-input AND gate. As long as at least one of the inputs is low, the output will be low. The output of the gate is high if, and only if, all four inputs are in the high state.

The truth table for this device is:

Truth Table

INPUTS				OUTPUT
A	B	C	D	
0	0	0	0	0
0	0	0	1	0
0	0	1	0	0
0	0	1	1	0
0	1	0	0	0
0	1	0	1	0
0	1	1	0	0
0	1	1	1	0
1	0	0	0	0
1	0	0	1	0
1	0	1	0	0
1	0	1	1	0
1	1	0	0	0
1	1	0	1	0
1	1	1	1	1

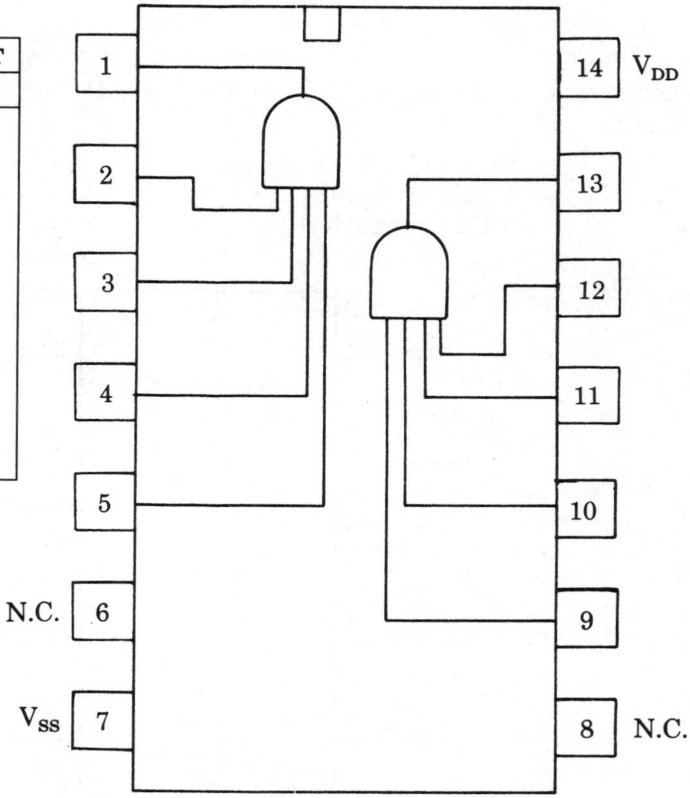

4082

4089 Binary Rate Multiplier

The 4089 is a 4-bit binary rate multiplier that provides an output pulse rate which is the input clock pulse rate multiplied by $1/16$ times the binary input number. For example, if 5 is the binary input number, there will be 5 output pulses for every 16 clock pulses.

The 4527 is a 4-bit BCD rate multiplier that provides an output pulse rate that is the input clock pulse rate multiplied by $1/10$ times the BCD input number. For example, if 5 is the BCD input number, there will be 5 output pulses for every 10 clock pulses.

These devices can be used to perform arithmetic operations. These operations include multiplication and division, A/D and D/A conversion, and frequency division.

Supply Voltage Range	3 to 15V
Noise Immunity	0.45 V$_{DD}$ typ.
TTL Compatibility	Fanout of 2 driving 74L or 1 driving 74LS

Pin diagram:

Pin	Left		Pin	Right
1	"15"		16	V$_{DD}$
2	C		15	B
3	D		14	A
4	SET TO "15"		13	CLEAR
5	$\overline{\text{OUT}}$		12	CASCADE
6	OUT		11	INHIBIT IN
7	INHIBIT OUT		10	STROBE
8	V$_{SS}$		9	CLOCK

4089

4093 Quad 2-Input NAND Schmitt Trigger

The 4093 consists of four Schmitt-trigger circuits. Each circuit functions as a 2-input NAND gate with Schmitt-trigger action on both inputs. The gate switches at different points for positive-going and negative-going signals. The difference between the positive (V_{T+}) and the negative voltage (V_{T-}) is the hysteresis voltage (V_H). All outputs have equal source and sink currents and conform to standard B-series output drive.

Supply Voltage Range   3 to 15V
Noise Immunity   Greater than 50%
Hysteresis Voltage (any input) $T_A = 25°C$
   Typical $V_{DD} = 5$ V $V_H = 1.5$ V
                           $V_{DD} = 10$ V $V_H = 2.2$ V
                           $V_{DD} = 15$ V $V_H = 2.7$ V
   Guaranteed $V_H = 0.1$ V_{DD}

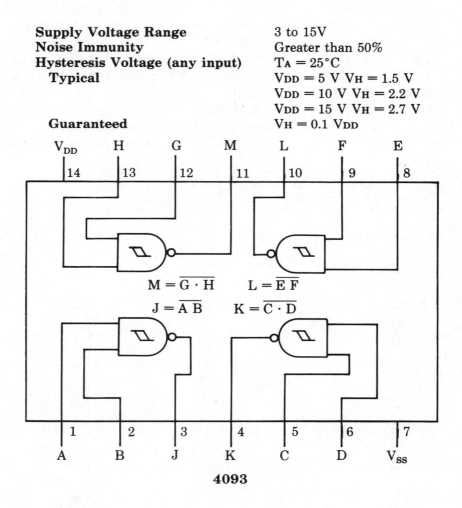

$M = \overline{G \cdot H}$ $L = \overline{E\ F}$

$J = \overline{A\ B}$ $K = \overline{C \cdot D}$

4093

4099, 4724 8-Bit Addressable Latches

The 4723 is a dual 4-bit addressable latch with common control inputs, including two address inputs (A0 and A1), an active low enable input ($\overline{E}$) and an active high clear input (CL). Each latch has a data input (D) and four outputs (Q0 through Q3). The 4724 and 4099 are 8-bit addressable latches with three address inputs (A0 through A2), an active low enable input ($\overline{E}$), active high clear input (CL), a data input (D), and eight outputs (Q0 through Q7).

Data is entered into a particular bit in the latch when that bit is addressed by the address inputs and the enable ($\overline{E}$) is low. Data entry is inhibited when enable ($\overline{E}$) is high.

When clear (CL) and enable ($\overline{E}$) are high, all outputs are low. When clear (CL) is high, enable ($\overline{E}$) is low, the channel demultiplexing occurs. The bit that is addressed has an active output that follows the data input while all unaddressed bits are held low. When operating in the addressable latch mode ($\overline{E}$ = CL = low), changing more than one bit of the address could impose a transient wrong address. Therefore, this action should only be done while in the memory mode ($\overline{E}$ = high, CL = low).

Supply Voltage Range	3 to 15 V
Noise Immunity	0.45 V_{DD} typ.
TTL Compatibility	Fanout of 2 driving 74L or 1 driving 74LS

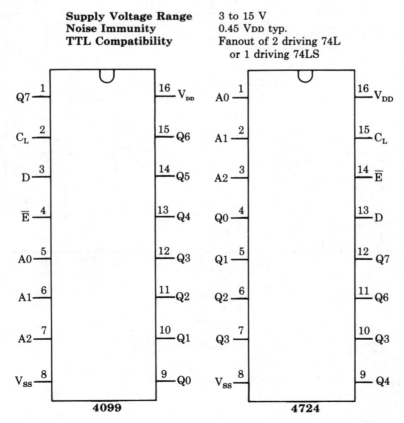

4099   4724

4510 BCD Up/Down Counter

The 4510 and 4516 are monolithic CMOS up/down counters which count in BCD and binary, respectively. The counters count up when the up/down input is at logic 1 and count down when the up/down input is at logic 0. A logic 1 preset-enable signal allows information at the parallel inputs to preset the counters to any state asynchronously with the clock. The counters are advanced one count at the positive-going edge of the clock if the carry-in, preset-enable, and reset inputs are at logic 0. Advancement is inhibited when any of these three inputs are at logic 1. The carry-out signal is normally at logic 1 state and goes to logic 0 when the counter reaches its maximum count in the up mode or its minimum count in the down mode, provided the carry input is at logic 0 state. The counters are cleared synchronously by applying a logic 1 voltage level at the reset input. All inputs are protected against static discharge by diode clamps to both V_{DD} and V_{SS}.

Supply Voltage Range	3 to 15 V
Noise Immunity	0.45 V_{DD} typ.
TTL Compatibility	Fanout of 2 driving 74L or 1 driving 74LS
Quiescent Power Dissipation	0.25 uW/package typ. @ Vcc = 5 V

Truth Table

CLOCK	RESET	PRESET ENABLE	CARRY IN	UP/DOWN	OUTPUT FUNCTION
X	1	X	X	X	Reset to zero
X	0	1	X	X	Set to P1, P2, P3, P4
⌐	0	0	0	1	Count up
⌐	0	0	0	0	Count down
⌐	0	0	X	X	No change
X	0	0	1	X	No change

⌐ = positive transition
⌐ = negative transition
X = don't care

4518, 4520 Dual Synchronous Up Counters

The 4518 dual BCD counter and the 4520 dual binary counter are implemented with complementary-MOS (CMOS) circuits constructed with N-channel and P-channel enhancement-mode transistors. Each counter consists of two identical, independent synchronous 4-stage counters. The counter stages are toggle flip-flops that increment on either the positive-edge of clock or negative-edge of enable, simplyifing the cascading of multiple stages. Each counter can be asynchronously cleared by a high level on the reset line. All inputs are protected against static discharge by diode clamps to both V_{DD} and V_{SS}.

Supply Voltage Range	3 to 15 V
Noise Immunity	0.45 V_{DD} typ.
TTL Compatibility	Fanout of 2 driving 74L or 1 driving 74LS
Counting Rate (typ.) at $V_{DD} = 10$ V	6 MHz

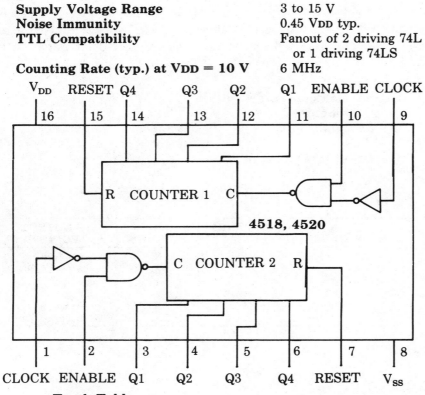

Truth Table

CLOCK	ENABLE	RESET	ACTION
⌐⌐/	1	0	Increment counter
0	⌐⌐	0	Increment counter
⌐⌐	X	0	No change
X	/	0	No change
/	0	0	No change
1	⌐⌐	0	No change
X	X	1	Q1 thru Q4 = 0

X = Don't Care

264

4527 BCD Rate Multiplier

The 4089 is a 4-bit binary rate multiplier that provides an output pulse rate that is the input clock pulse rate multiplied by $1/16$ times the binary input number. For example, if 5 is the binary input number, there will be 5 output pulses for every 16 clock pulses.

The 4527 is a 4-bit BCD rate multiplier that provides an output pulse rate that is in the input clock pulse rate multiplied by $1/10$ times the BCD input number. For example, if 5 is the BCD input number, there will be 5 output pulses for every 10 clock pulses.

These devices can be used to perform arithmetic operations. These operations include multiplication and division, A/D and D/A conversion and frequency division.

Supply Voltage Range	3 to 15 V
Noise Immunity	0.45 V_{DD} typ.
TTL Compatibility	Fanout of 2 driving 74L
	or 1 driving 74LS

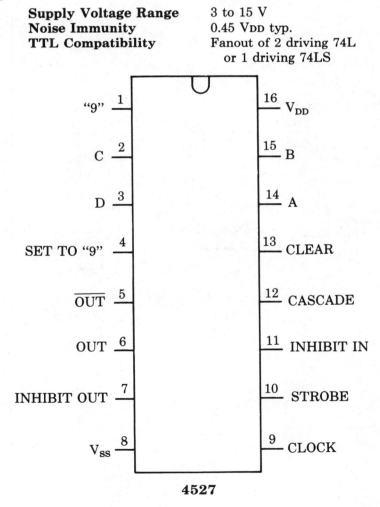

4527

74C00 Quad 2-Input NAND Gate

These logic gates employ complementary-MOS (CMOS) to achieve wide power-supply operating range, low power consumption, high noise immunity and symmetric-controlled rise and fall times. With features such as this, the 74C logic family is close to ideal for use in digital systems. Function and pinout compatibility with series 54/74 devices minimizes design time for those designers already familiar with the standard 54/74 logic family.

All inputs are protected from damage as a result of static discharge by diode clamps to V_{CC} and GND. See 7400, 7402, 7404, 7410, and 7420 data for more information on logic and pinouts.

Supply Voltage Range	3.0 to 15 V
Guaranteed Noise Margin	1.0 V
Noise Immunity	0.45 Vcc typ.
Power Consumption	10 nW/package typ.
TTL Compatibility	Fanout of 2 driving 74L

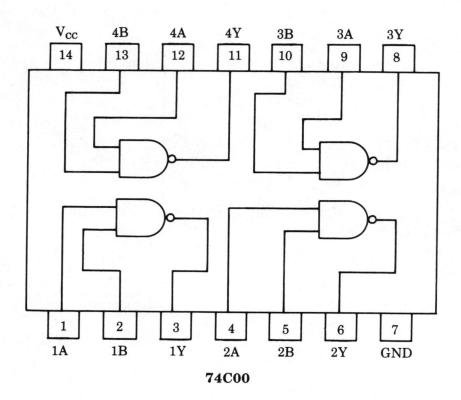

74C00

74C02 Quad 2-Input NOR Gate

These logic gates employ complementary-MOS (CMOS) to achieve wide power-supply operating range, low power consumption, high noise immunity and symmetric-controlled rise and fall times. With features such as this, the 74C logic family is close to ideal for use in digital systems. Function and pinout compatibility with series 54/74 devices minimizes design time for those designers already familiar with the standard 54/74 logic family.

   All inputs are protected from damage as a result of static discharge by diode clamps to V_{CC} and GND. See 7400, 7402, 7404, 7410, and 7420 data for more information on logic and pinouts.

Supply Voltage Range	3.0 to 15 V
Guaranteed Noise Margin	1.0 V
Noise Immunity	0.45 Vcc typ.
Power Consumption	10 nW/package typ.
TTL Compatibility	Fanout of 2 driving 74L

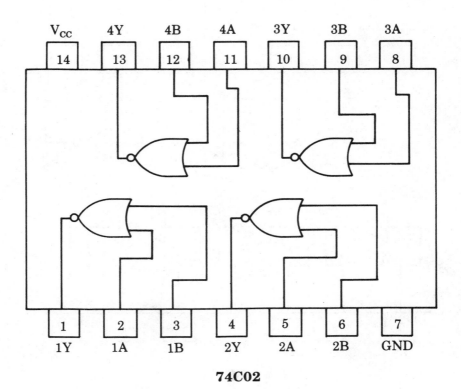

74C02

74C04 Hex Inverter

These logic gates employ complementary-MOS (CMOS) to achieve wide power-supply operating range, low power consumption, high noise immunity and symmetric-controlled rise and fall times. With features such as this, the 74C logic family is close to ideal for use in digital systems. Function and pinout compatibility with series 54/74 devices minimizes design time for those designers already familiar with the standard 54/74 logic family.

All inputs are protected from damage as a result of static discharge by diode clamps to V_{CC} and GND. See 7400, 7402, 7404, 7410, and 7420 data for more information on logic and pinouts.

Supply Voltage Range	3.0 to 15 V
Guaranteed Noise Margin	1.0 V
Noise Immunity	0.45 Vcc typ.
Power Consumption	10 nW/package typ.
TTL Compatibility	Fanout of 2 driving 74L

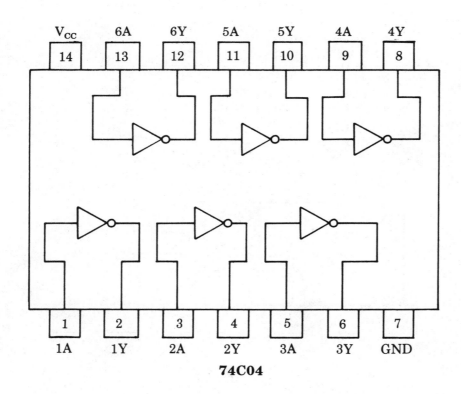

74C04

74C08 Quad 2-Input AND Gate

Employing complementary-MOS (CMOS) transistors to achieve wide power-supply operating range, low power consumption, and high noise margin, these gates provide basic functions used in the implementation of digital integrated-circuit systems. The N-channel and P-channel enhancement mode-transistors provide a symmetrical circuit with output swing essentially equal to the supply voltage. No dc power other than that caused by leakage current is consumed during static condition. All inputs are protected from damage as a result of static discharge by diode clamps to V_{CC} and GND. See 7408 and 7486 data for more information on logic and pinouts.

Supply Voltage Range	3.0 to 15 V
Guaranteed Noise Margin	1.0 V
Noise Immunity	0.45 Vcc typ.
TTL Compatibility	Fanout of 2 driving 74L
Power Consumption	10 nW/package typ.

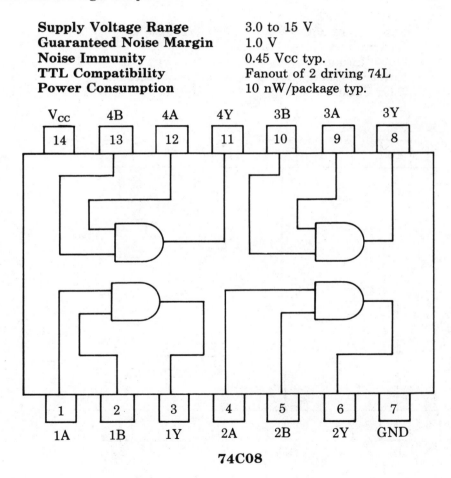

74C08

74C10 Triple 3-Input NAND Gate

These logic gates employ complementary-MOS (CMOS) to achieve wide power-supply operating range, low power consumption, high noise immunity and symmetric-controlled rise and fall times. With features such as this, the 74C logic family is close to ideal for use in digital systems. Function and pinout compatibility with series 54/74 devices minimizes design time for those designers already familiar with the standard 54/74 logic family.

All inputs are protected from damage as a result of static discharge by diode clamps to V_{CC} and GND. See 7400, 7402, 7404, 7410, and 7420 data for more information on logic and pinouts.

Supply Voltage Range	3.0 to 15 V
Guaranteed Noise Margin	1.0 V
Noise Immunity	0.45 Vcc typ.
Power Consumption	10 nW/package typ.
TTL Compatibility	Fanout of 2 driving 74L

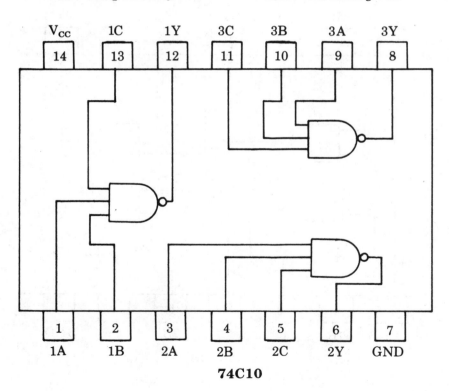

74C10

74C14 Hex Schmitt Trigger

The MM74C14 Hex Schmitt trigger is a monolithic complementary-MOS (CMOS) integrated circuit constructed with N-channel and P-channel enhancement transistors. The positive-going and negative-going threshold voltages, V_{T+} and V_{T-}, show low variation with respect to temperature (typ 0.0005 V per C at $V_{CC} = 10$ V), and hysteresis, $V_{T+} - V_{T-} \geq 0.2\ V_{CC}$ is guaranteed.

All inputs are protected from damage as a result of static discharge by diode clamps to V_{CC} and GND. See 7414 data for more information on logic and pinouts.

Supply Voltage Range	3.0 to 15 V
Noise Immunity	0.70 Vcc typ.
TTL Compatibility	Fanout of 2 driving 74L
Hysteresis	0.4 Vcc typ.
	0.2 Vcc guaranteed

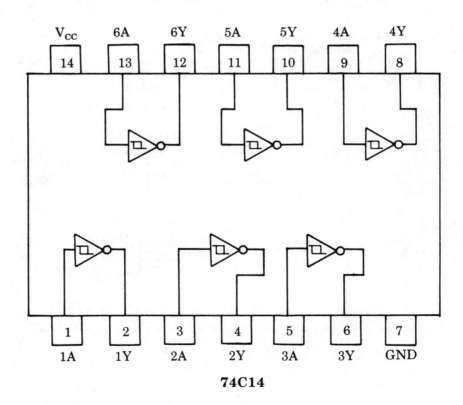

74C14

74C20 Dual 4-Input NAND Gate

These logic gates employ complementary-MOS (CMOS) to achieve wide power-supply operating range, low power consumption, high noise immunity and symmetric-controlled rise and fall times. With features such as this, the 74C logic family is close to ideal for use in digital systems. Function and pinout compatibility with series 54/74 devices minimizes design time for those designers already familiar with the standard 54/74 logic family.

All inputs are protected from damage as a result of static discharge by diode clamps to V_{CC} and GND. See 7400, 7402, 7404, 7410, and 7420 data for more information on logic and pinouts.

Supply Voltage Range	3.0 to 15 V
Guaranteed Noise Margin	1.0 V
Noise Immunity	0.45 Vcc typ.
Power Consumption	10 nW/package typ.
TTL Compatibility	Fanout of 2 driving 74L

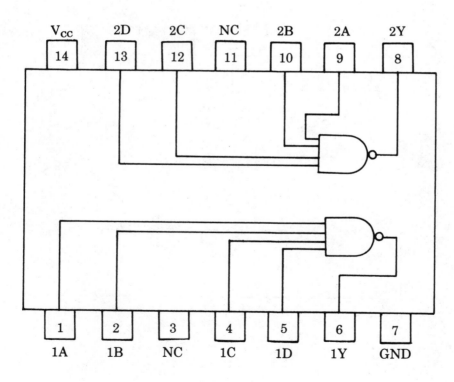

74C20

74C30 8-Input NAND Gate

The logic gate employs complementary-MOS (CMOS) to achieve wide power-supply operating range, low power consumption and high noise immunity. Function and pinout compatibility with series 54/74 devices minimizes design time for those designers familiar with the standard 54/74 logic family.

All inputs are protected from damage to static discharge by diode clamps to V_{CC} and GND. See 7430 data for more information on logic and pinouts.

Supply Voltage Range	3.0 to 15 V
Guaranteed Noise Margin	1.0 V
Noise Immunity	0.45 Vcc typ.
TTL Compatibility	Fanout of 2 driving 74L

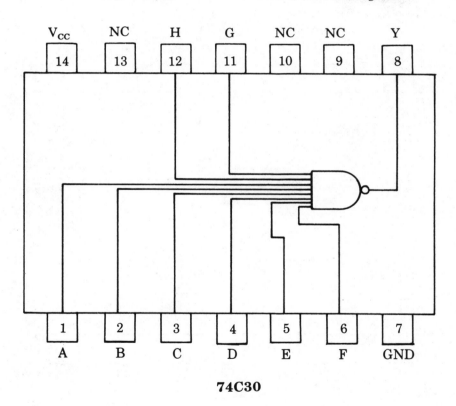

74C30

273

74C32 Quad 2-Input OR Gate

Employing complementary-MOS (CMOS) transistors to achieve low power and high noise margin, these gates provide the basic functions used in the implementation of digital integrated circuit systems. The N-channel and P-channel enhancement-mode transistors provide a symmetrical circuit with output swings essentially equal to the supply voltage. This results in high noise immunity over a wide supply-voltage range. No dc power other than that caused by leakage current is consumed during static conditions. All inputs are protected against static-discharge damage.

Supply Voltage Range	3.0 to 15 V
Noise Margin	1.0 V
Noise Immunity	0.45 Vcc typ.
TTL Compatibility	Fanout of 2 driving 74L

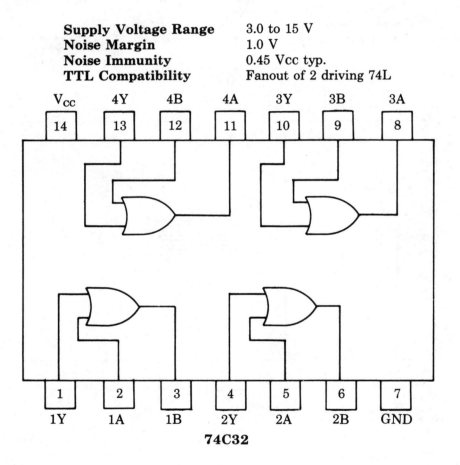

74C32

74C42 BCD-to-Decimal Decoder

The MM74C42 1-of-10 decoder is a monolithic complementary-MOS (CMOS) integrated circuit constructed with N-channel and P-channel enhancement transistors. This decoder produces a logic 0 at the output corresponding to a 4-bit binary input from zero to nine, and a logic 1 at the other outputs. For binary inputs from 10 to 15, all outputs are logic 1. See 7442 data for more information on logic and pinouts.

Supply Voltage Range	3 to 15 V
Fanout	Drive 2 LPTTL loads
Noise Immunity	0.45 Vcc (typ.)
Power	50 nW (typ.)
Speed of Operation	10 MHz (typ.) with 10 V_{CC}

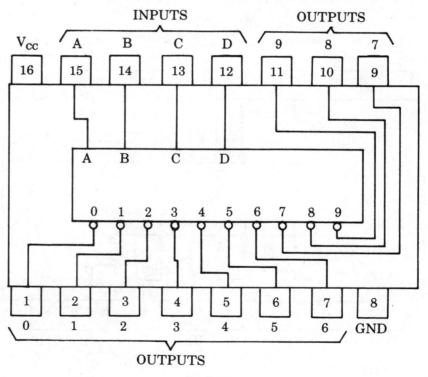

74C42

74C48 BCD-to-7-Segment Decoder

The MM74C48 BCD-to-7-segment decoder is a monolithic complementary-MOS (CMOS) integrated circuit constructed with N-channel and P-channel enhancement transistors. Seven NAND gates and one driver are connected in pairs to make binary-coded decimal (BCD) data and its complement available to the seven decoding AND-OR-INVERT gates. The remaining NAND gate and three input buffers provide test-blanking input/ripple-blanking output, and ripple-blanking inputs. See 7448 data for more information on logic and pinouts.

Supply Voltage Range	3.0 to 15V
Guaranteed Noise Margin	1.0 V
Noise Immunity	0.45 Vcc typ.
TTL Compatibility	Fanout of 2 driving 74L

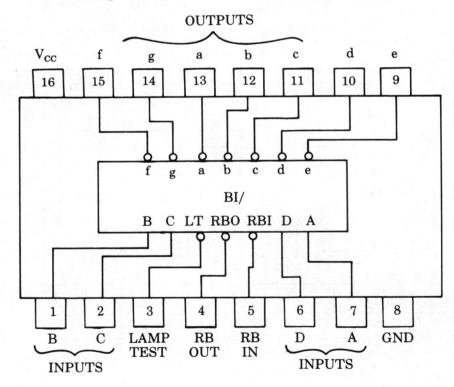

74C48

74C73 Dual JK Flip-Flops with Clear

These dual JK flip-flops are monolithic complementary-MOS (CMOS) integrated circuits constructed with N-channel and P-channel enhancement transistors. Each flip-flop has independent J, K, clock and clear inputs, and Q and $\overline{Q}$ outputs. The MM54C76/MM74C76 flip-flops also include preset inputs and are supplied in 16-pin packages. These flip-flops are edge-sensitive to the clock input and change state on the negative-going transition of the clock pulses. Clear or preset is independent of the clock and is accomplished by a low level on the respective input. See 7473, 7476, and 74107 data for logic information and pinouts.

Supply Voltage Range	3 to 15 V
Fanout	Drive 2 LPTTL loads
Noise Immunity	0.45 Vcc (typ.)
Power	50 nW (typ.)
Speed of Operation	10 MHz (typ.) with 10 V Supply

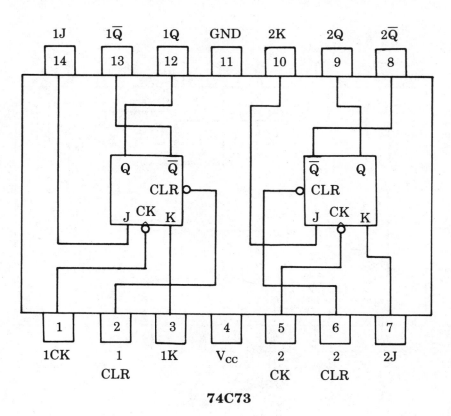

74C73

277

74C74 Dual D Flip-Flop

The MM74C74 dual D flip-flop is a monolithic complementary-MOS (CMOS) integrated circuit constructed with N-channel and P-channel enhancement transistors. Each flip-flop has independent data, preset, clear and clock inputs, and Q and $\overline{Q}$ outputs. The logic level present at the data input is transferred to the output during the positive-going transition of the clock pulse. Preset or clear is independent of the clock and accomplished by a low level at the preset or clear input. See 7474 data for more logic information and pinouts.

Supply Voltage Range	3 to 15 V
Fanout	Drive 2# LPTTL loads
Noise Immunity	0.45 Vcc (typ.)
Power	50 nW (typ.)
Speed of Operation	10 MHz (typ.) with 10 V supply

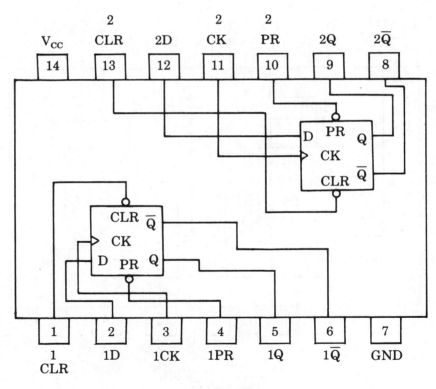

74C74

278

74C76 Dual JK Flip-Flops with Clear and Preset

These dual JK flip-flops are monolithic complementary-MOS (CMOS) integrated circuits constructed with N-channel and P-channel enhancement transistors. Each flip-flop has independent J, K, clock and clear inputs, and Q and $\overline{Q}$ outputs. The MM54C76/MM74C76 flip-flops also include preset inputs and are supplied in 16-pin packages. These flip-flops are edge-sensitive to the clock input and change state on the negative-going transition of the clock pulses. Clear or preset is independent of the clock and is accomplished by a low level on the respective input. See 7473, 7476, and 74107 data for logic information and pinouts.

Supply Voltage Range	3 to 15 V
Fanout	Drive 2 LPTTL loads
Noise Immunity	0.45 Vcc (typ.)
Power	50 nW (typ.)
Speed of Operation	10 MHz (typ.) with 10 V Supply

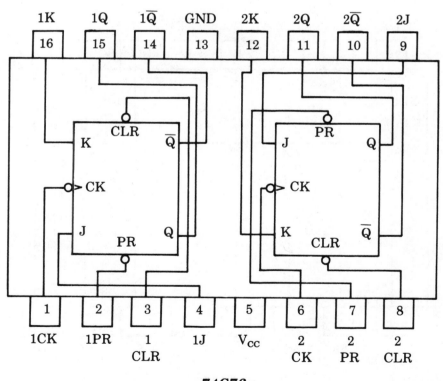

74C76

279

74C83 4-Bit Binary Full Adder

The MM74C83 4-bit binary full adder performs the addition of two 4-bit binary numbers. A carry input (C_O) is included. The sum (Σ) outputs are provided for each bit, and the resultant carry (C_4) is obtained from the fourth bit. Because the carry-ripple time is the limiting delay in the addition of a long word length, carry look-ahead circuitry has been included in the design to minimize this delay. Also, the logic levels of the input and output, including the carry, are in their true form. Thus the end-around carry is accomplished without the need for level inversion.

Supply Voltage Range	3 to 15 V
Guaranteed Noise Margin	1 V
Noise Immunity	0.45 Vcc typ.
TTL Compatibility	Fanout of 2 driving 74L
Carry Ripple (C_0 to C_4)	50 ns typ. @ Vcc = 10 V and CL = 50 pF
Summing	125 ns typ. @ Vcc = 10 V and C_L = 50 pF

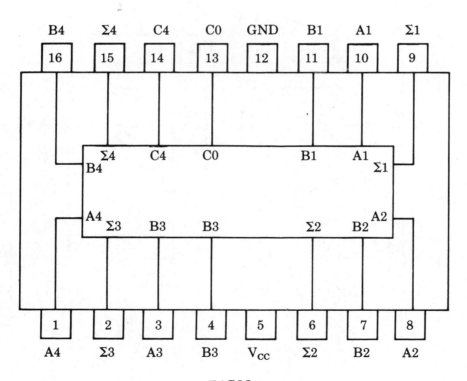

74C83

74C85 4-Bit Magnitude Comparator

The MM74C85 is a 4-bit magnitude comparator that performs comparison of straight binary or BCD codes. The circuit consists of eight comparing inputs (A0, A1, A2, A3, B0, B1, B2, and B3), three cascading inputs ($A > B$, $A < B$, and $A = B$), and three outputs ($A > B$, $A < B$, and $A = B$). This device compares two 4-bit words (A and B) and determines whether they are greater than, less than, or equal to each other by a high level on the appropriate output. For words greater than four bits, units can be cascaded by connecting the outputs ($A > B$, $A < B$, and $A = B$) of the least significant stage to the cascade inputs ($A > B$, $A < B$, and $A = B$) of the next significant stage. In addition, the least significant stage must have a high-level voltage ($V_{in(1)}$) applied to the $A = B$ input and low-level voltages ($V_{in(0)}$) applied to $A > B$ and $A < B$ inputs.

Supply Voltage Range	3.0 to 15 V
Guaranteed Noise Margin	1.0 V
Noise Immunity	0.45 Vcc typ.
TTL Compatibility	Fanout of 2 driving 74L

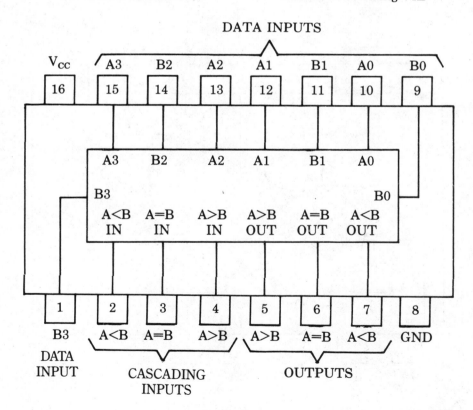

74C85

74C86 Quad 2-Input Exclusive-OR Gate

Employing complementary-MOS (CMOS) transistors to achieve a wide power-supply operating range, low power consumption and high noise margin, these gates provide basic functions used in the implementation of digital integrated circuit systems. The N-channel and P-channel enhancement-mode transistors provide a symmetrical circuit with output swing essentially equal to the supply voltage. No dc power other than that caused by leakage current is consumed during static condition. All inputs are protected from damage as a result of static discharge by diode clamps to V_{CC} and GND. See 7408 and 7486 data for more information on logic.

Supply Voltage Range	3.0 to 15 V
Guaranteed Noise Margin	1.0V
Noise Immunity	0.45 Vcc typ.
TTL Compatibility	Fanout of 2 driving 74L
Power Consumption	10 nW/package typ.

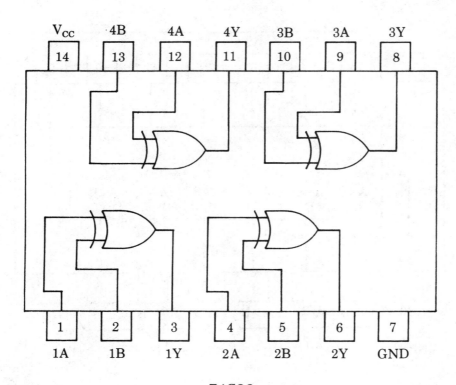

74C86

74C89 64-Bit 3-State Random-Access Read/Write Memory

The MM74C89 is a 16-word by 4-bit random access read/write memory. Inputs to the memory consist of four address lines, four data-input lines, a write-enable line and a memory-enable line. The four binary address inputs are decoded internally to select each of the 16 possible word locations. An internal address register latches the address information on the positive-to-negative transition of the memory-enable input. The four TRI-STATE® data-output lines working in conjunction with the memory-enable input provide easy memory expansion.

- **Address Operation** Address inputs must be stable t_{SA} prior to the positive to negative transition of memory enable. It is thus not necessary to hold address information stable for more than t_{HA} after the memory is enabled (positive-to-negative transition of memory enable). Note that the timing is different than the DM7489 in that a positive-to-negative transition of the memory enable must occur for the memory to be selected.
- **Write Operation** Information present at the data inputs is written into the memory at the selected address by bringing write enable and memory enable low.
- **Read Operation** The complement of the information that was written into the memory is nondestructively read out at the four outputs. This is accomplished by selecting the desired address and bringing memory enable low and write enable high. When the device is writing or disabled, the output assumes a TRI-STATE® (high-Z) condition. See 7489 for more logic information and pinouts.

Supply Voltage Range	3.0 to 15 V
Guaranteed Noise Margin	1.0 V
Noise Immunity	0.45 Vcc typ.
TTL Compatibility	Fanout of 2 driving 74L
Power Consumption	100 nW/package typ. @ Vcc = 5 V
Access Time	130 ns typ. at Vcc = 10 V

74C90 4-Bit Decade Counter

The MM74C90 decade counter and the MM74C93 binary counter are complementary-MOS (CMOS) integrated circuits constructed with N-channel and P-channel enhancement-mode transistors. The 4-bit decade counter can be reset to zero or preset to nine by applying appropriate logic level on the R_{01}, R_{02}, R_{91}, and R_{92} inputs. Also, a separate flip-flop on the A-bit enables the user to operate it as a divide-by-2, -5, or -10 frequency counter. The 4-bit binary counter can be reset to zero by applying high logic level on inputs R_{01} and R_{02}. Also, a separate flip-flop on the A-bit enables the user to operate it as a divide-by-2, -8, or -16 counter. Counting occurs on the negative-going edge of the input pulse. See 7490 and 7493 data for more information on logic. All inputs are protected against static-discharge damage.

Supply Voltage Range	3 to 15 V
Guaranteed Noise Margin	1 V
Noise Immunity	0.45 Vcc (typ.)
Low Power TTL Compatibility	Fanout of 2 driving 74L

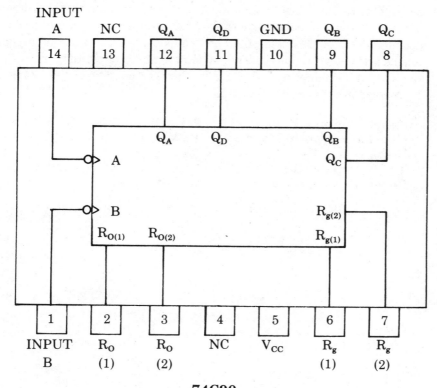

74C90

74C93 4-Bit Binary Counter

The MM74C90 decade counter and the MM74C93 binary counter are complementary-MOS (CMOS) integrated circuits constructed with N-channel and P-channel enhancement-mode transistors. The 4-bit decade counter can be reset to zero or preset to nine by applying appropriate logic level on the R_{01}, R_{02}, R_{91}, and R_{92} inputs. Also, a separate flip-flop on the A-bit enables the user to operate it as a divide-by-2, -5, or -10 frequency counter. The 4-bit binary counter can be reset to zero by applying high logic level on inputs R_{01} and R_{02}. Also, a separate flip-flop on the A-bit enables the user to operate it as a divide-by-2, -8, or -16 divider. Counting occurs on the negative-going edge of the input pulse. See 7490 and 7493 data for more information on logic. All inputs are protected against static-discharge damage.

Supply Voltage Range	3 to 15 V
Guaranteed Noise Margin	1 V
Noise Immunity	0.45 Vcc (typ.)
Low Power TTL Compatibility	Fanout of 2 driving 74L

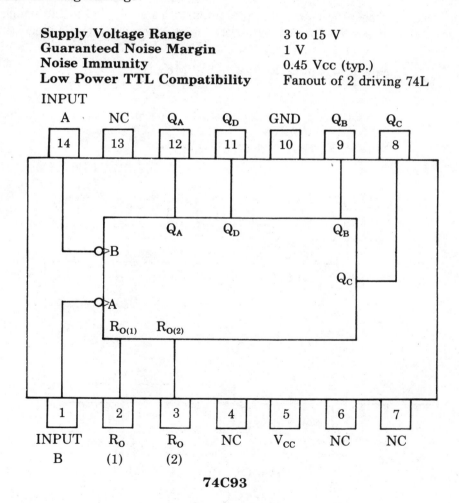

74C93

74C95 4-Bit Right-Shift/Left-Shift Register

This 4-bit shift register is a monolithic complementary-MOS (CMOS) integrated circuit composed of four D flip-flops. This register will perform right-shift or left-shift operations dependent upon the logical-input level to the mode control. A number of these registers can be connected in series to form an N-bit right-shift or left-shift register.

When a logic 0 level is applied to the mode control input, the output of each flip-flop is coupled to the D input of the succeeding flip-flop. Right-shift operation is performed by clocking at the clock 1 input, and serial data entered at the serial input, clock 2 and parallel inputs A through D are inhibited. With a logic 1 level applied to the mode control, outputs to succeeding stages are decoupled and parallel loading is possible. With external interconnection, left-shift operation can be accomplished by connecting the output of each flip-flop to the parallel input of the previous flip-flop and serial data can be entered at input D. See 7495 data for more information on logic.

Speed of Operation	10 MHz typ.
	$V_{CC} = 10$ V, $C_L = 50$ pF
Noise Immunity	0.45 V_{CC} typ.
Power	100 nW typ.
TTL Compatibility	Drive 2 LTTL loads
Supply Voltage Range	3 to 15 V

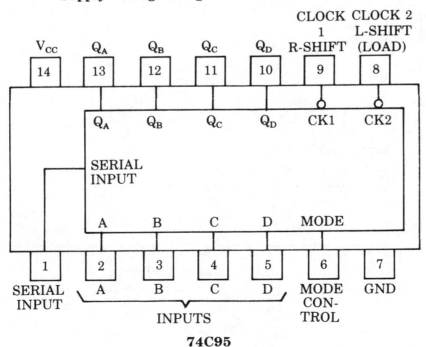

74C95

74C107 Dual JK Flip-Flops with Clear

These dual JK flip-flops are monolithic complementary-MOS (CMOS) integrated circuits constructed with N-channel and P-channel enhancement transistors. Each flip-flop has independent J, K, clock and clear inputs, and Q and $\overline{Q}$ outputs. The MM54C76/MM74C76 flip-flops also include preset inputs and are supplied in 16-pin packages. These flip-flops are edge-sensitive to the clock input and change state on the negative-going transition of the clock pulses. Clear or preset is independent of the clock and is accomplished by a low level on the respective input. See 7473, 7476, and 74107 data for logic information.

Supply Voltage Range	3 to 15 V
Fanout	Drive 2 LPTTL loads
Noise Immunity	0.45 Vcc (typ.)
Power	50 nW (typ.)
Speed of Operation	10 MHz (typ.) with 10 V Supply

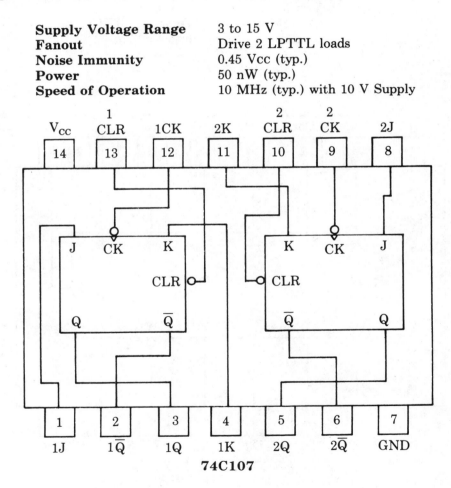

74C107

74C151 8-Channel Digital Multiplexer

The MM74C151 multiplexer is a monolithic complementary-MOS (CMOS) integrated circuit constructed with N-channel and P-channel enhancement transistors. This data selector/multiplexer contains on-chip binary decoding. Two outputs provide true (output Y) and complement (output W) data. A logic 1 on the strobe input forces W to a logic 1 and Y to a logic 0.

All inputs are protected against electrostatic effects. See 74151 data for more information on logic.

Supply Voltage Range	3 to 15 V
TTL Compatibility	Drive 2 LPTTL loads
Noise Immunity	0.45 Vcc typ.
Power	50 nW typ.

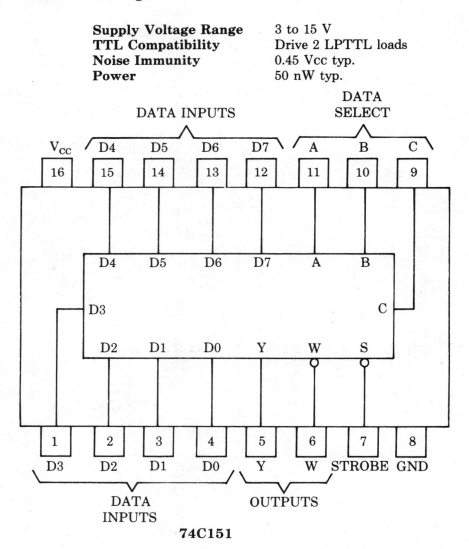

74C151

74C154 4-Line-to-16-Line Decoder/Demultiplexer

The MM74C154 one-of-16 decoder is a monolithic complementary-MOS (CMOS) integrated circuit constructed with N-channel and P-channel enhancement transistors. The device is provided with two strobe inputs, both of which must be in the logic 0 state for normal operation. If either strobe input is in the logic 1 state, all 16 outputs will go to the logic 1 state.

To use the product as a demultiplexer, one of the strobe inputs serves as a data-input terminal, while the other strobe input must be maintained in the logic 0 state. The information will then be transmitted to the selected output, as determined by the four-line input address. See 74154 data for more information on logic.

Supply Voltage Range	3 to 15 V
TTL Compatibility	Drive 2 LPTTL loads
Noise Margin	1 V guaranteed
Noise Immunity	0.45 Vcc typ.

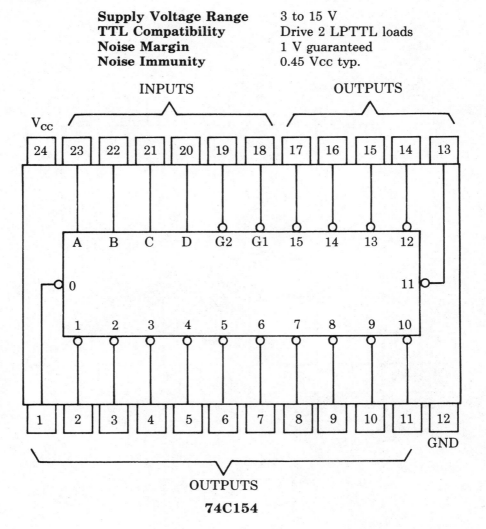

74C154

74C157 Quad 2-Input Multiplexers

These multiplexers are monolithic complementary-MOS (CMOS) integrated circuits constructed with N-channel and P-channel enhancement transistors. They consist of four 2-input multiplexers with a common select and enable inputs. When the enable input is at logic 0, the four outputs assume the values as selected from the inputs. When the enable input is at logic 1, the outputs assume logic 0. Select decoding is done internally, resulting in a single-select input only. See 74157 data for more information on logic.

Supply Voltage Range	3 to 15 V
Noise Immunity	0.45 Vcc typ.
Power	50 nW (typ.)
TTL Compatibility	Drive 2 LPTTL loads

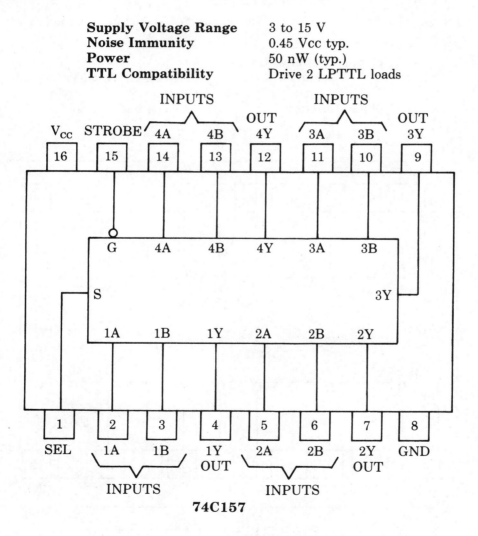

74C157

74C160 Decade Counter

These synchronous presettable-up counters are monolithic complementary-MOS (CMOS) integrated circuits constructed with N-channel and P-channel enhancement-mode transistors. They feature an internal carry look-ahead for fast-counting schemes and for cascading packages without additional gating.

A low level at the load input disables counting and causes the outputs to agree with the data input after the next positive clock edge. The clear function for the C162 and C163 is synchronous, and a low level at the clear input sets all four outputs low after the next positive clock edge. The clear function for the C160 and C161 is asynchronous, and a low level at the clear input sets all four outputs low, regardless of the state of the clock.

Counting is enabled when both count-enable inputs are high. Input T is fed forward to also enable the carry out. The carry output is a positive pulse with a duration approximately equal to the positive portion of Q_A and can be used to enable successive cascaded stages. Logic transitions at the enable-P or -T inputs can occur when the clock is high or low. See 74160, 74161, 74162, and 74163 for more logic information and pinouts.

Noise Margin	1 V guaranteed
Noise Immunity	0.45 Vcc typ.
TTL Compatibility	Drives 2 LPTTL loads
Supply Voltage Range	3 to 15 V

74C161 Binary Counter

These synchronous presettable-up counters are monolithic complementary-MOS (CMOS) integrated circuits constructed with N-channel and P-channel enhancement-mode transistors. They feature an internal carry look-ahead for fast-counting schemes and for cascading packages without additional gating.

A low level at the load input disables counting and causes the outputs to agree with the data input after the next positive clock edge. The clear function for the C162 and C163 is synchronous, and a low level at the clear input sets all four outputs low after the next positive clock edge. The clear function for the C160 and C161 is asynchronous, and a low level at the clear input sets all four outputs low, regardless of the state of the clock.

Counting is enabled when both count-enable inputs are high. Input T is fed forward to also enable the carry out. The carry output is a positive pulse with a duration approximately equal to the positive portion of Q_A and can be used to enable successive cascaded stages. Logic transitions at the enable-P or -T inputs can occur when the clock is high or low. See 74160, 74161, 74162, and 74163 for more logic information.

Noise Margin	1 V guaranteed
Noise Immunity	0.45 Vcc typ.
TTL Compatibility	Drives 2 LPTTL loads
Supply Voltage Range	3 to 15 V

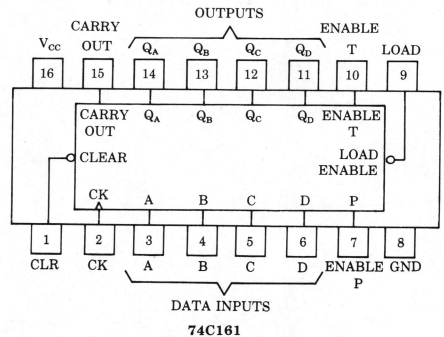

74C161

74C162 Decade Counter

These synchronous presettable-up counters are monolithic complementary-MOS (CMOS) integrated circuits constructed with N-channel and P-channel enhancement-mode transistors. They feature an internal carry look-ahead for fast-counting schemes and for cascading packages without additional gating.

A low level at the load input disables counting and causes the outputs to agree with the data input after the next positive clock edge. The clear function for the C162 and C163 is synchronous, and a low level at the clear input sets all four outputs low after the next positive clock edge. The clear function for the C160 and C161 is asynchronous, and a low level at the clear input sets all four outputs low, regardless of the state of the clock.

Counting is enabled when both count-enable inputs are high. Input T is fed forward to also enable the carry out. The carry output is a positive pulse with a duration approximately equal to the positive portion of Q_A and can be used to enable successive cascaded stages. Logic transitions at the enable-P or -T inputs can occur when the clock is high or low. See 74160, 74161, 74162, and 74163 for more logic information and pinouts.

Noise Margin	1 V guaranteed
Noise Immunity	0.45 Vcc typ.
TTL Compatibility	Drives 2 LPTTL loads
Supply Voltage Range	3 to 15 V

74C163 Binary Counter

These synchronous presettable-up counters are monolithic complementary-MOS (CMOS) integrated circuits constructed with N-channel and P-channel enhancement-mode transistors. They feature an internal carry look-ahead for fast-counting schemes and for cascading packages without additional gating.

A low level at the load input disables counting and causes the outputs to agree with the data input after the next positive clock edge. The clear function for the C162 and C163 is synchronous, and a low level at the clear input sets all four outputs low after the next positive clock edge. The clear function for the C160 and C161 is asynchronous, and a low level at the clear input sets all four outputs low, regardless of the state of the clock.

Counting is enabled when both count-enable inputs are high. Input T is fed forward to also enable the carry out. The carry output is a positive pulse with a duration approximately equal to the positive portion of Q_A and can be used to enable successive cascaded stages. Logic transitions at the enable-P or -T inputs can occur when the clock is high or low. See 74160, 74161, 74162, and 74163 for more logic information.

Noise Margin	1 V guaranteed
Noise Immunity	0.45 Vcc typ.
TTL Compatibility	Drives 2 LPTTL loads
Supply Voltage Range	3 to 15 V

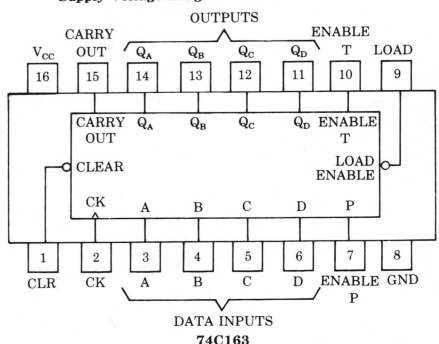

74C163

74C164 8-Bit Parallel-Out Serial Shift Register

The MM74C164 shift registers is a monolithic complementary-MOS (CMOS) integrated circuit constructed with N-channel and P-channel enhancement transistors. These 8-bit shift registers have gated serial inputs and clear. Each register bit is a D-type master-slave flip-flop. A high-level input enables the other input, which will then determine the state of the flip flop.

Data is serially shifted in and out of the 8-bit register during the positive-going transition of clock pulse. Clear is independent of the clock and accomplished by a low level at the clear input. All inputs are protected against electrostatic effects. See 74164 data for more information on logic.

Voltage Range	3 to 15 V
TTL Compatibility	Drive 2 LPTTL loads
Noise Immunity	0.45 Vcc typ.
Power	50 nW typ.
Speed of Operation	8.0 MHz typ. with 10 V supply

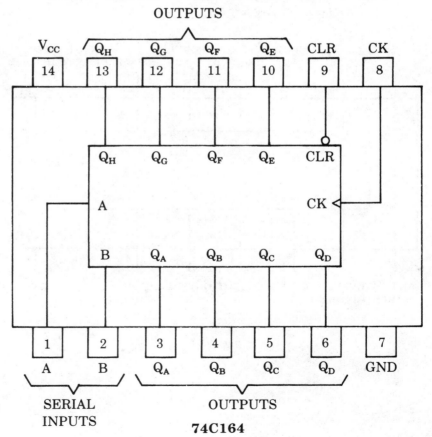

74C164

74C173 Tri-State® Quad D Flip-Flop

The MM74C173 TRI-STATE® Quad D flip-flop is a monolithic complementary-MOS (CMOS) integrated circuit constructed with N-channel and P-channel enhancement transistors. The four D-type flip-flops operate synchronously from a common clock. The TRI-STATE® output allows the device to be used in bus-organized systems. The outputs are placed in the TRI-STATE® mode when either of the two output-disable pins are in the logic 1 level. The input disable allows the flip-flop to remain in their present states without disrupting the clock. If either of the two input disables are taken to a logic 1 level, the Q outputs are fed back to the inputs. In this manner, the flip-flops do not change state.

Clearing is enabled by taking the input to a logic 1 level. Clocking occurs on the positive-going transition. See 74173 data for more information on logic.

Supply Voltage Range	3 to 15 V
TTL Compatibility	Drive 2 LPTTL loads
Noise Immunity	0.45 Vcc typ.
Power	
Speed of Operation	

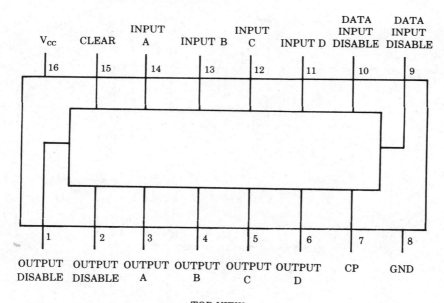

TOP VIEW

74C173

74C192 Synchronous 4-Bit Up/Down Decade Counter

These up/down counters are monolithic complementary-MOS (CMOS) integrated circuits. The MM74C192 is a BCD counter. The MM74C193 is a binary counter.

Counting up and counting down is performed by two count inputs, one being held high while the other is clocked. The outputs change on the positive-going transition of this clock.

These counters feature preset inputs that are set when load is a logic 0 and a clear which forces all outputs to 0 when it is at logic 1. The counters also have carry and borrow outputs so that they can be cascaded using no external circuitry. See 74192 and 74193 data for logic information.

Noise Margin	1 V guaranteed
TTL Compatibility	Drive 2 LPTTL loads
Supply Range	3 to 15 V
Noise Immunity	0.45 Vcc typ.

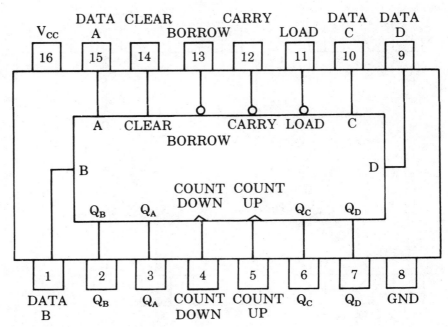

INPUTS: 1, 4, 5, 9, 10, 11, 14, 15
OUTPUTS: 2, 3, 6, 7, 12, 13

74C192

74C193 Synchronous 4-Bit Up/Down Binary Counter

These up/down counters are monolithic complementary-MOS (CMOS) integrated circuits. The MM74C192 is a BCD counter. The MM74C193 is a binary counter.

Counting up and counting down is performed by two count inputs, one being held high while the other is clocked. The outputs change on the positive-going transition of this clock.

These counters feature preset inputs that are set when load is a logic 0 and a clear which forces all outputs to 0 when it is at logic 1. The counters also have carry and borrow outputs so that they can be cascaded using no external circuitry. See 74192 and 74193 data for logic information.

Noise Margin	1 V guaranteed
TTL Compatibility	Drive 2 LPTTL loads
Supply Range	3 to 15 V
Noise Immunity	0.45 Vcc typ.

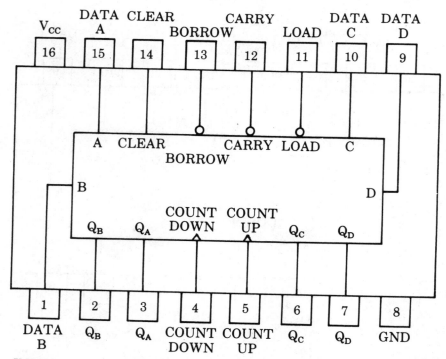

INPUTS: 1, 4, 5, 9, 10, 11, 14, 15
OUTPUTS: 2, 3, 6, 7, 12, 13

74C193

74C195 4-Bit Register

The MM74C195 CMOS 4-bit register features parallel inputs, parallel outputs, J-K serial inputs, shift/load control input and a direct-overriding clear. Two modes of operation are possible: parallel load and shift in direction Q_A towards Q_D.

Parallel loading is accomplished by applying the four bits of data and taking the shift/load control input low. The data is loaded into the associated flip-flops and appears at the outputs after the positive transition of the clock input. During parallel loading, serial data flow is inhibited.

Serial shifting is accomplished synchronously when the shift/load control input is high. Serial data for this mode is entered at the J-$\overline{K}$ inputs. These inputs allow the first stage to perform as a J-$\overline{K}$-, D-, or T-type flip-flop as shown in the truth table. See 74195 data for logic information.

Speed of Operation	8.5 MHz (typ.) with 10 V supply and 50 pF load
Noise Immunity	0.45 Vcc (typ.)
Power	100 nW (typ.)
TTL Compatible	Drive 2 LPTTL loads

OUTPUTS

V_{CC}	Q_A	Q_B	Q_C	Q_D	$\overline{Q}_D$	CLOCK	SHIFT/ LOAD
16	15	14	13	12	11	10	9

Q_A Q_B Q_C Q_D $\overline{Q}_D$ CK

CLEAR

SHIFT/ LOAD

J $\overline{K}$ A B C D

1	2	3	4	5	6	7	8
CLEAR	J	$\overline{K}$	A	B	C	D	GND

SERIAL INPUTS

PARALLEL INPUTS

74C195

74C922 16-Key Encoder

These CMOS key encoders provide all the necessary logic to fully encode an array of SPST switches. The keyboard scan can be implemented by either an external clock or external capacitor. These encoders also have on-chip pullup devices that permit switches with up to 50 kΩ of resistance to be used. No diodes in the switch array are needed to eliminate ghost switches. The internal debounce circuit needs only a single external capacitor and can be defeated by omitting the capacitor. A data-available output goes to a high level when a valid keyboard entry has been made. The data available output returns to a low level when the entered key is released, even if another key is depressed. The data available will return high to indicate acceptance of the new key after a normal debounce period; this two-key roll over is provided between any two switches.

An internal register remembers the last key pressed, even after the key is released. The TRI-STATE® outputs provide for easy expansion and bus operation and are LPTTL compatible.

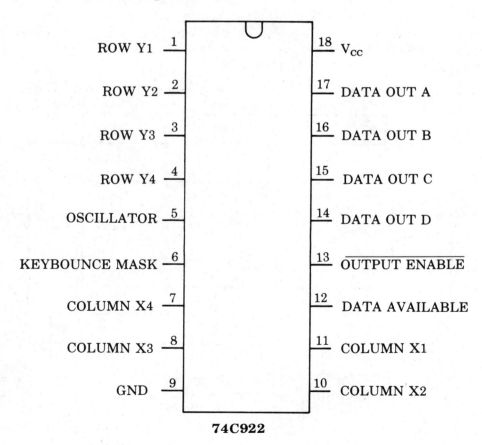

ROW Y1 — 1	18 — V_{CC}	
ROW Y2 — 2	17 — DATA OUT A	
ROW Y3 — 3	16 — DATA OUT B	
ROW Y4 — 4	15 — DATA OUT C	
OSCILLATOR — 5	14 — DATA OUT D	
KEYBOUNCE MASK — 6	13 — $\overline{\text{OUTPUT ENABLE}}$	
COLUMN X4 — 7	12 — DATA AVAILABLE	
COLUMN X3 — 8	11 — COLUMN X1	
GND — 9	10 — COLUMN X2	

74C922

74C923 20-Key Encoder

These CMOS key encoders provide all the necessary logic to fully encode an array of SPST switches. The keyboard scan can be implemented by either an external clock or external capacitor. These encoders also have on-chip pullup devices that permit switches with up to 50 kΩ of resistance to be used. No diodes in the switch array are needed to eliminate ghost switches. The internal debounce circuit needs only a single external capacitor and can be defeated by omitting the capacitor. A data-available output goes to a high level when a valid keyboard entry has been made. The data available output returns to a low level when the entered key is released, even if another key is depressed. The data available will return high to indicate acceptance of the new key after a normal debounce period; this two-key roll over is provided between any two switches.

An internal register remembers the last key pressed even after the key is released. The TRI-STATE® outputs provide for easy expansion and bus operation and are LPTTL compatible.

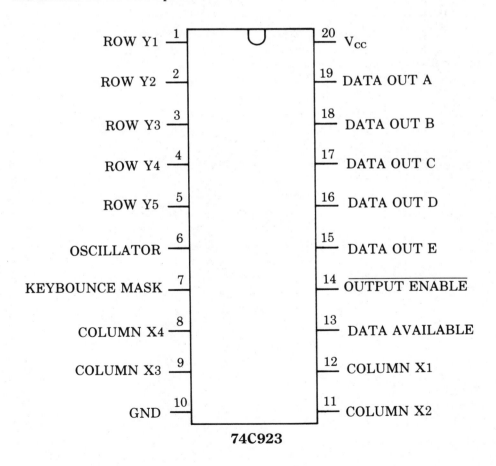

ROW Y1	1		20	V_{CC}
ROW Y2	2		19	DATA OUT A
ROW Y3	3		18	DATA OUT B
ROW Y4	4		17	DATA OUT C
ROW Y5	5		16	DATA OUT D
OSCILLATOR	6		15	DATA OUT E
KEYBOUNCE MASK	7		14	$\overline{\text{OUTPUT ENABLE}}$
COLUMN X4	8		13	DATA AVAILABLE
COLUMN X3	9		12	COLUMN X1
GND	10		11	COLUMN X2

74C923

Truth Table

SWITCH POSITION		0 Y1,X1	1 Y1,X2	2 Y1,X3	3 Y1,X4	4 Y2,X1	5 Y2,X2	6 Y2,X3	7 Y2,X4	8 Y3,X1	9 Y3,X2	10 Y3,X3	11 Y3,X4
D A T A	A	0	1	0	1	0	1	0	1	0	1	0	1
	B	0	0	1	1	0	0	1	1	0	0	1	1
	C	0	0	0	0	1	1	1	1	0	0	0	0
O U T	D	0	0	0	0	0	0	0	0	1	1	1	1
	E*	0	0	0	0	0	0	0	0	0	0	0	0

SWITCH POSITION		12 Y4,X1	13 Y4,X2	14 Y4,X3	15 Y4,X4	16 Y5*,X1	17 Y5*,X2	18 Y5*,X3	19 Y5*X4
D A T A	A	0	1	0	1	0	1	0	1
	B	0	0	1	1	0	0	1	1
	C	1	1	1	1	0	0	0	0
O U T	D	1	1	1	1	0	0	0	0
	E*	0	0	0	0	1	1	1	1

*Omit for MM54C922/MM74C922

74C927, 74C928 4-Digit Counters
with Multiplexed 7-Segment Output Drivers

These CMOS counters consist of a 4-digit counter, an internal-output latch, NPN-output sourcing drivers for a 7-segment display, and an internal multiplexing circuit with 4 multiplexing outputs. The multiplexing circuit has its own free-running oscillator, and requires no external clock. The counters advance on the negative edge of the clock. A high signal on the reset input will reset the counter to zero, and reset the carry-out low. A low signal on the latch-enable input will latch the number in the counters into the internal-output latches. A high signal on the display-select input will select the number in the counter to be displayed; a low-level signal on the display select will select the number in the output latch to be displayed.

The MM74C925 is a 4-decade counter and has latch enable, clock, and reset inputs. The MM74C926 is like the MM74C925, except that it has a display

Supply Voltage Range	3 to 6 V
Guaranteed Noise Margin	1 V
Noise Immunity	0.45 Vcc typ.
Segment Sourcing Current	40 mA @ Vcc − 1.6 V, Vcc = 5 V

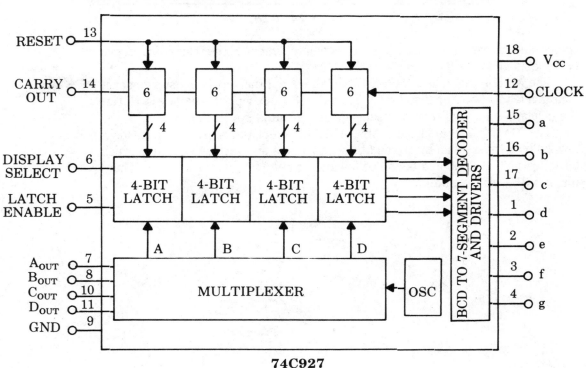

74C927

303

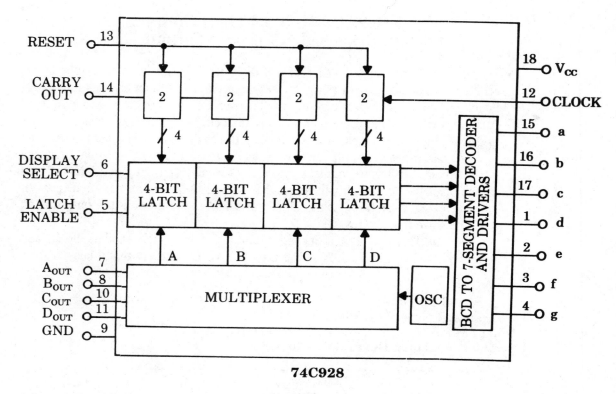

74C928

select and a carry-out used for cascading counters. The carry-out signal becomes high at 6000 and low at 0000.

The MM74C927 is like the MM74C926, except the second most significant digit divides by 6 rather than by 10. Thus, if the clock input frequency is 10 Hz, the display would read tenths of seconds and minutes (i.e., 9:59.9).

The MM74C928 is like the MM74C926, except the most significant digit divides by 2 rather than by 10, and the carry-out is an overflow indicator, which becomes high at 2000 and becomes low only when the counter is reset. Thus, this is a $3^{1}/_{2}$-digit counter.

MM74C946 4$^{1}/_{2}$-Digit
Counter/Decoder/LCD Display Driver

The MM74C96 is designed to directly drive up to 4$^{1}/_{2}$ digits of a 7-segment LCD display. This chip was designed to maximize display contrast and display life. It also consumes very low power. In the quiescent state, this device is rated for 100 μW (0.0001 watt).

The MM74C946 features a carry output to permit cascading additional stages in four-digit blocks. Leading-zero blanking input and output are provided to ensure correct leading-zero blanking when multiple counters are cascaded.

An on-chip Schmitt trigger is included at the clock input. This aids the MM74C946 in reliable operation in noisy environments, or with slow-changing input signals.

An on-chip backplane oscillator/driver is also included in this device. This section can be disabled, permitting slaving of multiple devices to a common external backplane signal.

Pin	Signal	Signal	Pin
1	V$_{cc}$	D1	40
2	E1	C1	39
3	G1	B1	38
4	F1	A1	37
5	BACKPLANE	OSCILLATOR	36
6	A2	GND	35
7	B2	STORE	34
8	C2	RESET	33
9	D2	CLOCK	32
10	E2	ENABLE	31
11	G2	LZ0	30
12	F2	LZ1	29
13	A3	CARRY	28
14	B3	½-DIGIT	27
15	C3	F4	26
16	D3	G4	25
17	E3	E4	24
18	G3	D4	23
19	F3	C4	22
20	A4	B4	21

74C946

80C95, 80C97 3-State Hex Buffers

These gates are monolithic complementary-MOS (CMOS) integrated circuits constructed with N-channel and P-channel enhancement-mode transistors. The MM80C95 and the MM80C97 convert CMOS or TTL outputs to TRI-STATE® outputs with no logic inversion. The MM80C96 and MM80C98 provide the logic opposite of the input signal. The MM80C95 and MM80C96 have common TRI-STATE® controls for all six devices. The MM80C97 and MM80C98 have two TRI-STATE® controls; one for two devices and one for the other four devices. Inputs are protected from damage as a result of static discharge by diode clamps to V_{CC} and GND.

Supply Voltage Range	3.0 to 15 V
Guaranteed Noise Margin	1.0 V
Noise Immunity	0.45 Vcc (typ.)
TTL Compatibility	Drive 1 TTL load

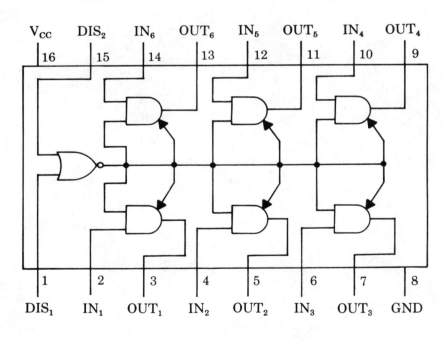

80C95

80C96, 80C98 3-State Hex Inverters

These gates are monolithic complementary-MOS (CMOS) integrated circuits constructed with N-channel and P-channel enhancement-mode transistors. The MM80C95 and the MM80C97 convert CMOS or TTL outputs to TRI-STATE® outputs with no logic inversion. The MM80C96 and MM80C98 provide the logic opposite of the input signal. The MM80C95 and MM80C96 have common TRI-STATE® controls for all six devices. The MM80C97 and MM80C98 have two TRI-STATE® controls: one for two devices and one for the other four devices. Inputs are protected from damage as a result of static discharge by diode clamps to V_{CC} and GND.

Supply Voltage Range	3.0 to 15 V
Guaranteed Noise Margin	1.0 V
Noise Immunity	0.45 Vcc (typ.)
TTL Compatibility	Drive 1 TTL load

3
SECTION

Special-Purpose CMOS

The CMOS devices presented in this section are more specialized and sophisticated than those in the preceding section. Certain exotic ICs of the CMOS family are quite popular today in both industrial and hobbyist applications. A handful of special-purpose CMOS chips are covered here, with information that is normally supplied with any CMOS devices.

Special-Purpose CMOS Listing

BA820 8-Bit Serial-In/Parallel-Out Driver

The BA820 is a monolithic driver, intended for such applications as driving LED character displays and thermal heads in printers. The chip features a single input. Data is entered serially. The output data can be taken from eight parallel outputs, or from a single serial output.

Multiple BA820's can be connected in tandem for a greater number of parallel outputs. The serial data output of the preceding stage is connected to the serial data input of the following stage.

The BA820's inputs are compatible with both TTL and CMOS circuitry.

Supply Voltage Range	4.5 to 5.5 V
	12 V max at output pins $\overline{Q}_0 - \overline{Q}_7$
Power dissipation	550 mW max.
Max. data transfer speed	200 kHz min.

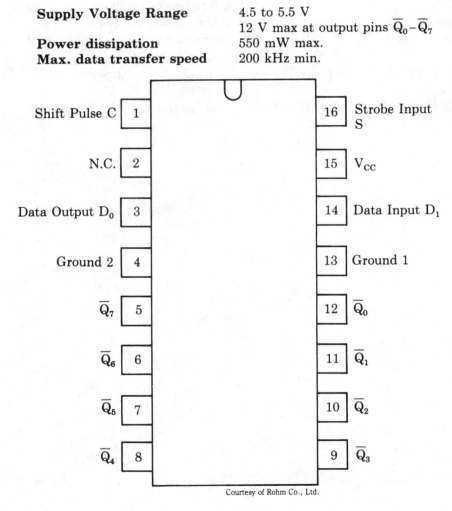

Courtesy of Rohm Co., Ltd.

BA820

MC1408, MC1508, 8-Bit Multiplying D/A Converter

The MC1408/MC1508 is a digital-to-analog converter that accepts an 8-bit digital word at its inputs, and converts it into a linear output current. The unusual feature of this device is that it has an additional analog input. The voltage applied to this input serves as a constant multiplier. The output current of the MC1408/MC1508 is the linear product of the 8-bit digital input and the analog input voltage.

This chip is very fast and very accurate in its operation. Its noninverting digital inputs are both TTL and CMOS compatible.

Standard Supply Voltages

V_{cc}	+4.5 to +5.5 V
V_{ee}	−5.0 to −15 V
Output Voltage Swing	+0.4 to −5.0 V
Settling Time	300 ns typ.
Multiplying Input Slew Rate	4.0 mA/μs

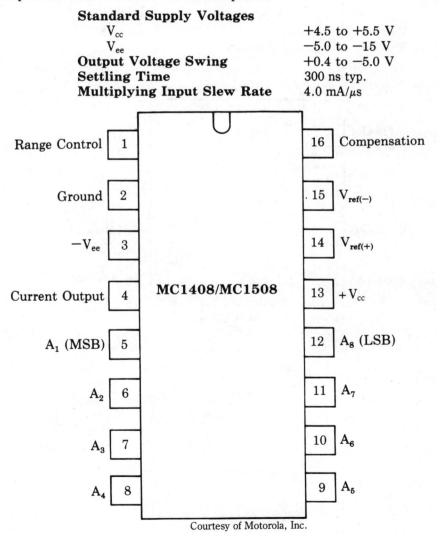

Courtesy of Motorola, Inc.

311

MM5368 CMOS Oscillator Divider

The MM5368 accepts a square-wave input signal from an oscillator (or other signal source), and divides the signal frequency to three much lower output frequencies.

The input signal at pin #6 should be a floating 16-kHz (16,000 Hz) square wave. The same signal is buffered and can be tapped off at pin #5. A 10 Hz signal is available at pin #3 and pin #4 offers a 1-Hz signal. The signal frequency at pin #1 can be either 50 Hz or 60 Hz, depending on the logic state at the select input (pin #7).

Supply Voltage Range	3 to 15 V
Voltage at any pin	-0.3 V to V_{dd} to $+0.3$ V
Maximum Input Frequency	
$V_{dd} = 3$ V	64 kHz
$V_{dd} = 15$ V	500 kHz

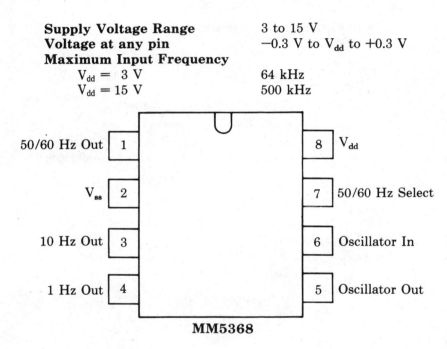

MM5368

MM5452/MM5453 Liquid Crystal Display Driver

The MM5452/MM5453 is designed to drive 7-segment liquid crystal displays from digital-input values.

Although this chip is a CMOS device, its inputs are TTL-compatible. Input data is accepted in serial form.

The primary difference between the MM5452 and the MM5453 is that the MM5453 has a 33-bit output, while the MM5452 has only a 32-bit output. The thirty-third output bit in the MM5452 is replaced by a data-enable pin, which might be required in certain applications.

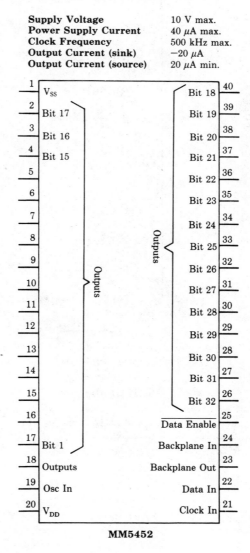

Supply Voltage	10 V max.
Power Supply Current	40 μA max.
Clock Frequency	500 kHz max.
Output Current (sink)	-20 μA
Output Current (source)	20 μA min.

MM5452

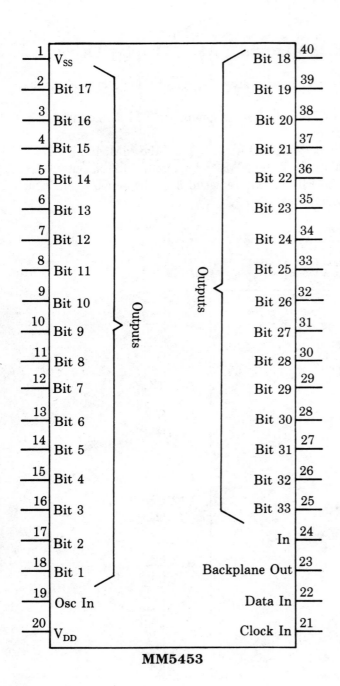

1	V_SS	Bit 18	40
2	Bit 17	Bit 19	39
3	Bit 16	Bit 20	38
4	Bit 15	Bit 21	37
5	Bit 14	Bit 22	36
6	Bit 13	Bit 23	35
7	Bit 12	Bit 24	34
8	Bit 11	Bit 25	33
9	Bit 10	Bit 26	32
10	Bit 9	Bit 27	31
11	Bit 8	Bit 28	30
12	Bit 7	Bit 29	29
13	Bit 6	Bit 30	28
14	Bit 5	Bit 31	27
15	Bit 4	Bit 32	26
16	Bit 3	Bit 33	25
17	Bit 2	In	24
18	Bit 1	Backplane Out	23
19	Osc In	Data In	22
20	V_DD	Clock In	21

$$V_{SS}$$

Outputs

Outputs

MM5453

LS7210 Programmable Digital Delay Timer

The LS7210 can digitally generate time delay periods ranging from a low of 6 ms (0.006 s) up to theoretical infinity. The chip is programmed via a 5-bit digital input. Two digital control inputs select from four different operating modes:

- Delayed operate
- Delayed release
- Dual delay
- One-shot

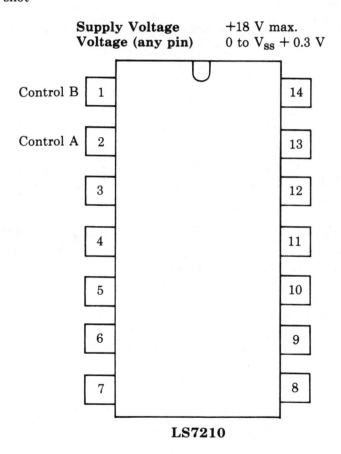

Supply Voltage   +18 V max.
Voltage (any pin)   0 to V_{SS} + 0.3 V

LS7210

7555 CMOS Timer

The 7555 is a CMOS version of the popular 555 timer IC, which is described in section 8 of this book.

The advantages of the CMOS version include a wider range of acceptable supply voltages and lower power consumption. The CMOS 7555 is more stable than the standard 555, permitting longer timing cycles.

Like the ordinary 555 timer, the 7555 CMOS timer can be used in both monostable-multivibrator and astable-multivibrator applications.

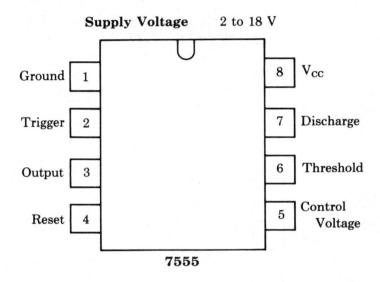

Supply Voltage   2 to 18 V

Ground — 1	8 — V_{cc}
Trigger — 2	7 — Discharge
Output — 3	6 — Threshold
Reset — 4	5 — Control Voltage

7555

14410 Tone Encoder

The 14410 2-of-8 tone encoder is constructed with complementary-MOS (CMOS) enhancement-mode devices. It is designed to accept digital inputs in a 2-of-8 code format and to digitally synthesize the high-band and low-band sine waves specified by telephone tone dialing systems. The inputs are normally originated from a 4-by-4 matrix keypad, which generates four row and four column input signals in a 2-of-8 code format (1 row and 1 column are simultaneously connected to V_{SS}). The master clocking for the 14410 is achieved from a crystal-controlled oscillator that is included on the chip. Internal clocks, which operate the logic, are enabled only by one or more row and column signals being activated simultaneously. The two sine-wave outputs have NPN bipolar structures on the same substrate, which allows for low output impedance and large source currents. This device can be used in telephone tone dialers, radio and mobile telephones, process control, point-of-sale terminals and credit-card verification terminals.

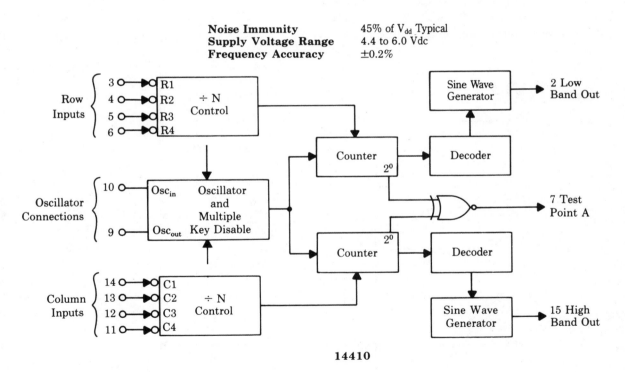

Noise Immunity	45% of V_{dd} Typical
Supply Voltage Range	4.4 to 6.0 Vdc
Frequency Accuracy	±0.2%

14410

14411 Bit-Rate Generator

The 14411 bit-rate generator is constructed with complementary-MOS (CMOS) enhancement-mode devices. It utilizes a frequency divider network to provide a wide range of output frequencies.

A crystal-controlled oscillator is the clock source for the network. A two-bit address is provided to select one of four multiple output clock rates.

Applications include a selectable frequency source for equipment in the data communications market, such as teletypes, printers, CRT terminals and microprocessor systems. It features:

- Single 5.0 V_{DC} ($\pm 5\%$) power supply
- Internal oscillator crystal-controlled for stability (1.8432 MHz)
- Sixteen different output clock rates
- 50% output duty cycle
- Programmable time bases for 1-of-4 multiple output rates
- Buffered outputs compatible with low-power TTL
- Noise immunity = 45% of V_{DD} typical
- Diode protection on all inputs

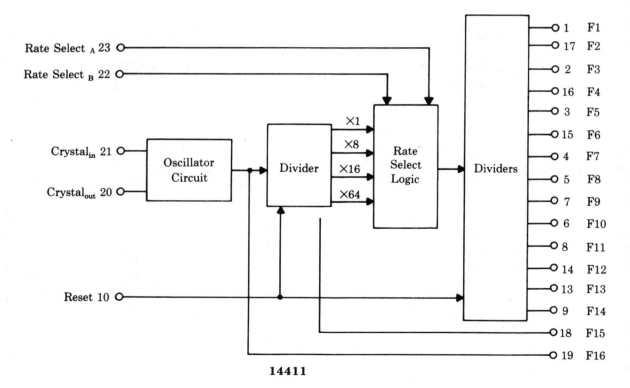

14411

14415 Timer/Driver

The 14415 quad timer/driver is constructed with complementary-MOS (CMOS) enhancement-mode devices. The output pulse width of each digital timer is a function of the input clock frequency. Once the proper input sequence is detected, the output buffer is set (turned on), and after 100 clock pulses are counted, the output buffer is reset (turned off).

The 14415 was designed specifically for application in high-speed line printers to provide the critical timing of the hammer drivers, but can be used in many applications requiring precision pulse widths. It features:

- Four precision digital time delays
- Schmitt-trigger clock conditioning
- NPN bipolar output drivers
- Timing disable capability using inhibit output
- Positive- or negative-edge strobing on the inputs
- Synchronous polynomical counters used for delay counting
- Power-supply operating range
  - = 3.0 to 18 V_{DC} (14415EFL)
  - = 3.0 to 16 V_{DC} (14415FL/FP)
  - = 3.0 to 6.0 V_{DC} (14415EVL/VL/VP)

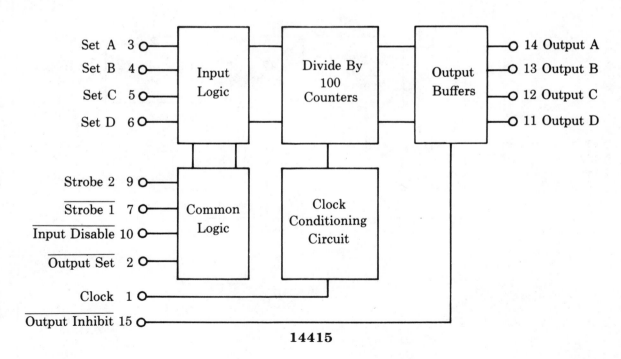

14415

14435 A/D Subsystem

The 14435 A/D logic is designed specifically for use in a dual-slope integration A/D converter system. The device consists of $3^1/2$ digits of BCD counters, 13 memory latches, and output multiplexing circuitry. An internal clock oscillator is provided to generate system timing and to set the output-multiplexing rate. A single capacitor is required to set the oscillator frequency. It features:

- On-chip clock to control digit select, multiplexing and BCD counters simultaneously
- Multiplexed BCD output
- Built-in 100-count delay for accurate system conversion of low-level inputs
- System overrange output
- Supply voltage range
  = 3.0 to 18 V_{DC} (14435EFL)
  = 3.0 to 16 V_{DC} (14435FL/FP)
  = 3.0 to 6.0 V_{DC} (14435EVL/VL/VP)

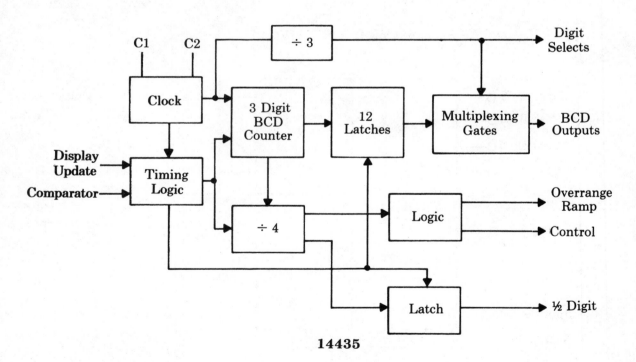

14435

320

14490 Contact Bounce Eliminator

The 14490 is constructed with complementary-MOS (CMOS) enhancement-mode devices, and is used for the elimination of extraneous level changes that result when interfacing with mechanical contacts. The digital contact bounce-eliminator circuit takes an input signal from a bouncing contact and generates a clean digital signal four clock periods after the input has stabilized. The bounce-eliminator circuit will remove bounce on both the make and the break of a contact closure.

The clock for operation of the 14490 is derived from an internal RC oscillator which requires only an external capacitor to adjust for the desired operating frequency (bounce delay). The clock can also be driven from an external clock source or the oscillator of another 14490. It features:

- Noise immunity = 45% of V_{DD} Typical
- Supply voltage range
    = 3.0 to 18 V_{DC} (14490EFL)
    = 3.0 to 16 V_{DC} (14490FL/FP)
    = 3.0 to 6.0 V_{DC} (14490EVL/VL/VP)

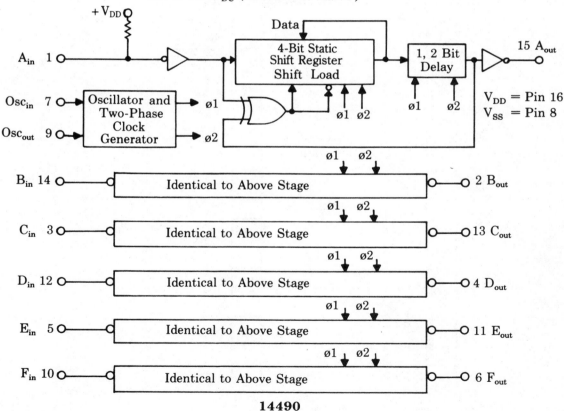

14490

MM58174A Microprocessor Compatible Real-Time Clock

Designed primarily for business-oriented microprocessor/computer systems, the MM58174A functions as a real-time (seconds, minutes, and hours) clock and calendar. The interrupt timer within this chip can be programmed to any one of three times.

The chip can be kept operating and accurately keeping time with a very low standby power. Battery-operated standby is very practical with this device. A minimum of 2.2 volts must be maintained to keep the MM58174A's time-keeping functions running.

This IC was designed to use a 32.768 kHz (32,768 Hz) crystal-controlled oscillator as the timebase signal source.

Supply Voltage	6.5 V max.	
	5.5 V typ.	
Internal Resistor to V_{dd}		
For $\overline{WR}$	100,000 Ω	
For $\overline{CS}$	100,000 Ω	
Voltage at Any Pin	+0.3 V to V_{ss} − 0.3 V	

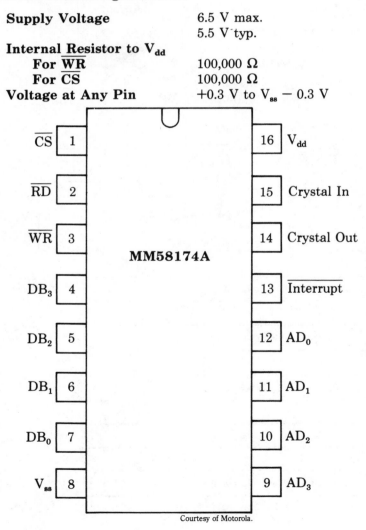

	MM58174A	
$\overline{CS}$	1	16 V_{dd}
$\overline{RD}$	2	15 Crystal In
$\overline{WR}$	3	14 Crystal Out
DB_3	4	13 $\overline{Interrupt}$
DB_2	5	12 AD_0
DB_1	6	11 AD_1
DB_0	7	10 AD_2
V_{ss}	8	9 AD_3

Courtesy of Motorola.

MC145040 / MC145041 8-Bit A/D Converters with Serial Interface

The MC145040 and MC145041 perform fast and accurate analog-to-digital conversions. The output is in the form of an 8-bit digital word.

A single-ended power supply is used with both chips, and no external trimming circuitry is required.

With the MC145040, an external clock input (A/D CLK) is used to operate the dynamic A/D conversion sequence.

The MC145041 features an internal clock, and the clock input pin is replaced with an end-of-conversion (EOF) output signal.

Supply Voltage   4.5 to 5.5 V
Power Consumption   11 mW

Successive Approximation Conversion Time

MC145040	10 μs (with 2 MHz A/D CLK)
MC145041	20 μs max. (Internal Clock)

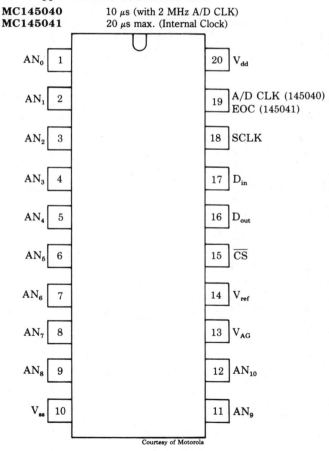

Courtesy of Motorola

MC145040/MC145041

MC145160 / MC145166 / MC145167 Dual PLL for Cordless Telephones

The MC145160, MC145166, and MC145167 are dual phase-locked loop (PLL) frequency synthesizers. They were designed primarily for use in 46/49 MHz cordless telephone systems. Each of these chips contain two ROM programmable counters for receive and transmit loops, and two independent phase-detector circuits.

The receive and transmit circuits share a common-reference oscillator and reference divider.

The MC145167 is designed for easy interfacing with a microprocessor. It provides the same features as the MC145166, but it accepts channel programming via a clocked, serial-data input, rather than parallel BCD inputs. Both the MC145166 and the MC145167 transmit at the oscillator's fundamental frequency.

The MC145160 transmits at half the fundamental frequency and also features a 4-kHz tone output. The channel programming for this chip, as for the MC145166, is accepted in the form of parallel BCD inputs.

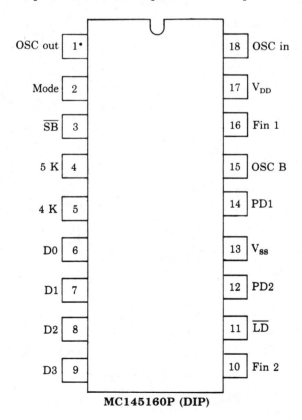

OSC out	1•		18	OSC in
Mode	2		17	V_{DD}
$\overline{SB}$	3		16	Fin 1
5 K	4		15	OSC B
4 K	5		14	PD1
D0	6		13	V_{SS}
D1	7		12	PD2
D2	8		11	$\overline{LD}$
D3	9		10	Fin 2

MC145160P (DIP)

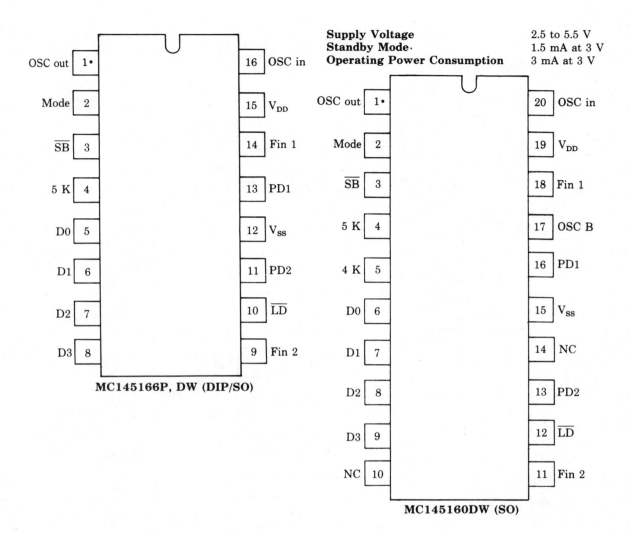

Supply Voltage		2.5 to 5.5 V	
Standby Mode		1.5 mA at 3 V	
Operating Power Consumption		3 mA at 3 V	

MC145166P, DW (DIP/SO)

MC145160DW (SO)

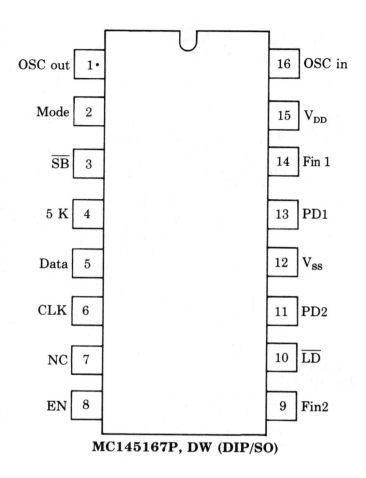

MC145167P, DW (DIP/SO)

DUAL PLL OPTIONS

Part number	Options			
	4 KHz Output	Transmit Frequency	Channel Programming	Package Lead count
MC145160	Yes	Half of fundamental	BCD	18/20
MC145166	No	Fundamental	BCD	16
MC145167	No	Fundamental	Serial	16

4
SECTION

Memories

With the increased emphasis on digital circuitry in today's world of electronics, microprocessors are turning up in many applications, both in general-purpose computers and dedicated devices of various types. In order for any sort of microprocessor to be of any use, it must have data and programming information, which is almost always stored in some type of memory device.

In this section, we will look at a number of RAM (Random-Access Memory) and EPROM (Erasable-Programmable Read-Only Memory) ICs.

Memory ICs

X2004 4 K Nonvolatile Static RAM

A static RAM (random-access memory) retains its stored data as long as power is continuously supplied to the circuitry. Unlike a dynamic RAM, a static RAM does not require periodic refreshing of the stored data. Most RAM chips are volatile. That is, it will irretrievably lose its contents if power is interrupted.

The X2004 is designed to be nonvolatile. Basically, this chip consists of a high-speed static RAM overlaid bit-for-bit with a nonvolatile electrically erasable PROM (EEPROM).

The design of this chip permits easy transfer from RAM to EEPROM (store) and from EEPROM to RAM (recall). The manufacturer claims that data can be reliably stored within the EEPROM for up to 100 years.

The maximum time required for a store (or write) operation is 10 ms. Recall operations can be made even faster. The rated maximum recall time is 5 μs.

The X2004 operates from a single-ended 5-volt power supply.

This RAM chip holds up to 4 K (4096 bits) of data.

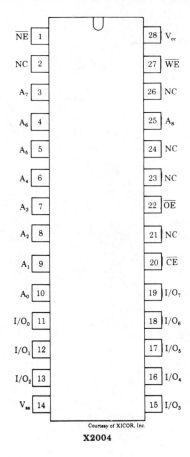

Courtesy of XICOR, Inc.

X2004

X2201A 1 K Nonvolatile Static RAM

A static RAM (random-access memory) retains its stored data as long as power is continuously supplied to the circuitry. Unlike a dynamic RAM, a static RAM does not require periodic refreshing of the stored data. Most RAM chips are volatile. That is, it will irretrievably lose its contents if power is interrupted.

The X2201A is designed to be nonvolatile. Basically, this chip consists of a high-speed static RAM overlaid bit-for-bit with a nonvolatile electrically erasable PROM (EEPROM).

The design of this chip permits easy transfer from RAM to EEPROM (store) and from EEPROM to RAM (recall). The manufacturer claims that data can be reliably stored within the EEPROM for up to 100 years.

The maximum time required for a store (or write) operation is 10 ms. Recall operations can be made even faster. The rated typical recall time is 1 μs.

The X2201A operates from a single-ended 5-volt power supply and is fully compatible with TTL and CMOS circuits.

This RAM chip holds up to 1 K (1024 bits) of data.

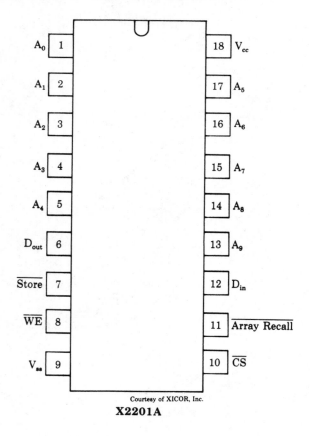

Courtesy of XICOR, Inc.

X2201A

X2210 256-Bit Nonvolatile Static RAM

The X2210 is a smaller version of the X2201A and the X2004 discussed previously. Once again, the internal RAM is overlaid bit-for-bit with EEPROM for nonvolatile storage of data. The total data storage capacity of this chip is 256 bits, or $1/2$ K.

The maximum time required for a store (or write) operation is 10 ms. Recall operations can be made even faster. The rated typical recall time is $1\mu s$.

The X2201A operates from a single-ended 5-volt power supply and is fully compatible with TTL and CMOS circuits.

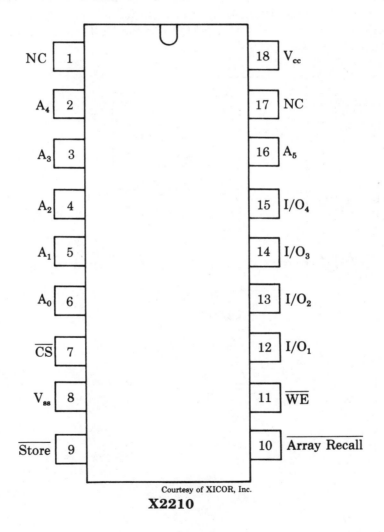

Courtesy of XICOR, Inc.

X2210

X2402 2 K Electrically Erasable EPROM

An EPROM is an erasable-programmable read-only memory. Customized data can be permanently stored by the user. Individual bits cannot be changed once they are written, but the entire chip can be erased as a whole.

The earliest EPROMs were erased by exposure to an ultraviolet light. Newer devices can be erased with a special electrical signal. This system is more reliable and more convenient.

The X2402 EEPROM offers a 2 K (2048 bits) of data storage, arranged as 8 pages of 256 bits each. A 2-wire serial interface is used with this chip, and the write cycle is self-timed. Typically, a write cycle will take about 5 ms.

The manufacturer claims that data stored in the X2402 can be held for up to 100 years.

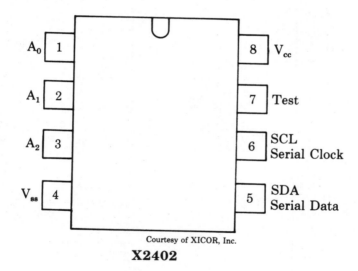

Courtesy of XICOR, Inc.

X2402

X2404 4 K Electrically Erasable EPROM

Unlike early EPROMs (erasable-programmable read-only memory), modern EEPROMS do not need exposure to an ultraviolet light source to erase their data contents. The data in an EEPROM can be erased with a special electrical signal. This system is more reliable and convenient.

The X2404 EEPROM is essentially the equivalent to 2 X2402s in a single 8-pin housing. It offers 4 K (4096 bits) of data storage, arranged as 2 groups of 8 pages of 256 bits each.

A 2-wire serial interface is used with this chip, and the write cycle is self-timed. Typically, a write cycle will take about 5 ms.

The manufacturer claims that data stored in the X2404 can be held for up to 100 years.

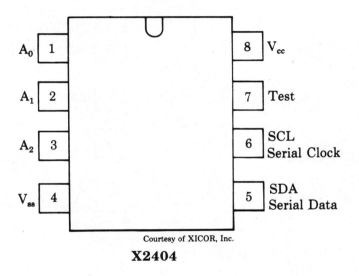

Courtesy of XICOR, Inc.

X2404

X24C16 16 K Electrically Erasable EPROM

Unlike early EPROMs (erasable-programmable read-only memory), modern EEPROMS do not need exposure to an ultraviolet light source to erase their data contents. The data in an EEPROM can be erased with a special electrical signal. This system is more reliable and convenient.

The X24C16 EEPROM is essentially the equivalent to 4 X2402s in a single 8-pin housing. It offers 16 K (16,384 bits) of data storage, arranged as 4 groups of 8 pages of 256 bits each.

A 2-wire serial interface is used with this chip, and the write cycle is self-timed. Typically, a write cycle will take about 5 ms.

The manufacturer claims that data stored in the X24C16 can be held for up to 100 years.

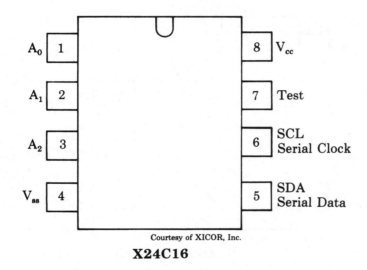

Courtesy of XICOR, Inc.

X24C16

X2804A 4 K Electrically Erasable EPROM

An EPROM is an erasable-programmable read-only memory. Customized data can be permanently stored by the user. Individual bits cannot be changed once they are written, but the entire chip can be erased as a whole.

The earliest EPROMS were erased by exposure to an ultraviolet light. Newer devices can be erased with a special electrical signal. This system is more reliable and convenient.

The X2804A EEPROM offers 4 K (4096 bits) of data storage, arranged as 8 pages of 512 bits each. The X2804A operates from a single-ended power supply and is TTL-compatible.

This chip features very low power dissipation. The current consumption in the standby mode is rated at a maximum of 50 mA. Even in the active mode, this IC's current consumption is rated for no more than 80 mA.

The manufacturer claims that data stored in the X2804A can be held for up to 100 years.

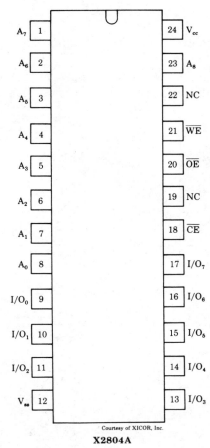

Courtesy of XICOR, Inc.

X2804A

MM4270 4 K Extended-Temperature-Range Dynamic RAM

The MM4270, manufactured by National Semiconductor, is a dynamic, rather than a static RAM (random-access memory). This term means that the data must be periodically refreshed (automatically read and rewritten), or it will be lost.

This chip holds up to 4 K (4,096 bits) of data. The input/output pin is a three-state connection. Besides the standard high and low states, it also has a third, high-impedance "don't-care" state.

A very novel feature of the MM4270 is pin #5, which is labelled *TSP*, or *tri-share port*. This multifunction control input, along with the common input/output permits the full 4 K RAM to fit into a standard 18-pin package. The TSP pin controls several functions, including:

- read/write
- V_{CC}
- Logic chip select

The supply for the output buffer is V_{DD}, rather than V_{CC}, so no special driver circuitry is needed.

The MM4270 requires two power-supply voltages—+12 volts, and −5 volts. Access time for this chip is rated for no more than 270 ns. The minimum rated value for the cycle time is 470 ns.

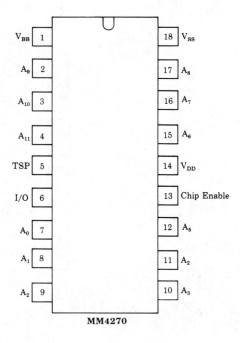

MM4270

BR6116 2 K × 8 High-Speed CMOS SRAM

The BR6116 is a 16 K (16,384 bits) static RAM (random-access memory). No refreshing circuitry is required with a static RAM. The memory is internally arranged as 2 K (2,048) words of 8 bits each.

CMOS circuitry is used throughout this chip for high performance and relatively low power consumption. Three-state outputs are used. Besides the standard high and low states, it has a third, high-impedance ''don't-care'' state.

Even though the BR6116 is a CMOS device, its inputs and outputs are TTL-compatible.

This IC is designed to be operated from a single-ended + 5-volt power supply. In normal operation, the power consumption of this chip is typically about 250 mW. In the standby mode, the BR6116's power consumption drops to a typical value of just 5 μW.

Access time for this chip is quite fast. The typical rating is 90 ns, with 120 ns as the maximum. The access and cycle times are equal.

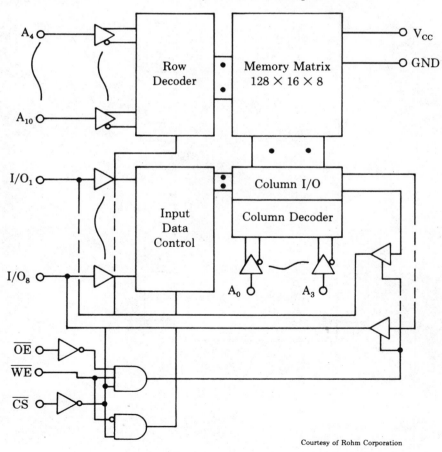

Courtesy of Rohm Corporation

337

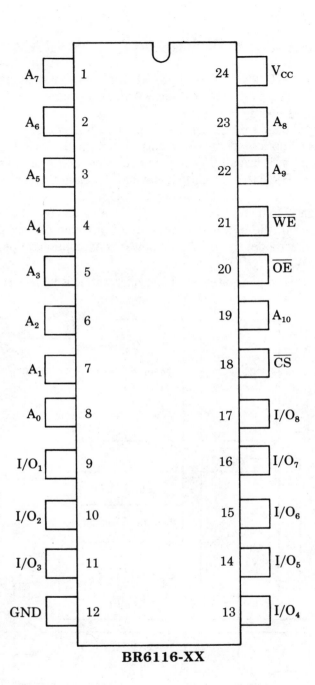

BR6116-XX

BR6116-100 2 K × 8 High-Speed CMOS SRAM

The BR6116-100 is a 16 K (16,384 bits) static RAM (random-access memory). No refreshing circuitry is required with a static RAM. Not surprisingly, this chip is quite similar to the BR6116 presented earlier. As with the BR6116, the memory in the BR6116-100 is internally arranged as 2 K (2,048) words of 8 bits each.

CMOS circuitry is used throughout this chip for high performance and relatively low power consumption. Three-state outputs are used. Besides the standard high and low states, it has a third, high-impedance ''don't-care'' state.

Even though the BR6116-100 is a CMOS device, its inputs and outputs are TTL-compatible.

This IC is designed to be operated from a single-ended + 5-volt power supply. In normal operation, the power consumption of this chip is typically about 175 mW. In the standby mode, the BR6116-100's power consumption drops to a typical value of just 5 μW.

The access time for this chip is quite fast. The maximum rating is 100 ns. The access and cycle times are equal.

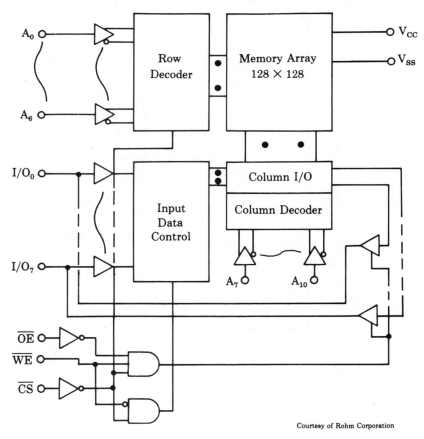

Courtesy of Rohm Corporation

339

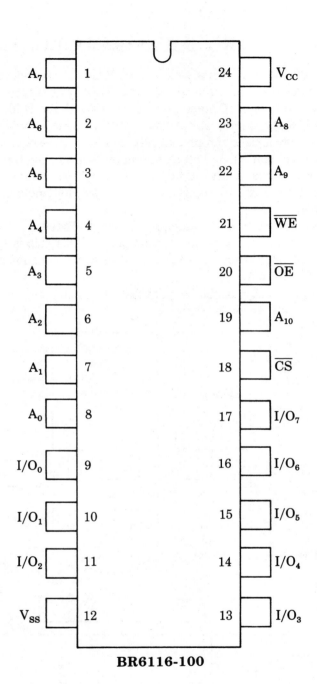

A_7	1		24	V_{CC}
A_6	2		23	A_8
A_5	3		22	A_9
A_4	4		21	$\overline{WE}$
A_3	5		20	$\overline{OE}$
A_2	6		19	A_{10}
A_1	7		18	$\overline{CS}$
A_0	8		17	I/O_7
I/O_0	9		16	I/O_6
I/O_1	10		15	I/O_5
I/O_2	11		14	I/O_4
V_{SS}	12		13	I/O_3

BR6116-100

BR6264 8 K × 8 High-Speed CMOS SRAM

The BR6264 is a 64 K (65,536 bits) static RAM (random-access memory). No refreshing circuitry is required with a static RAM. The memory is internally arranged as 8 K (8,192) words of 8 bits each.

CMOS circuitry is used throughout this chip for high performance and relatively low power consumption. Three-state outputs are used. Besides the standard high and low states, there is a third, high-impedance "don't-care" state.

Even though the BR6264 is a CMOS device, its inputs and outputs are TTL-compatible. This IC is designed to be operated from a single-ended +5-volt power supply.

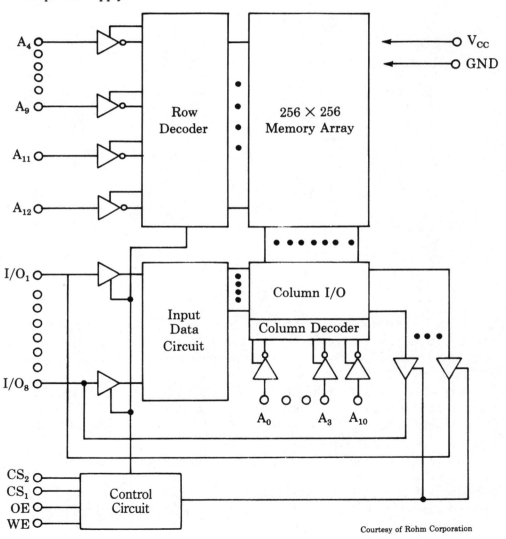

Courtesy of Rohm Corporation

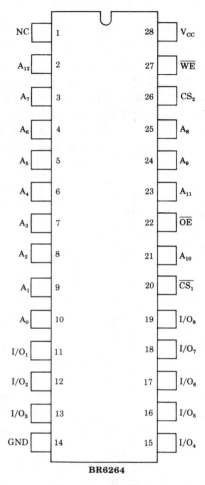

NC	1	28	V_{CC}
A_{12}	2	27	$\overline{WE}$
A_7	3	26	CS_2
A_6	4	25	A_8
A_5	5	24	A_9
A_4	6	23	A_{11}
A_3	7	22	$\overline{OE}$
A_2	8	21	A_{10}
A_1	9	20	$\overline{CS_1}$
A_0	10	19	I/O_8
I/O_1	11	18	I/O_7
I/O_2	12	17	I/O_6
I/O_3	13	16	I/O_5
GND	14	15	I/O_4

BR6264

There are two versions of the BR6264 available. In the standard version, the normal current consumption is rated for a maximum of 90 mA. In the standby mode, the standard BR6264's current consumption drops to a maximum value of just 2 mA.

A low-power version of the BR6264 is also available. In this version of the chip, the maximum current consumption in normal operation is rated for 85 mA. In the standby mode, the current consumed by the low-power BR6264 is rated for a maximum value of 100 μA.

The access time for this chip is quite fast. The typical rating is 100 ns, with 120 ns as the maximum.

This IC features two chip-select inputs, to permit convenient battery back-up applications. In addition, an output enable is included to make interfacing as easy as possible.

BR93C46 1 K Serial Electrically Erasable EPROM

The BR93C46 is an electrically erasable EPROM (erasable-programmable read-only memory). Early EPROM chips could be erased only by exposure to a strong ultraviolet light. The BR93C46 is designed to be erased with a special electrical signal. If no erase signal is applied, the manufacturer claims data can be retained by the chip for up to 10 years, with or without power applied.

The BR93C46 is rated for up to 10,000 erasures or rewrites per register. The memory in this chip totals 1 K (1,024 bits), arranged as 64 registers of 16 bits apiece.

The BR93C46 is designed to be operated from a single-ended +5-volt power supply. It can be used with either CMOS or TTL circuitry.

Very little power is consumed by this device. In the active mode, the maximum current drawn is rated as a mere 3 mA. In a CMOS circuit, the standby current is rated for no more than 400 μA. In a TTL circuit, the standby current is rated for a maximum value of 1 mA.

The chip names are defined as follows:

CS	Chip Select
DI	Serial Data Input
DO	Serial Data Output
GND	Ground
PE	Program Enable
PRE	Protect Register Enable
SK	Serial Data Clock
V$_{CC}$	Supply Voltage

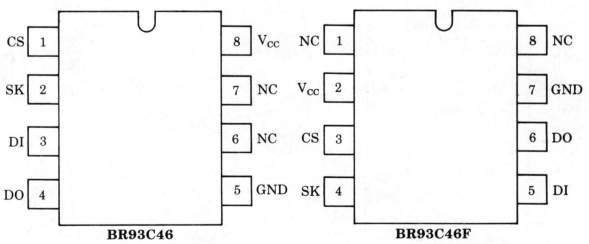

BR93C46   **BR93C46F**

Courtesy of Rohm Corporation

Caution: Note the difference in pinouts.

BR93CS46 1 K Serial Electrically Erasable EPROM

The BR93CS46 is an electrically erasable EPROM (erasable-programmable read-only memory). Early EPROM chips could be erased only by exposure to a strong ultraviolet light. The BR93CS46 is designed to be erased with a special electrical signal. If no erase signal is applied, the manufacturer claims data can be retained by the chip for up to 10 years, with or without power applied.

The BR93CS46 is rated for up to 10,000 erasures or rewrites per register. The memory in this chip totals 1 K (1,024 bits), arranged as 64 registers of 16 bits apiece. The BR93CS46 is designed to be operated from a single-ended power supply of +3 to +5 volts.

Very little power is consumed by this device. In the active mode, the maximum current drawn is rated as a mere 1 mA. In the standby mode, the current drawn is rated for no more than 25 μA.

The BR93CS46 features auto-increment of the register address to permit continuous READ operations.

The chip names are defined as follows:

CS	Chip Select
DI	Serial Data Input
DO	Serial Data Output
GND	Ground
NC	No Connection
SK	Serial Data Clock
V_{CC}	Supply Voltage

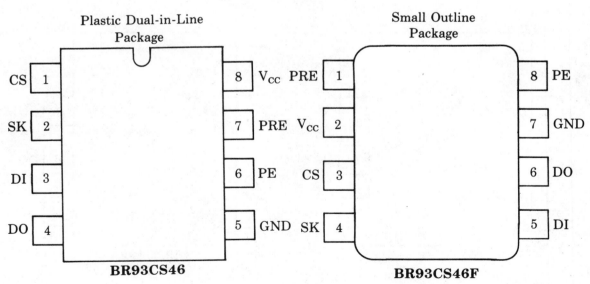

Plastic Dual-in-Line Package

Small Outline Package

BR93CS46

BR93CS46F

Courtesy of Rohm Corporation

Caution: Note the difference in pinouts.

344

5
SECTION

Operational amplifiers

For the linear or analog ICs presented in the remaining sections of this book, pinouts, a schematic or block diagram (where possible), a description, and a list of features, particular specifications, and absolute maximum ratings are included.

Operational amplifiers, or *op amps* are by far the most commonly used and versatile of all types of linear ICs. For this reason they deserve a section of their own.

Basically, an op amp is a differential voltage amplifier. When a single input is used, it may be used in either the inverting or the noninverting mode.

An ideal op amp has infinite open-loop gain. A practical op amp has very high, but finite open-loop gain. In most practical circuits, the gain is limited by providing a suitable negative feedback path between the op amp's output and it's inverting input.

To help you learn about op amp ICs, a mini-glossary precedes our description of the most popular devices.

Op Amp Chip Listing

Operational Amplifiers

input bias current   The average of the two input currents.

input offset current   The absolute value of the difference between the two input currents for which the output will be driven higher than or lower than specified voltages.

input offset voltage   The absolute value of the voltage between the input terminals required to make the output voltage greater than or less than specified voltages.

input voltage range   The range of voltage on the input terminals (common-mode) over which the offset specifications apply.

logic threshold voltage   The voltage at the output of the comparator at which the loading logic circuitry changes it digital state.

negative output level   The negative dc output voltage with the comparator saturated by a differential input equal to or greater than a specified voltage.

output leakage current   The current into the output terminal with the output voltage within a given range and the input drive equal to or greater than a given value.

output resistance   The resistance seen looking into the output terminal with the dc output level at the logic threshold voltage.

output sink current   The maximum negative current that can be delivered by the comparator.

positive output level   The high output voltage level with a given load and the input drive equal to or greater than a specified value.

power consumption   The power required to operate the comparator with no output load. The power will vary with signal level, but is specified as a maximum for the entire range of input signal conditions.

response time   The interval between the application of an input step function and the time when the output crosses the logic threshold voltage. The input step drives the comparator from some initial, saturated input voltage to an input level just barely in excess of that required to bring the output from saturation to the logic threshold voltage. This excess is referred to as the voltage overdrive.

saturation voltage   The low-output voltage level with the input drive equal to or greater than a specified value.

strobe current   The current out of the strobe terminal when it is at the zero logic level.

strobed output level   The dc output voltage, independent of input conditions, with the voltage on the strobe terminal equal to or less than the specified low state.

strobe on voltage   The maximum voltage on either strobe terminal required to force the output to the specified high state independent of the input voltage.

strobe off voltage The minimum voltage on the strobe terminal that will guarantee that it does not interfere with the operation of the comparator.

strobe release time The time required for the output to rise to the logic threshold voltage after the strobe terminal has been driven from 0 to the logic 1 level.

supply current The current required from the positive or negative supply to operate the comparator with no output load. The power will vary with input voltage, but is specified as a maximum for the entire range of input voltage conditions.

voltage gain The ratio of the change in output voltage to the change in voltage between the input terminals producing it.

LM11 Operational Amplifier

The LM11 is one of the oldest operational amplifier ICs still available. It's specifications don't quite match those of some more-modern devices, but it can still be used in a great many practical applications, with excellent results.

In most applications, the LM11 will require external frequency compensation. A special pin for this purpose is included on the chip.

Internal output protection permits the output to be short-circuited indefinitely, without damage to the IC.

Absolute maximum ratings

Total supply voltage	40 V	(±20 V)
Input Current	±10 mA	
Power Dissipation	500 mW	
Common-Mode Rejection		
LM11	130 dB	typ.
LM11C	130 dB	typ.
LM11CL	110 dB	typ.
Supply-Voltage Rejection		
LM11	118 dB	typ.
LM11C	118 dB	typ.
LM11CL	100 dB	typ.
Supply Current	0.3 mA	typ.

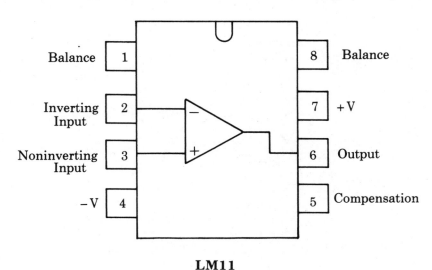

LM11

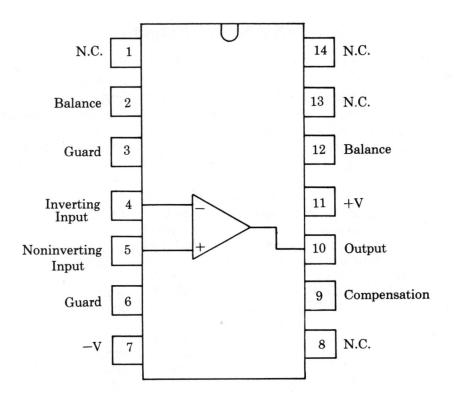

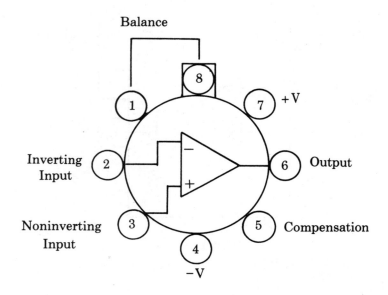

Balance

LM101 Operational Amplifier

The LM101 is another one of the oldest operational amplifier ICs still available. Before the 741 came along, the 101 was the de facto standard that all other op amps were compared to.

The 101's specifications don't quite match some more modern devices, but it can still be used in a great many practical applications with excellent results.

In most applications, the 101 will require external phase compensation and offset nulling. Special pins for this purpose are included on the chip.

Supply Voltage	10 V ($\pm$5V) min.
	40 V ($\pm$20 V) max.
Power Dissipation	50 mW typ.
Common-Mode Rejection	90 dB typ.
Power-Supply Rejection	90 dB typ.
Open-Loop Voltage Gain	160,000 max.

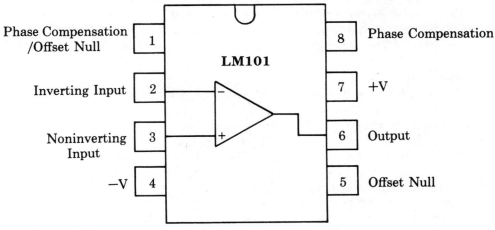

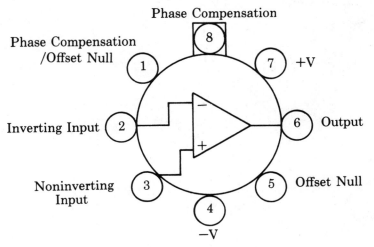

LM124/LM224/LM324, LM124A/LM224A/LM324A, LM2902 Low-Power Quad Operational Amplifiers

The LM124 series consists of four independent, high-gain, internally frequency-compensated operational amplifiers that were designed specifically to operate from a single power supply over a wide range of voltages. Operation from split power supplies is also possible and the low power-supply current drain is independent of the magnitude of the power-supply voltage.

Application areas include transducer amplifiers, dc-gain blocks and all the conventional op-amp circuits, which now can be more easily implemented in single power-supply systems. For example, the LM124 series can be directly operated from the standard $+5$ V_{dc} power-supply voltage that is used in digital systems. The voltage will easily provide the required interface electronics without requiring additional ± 15 V_{dc} power supplies.

In the linear mode, the input common-mode voltage range includes ground and the output voltage can also swing to ground, even though operated from only a single power-supply voltage. The unity-gain cross frequency is temperature-compensated. The input bias current is also temperature-compensated.

Dc Voltage Gain	100 dB
Bandwidth (Unity Gain)	1 MHz
Power Supply Range:	
Single Supply	3 to 30 Vdc
or Dual Supplies	$\pm$ 1.5 to $\pm$ 15 Vdc
Supply Current Drain	800 μA – Essentially independent of supply voltage (1 mW/op amp at $+$ 5 Vdc)
Input Biasing Current	45 nAdc
Input Offset Voltage	2 mVdc
Offset Current	5 nAdc
Output Voltage Swing	0 to V+ $-$ 1.5 Vdc

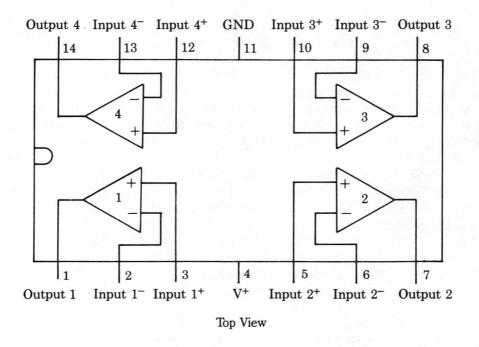

Output 4 · Input 4⁻ Input 4⁺ GND Input 3⁺ Input 3⁻ Output 3

Top View

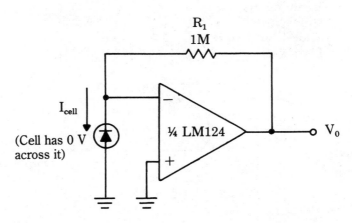

LM124

353

353 Wide-Bandwidth Dual-JFET Operational Amplifier

The 353 contains two high-quality operational-amplifier stages in a single 8-pin package. These op amps are easy to use because they have no special-purpose pins. All eight pins are taken up with the supply-voltage connections, and the inputs and outputs for each of the two operational-amplifier stages. Except for the power-supply connections, the two op-amp stages are completely independent of each other.

The 353 features full internal-frequency and phase compensation.

The 353 operational amplifiers use well-matched high-voltage JFET input devices, so they exhibit an extremely high input impedance, and very low input-bias and offset currents. Other advantages of the 353 are minimal offset-voltage drift and very low noise. These features make op amps very well suited to high-fidelity audio and data-transmission applications.

Thanks to internal output-protection circuitry, the output of either op amp in the 353 can be safely short-circuited for an indefinite period of time.

Supply Voltage	36 V ($\pm$18 V) max.
Power Dissipation	500 mW typ.
Input Voltage	$\pm$ 15 V max.
Differential-Input Voltage	$\pm$ 30 V max.
Wide-Gain Bandwidth	4 MHz
Slew Rate	13 V/μS

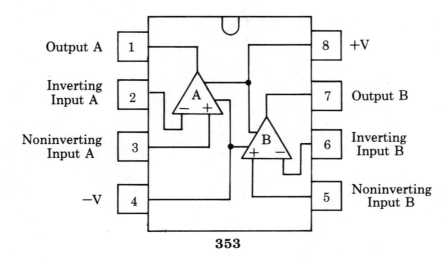

353

354

LM709/LM709A/LM709C Operational Amplifier

The LM709 series is a monolithic operational amplifier intended for general-purpose applications. Operation is completely specified over the range of voltages commonly used for these devices. The design, in addition to providing high gain, minimizes both offset voltage and bias currents. Further, the class-B output stage gives a large output capability with minimum power drain.

External components are used to frequency-compensate the amplifier. Although the specified unity-gain compensation network will make the amplifier unconditionally stable in all feedback configurations, compensation can be tailored to optimize high-frequency performance for any gain setting.

Since the amplifier is built on a single silicon chip, it provides low offset and temperature drift at a minimum cost. It also ensures negligible drift as a result of temperature gradients in the vicinity of the amplifier.

The LM709C is the industrial version of the LM709. It is identical to the LM709/LM709A, except that it is specified for operation from 0°C to +70°C.

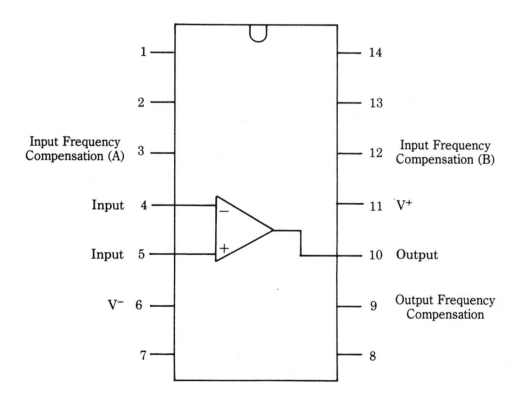

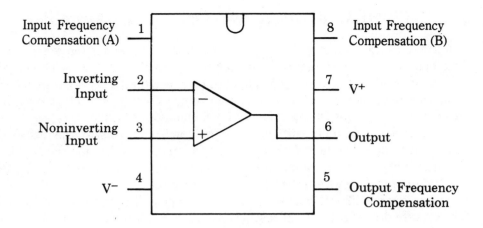

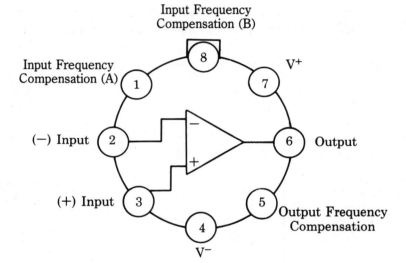

Note: Pin 4 connected to case.

LM709

BA718 Dual Operational Amplifier

The 718 contains a pair of independent operational amplifiers in a single 9-pin SIP (single inline package) housing. These op amps are very easy to use because the only connections made to the chip are the supply voltages and the inverting and noninverting inputs and output for each op amp.

The 718's op amp feature internal phase compensation. The op amp outputs are short-circuit protected.

This device can be operated from either a dual-polarity or a single-polarity power supply. Even if a single-ended (positive) supply voltage is used with the 718, a negative voltage can be included in the common-mode input voltage range.

Supply Voltage	3 to 18 V
	$\pm$ 1.5 to $\pm$ 9 V
Current Consumption	1.5 mA (typ.)
Power Dissipation	450 mW (max.)
Common-Mode Rejection Ratio	90 dB (typ.)
Differential Input Voltage	18 V (max.)

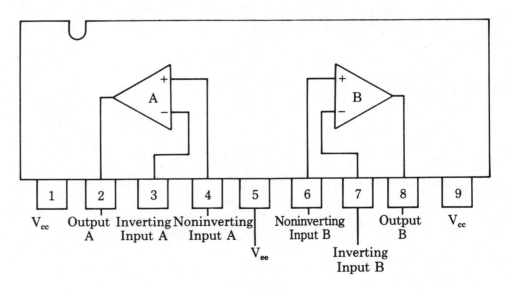

BA718

BA728, BA728F Dual Operational Amplifier

The 728 contains a pair of independent operational amplifiers in a single 8-pin DIP (dual-inline package) housing. Other than the packaging, the 728 is identical to the 718, discussed previously.

The op amps within the 728 are very easy to use because the only connections made to the chip are the supply voltages and the inverting and noninverting inputs and output for each op amp.

The 728's op amps feature internal-phase compensation. The op-amp outputs are short-circuit protected.

This device can be operated from either a dual-polarity or a single-polarity power supply. Even if a single-ended (positive) supply voltage is used with the 728, a negative voltage can be included in the common-mode input voltage range.

Supply Voltage	3 to 18 V
	$\pm$ 1.5 to $\pm$ 9 V
Current Consumption	1.5 mA (typ.)
Power Dissipation	450 mW (max.)
Common-Mode Rejection Ratio	90 dB (typ.)
Differential Input Voltage	18 V (max.)

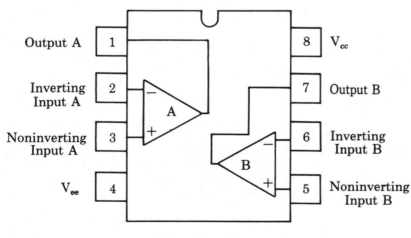

BA728/BA728F

LM741/LM741A/LM741C/LM741E Operational Amplifier

The LM741 series are general-purpose operational amplifiers that feature improved performance over industry standards, like the LM709. They are direct, plug-in replacements for the 709C, LM201, MC1439, and 748 in most applications.

The amplifiers offer many features that make their application nearly foolproof: overload protection on the input and output, no latch-up when the common-mode range is exceeded, as well as freedom from oscillations. The LM741C/LM741E is identical to the LM741/LM741A, except that the LM741C/LM741E has its performance guaranteed over a 0°C to +70°C temperature range, instead of −55°C to +125°C.

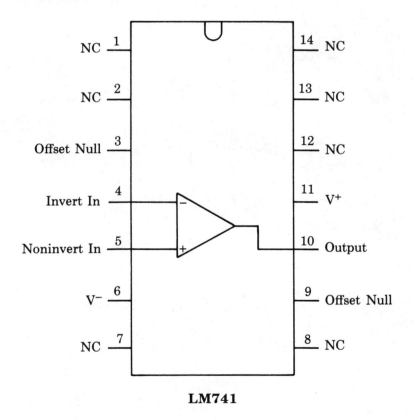

LM741

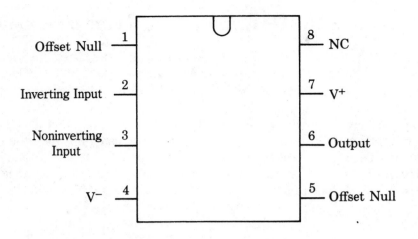

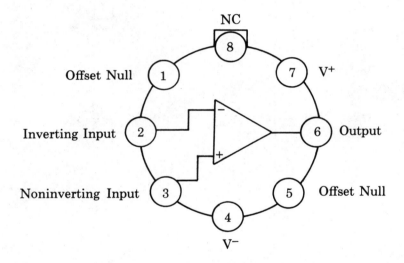

Note: Pin 4 connected to case.

LM747/LM747A/LM747C/LM747E
Dual Operational Amplifier

The LM747 series are general-purpose dual operational amplifiers. The two amplifiers share a common-bias network and power-supply leads. Otherwise, their operation is completely independent. Features include:

- No frequency compensation required
- Short-circuit protection
- Wide common-mode and differential voltage ranges
- Low power consumption
- No latch-up
- Balanced offset null

The LM747C/LM747E is identical to the LM747/LM747A except that the LM747C/LM747E has its specifications guaranteed over the temperature range from 0°C to +70°C instead of −55°C to +125°C.

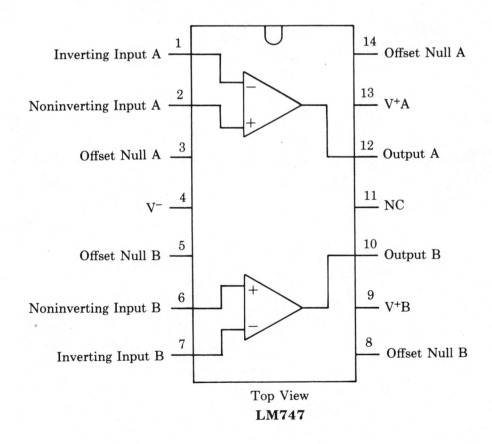

Top View
LM747

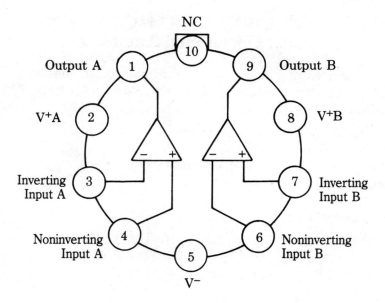

NC

Output A   1

Output B

V^+A 2

8   V^+B

Inverting
Input A   3

7   Inverting
Input B

Noninverting
Input A   4

6   Noninverting
Input B

5

V^-

Top View

LM748/LM748C Operational Amplifier

The LM748/LM748C is a general-purpose operational amplifier built on a single silicon chip. The resulting close match and tight thermal coupling gives low offsets and temperature drift as well as fast recovery from thermal transients. In addition, the device features:

- Frequency compensation with a single 30 pF capacitor
- Operation from ±5 to ±20 V
- Low current drain—1.8 mA at ±20 V
- Continuous short-circuit protection
- Operation as a comparator with differential inputs as high as ±30 V
- No latch-up when common mode range is exceeded.
- Same pin configuration as the LM101.

The unity-gain compensation specified makes the circuit stable for all feedback configurations, even with capacitive loads. However, it is possible to optimize compensation for best high-frequency performance at any gain. As a comparator, the output can be clamped at any desired level to make it compatible with logic circuits.

The LM748 is specified for operation over the −55°C to ±125°C military temperature range. The LM748C is specified for operation over the 0°C to +70°C temperature range.

Inverting Amplifier with Balancing Circuit

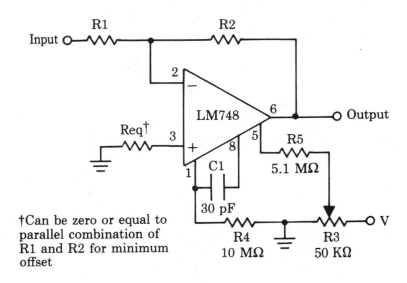

†Can be zero or equal to parallel combination of R1 and R2 for minimum offset

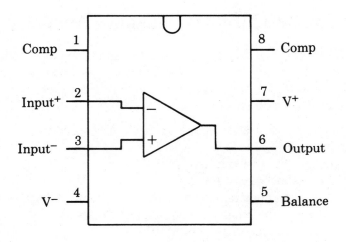

Top View

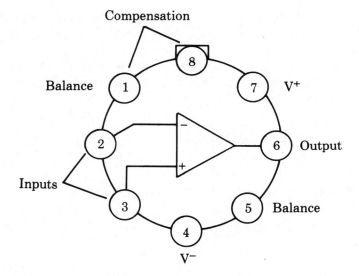

Compensation

Balance

Inputs

V⁺

Output

Balance

V⁻

Note: Pin 4 connected to case.

LM748

LM1458/LM1558 Dual Operational Amplifier

The LM1458 and LM1558 are general-purpose dual operational amplifiers. The two amplifiers share a common-bias network and power-supply leads. Otherwise, their operation is completely independent. Features include:

- No frequency compensation required
- Short-circuit protection
- Wide common-mode and differential voltage ranges
- Low-power consumption
- 8-lead TO-5 and 8-lead mini-DP
- No latch-up when the input common-mode range is exceeded

The LM1458 is identical to the LM1558 except that the LM1458 has its specifications guaranteed over the temperature range from 0°C to 70°C instead of the −55°C to +125°C range of the LM1558.

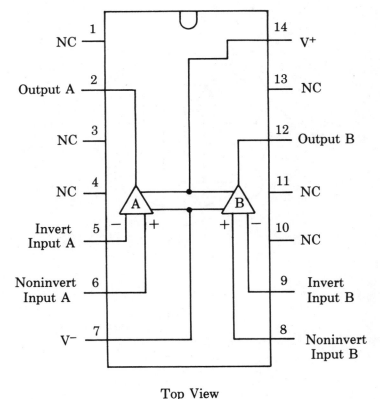

Top View

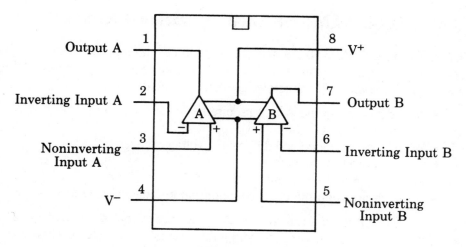

Output A   1   8   V⁺

Inverting Input A   2   7   Output B

Noninverting Input A   3   6   Inverting Input B

V⁻   4   5   Noninverting Input B

Top View

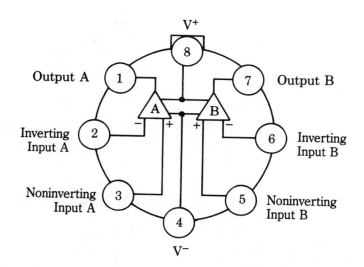

Top View

LM1558

LM1900/LM2900/LM3900, LM3301, LM3401
Quad Amplifier

The LM1900 series consists of four independent, dual input, internally compensated amplifiers that were designed specifically to operate from a single power supply voltage and to provide a large output voltage swing. These amplifiers make use of a current mirror to achieve the noninverting input function. They are used as ac amplifiers; RC active filters; low-frequency triangle-square- and pulse-wave generation circuits; tachometers and low-speed high-voltage digital logic gates. Features include:

- Wide single supply voltage range or dual supplies 4 to 36 V_{dc}
  ±2 to ±18 V_{dc}
- Supply current drain independent of supply voltage
- Low input-biasing current   30nA
- High open-loop gain   70dB
- Wide bandwidth   2.5 MHz (unity gain)
- Large output voltage swing $(V+ -1) V_{p-p}$
- Internally frequency compensated for unity gain
- Output short-circuit protection

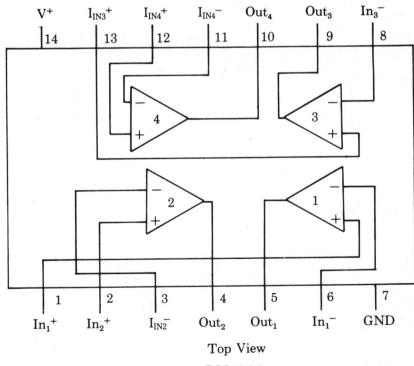

Top View

LM1900

CA3008-Operational Amplifier

The CA3008 is a general-purpose amplifier used in narrow-band and band-pass amplifier, feedback amplifier, dc and video amplifier, multivibrator, oscillator, comparator, and servo-driver applications. It comes in a 14-lead ceramic-and-metal flat package.

Max. Positive dc Supply Voltage	+10 V
Max. Negative dc Supply Voltage	−10 V
Max. Input Signal Voltage (single-ended)	+, −4 V
Max. Total Device Dissipation	300 mW
Typ. Input Offset Voltage	1.08 mV
Typ. Input Offset Current	0.54 μA
Typ. Input Bias Current	5.3 μA

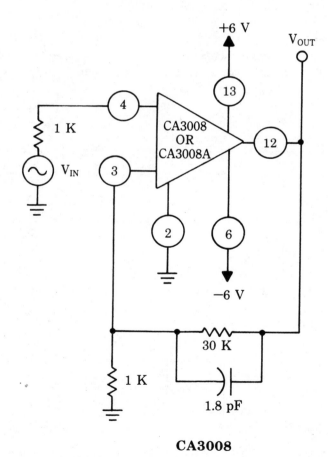

CA3008

CA3037A-Operational Amplifier

The CA3037A is a general-purpose amplifier used in narrow-band and band-pass amplifier, feedback amplifier, dc and video amplifier, multivibrator, oscillator, comparator, and servo-driver applications. It comes in a 14-lead TO-116 dual-in-line ceramic package.

Typ. Input Offset Voltage	0.9 mV
Typ. Input Offset Current	0.3 μA
Typ. Input Bias Current	2.5 μA
Typ. Input Impedance	20 kΩ
Typ. Output Impedance	160 Ω
Typ. Noise Figure	8.3 dB

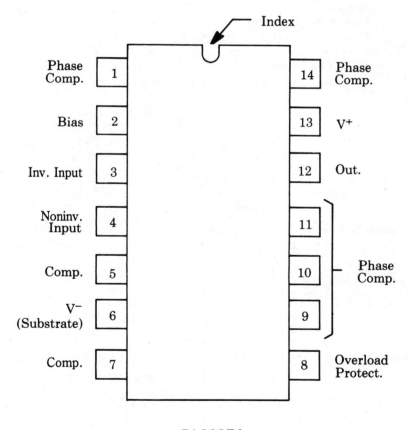

CA3037A

BA4560 Dual High-Slew-Rate Operational Amplifier

The 4560 contains a pair of high-quality operational amplifiers in a simple 8-pin DIP housing.

These two op amps are very easy to use because there are no special-purpose pins. All eight pins are taken up with the supply-voltage connections, and the inputs and outputs for each of the two op-amp stages. Except for the power-supply connections, the two op-amp stages are completely independent of each other.

The op amp within the 4560 offer excellent frequency response, slew rate, and high output-current capacity.

Supply Voltage	36 V ($\pm$ 18 V) max.
Power Dissipation	500 mW max.
Differential Input Voltage	$\pm$ 30 V max.
Slew Rate	4 V/μS
Gain-Bandwidth Product	10 MHz
Common-Mode Rejection Ratio	90 dB typ.

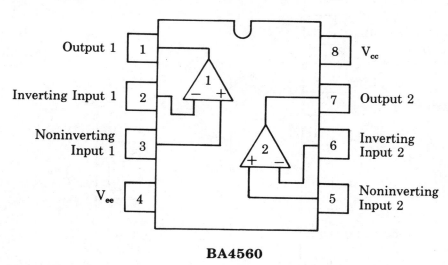

BA4560

BA4561 High-Slew-Rate Operational Amplifier

The 4561 contains a pair of high-quality operational amplifiers in a simple 9-pin SIP (single-inline package) housing. All 9 pins are arranged in one continuous row. The packaging is the only difference between the 4561 and the 4560 (discussed previously). Electrically, they are identical. The V_{cc} connection is provided twice on the 4561.

These two op amps are very easy to use because there are no special-purpose pins. All eight pins are taken up with the supply-voltage connections, and the inputs and outputs for each of the two op-amp stages. Except for the power-supply connections, the two op-amp stages are completely independent of one another.

The op amps within the 4561 offer excellent frequency response, slew rate, and high output-current capacity.

Supply Voltage	36 V ($\pm$ 18 V max.
Power Dissipation	500 mW max.
Differential Input Voltage	$\pm$ 30 V max.
Slew Rate	4 V/μS
Gain-Bandwidth Product	10 MHz
Common-Mode Rejection Ratio	90 dB typ.

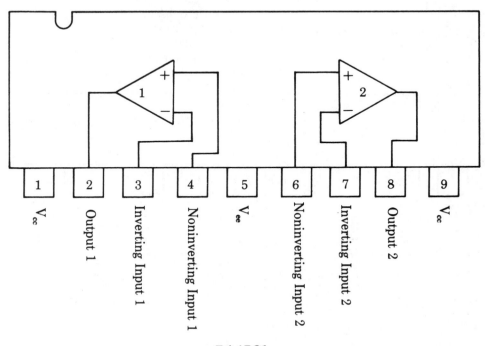

BA4561

BA6110 Voltage-Controlled Operational Amplifier

The 6110 is contained within a simple 9-pin SIP (single-inline package) housing. All nine pins are arranged in one continuous row.

The forward transconductance (gm) of the 6110 op amp is programmable over a wide range with high linearity. In effect, the op amp's gain can be controlled via an external signal; thus, this is a voltage-controlled op amp. Actually, the control signal is accepted by the chip in the form of a current, but by simply adding a resistor in series with the control input (pin #4), a more convenient control voltage can be used.

The open-loop gain of the 6110 is set by the applied control current and external gain resistor (R1).

The 6110 also features an on-chip low-impedance output buffer. This internal buffer can be used to simplify external circuitry and to minimize the overall parts count of the complete circuit.

The op amp used in the 6110 is a high-quality device, featuring low noise, low distortion, and low offset.

Supply Voltage	34 V ($\pm$17 V) max.
Power Dissipation	500 mW max.
Quiescent Current	0.9 mA min.
	3.0 mA typ.
	6.0 mA max.
Forward Transconductance	4800 $\mu\Omega$ min.
	8000 $\mu\Omega$ typ.
	12000 $\mu\Omega$ max.

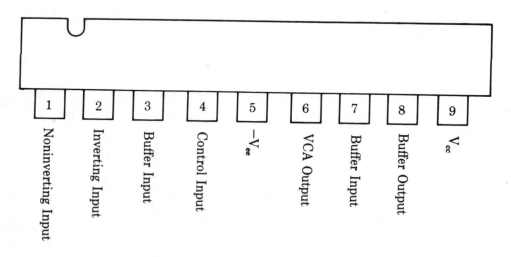

1. Noninverting Input
2. Inverting Input
3. Buffer Input
4. Control Input
5. $-V_{ee}$
6. VCA Output
7. Buffer Input
8. Buffer Output
9. V_{cc}

BA6110

BA14741A, BA14741AF Quad Operational Amplifier

The 14741 contains four independent high-grade operational amplifiers in a single 14-pin DIP housing. These op amps are very easy to use because there are no special-purpose pins. All eight pins are taken up with the supply-voltage connections, and the inputs and outputs for each of the four op-amp stages.

The four op amps within the 14741 feature internal-phase compensation.

Unlike most other (especially earlier) op-amp chips, the 14741 can be operated from either a dual-polarity (+), or a single-polarity (+) power supply.

Supply Voltage Range	$\pm$ 2 to $\pm$ 18 V
Power Dissipation	
BA14741A	600 mW max.
BA14741AF	450 mW max.
Slew Rate	1.0 V/μS
Output Voltage	$\pm$ 12.5 V typ.
Common-Mode Rejection Ratio	100 dB typ.

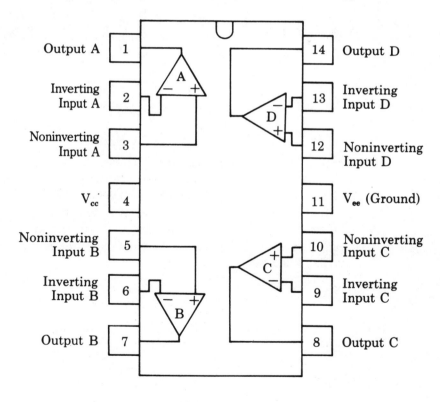

BA14741A/BA14741AF

6
SECTION

Audio amplifiers

Probably the most commonly used type of electronic circuit is the amplifier. Almost all electronic systems of any complexity include at least one amplifier stage.

In this section we will look at ICs designed for the amplification of signals within the audio-frequency (af) range. In section 7, we will move on to radio-frequency (rf) amplifiers and related devices.

Audio Amplifier IC Listing

LM377 Dual 2-Watt Audio Amplifier

The LM377 is a monolithic dual power amplifier which offers high quality performance for stereo phonographs, tape players, recorders AM-FM stereo receivers, etc. The LM377 will deliver 2 W per channel into 8 Ω or 16 Ω loads. The amplifier is designed to operate with a minimum of external components and contains an internal bias regulator to bias each amplifier. Device overload protection consists of both internal current limit and thermal shutdown. Features include:

- Avo typical 90 dB
- 2 W per channel
- 70-dB ripple rejection
- 75-dB channel separation
- Internal stabilization
- Self-centered biasing
- 3 MΩ input impedance
- 10 to 26 V operation
- Internal current limiting
- Internal thermal protection

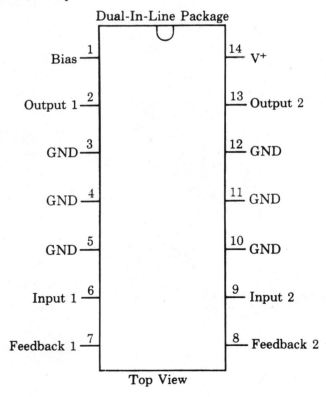

Dual-In-Line Package

Bias — 1	14 — V+
Output 1 — 2	13 — Output 2
GND — 3	12 — GND
GND — 4	11 — GND
GND — 5	10 — GND
Input 1 — 6	9 — Input 2
Feedback 1 — 7	8 — Feedback 2

Top View

Simple Stereo Amplifier

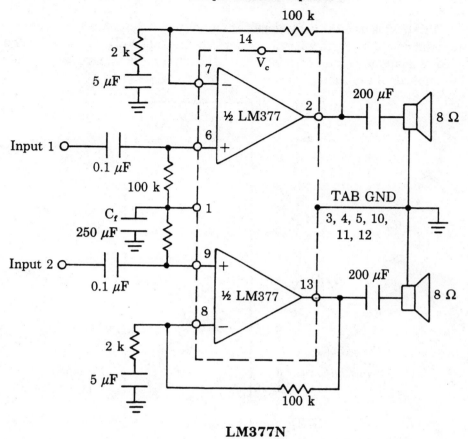

LM377N

LM380 Audio Power Amplifier

The LM380 is a power audio amplifier for consumer application. In order to hold system cost to a minimum, gain is internally fixed at 34 dB. A unique input stage allows inputs to be ground referenced. The output is automatically self-entering to one-half of the supply voltage.

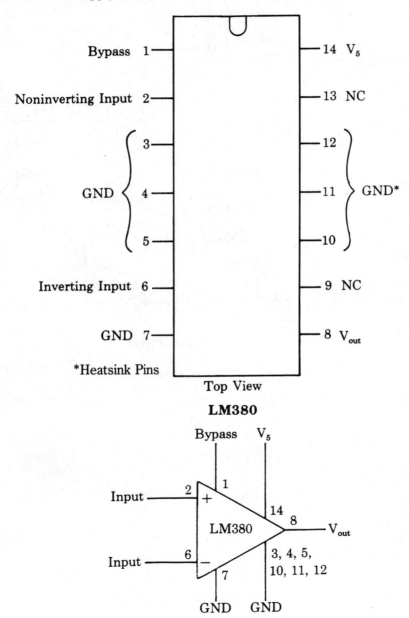

Top View

LM380

The output is short-circuit proof with internal thermal limiting. The package outline is standard dual-in-line. A copper lead frame is used with the center three pins on either side, comprising a heat sink. This makes the device easy to use in standard pc layout.

Uses include simple phonograph amplifiers, intercoms, line drivers, teaching-machine outputs, alarms, ultrasonic drivers, TV sound systems, AM-FM radio, small servo drivers, power converters, etc.

A selected part for more power on higher supply voltages is available as the LM384. Features include:

- Wide supply-voltage range
- Low quiescent power drain
- Voltage gain fixed at 50
- High peak-current capability
- Input referenced to GND
- High input impedance
- Low distortion
- Quiescent output voltage is at one-half of the supply voltage
- Standard dual-in-line package

LM381/LM381A Low-Noise Dual Preamplifier

The LM381/LM381A is a dual pre-amp for the application of low-level signals in applications requiring optimum noise performance. Each of the two amplifiers is completely independent, with individual internal power supply decoupler-regulator, providing 120-dB supply rejection and 60-dB channel separation. Other outstanding features include high gain (112 dB), large output voltage swing (V_{CC} − 2 V) p-p, and wide power bandwidth (75 kHz, 20 V) p-p. The LM381/LM381A operates from a single supply across the wide range of 9 to 40 V.

Either differential input or single-ended input configurations can be selected. The amplifier is internally compensated with the provision for additional external compensation for narrow-band applications.

- Low noise—0.5 μV total input noise
- High gain—112-dB open loop
- Single supply operation
- Wide supply range—9 V to 40 V
- Power supply rejection—120 dB
- Large output voltage swing (V_{CC} to 2 V) p-p
- Wide bandwidth—15 MHz unity gain
- Power bandwidth—75 kHz, 20 V p-p
- Internally compensated
- Short-circuit protected

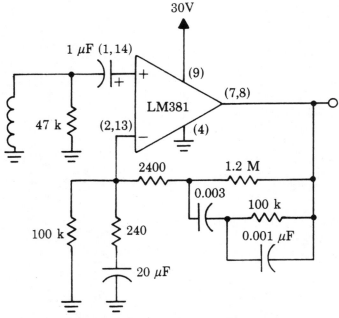

Typical Magnetic Phono Preamp

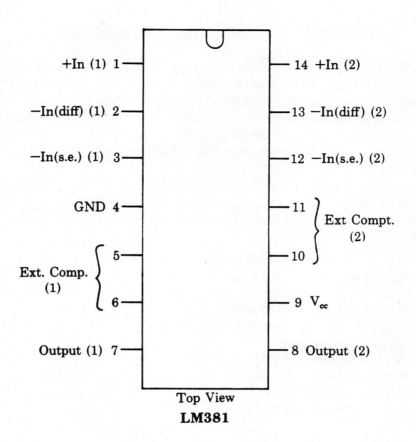

Top View
LM381

LM382 Low-Noise Dual Preamplifier

The LM382 is a dual preamplifier for the amplification of low-level signals in applications requiring optimum noise performance. Each of the two amplifiers is completely independent, with individual internal power supply decoupler regulators, providing 120-dB supply rejection and 60-dB channel separation. Other outstanding features include high gain (100 dB), and wide power bandwidth (75 kHz, 20 V) p-p. The LM382 operates from a single supply across the wide range of 9 to 40 V.

A resistor matrix is provided on the chip to allow the user to select a variety of closed-loop gain options and frequency-response characteristics such as flatband, NAB, or RIAA equalization. The circuit is supplied in the 14-lead dual-inline package.

- Low noise—0.8-μV total equivalent input noise
- High gain—100-dB open loop
- Single supply operation
- Wide supply range—9 to 40 V
- Power supply rejection—120 dB
- Large output voltage swing
- Wide bandwidth—15 MHz unity gain
- Power bandwidth—75 kHz, 20 V p-p
- Internally compensated
- Short-circuit protected

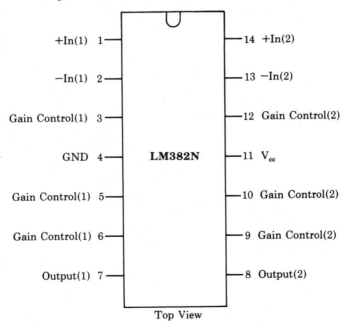

Top View

LM386 Low-Voltage Audio Power Amplifier

The '386 is closely related to the '380 (discussed earlier in this section). The big advantage of the '386 is that it is designed for very low power requirements, making this chip an excellent choice for battery-powered applications.

The '386 can be reliably driven from a power source as low as 4 volts. In the quiescent (no input signal) state, the power consumption is a mere 18 mW, assuming a 6-volt power supply is being used.

In many practical circuits using the '386, overall parts count tends to be quite low. The amplifier's gain is internally set to 20. If more gain is required, the circuit can easily be modified by adding an external resistor and capacitor between pins 1 and 8. The gain can be increased by up to 200.

The '386's inputs are referenced to ground. Internal circuitry within the device automatically bias the output signal to one half the supply voltage.

The amplifier is designed to drive low-impedance loads, such as 8-Ω or 16-Ω speakers, directly.

Supply Voltage	+15 V Max.
Power Dissipation	660 mW Max.
Quiescent Current Consumption	3 mA typ.

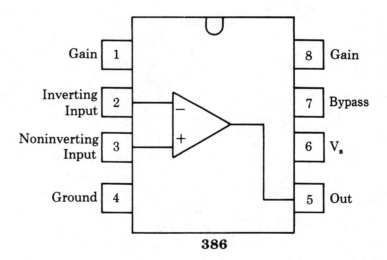

386

LM1303 Stereo Preamplifier

The LM1303 consists of two identical operational amplifiers constructed on a single silicon chip. Intended for amplification of low-level stereo signals, the LM1303 features low input noise voltage, high open-loop voltage gain, large output voltage swing and short circuit protection.

Output Voltage Swing	4.0 V rms min.
Open-Loop Voltage Gain	6,000 min.
Channel Separation	60 dB min. at 10 kHz

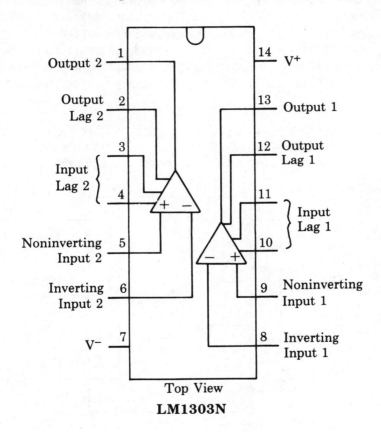

Top View
LM1303N

TDA1520A 20-Watt Hi-Fi Audio Amplifier

Most audio-amplifier ICs can only put out fairly small amounts of power—typically just a watt or two, or even less. The TDA1520A is designed for more "heft." This amplifier IC can drive 4-Ω or 8-Ω speakers with up to 20 watts.

The power supply for this chip can be either symmetrical or asymmetrical. Of course, to achieve the relatively high power output levels of the TDA1520A, a rather large power supply is required.

Supply Voltage	50 V Max.
Total Quiescent Current	
(Supply Voltage = 33 V)	70 mA Max.
Closed-Loop Voltage Gain	30 dB Max.

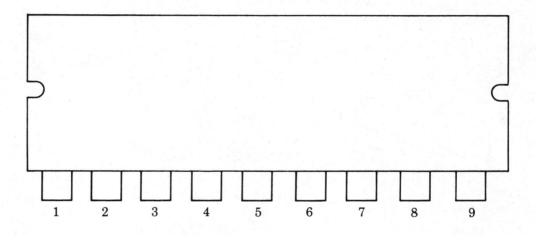

1 Noninverting Input
2 Input Ground (Substrate)
3 Compensation
4 Negative Supply (Ground)
5 Output
6 Positive Supply (V_p)
7 No Connection
8 Ripple Rejection
9 Inverting Input (Feedback)

TDA1520A

CA3007 Audio Amplifier

The CA3007 is a special-purpose audio amplifier used in audio-driver applications, sound systems, and communications equipment. It comes in a 12-lead TO-5 package.

Max. Positive Dc Supply Voltage	+ 10 V
Max. Negative Dc Supply Voltage	− 10 V
Max. Input Signal Voltage:	
Single-ended	± 2.5 V
Common mode	± 2.5 V
Max. Total Device Dissipation	300 mW
Typ. Input Unbalance Voltage	0.57 mV
Typ. Input Unbalance Current	0.57 μA
Typ. Input Bias Current	11 μA

TCA5550 Stereo Sound-Control System

The TCA5550 is designed to perform several "front end" audio applications in a single chip, including stereo balance, volume, and tone (bass and treble) control.

The chip is designed to accept simple dc voltage inputs, to permit convenient control over the functions with four inexpensive and readily available potentiometers. The use of dc voltages as control signals, also makes the '5550 well-suited for use in remote-control applications.

The overall frequency response for the bass and treble tone controls are set by a single external capacitor for each control in each channel. Separate response-setting capacitors are used for the bass and treble sections, for maximum flexibility.

The distortion introduced by this chip is very low. The manufacturer claims a distortion rating of 0.1% at nominal input level, assuming unity gain, and all tone controls set to a "flat" response.

The volume-control range of the TCA5550 can cover up to 75 dB. This chip also has a wide dynamic range, accepting input signals ranging from 100 mV to 500 mV rms.

Max. Supply Voltage	18 V
Min. Supply Voltage	10 V
Max. Power Dissipation	1.25 W
Supply Current	
Min. Gain	30 mA
Max. Gain	15 mA
Typ. Input Impedance	100,000 Ω
Typ. Output Impedance	300 Ω
Min. Channel Separation	45 dB

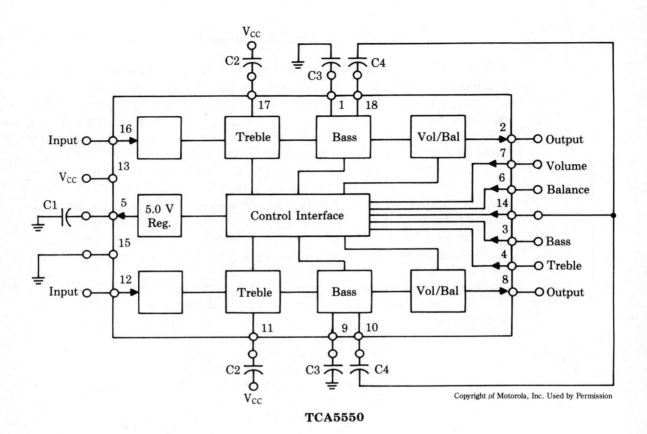

Copyright of Motorola, Inc. Used by Permission

TCA5550

388

MC13060 Mini-Watt Audio-Output Amplifier

The '13060 is a rugged and versatile general-purpose audio amplifier capable of a two-watt output. The output is independent of the supply voltage over a fairly wide range. The chip can be powered by supply voltages ranging from 6 to 35 vdc.

The output signal voltage and the power-supply current drain are very linearly related. Both are quite constant over a wide range of supply voltages.

The gain of the amplifier is determined by external components. Circuits using the '13060 are generally quite simple, with a minimal component count. The device is very easy to use. Four of the eight pins are simply shorted to ground for heat-sinking, leaving just four active pins. The chip features self-protecting thermal-shutdown circuitry.

Max. Supply Voltage	35 V
Max. Audio Input (pin 5)	1 V
Typ. Quiescent Current	13 mA
Typ. Gain	50 V/V
Typ. Input Impedance	28 kΩ

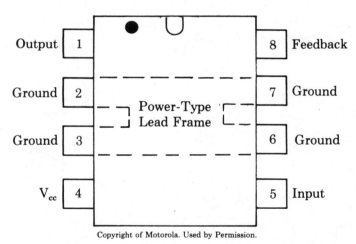

MC13060

MC34119 Low-Power Audio Amplifier

The MC34119 is a low-power audio amplifier, with an output power of up to 250 mW with a 32-Ω load. This chip was designed primarily for use in telephone applications, such as in speakerphones.

This amplifier provides differential speaker outputs to maximize output swing even at low supply voltages. The '34119 requires a minimum of 2.0 volts to operate. Coupling capacitors to the speaker are not required with this amplifier chip.

The maximum open-loop gain for this IC is 80 dB. This gain can be reduced with closed-loop feedback, simply by adding a pair of external resistors to the circuit. The amplifier gain is adjustable from 0 to more than 46 dB for the voice frequencies.

An unusual feature of this amplifier IC is the chip-disable pin. This input permits powering down, and/or muting of the input signal.

Two package styles are used with the MC34119—a standard 8-pin DIP housing, and an 8-pin surface-mount package.

Max. Supply Voltage	+18 V
Min. Volts	**−1**
Preferred range	+2 to +16 V
Typ. Quiescent Current	2.7 mA
Typ. Total Harmonic Distortion	0.5%
Output Load Impedance	8 Ω mim.
	100 Ω max.
Max. Peak Load Current	± 200 mA

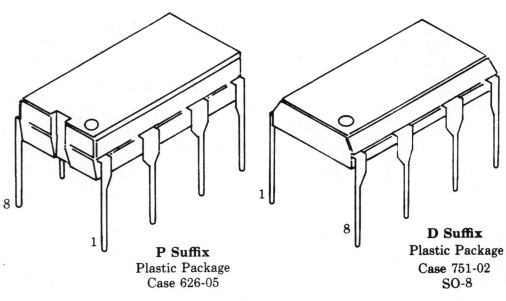

8

1

P Suffix
Plastic Package
Case 626-05

1

8

D Suffix
Plastic Package
Case 751-02
SO-8

Block Diagram and Typical Application Circuit

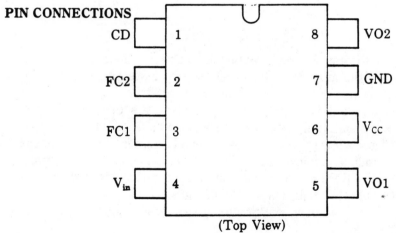

* = Optional

Differential Gain $= 2 \times \dfrac{R_f}{R_i}$

PIN CONNECTIONS

CD	1	8	VO2
FC2	2	7	GND
FC1	3	6	V_{CC}
V_{in}	4	5	VO1

(Top View)

ORDERING INFORMATION		
Device	**Temperature Range**	**Package**
MC34119P	−20°C to + 70°C	Plastic DIP
MC34119D		Plastic SOIC

391

7
SECTION

Rf amplifiers & related devices

Probably the most commonly used type of electronic circuit is the amplifier. Almost all electronic systems of any complexity include at least one amplifier stage.

In this section we will look at ICs designed for the amplification of signals within the radio-frequency (rf) range, and a few related devices. These ICs are intended for use in radio and television receivers and communications systems.

Because rf circuits operate at much higher signal frequencies than audio circuits, greater care must be taken when working on circuit layouts, lead lengths, and heatsinks.

Rf IC Listing

LM733, LM733C	Differential Video Amplifier
TDA1190P, TDA3190P	TV Sound System
LM1304, LM1305, LM1307, LM1307F	FM Multiplex Stereo Demodulator
LM1310	Phase-Locked-Loop FM Stereo Demodulator
MC1330A1P	Low-Level Video Detector
MC1350	IF Amplifier
LM1351	FM Detector, Limiter, and Audio Amplifier
MC1374	TV Modulator Circuit
MC1377	Color Television RGB-to-PAL/NTSC Encoder
MC1378	Color-Television Composite-Video-Overlay Synchronizer
MC1391P	TV Horizontal Processor
BA1404	Stereo Transmitter
MC1496/MC1596	Balanced Modulator/Demodulator
MC2831A	Low-Power FM Transmitter System
MC2833	Low-Power FM Transmitter System
CA3001	Video- and Wideband Amplifier
CA3002	If Amplifier
CA3005	Rf Amplifier
CA3011	FM If Amplifier
CA3013	FM If Amplifier/Discriminator/Af Amplifier
CA3023	Video- and Wideband Amplifier
TDA3301, TDA3303	TV-Color Processor
TDA3330	TV-Color Processor
TDA3333	TV Color-Difference Demodulator
MC3356	Wideband FSK Receiver
MC3357	Low-Power FM If
MC3362	Low-Power Narrowband FM If
MC3363	Low-Power Dual-Conversion FM Receiver
MC3367	Low-Voltage Narrowband-FM Receiver
TDA4500A	FM Stereo Demodulator
TDA7000	FM Receiver
MC10320	Triple 4-Bit Color Palette Video DAC
MC13001XP	Monomax® Black & White TV Subsystem

MC13010P	TV Parallel Sound If/AFT
MC13014P	Monomax® Companion Audio/Vertical Subsystem
MC13020P	C-Quam® AM Stereo Decoder
MC13021	C-Quam® AM Stereo Tuning Stabilizer
MC13022	C-Quam® Advanced Medium-Voltage AM Stereo Decoder
MC13024	C-Quam Low-Voltage AM Stereo Receiver
MC13041	AM Receiver Subsystem
MC13055	Wideband FSK Receiver
MC44802	PLL Tuning Circuit with 1.3 GHz Prescaler

LM733/LM733C Differential Video Amplifier

The LM733/LM733C is a two-stage, differential input, differential output, wideband video amplifier. The use of internal series-shunt feedback gives wide bandwidth with low phase distortion and high gain stability. Emitter-follower outputs provide a high current drive, low-impedance capability. Its 120-MHz bandwidth and selectable gains of 10, 100, and 400, without need for frequency compensation, make it a very useful circuit for memory element drivers, pulse amplifiers, and wideband linear gain stages.

The LM733 is specified for operation over the $-55°C$ to $+125°C$ military temperature range. The LM733C is specified for operation over the $0°C$ to $+70°C$ temperature range. Features include:

- 120-MHz bandwidth
- 250 $k\Omega$ input resistance
- Selectable gains of 10, 100, 400
- No frequency compensation
- High common-mode rejection ratio at high frequencies

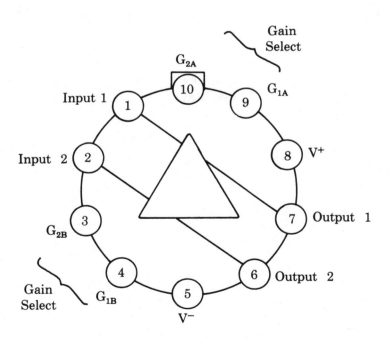

Note: Pin 5 connected to case.
Top View
LM733H

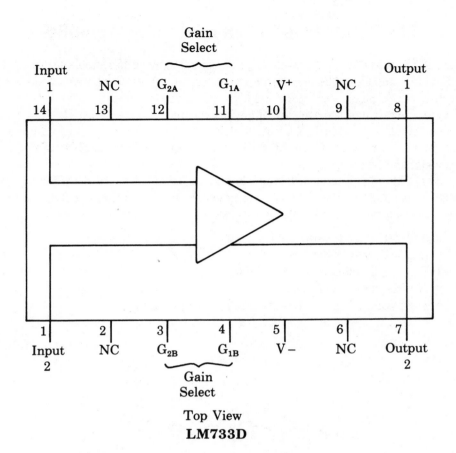

Gain
Select

Input
1   NC G_{2A} G_{1A} V$^+$ NC   Output
1

14   13   12   11   10   9   8

1   2   3   4   5   6   7

Input   NC G_{2B} G_{1B} V$-$ NC   Output
2   2

Gain
Select

Top View
LM733D

TDA1190P, TDA3190P TV Sound System

The TDA3190P/1190P could have been included in section 6, since it is basically an audio amplification system, but it is included here instead, because it is designed for TV sound-system applications. It even includes an on-chip FM detector and related circuitry to demodulate television audio signals.

The functional stages within these devices include:

- If limiter
- If amplifier
- Low-pass filter
- FM detector
- Dc volume control
- Audio preamplifier
- Audio power amplifier

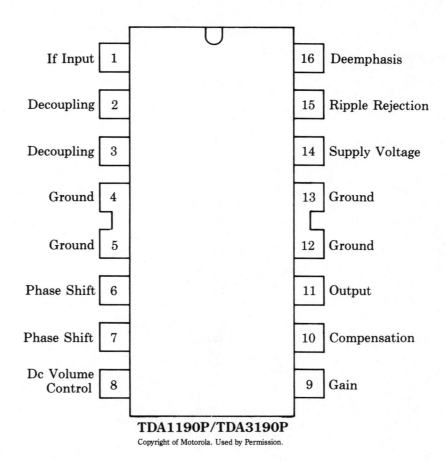

TDA1190P/TDA3190P

The audio power amplifier stage in the TDA3190P can put out up to 4.2 Watts (assuming that the supply voltage is 24 V, and the output load impedance is 16 Ω).

The dc volume-control input permits an external dc voltage to set the amplifier gain, or output volume. This feature can be particularly handy in remotely controlled systems. The volume-control response is linear.

The TDA1190P is a low-power version of the TDA3190P.

Supply Voltage
  TDA1190P   9.0 V min.
                    22 V max.
  TDA3190P   9.0 V min.
                    22 V max.

Output Power
  TDA1190P   1.3 W max.
                    (V_{CC} = 18 V R1 = 32 Ω)
  TDA3190P   4.2 W
                    (V_{CC} = 24 V R1 = 16 Ω)

LM1304, LM1305, LM1307, LM1307E
FM Multiplex Stereo Demodulator

The LM1304, LM1305, LM1307, and LM1307E are designed to derive the left- and right-channel audio information from the detected composite stereo signal. The LM1304 eliminates the need for an external stereo-channel separation control. The LM1305 is similar to the LM1304, but permits the use of an external stereo channel separation control for maximum separation. The LM1307 is also similar to the LM1304, but it does not have the audio mute control or the stereo/mono switch. The LM1307E is similar to the LM1307, but it has the option of emitter-follower output drivers for buffers or high-current applications. Features include:

- Operation over a wide power-supply range
- Built-in stereo-indicator lamp driver—100 mA typical
- Automatic switching between stereo and monaural
- Audio mute control

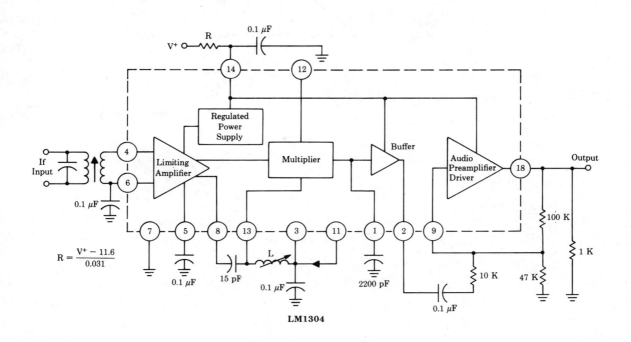

LM1304

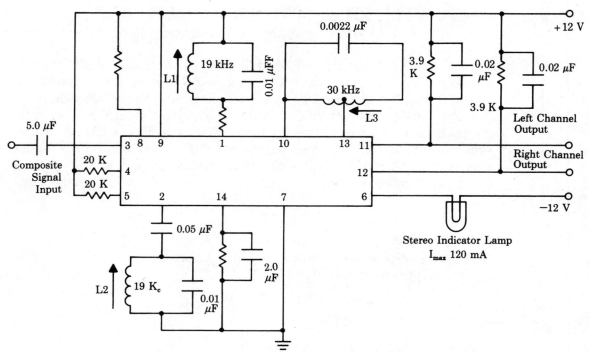

L1,L2: 333 turns, Q_u — 55 8.0 mH nominal Miller No. 1361 or equivalent
L3: 420 turns No. 38 AWG, tap at 42 turns, $Q_u = 55$ 8.0 mH nominal.
Miller No. 1362 or equivalent.
*$R_A = 180 \, \Omega$ nominal, adjusted for lamp sensitivity to 19 kHz pilot

LM1310 Phase-Locked-Loop FM Stereo Demodulator

The LM1310 is an integrated FM stereo demodulator using phase-locked-loop techniques to regenerate the 38-kHz subcarrier. A second version also available is the LM1800, which adds superb power-supply rejection and buffered (emitter-follower) outputs to the basic phase-locked decoder circuit. The features available in these integrated circuits make possible a system that can deliver high-fidelity sound within the cost restraints of inexpensive stereo receivers. Features include:

- Automatic stereo/monaural switching
- No coils, all tuning performed with single potentiometer
- Wide supply operating voltage range
- Excellent channel separation

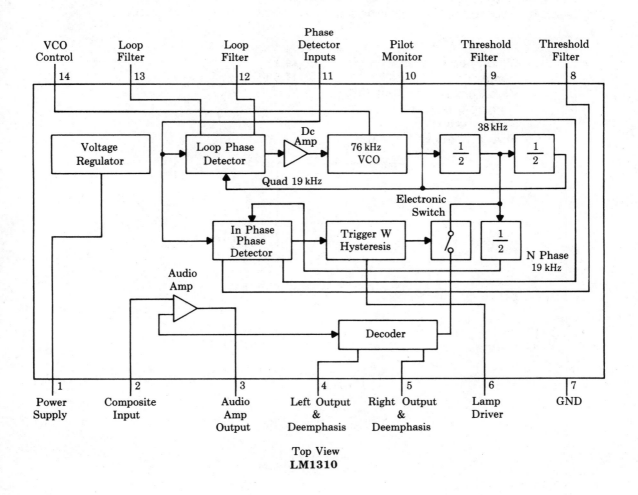

Top View
LM1310

MC1330A1P, Low-Level Video Detector

The MC1330A1P is intended for use in the video section of television receivers. This chip features a very wide bandwidth and quiet linear video (amplitude and phase) characteristics.

This device can be used in either color or black and white TV receivers.

The circuitry within the MC1330A1P low-level video detector IC replaces the following discrete circuit stages:

- Third if amplifier
- Video detector
- Video buffer
- AFC buffer

The video input signal to this chip is divided into two channels—a linear amplifier and a limiting amplifier that provides the switching carrier for the detector.

Max. Supply Voltage	24 V
Supply Current	17.5 mA (t@)
Zero Signal Dc Output Voltage	7.0 to 8.2 Vdc
Conversion Gain	33 dB (t@)
Video Output	8.0 V p-p
Min. Frequency Response	8.0 MHz

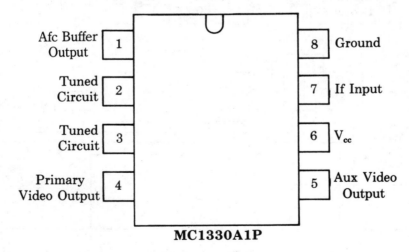

MC1330A1P

MC1350 If Amplifier

The MC1350 is a monolithic if amplifier, featuring a wide-range AGC (automatic gain control). It is intended for use with video if signals in a television receiver.

Max.Supply Voltage	18 V
Output Supply Voltage	18 V
Differential Input Voltage	5.0 V
Power Gain 45 MHz	50 dB
58 MHz	48 dB
Min. AGC Range	60 dB (0 to 45 MHz)

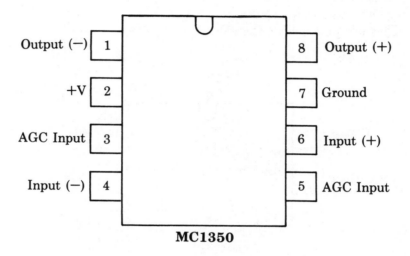

MC1350

LM1351 FM Detector, Limiter, and Audio Amplifier

The LM1351 is a monolithic integrated circuit FM detector, limiter, and audio amplifier that requires a minimum of external components for operation. It includes three stages of if limiting and a balanced product detector. The audio amplifier is capable of driving a single external transistor class-A audio-output stage. Features include:

- Direct replacement for MC1351
- Simple detector alignment: one coil or ceramic filter.
- Sensitivity—3-dB limiting voltage at 80 μV typ.
- Low harmonic distortion
- High if voltage gain
- High audio preamplifier open-loop gain

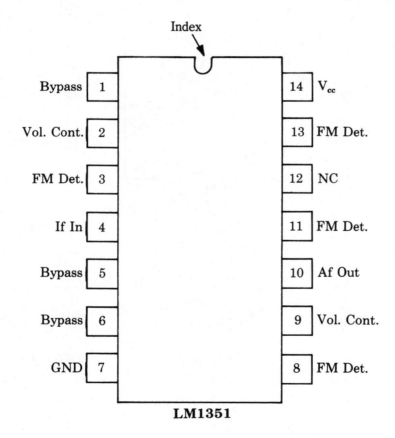

MC1374 TV Modulator Circuit

The MC1374 is designed to generate a TV signal from audio and video inputs. The internal circuits within this chip include:

- FM audio modulator
- Sound carrier oscillator
- Rf oscillator
- Rf dual-input modulator

The MC1374 features a wide dynamic range and low-distortion audio. The gain of the rf modulator can be externally adjusted. The output signal can use either positive or negative sync, depending upon the requirements of the specific application.

A single-ended power-supply voltage is used with the 1374. This voltage can be anything from +5 to +14 volts, although it is recommended that the supply voltage not exceed +12 volts in normal operation.

The output signal can be set for TV channel 3 or 4. It is best to select a channel that is not used by a local broadcaster in your area.

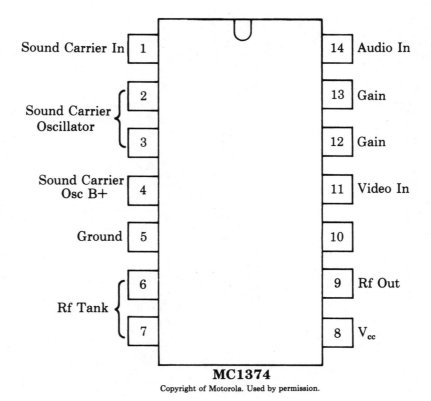

MC1374

Copyright of Motorola. Used by permission.

405

Typical applications for the 1374 include:

- Video tape players
- Video disc players
- Computer monitors
- Video games
- Cable- or satellite-subscription decoders

Supply Voltage	+14 V max.
	+5 V min.
Power Dissipation	1250 mW max.
Rf Output	170 mV p-p typ.
(pin 9 resistor = 75 Ω No external load)	
Min. Video Bandwidth	30 MHz (75-Ω input source)
Typ.AM-Oscillator Frequency Range	105 MHz
Typ. Frequency Range of Modulator	4.5 MHz

MC1377 Color Television RGB-to-PAL/NTSC Encoder

The MC1377 accepts baseband red, blue, green, and sync inputs, and generates a composite video signal. Either the PAL or NTSC standard can be easily selected, simply by applying an appropriate control signal pin #20.

The external circuitry used with this chip does not have to be extensive. A complete circuit can include only a handful of external parts. On the other hand, the 1377 does have sufficient pinouts for more-sophisticated external circuitry and a fully implemented, top-quality composite signal.

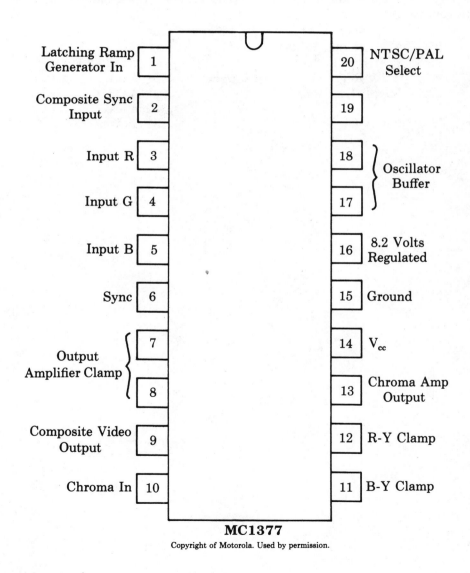

Latching Ramp Generator In	1	20 NTSC/PAL Select
Composite Sync Input	2	19
Input R	3	18 Oscillator Buffer
Input G	4	17
Input B	5	16 8.2 Volts Regulated
Sync	6	15 Ground
Output Amplifier Clamp	7	14 V_{cc}
	8	13 Chroma Amp Output
Composite Video Output	9	12 R-Y Clamp
Chroma In	10	11 B-Y Clamp

MC1377

The internal circuits within this device include:

- Color subcarrier oscillator
- Voltage-controlled 90° phase shifter
- Two DSB-suppressed-carrier chroma modulators
- RGB-input matrices
- Blanking-level clamps

An external reference oscillator can be used, or the on-chip oscillator can be selected.

Typical applications for the MC1377 include color video cameras and graphics generators.

Max. Supply Voltage	+15 V
Preferred Range	+10.8 to 13.2 V
8.2 V Regulator Output Current	10 mA max.
Supply Current	32 mA typ.
	40 mA max.
Power Dissipation	1250 mW max.

MC1378 Color-Television Composite-Video-Overlay Synchronizer

The MC1378 is a bipolar composite video overlay encoder and microcomputer synchronizer. It's internal circuitry includes quadrature color modulators, RGB matrices, blanking-level clamps, and a complete complement of synchronizers to lock a microcomputer-based video source to any remote video source. Except for the microcomputer synchronizers, the MC1378 is quite similar to the MC1377, discussed previously.

All necessary reference oscillators are included on-chip. The device can be operated in either the PAL or NTSC modes, with 625 or 525 lines. The MC1378 was specifically designed for use with the Motorola RMS (Raster Memory System), but it can be applied to other controllable video sources. It will work with nonstandard video.

The MC1378 can be operated from a standard, single-ended 5.0-volt power supply.

Max. Supply Voltage	+6.0 V
Preferred Range	+4.75 to 5.25 V
Max. Power Dissipation	1250 mW
Typ. Supply Current	100 mA

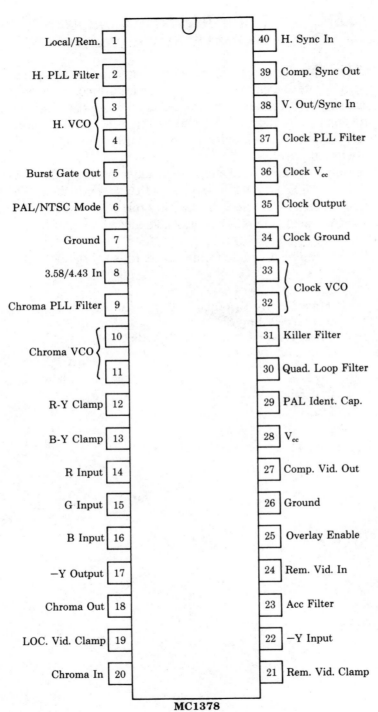

MC1378

Copyright of Motorola, used by permission.

410

MC1391P TV Horizontal Processor

The MC1391P contains the horizontal circuitry for all types of television receivers. The on-chip circuits include:

- Phase detector
- Oscillator
- Predriver

This device features low thermal frequency drift and $\pm$ 300 Hz typical pull-in capability. The hold control capability can be externally preset.

The MC1391P can be used for driving either transistor or tube television circuits, because the output duty cycle is variable.

Supply Current	40 mA max.
	20 mA typ.
Max. Output Current	30 mA
Max. Output Voltage	40 V
Max.Power Dissipation	625 mW
Regulated Voltage (pin 6)	8.0 V min.
	8.6 V typ.
	9.4 V max.

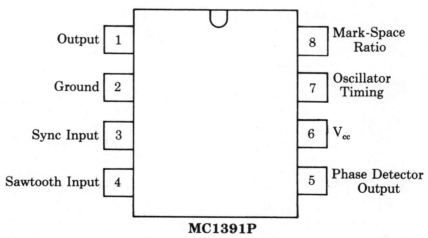

MC1391P

Copyright of Motorola, used by permission.

BA1404 Stereo Transmitter

The BA1404 is basically an FM stereo transmitter on a chip. The stereo modulator creates a stereo composite signal, which consists of a main (L + R) signal and a sub (L − R) signal, along with the appropriate pilot signals, derived from a 38-kHz quartz-controlled oscillator.

The carrier signal generated by this chip can be set within the standard FM broadcast band (76 MHz to 108 MHz).

The circuitry within the BA1404 includes:

- Stereo modulator
- FM modulator
- Rf amplifier

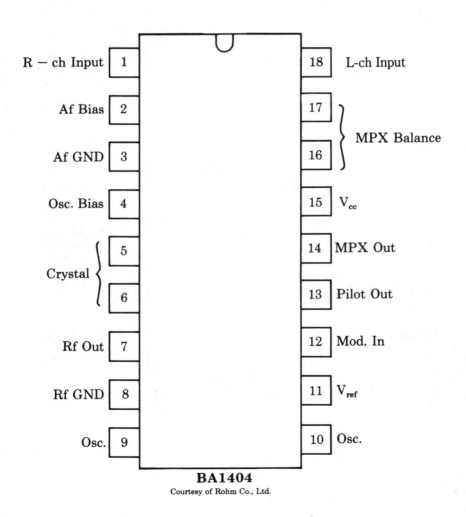

BA1404
Courtesy of Rohm Co., Ltd.

This chip consumes very little power at a relatively low supply voltage. In most applications, few external components are required because just about everything is included on chip. The BA1404 is ideal in applications demanding small circuit size, such as in wireless microphones. It can also be used in other low-power FM-stereo transmission applications.

Max. Supply Voltage	+36 V
Max. Power Dissipation	500 mW
Typ. Quiescent Current	3 mA
Typ. Channel Separation	45 dB
Typ. Input Impedance	540 Ω
Typ. Rf Maximum Output Voltage	600 mV

LM1496/LM1596 Balanced Modulator/Demodulator

The LM1496/LM1596 are double-balanced modulator/demodulators that produce an output voltage proportional to the product of an input (signal) voltage and a switching (carrier) signal. Typical applications include suppressed-carrier modulation, amplitude modulation, synchronous detection, FM or PM detection, and broadband frequency doubling and chopping.

The LM1596 is specified for operation over the $-55°C$ to $+125°C$ military temperature range. The LM1496 is specified for operation over the $0°C$ to $+70°C$ temperature range. Features include:

- Excellent carrier suppression
  65 dB typical at 9.5 MHz
  50 dB typical at 10 MHz
- Adjustable gain and signal handling
- Fully balanced inputs and outputs
- Low offset and drift
- Wide frequency response up to 100 MHz

Dual-In-Line Package

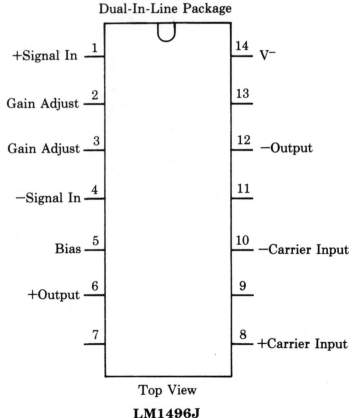

Top View

LM1496J

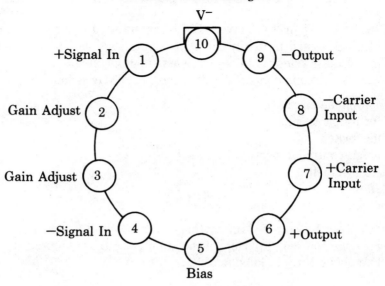

Metal Can Package

V⁻

+Signal In — 1

Gain Adjust — 2

Gain Adjust — 3

−Signal In — 4

Bias — 5

6 — +Output

7 — +Carrier Input

8 — −Carrier Input

9 — −Output

10

Top View

Note: Pin 10 is connected electrically to the case through the device substrate.

LM1496H

MC2831A Low-Power FM Transmitter System

The MC2831A is a virtually complete FM transmitter subsystem in a single 16-pin chip. It is designed primarily for applications such as FM communication equipment, cordless telephones, and wireless microphones.

The internal circuits contained within the MC2831A include:

- Microphone amplifier
- Pilot-tone oscillator
- Tone switch
- Voltage-controlled oscillator
- Battery monitor
- Buffer
- Variable-reactance stage

This chip can be powered off anything from 3.0 to 8.0 volts dc, with very little power consumption. Typically, if the supply voltage is 4 volts, the current drain will be about 4 mA at full operation.

Max. Supply Voltage	10 Vdc
Operating Supply Voltage Range	3 to 8 Vdc
Typ. Drain Current	
Pin #4	3.6 mA
Pin #12	290 μA
Typ. Microphone Amplifier Voltage Gain	30 dB (Closed loop)
Typ. Output Rf Voltage	
(F_o = 16.6 MHz)	40 mV rms

16

1

P Suffix
Case 648-06

16

1

D Suffix
Case 751B-03
SO-16

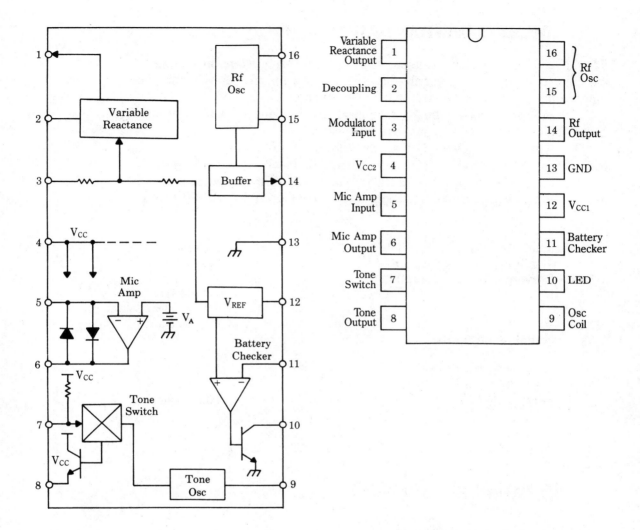

MC2833 Low-Power FM Transmitter System

The MC2833 is a virtually complete FM transmitter subsystem on a single 16-pin chip. It is designed primarily for applications such as FM communication equipment, cordless telephones, and wireless microphones.

The on-chip circuits in the MC2833 include a microphone amplifier, voltage-controlled oscillator, and two auxiliary transistors.

This chip can be powered off anything from 2.8 to 9.0 volts dc, with very little power consumption. Typically, the current drain will be about 2.8 mA.

Using direct rf output, the MC2833 offers -30 dBm power output to 60 MHz. The on-chip transistor amplifiers can be used for up to $+10$ dBm power output.

Max. Supply Voltage	10 Vdc
Operating Supply Voltage Range	2.8 to 9.0 Vdc
Drain Current (No input signal)	
Pin #10	2.9 mA typ.
	1.7 mA min.
	4.3 mA max.
Typ. Microphone Amplifier Voltage Gain (Closed loop)	
V_{in} = 3.0 mV rms	
F_{in} = 1.0 kHz	30 dB
Typ. Output Rf Voltage	
F_o = 16.6 MHz	90 mV rms

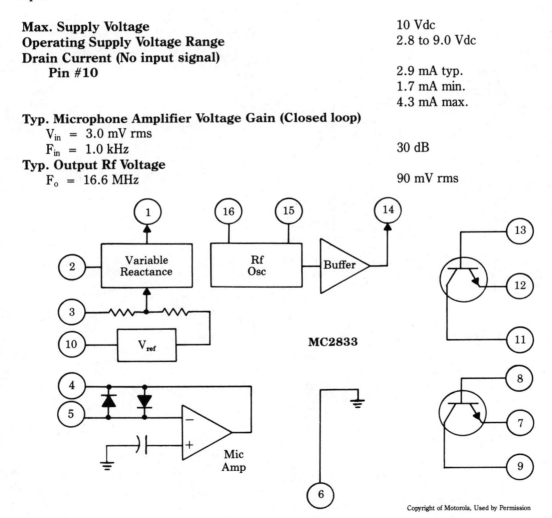

MC2833

418

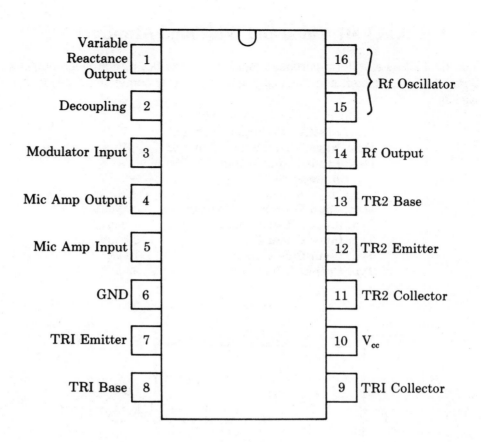

CA3001 Video and Wideband Amplifier

The CA3001 is a general-purpose amplifier used in dc, if, and video-amplifier, Schmitt-trigger, mixer, and modulator applications. It comes in a 12-lead TO-5 package.

Max. Positive Dc Supply Voltage	$+10$ V
Max. Negative Dc Supply Voltage	-10 V
Max. Input Signal Voltage	
Single-ended	± 2.5 V
Common-mode	± 2.5 V
Max. Total Device Dissipation	300 mW
Typ. Input Offset Voltage	1.5 mV
Typ. Input Offset Current	3.4 μA
Typ. Input Bias Current	10 μA
Typ. Output Offset Voltage	52 mV

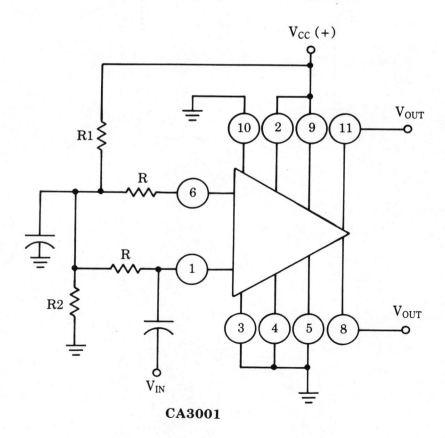

CA3001

CA3002 IF Amplifier

The CA3002 is a general-purpose amplifier used in video amplifier, product, and AM-detector applications. It comes in a 10-lead TO-5 package.

Max. Positive Dc Supply Voltage	$+10$ V
Max. Negative Dc Supply Voltage	-10 V
Max. Input Signal Voltage (single-ended)	±3.5 V
Max. Total Device Dissipation	300 mW
Typ. Input Unbalance Voltage	2.2 mV
Typ. Input Unbalance Current	2.2 μA
Typ. Input Bias Current	20 μA

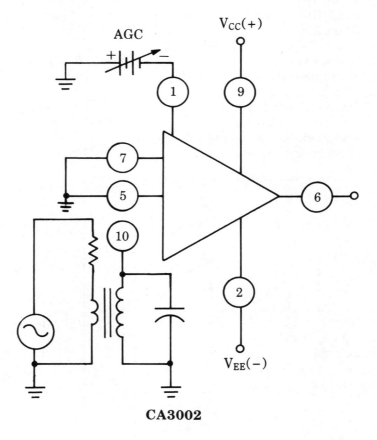

CA3002

CA3005 Rf Amplifier

The CA3005 is a general-purpose amplifier used in push-pull input and output, wideband and narrow-band amplifier, agc, detector, mixer, limiter, modulator, and cascode amplifier applications. It comes in a 12-lead TO-5 package.

Max. Positive Dc Supply Voltage	V_{CC} + 12 V
Max. Negative Dc Supply Voltage	V_{EE} − 12 V
Max. Input-Signal Voltage:	
Single-ended	±3.5 V
Common-mode	+3.5 to −2.5 V
Max. Total Device Dissipation	300 mW
Typ. Input Offset Voltage	2.6 mV
Typ. Input Offset Current	1.4 μA
Typ. Input Bias Current	19 μA
Typ. Power Gain (f = 100 MHz):	
Cascode Circuit	20 dB
Differential-Amplifier Circuit	16 dB
Noise Figure (f = 100 MHz):	
Cascode Circuit	27.80 dB
Differential-Amplifier Circuit	7.8 dB
Common-Mode Rejection Ratio (f = 1 kHz)	101 dB
Useful Frequency Range	Dc to 120 MHz

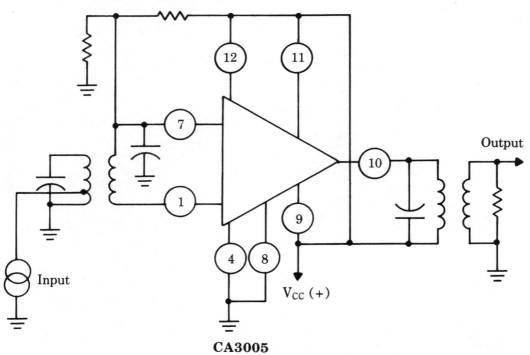

CA3005

CA3011 FM If Amplifier

The CA3011 is a special-purpose amplifier used in if amplifiers for FM broadcast and TV-sound applications. It comes in a 10-lead TO-5 package.

Max. Positive Dc Supply Voltage	+10 V
Max. Recommended Minimum Dc Supply Voltage (V_{CC})	5.5 V
Max. Input Signal Voltage (single-ended)	±3 V
Max. Total Device Dissipation	300 mW
Typ. Device Dissipation	120 mW
Typ. Voltage Gain:	
f = 1 MHz	70 dB
f = 4.5 MHz	67 dB
f = 10.7 MHz	61 dB
Typ. Noise Figure (f = 4.5 MHz)	8.7 dB
Typ. Useful Frequency Range	100 kHz to > 20 MHz

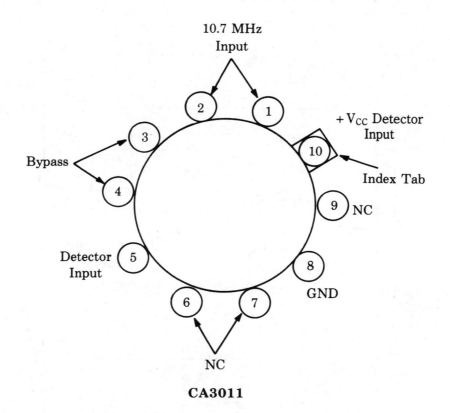

CA3011

CA3013 FM If Amplifier/Discriminator/AF Amplifier

The CA3013 is a special-purpose amplifier used in if amplifier, AM and noise limiter, FM detector, and AF preamplifier applications. It comes in a 10-lead TO-5 package.

Max. Positive Dc Supply Voltage	+10 V
Max. Recommended Minimum Dc Supply Voltage (V_{CC})	5.5 V
Max. Input Signal Voltage (Between terminals 1 and 2)	±3 V
Max. Total Device Dissipation	300 mW
Typ. Device Dissipation	120 mW
Typ. Voltage Gain:	
f = 1 MHz	70 dB
f = 4.5 MHz	67 dB
f = 10.7 MHz	60 dB
Typ. Noise Figure (f = 4.5 MHz)	8.7 dB
Typ. Useful Frequency Range	100 kHz to > 20 MHz

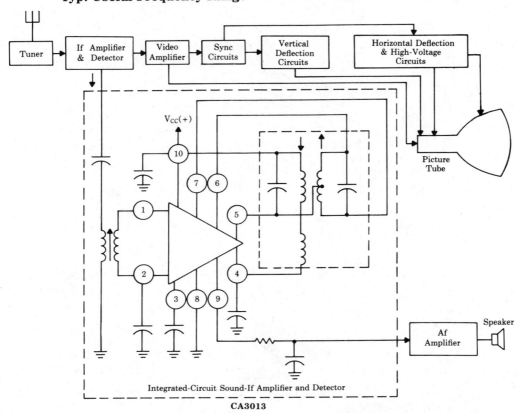

Integrated-Circuit Sound-If Amplifier and Detector

CA3013

424

CA3023 Video and Wideband Amplifier

The CA3023 is a general-purpose amplifier used in gain-controlled linear amplifier, AM/FM if amplifier, video amplifier, and limiter applications. It comes in a 12-lead TO-5 package.

Typ. Device Dissipation	35 mW
Typ. Quiescent Output Voltage	1.3 V
Typ. AGC Source Current (V_{agc} = 6 V)	0.8 mA
Typ. Voltage Gain (f = 5 MHz)	53 dB
$-$ 3 dB Bandwidth	16 MHz
Typ. Input Resistance (f = 10 MHz)	300 Ω
Typ. Input Capacitance (f = 10 MHz)	13 pF
Typ. Output Resistance (f = 10 MHz)	100 Ω
Typ. Noise Figure (f = 1 MHz)	6.5 dB
Typ. AGC Range (f = 10 MHz)	33 dB
Typ. Useful Frequency Range	Dc to 40 MHz
Typ. Maximum Output Voltages (f = 10 MHz)	0.5 V rms

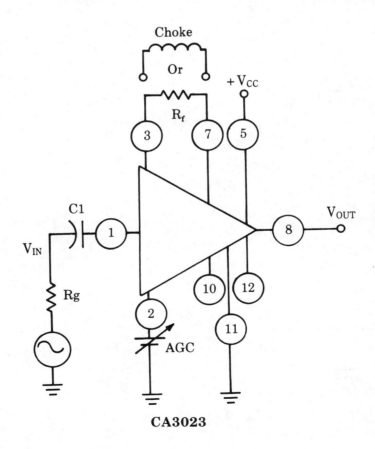

CA3023

TDA3301, TDA3303, TV Color Processor

The TDA3301 and the TDA3303 convert composite video signals into the three separate color signals (red, blue, and green). The only external-output circuitry required is a simple driver amplifier to interface with the picture tube in a television set or color monitor. The composite input signals can be in either the NTSC (American) or PAL (European) video formats.

These chips feature high-bandwidth on-screen display inputs, making them good choices for such video applications as computer monitors, text displays, video games, and cameras.

The TDA3301 differs from the TDA3303 in its user-control laws and phase-shift control, which operates in either the PAL or the NTSC format.

Supply Voltage	+10.8 V min.
	+12 V typ.
	+13.2 V max.
Typ. Power Dissipation	600 mW
Supply Current	45 mA typ.
	60 mA max.

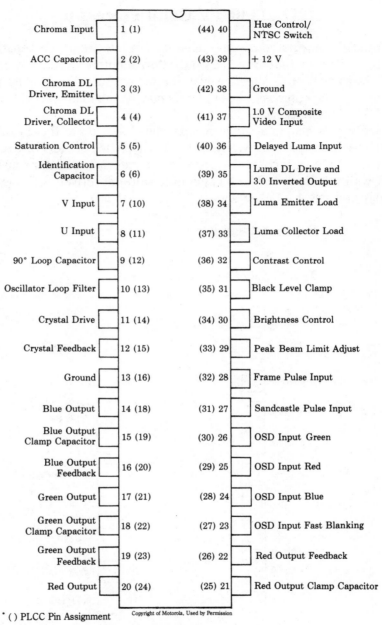

Chroma Input	1 (1)	(44) 40	Hue Control/ NTSC Switch
ACC Capacitor	2 (2)	(43) 39	+ 12 V
Chroma DL Driver, Emitter	3 (3)	(42) 38	Ground
Chroma DL Driver, Collector	4 (4)	(41) 37	1.0 V Composite Video Input
Saturation Control	5 (5)	(40) 36	Delayed Luma Input
Identification Capacitor	6 (6)	(39) 35	Luma DL Drive and 3.0 Inverted Output
V Input	7 (10)	(38) 34	Luma Emitter Load
U Input	8 (11)	(37) 33	Luma Collector Load
90° Loop Capacitor	9 (12)	(36) 32	Contrast Control
Oscillator Loop Filter	10 (13)	(35) 31	Black Level Clamp
Crystal Drive	11 (14)	(34) 30	Brightness Control
Crystal Feedback	12 (15)	(33) 29	Peak Beam Limit Adjust
Ground	13 (16)	(32) 28	Frame Pulse Input
Blue Output	14 (18)	(31) 27	Sandcastle Pulse Input
Blue Output Clamp Capacitor	15 (19)	(30) 26	OSD Input Green
Blue Output Feedback	16 (20)	(29) 25	OSD Input Red
Green Output	17 (21)	(28) 24	OSD Input Blue
Green Output Clamp Capacitor	18 (22)	(27) 23	OSD Input Fast Blanking
Green Output Feedback	19 (23)	(26) 22	Red Output Feedback
Red Output	20 (24)	(25) 21	Red Output Clamp Capacitor

* ( ) PLCC Pin Assignment

TDA3301/TDA3303

TDA3330 TV Color Processor

The TDA3330 converts composite video signals into the three separate color signals (red, blue, and green). The only external output circuitry required is a simple driver amplifier to interface with the picture tube in a television set, or color monitor. The composite input signals may be in either the NTSC (American) or PAL (European) video formats.

Basically, this chip is a somewhat simplified version of the TDA3301 and TDA3303 discussed previously. The simplified approach of the TDA3330 makes it very well suited to low cost CTV systems. No external oscillator adjustment is required with this device. The on-chip oscillators are driven with inexpensive and readily available 4.43 MHz and 3.58 MHz crystals.

Supply Voltage   +10.8 V min.
    +12 V typ.
    +13.2 V max.

Typ. Supply Current   50 mA

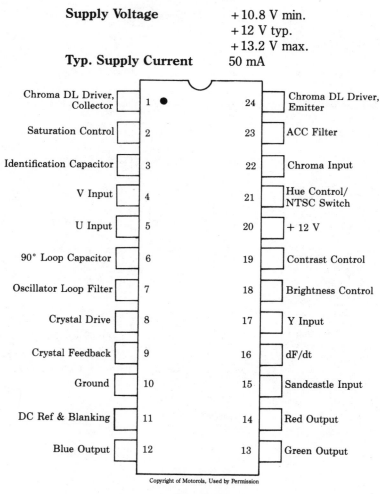

Pin	Left		Pin	Right
1	Chroma DL Driver, Collector		24	Chroma DL Driver, Emitter
2	Saturation Control		23	ACC Filter
3	Identification Capacitor		22	Chroma Input
4	V Input		21	Hue Control/ NTSC Switch
5	U Input		20	+ 12 V
6	90° Loop Capacitor		19	Contrast Control
7	Oscillator Loop Filter		18	Brightness Control
8	Crystal Drive		17	Y Input
9	Crystal Feedback		16	dF/dt
10	Ground		15	Sandcastle Input
11	DC Ref & Blanking		14	Red Output
12	Blue Output		13	Green Output

TDA3330

TDA3333 TV Color Difference Demodulator

The TDA3333 chip accepts an input composite video signal in either the NTSC (American) or PAL (European) format and demodulates it into the two color-difference signals—R/Y and B/Y.

No external oscillator adjustment is required with this device. The on-chip oscillators are driven with inexpensive and readily available 4.43 MHz and 3.58 MHz crystals.

The TDA3333 also features on-chip hue control for NTSC signals.

Supply Voltage	+10.8 V min.
	+12 V typ.
	+13.2 V max.
Dc Output	
Typ. B/Y	9.2 V
Typ. R/Y	10.1 V
Output Resistance	
Typ. B/Y	100 Ω
Typ. R/Y	80 Ω

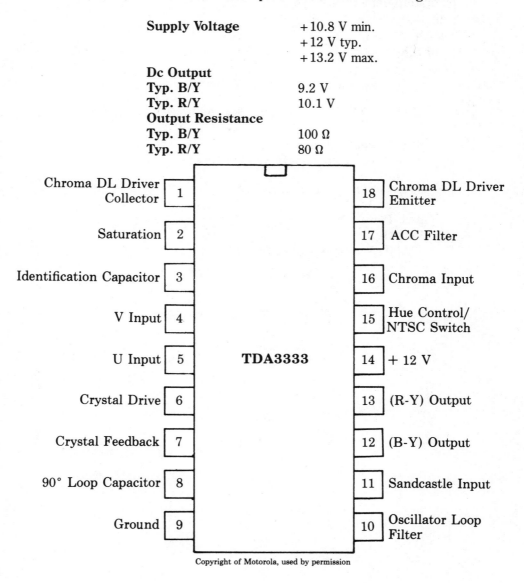

Chroma DL Driver Collector	1		18	Chroma DL Driver Emitter
Saturation	2		17	ACC Filter
Identification Capacitor	3	**TDA3333**	16	Chroma Input
V Input	4		15	Hue Control/NTSC Switch
U Input	5		14	+ 12 V
Crystal Drive	6		13	(R-Y) Output
Crystal Feedback	7		12	(B-Y) Output
90° Loop Capacitor	8		11	Sandcastle Input
Ground	9		10	Oscillator Loop Filter

429

MC3356 Wideband FSK Receiver

The MC3356 is designed for use in a receiver in a communication system using FSK (frequency shift keying).

The circuitry within this chip includes:

- Oscillator
- Mixer
- Limiting if amplifier
- Quadrature detector
- Audio buffer
- Squelch
- Meter drive
- Squelch status output
- Data shaper comparator

The MC3356 can reliably handle data rates up to 500 kilobaud.

Max. Supply Voltage	+15 V
Operating Power Supply Voltage Range	
Pins 6 and 10	3 to 9 V
Operating Rf Supply Voltage Range	
Pin 4	3 to 12 V
Max. Power Dissipation	125 mW
Sensitivity	
30 μV rms at 100 MHz	3 dB

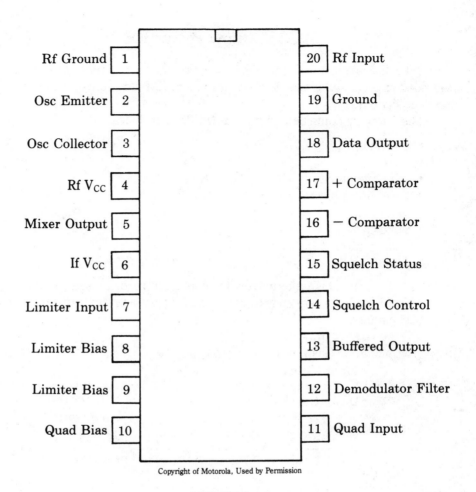

Rf Ground	1	20	Rf Input
Osc Emitter	2	19	Ground
Osc Collector	3	18	Data Output
Rf V_{CC}	4	17	+ Comparator
Mixer Output	5	16	− Comparator
If V_{CC}	6	15	Squelch Status
Limiter Input	7	14	Squelch Control
Limiter Bias	8	13	Buffered Output
Limiter Bias	9	12	Demodulator Filter
Quad Bias	10	11	Quad Input

MC3356

MC3357 Low-Power FM If

The MC3357 is a virtually complete if section for an FM receiver. The primary intended application for this device is for use in FM dual-conversion communications equipment.

The circuitry contained within the MC3357 includes:

- Oscillator
- Mixer
- Limiting amplifier
- Quadrature discriminator
- Active filter
- Squelch
- Scan control
- Mute switch

The if passband is quite narrow for maximum receiver selectivity.

This 16-pin IC is very easy to use, requiring just a few external parts in most practical circuits.

Max. Supply Voltage	12 V
Operating Supply Voltage Range	4 to 8 V
Input Voltage	
(V_{CC} = 6 V or greater)	1 V rms max.
Drain Current	
(V_{CC} = 6 V)	3 mA typ.

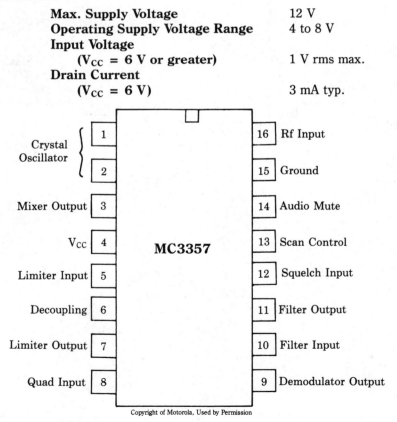

Copyright of Motorola, Used by Permission

MC3362 Low-Power Dual-Conversion FM Receiver

The MC3362 is just about a complete dual-conversion FM receiver in a single 24-pin package. Only a few external parts are required in most practical circuits.

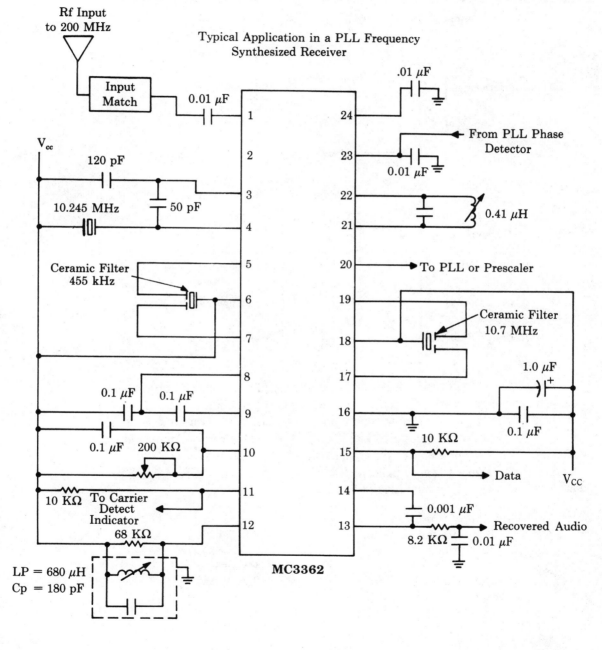

Typical Application in a PLL Frequency Synthesized Receiver

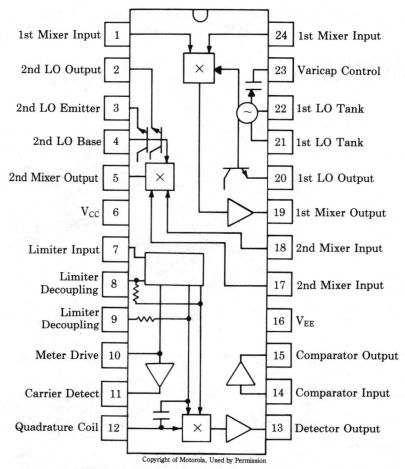

1st Mixer Input	1		24	1st Mixer Input
2nd LO Output	2		23	Varicap Control
2nd LO Emitter	3		22	1st LO Tank
2nd LO Base	4		21	1st LO Tank
2nd Mixer Output	5		20	1st LO Output
V_CC	6		19	1st Mixer Output
Limiter Input	7		18	2nd Mixer Input
Limiter Decoupling	8		17	2nd Mixer Input
Limiter Decoupling	9		16	V_EE
Meter Drive	10		15	Comparator Output
Carrier Detect	11		14	Comparator Input
Quadrature Coil	12		13	Detector Output

Copyright of Motorola, Used by Permission

The MC3362 features buffered first and second local-oscillator outputs and a comparator circuit for FSK (frequency shift keying) detection.

This chip is capable of a very wide input bandwidth. Using the on-chip local oscillator, the bandwidth can be as high as 200 MHz. This can be increased to 450 MHz if an appropriate external local oscillator is used.

A received signal strength indicator (RSSI) is included in this IC's circuitry. This indicator has a dynamic range of 60 dB.

Max. Supply Voltage	8 V
Recommended Range	2 to 7 V
Input Voltage	
(V_{CC} = > 5 V)	1 V rms max.
Input for 20 dB (S + N)/N	0.7 μV rms typ.
Drain Current (Carrier Detect Low)	
	4.5 mA typ.
	7.0 mA max.

434

MC3363 Low-Power Dual-Conversion FM Receiver

The MC3363 contains a nearly complete narrowband-FM receiver in a single chip designed to operate in the VHF band. The circuitry is a dual-conversion receiver.

The subcircuits contained within this chip include:

- Rf amplifier transistor
- Oscillators
- Mixers
- Quadrature detector
- Meter drive/carrier detect
- Mute circuitry

In addition, the MC3363 features a buffered first-local-oscillator output. This output signal is useful in frequency synthesizers. The MC3363 also contains a data-slicing comparator for FSK (frequency shift keying) detection.

This receiver has an impressively wide input bandwidth. If the internal local oscillator is used, the input bandwidth is 200 MHz. In some applications, it might be preferable to use an external local oscillator. Depending on the oscillator circuitry employed, the input bandwidth can be increased to 450 MHz.

Max. Supply Voltage	8 V
Recommended Operating Voltage Range	2 V to 7 V
Input Voltage	
(V_{CC} = 5 V)	1 V rms max.
Drain Current (Carrier Detect Low)	4.5 mA typ.
	8.0 mA max.
Carrier Detect Threshold (Below V_{CC})	0.53 V min.
	0.64 V typ.
	0.77 V max.
Mute Output Impedance	
Typ. High	10 Ω
Typ. Low	25 Ω

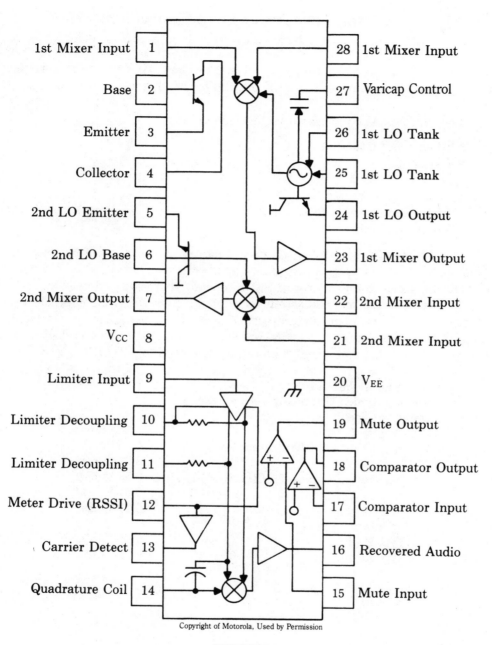

1st Mixer Input — 1

Base — 2

Emitter — 3

Collector — 4

2nd LO Emitter — 5

2nd LO Base — 6

2nd Mixer Output — 7

V_{CC} — 8

Limiter Input — 9

Limiter Decoupling — 10

Limiter Decoupling — 11

Meter Drive (RSSI) — 12

Carrier Detect — 13

Quadrature Coil — 14

28 — 1st Mixer Input

27 — Varicap Control

26 — 1st LO Tank

25 — 1st LO Tank

24 — 1st LO Output

23 — 1st Mixer Output

22 — 2nd Mixer Input

21 — 2nd Mixer Input

20 — V_{EE}

19 — Mute Output

18 — Comparator Output

17 — Comparator Input

16 — Recovered Audio

15 — Mute Input

MC3363

MC3367 Low-Voltage Narrowband-FM Receiver

The MC3367 contains a nearly complete narrowband-FM receiver in a single chip. It is designed to operate at frequencies up to 75 MHz for narrowband audio and data applications.

The chief advantage of this device is its extremely low power consumption. Battery power as low as 1.1 V can be used with the MC3367.

Internal circuitry within the MC3367 includes:

- Oscillator
- Mixer
- If amplifiers
- Limiting if circuitry
- Quadrature discriminator
- Voltage regulator
- Low-battery detection circuitry.

The MC3367 also contains a receiver enable circuit to permit a power-down "sleep mode," and a pair of undedicated buffer amplifiers to allow simultaneous audio and data reception. Another on-chip feature of the MC3367 is a comparator for enhancing FSK (frequency shift keying) data reception.

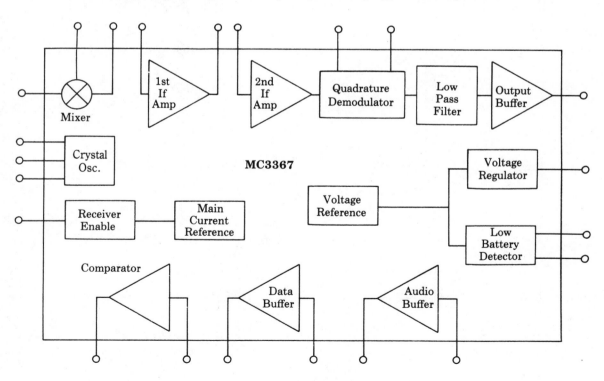

Max. Supply Voltage		5 V	
Recommended Operating Voltage Range		1.1 to 3.0 V	
Power Consumption		1.5 to 5.0 mW	
Input Bandwidth		75 MHz	
Input Limiting Voltage		$(-3.0$ dB$)$ 0.2 μV rms	
Voltage-Regulator Source Current		3.0 mA max.	
Min. Comparator Capability		25 kHz (50 kilobaud)	

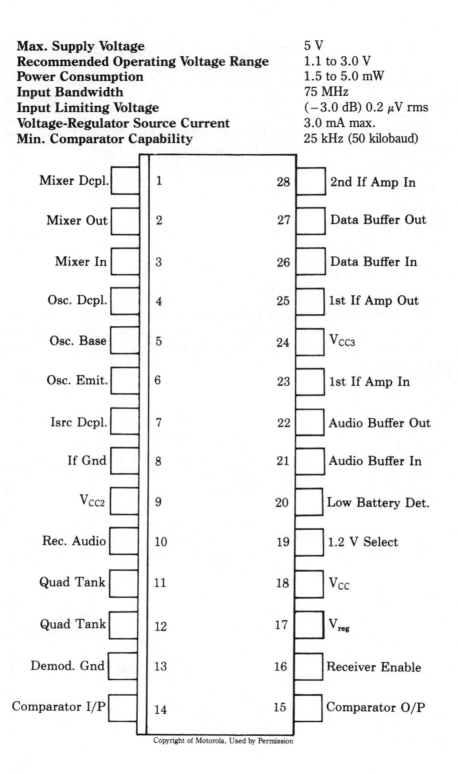

Mixer Dcpl.	1	28	2nd If Amp In
Mixer Out	2	27	Data Buffer Out
Mixer In	3	26	Data Buffer In
Osc. Dcpl.	4	25	1st If Amp Out
Osc. Base	5	24	V_{CC3}
Osc. Emit.	6	23	1st If Amp In
Isrc Dcpl.	7	22	Audio Buffer Out
If Gnd	8	21	Audio Buffer In
V_{CC2}	9	20	Low Battery Det.
Rec. Audio	10	19	1.2 V Select
Quad Tank	11	18	V_{CC}
Quad Tank	12	17	V_{reg}
Demod. Gnd	13	16	Receiver Enable
Comparator I/P	14	15	Comparator O/P

TDA4500A FM Stereo Demodulator

The TDA4500A is an FM Stereo Demodulator, designed primarily for use in Hi-Fi stereo receivers and car radios. It features excellent channel separation maintained over the entire audio frequency range (fixed or adjustable) and transient free Mono/Stereo switching. In the Mono mode, gains up to 6 dB are available.

No bulky and expensive inductors are required in circuits using the TDA4500A.

The TDA4500A offers very low distortion for high fidelity reproduction. The distortion is rated at 0.3% THD at 2.5 V peak-to-peak composite input signal.

Supply Voltage	16 V max.
	8 V min.
Max. Power Dissipation	1.8 W
Min. Stereo Channel Separation	
Unadjusted	30 dB
Optimized on other channel	40 dB
Monaural Voltage Gain	0.8 min.
	1.0 typ.
	1.2 max.
Typ. Signal-to-Noise Ratio	90 dB
Typ. Capture Range	$\pm 5.0\%$

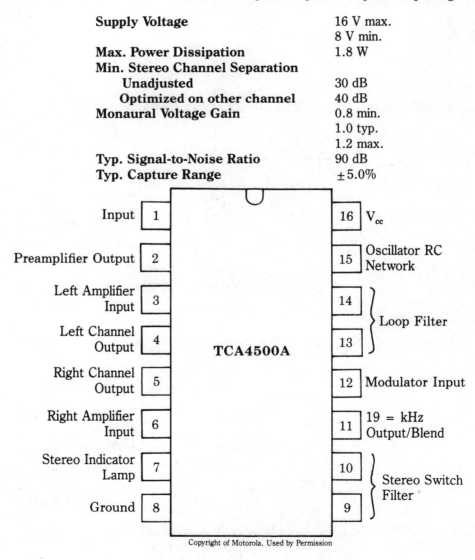

TDA7000 FM Receiver

The TDA7000 is a virtually complete monaural FM receiver in a single IC chip. Thanks to its low-power requirements and the minimum of external components required, this device is ideal for use in portable applications, where space, power requirements, and overall circuit cost are important factors.

The TDA7000 uses PLL (phase-locked loop) tuning to an intermediate frequency (if) of 70 kHz.

The circuitry contained within this chip includes:

- Rf input stage
- Mixer
- Local oscillator
- If amplifier/limiter
- Phase demodulator
- Mute detector and switch

Max. Supply Voltage	12 V
Max. Supply Current (V_{CC} = 4.5 V)	8 mA
Max. Power Dissipation	1.8 W

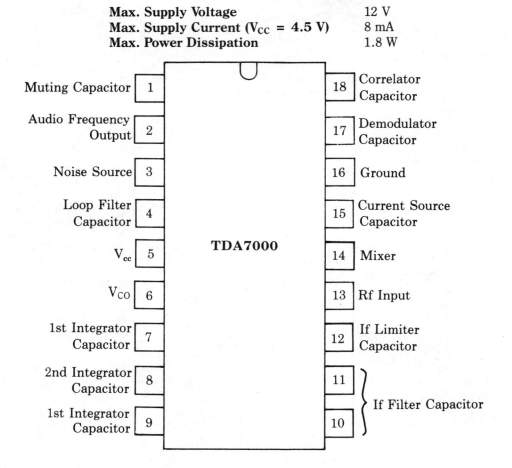

Left Pin		Right Pin	
Muting Capacitor	1	18	Correlator Capacitor
Audio Frequency Output	2	17	Demodulator Capacitor
Noise Source	3	16	Ground
Loop Filter Capacitor	4	15	Current Source Capacitor
V_{cc}	5	14	Mixer
V_{CO}	6	13	Rf Input
1st Integrator Capacitor	7	12	If Limiter Capacitor
2nd Integrator Capacitor	8	11	If Filter Capacitor
1st Integrator Capacitor	9	10	If Filter Capacitor

TDA7000

MC10320 Triple 4-Bit Color Palette Video DAC

The MC10320 is a high-resolution color graphics display system in a single 28-pin IC. It uses a triple 4-bit digital-to-analog converter and a 16×12 color look-up table. The output signals from this chip are in the form of EIA-343-A compatible red, green, and blue video signals. The output signals can directly drive single- or double-terminated 50-Ω or 75-Ω cables directly.

Thanks to the on-chip 16×12 color look-up table, up to 16 color combinations (out of a palette of 4096 possible colors) can be displayed on the screen at any one time. The color look-up table can be updated whenever and as often as desired.

The MC10320 is capable of a maximum pixel rate of 125 MHz. A variation on this chip is the MC10320-1, which offers a maximum pixel rate of 90 MHz.

The MC10320 or the MC10320-1 can be operated from either a single- or a dual-polarity power supply, depending on the external circuitry used with the chip.

Supply Voltages	
V_{CC1} **(measured to V_{EE1})**	-0.5 to 7.0 V
V_{CC2} **(measured to V_{EE2})**	-0.5 to 7.0 V
V_{EE1} **(measured to V_{EE2})**	-0.5 to 7.0 V
Recommended Supply Voltage Ranges	
Single Polarity	
V_{CC1}, V_{CC2}	4.5 V min.
	5.0 V typ.
	5.5 V max.
V_{EE1}, V_{EE2}	0
OR	
V_{CC1}, V_{CC2}	0
V_{EE1}, V_{EE2}	-4.5 V min.
	-5.0 V typ.
	-5.5 V max.
Dual Polarity	
V_{CC1}	4.5 V min.
	5.0 V typ.
	5.5 V max.
V_{CC2}	0
V_{EE1}	0
V_{EE2}	-4.5 V min.
	-5.0 V typ.
	-5.72 V max.
Typ. Supply Sensitivity	34 dB
Typ. Power Dissipation	684 mW

(Top View)

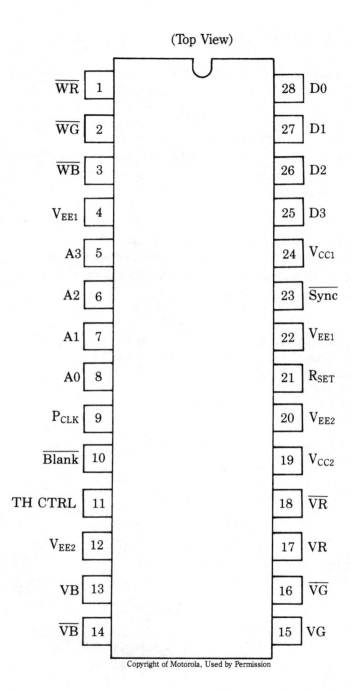

$\overline{WR}$	1
$\overline{WG}$	2
$\overline{WB}$	3
V_{EE1}	4
A3	5
A2	6
A1	7
A0	8
P_{CLK}	9
$\overline{Blank}$	10
TH CTRL	11
V_{EE2}	12
VB	13
$\overline{VB}$	14

28	D0
27	D1
26	D2
25	D3
24	V_{CC1}
23	$\overline{Sync}$
22	V_{EE1}
21	R_{SET}
20	V_{EE2}
19	V_{CC2}
18	$\overline{VR}$
17	VR
16	$\overline{VG}$
15	VG

ORDERING INFORMATION

Maximum Pixel Rate	Device
125 MHz	MC10320L
90 MHz	MC10320L-1

MC10320/MC10320-1

MC13001XP MONOMAX® Black and White TV Subsystem

The MC13001XP is part of Motorola's MONOMAX® series. It is virtually a complete, full-performance black and white television receiver in a single 28-pin IC.

The video if detector is fully on-chip. No external coils are required. In fact, this part of the device has no pins, except for the inputs. The MC13001XP features a minimum of pins and external circuitry requirements. The on-chip oscillator does not require external precision capacitors.

On-chip features of the MC13001XP include:

- Noise and video processing
- Black-level clamp
- Dc contrast
- Beam limiter
- High-performance vertical countdown
- 2-Loop horizontal system with low-power start-up mode
- Noise-protected sync and gated-AGC system

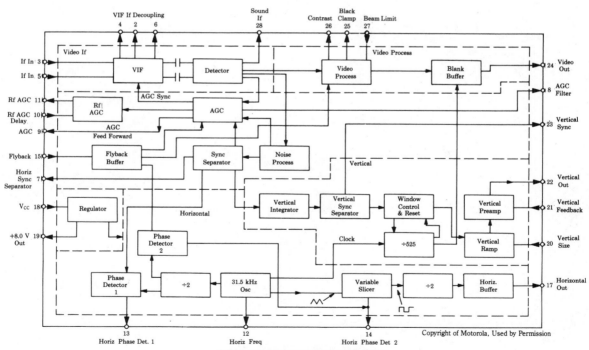

MC13001XP/MC13002XP

The MC13001 is designed to work with Motorola's TDA1190P or TDA3190P sound-if and audio-output devices. The MC13001XP is also designed to operate with the 525-line NTSC (American) video system. A similar device, the MC13002XP, is available for use with the 625-line CCIR system.

Max. Supply Voltage	+16 V
Max. Power Dissipation	1 W
Max. Power Supply Current	76 mA
Regulator Voltage	7.2 V min.
	8.2 V typ.
	8.8 V max.

MC13010P TV Parallel-Sound If/AFT

The MC13010P is an 18-pin IC designed to enhance the performance of a color TV in the audio and video/chroma system. Normally, bandpass compromises must be made to trade off 920 kHz video beat with sound performance. This chip eliminates the need for such compromises.

Other features of the MC13010P include:

- Surface -wave (SAW) filter
- Low-noise preamplifier for SAW-filter
- AFT circuit
- Wideband if amplification with mean level AGC
- Intercarrier detector for sound carrier output
- AFT discriminator with output polarity selection

Max. Supply Voltage	16 V
Supply Current	30 mA min.
	60 mA max.
Max. Power Dissipation	1.1 W
Regulator Voltage (Pin #12)	7.6 V min.
	8.2 V typ.
	8.8 V max.
Regulator Output Current	30 mA max.
Rf Supply Voltage (Pin #18)	5.8 V min.
	6.5 V typ.
	7.2 V max.

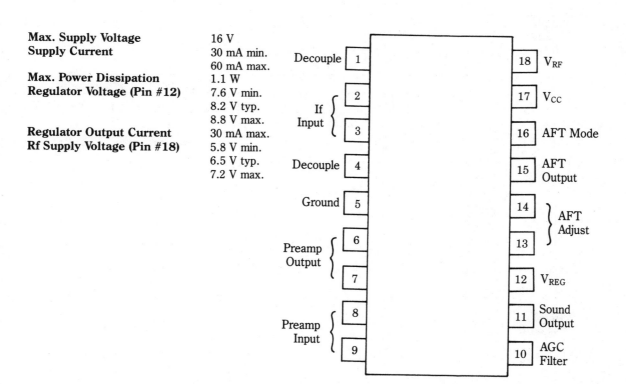

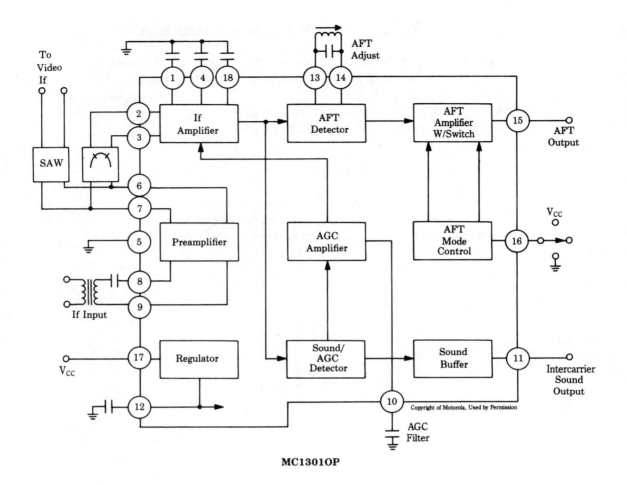

To Video If

If Input

V_CC

1 4 18

13 14 AFT Adjust

2 If Amplifier

3

SAW

6

7

5 Preamplifier

8

9

17 Regulator

12

AFT Detector

AGC Amplifier

Sound/ AGC Detector

AFT Amplifier W/Switch

AFT Mode Control

Sound Buffer

15 AFT Output

V_CC

16

11 Intercarrier Sound Output

10 AGC Filter

Copyright of Motorola, Used by Permission

MC1301OP

446

MC13014P Monomax® Companion Audio/Vertical Subsystem

The MC13014P was designed to complement Motorola's Monomax® family of television receiver ICs. This chip provides the complete output stages for the audio and vertical sections of the receiver. Very few external components are required in most circuits using the MC13014P. It contains all of the active components and most of the passive components needed for most typical applications.

Another advantage of this device is that it is adaptable to suit a wide variety of power-supply configurations.

Power-Supply Voltage (Pins #1, 7, and 16)	+40 V max.
Power-Supply Voltage, Audio Section (Pin #14)	+35 V max.
Power-Supply Current (No signal)	
(Pin #14)	11 mA typ.
	19 mA max.
Max. Audio Output	750 mW
Typ. Gain	50 V/V

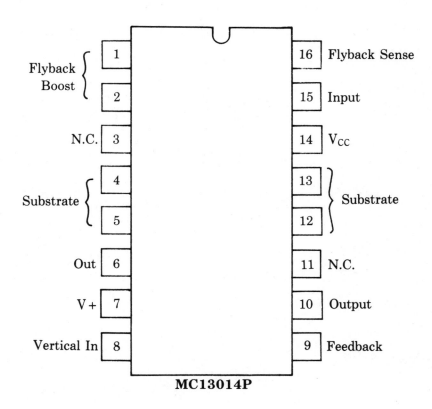

MC13014P

Block Diagram, Typical Application, Monochrome TV Receiver

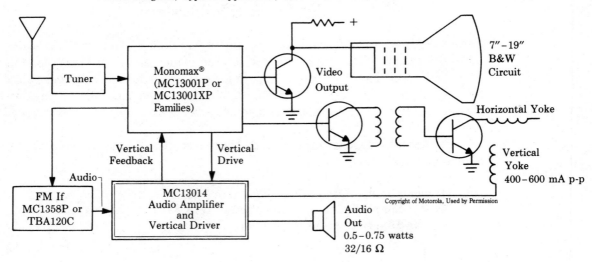

MC13020P C-Quam® AM Stereo Decoder

The MC13020P is complete, full-feature AM stereo decoder and pilot detection system, in a single 20-pin IC. Motorola's C-Quam® system of AM stereo decoding is used in this chip.

The MC13020P employs constant full-wave envelope signal detection for the L + R (mono) signal. The 1-R signal is decoded only in the presence of a valid stereo transmission, as indicated by a 25-Hz pilot signal.

In a practical circuit using the MC13020P, few external components are required. No coils are needed. In most applications, no external adjustments are necessary.

Max. Supply Voltage	+14 V
Recommended Operating Range	+6 to +10 V
Max. Power Dissipation	1.25 W
Pilot-Lamp Current (Pin #15)	50 mA max.

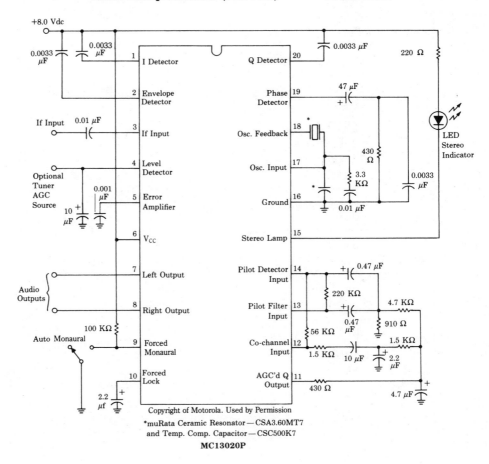

Copyright of Motorola. Used by Permission
*muRata Ceramic Resonator — CSA3.60MT7
and Temp. Comp. Capacitor — CSC500K7

MC13020P

MC13021 C-Quam® AM Stereo Tuning Stabilizer

The MC13021 is designed for use in high-quality AM stereo receivers, using Motorola's C-Quam® system.

An AM stereo receiver requires a very high degree of local oscillator stability in the front end, particularly with respect to any mechanical vibration in the audible range. Mechanical vibration at an audible frequency could affect the frequency stability of many oscillator circuits. These vibrations can generate significant unwanted audio noise via the L-R or stereo-information channel. To avoid such problems, PLL (Phase-Locked Loop) synthesized tuners are used in most quality AM stereo receivers. Unfortunately, this approach tends to be rather expensive.

The MC13021 offers a relatively low-cost alternative, providing PLL stability in conventional mechanically tuned receivers. The oscillator drive comes out at two levels to accommodate inductively or capacitively tuned systems.

The MC13021 is designed to work with the MC13020P C-Quam® decoder, (discussed earlier) and any discrete or IC AM front end, such as the MC13041 (discussed later in this section).

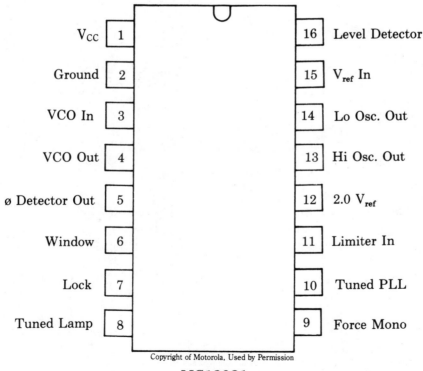

V_CC	1	16	Level Detector
Ground	2	15	V_{ref} In
VCO In	3	14	Lo Osc. Out
VCO Out	4	13	Hi Osc. Out
ø Detector Out	5	12	2.0 V_{ref}
Window	6	11	Limiter In
Lock	7	10	Tuned PLL
Tuned Lamp	8	9	Force Mono

MC13021

450

MC13022 C-Quam® Advanced Medium-Voltage AM Stereo Decoder

The MC13022 is designed to decode AM stereo signals, using Motorola's C-Quam® system. It can be used with good results in home, portable, and automotive applications.

Max. Supply Voltage	+12 V
Recommended Operating Range	+4 to 10 V
Max. Power Dissipation	1.25 W
Typ. Supply Line Current (Pin #25)	18 mA
Max. Pilot Lamp Current (Pin #21)	30 mA

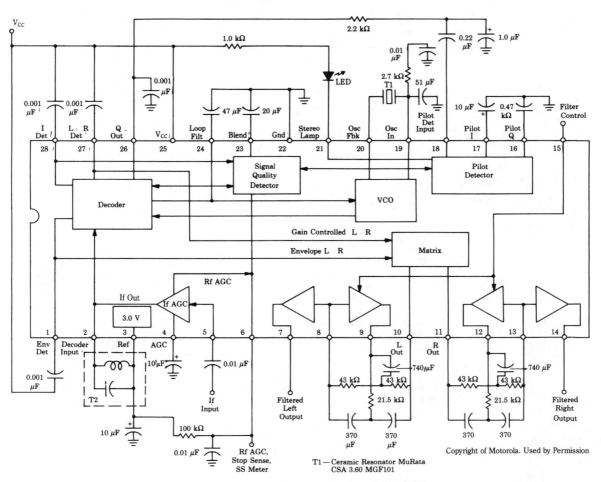

T1 — Ceramic Resonator MuRata
CSA 3.60 MGF101

T2 — Broad Resonance @ 450 kHz
Effective Rp of 8.0 to 12 kΩ
(Part No. to be Determined)

Copyright of Motorola. Used by Permission

MC13022

451

MC13024 Low-Voltage C-Quam®
AM Stereo Receiver

The MC13024 is a virtually complete AM stereo receiver in a single 24-pin IC. Only a minimum of external components are required. This receiver uses the Motorola C-Quam® system of AM stereo decoding.

This chip's primary intended applications are in manually tuned portable and pocket radios. The on-chip circuitry includes just about everything from the antenna input to the left and right audio outputs.

Supply Voltage	+8.0 V max.
	+1.8 V min.
Typ. Current Drain	5.0 mA
Typ. Distortion	<1%
Typ. Channel Separation	>25 dB

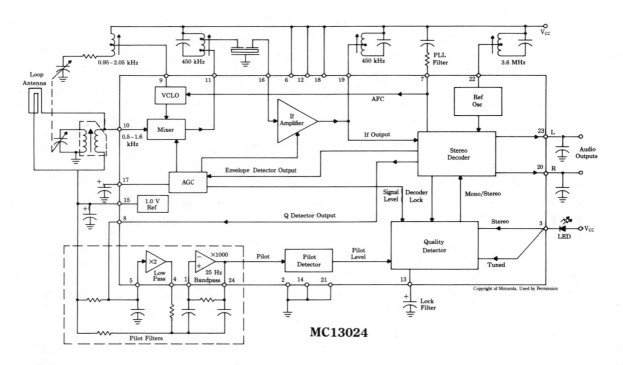

MC13024

MC13041 AM Receiver Subsystem

The MC13041 is designed as the core of an AM broadcast receiver. Combined with the MC13020 (discussed earlier in this section), this chip can be the heart of a very high quality stereo AM radio (using the Motorola C-Quam® system). The manufacturer claims that the MC13041 is ideal as the front end for AM stereo radios using electronic tuning.

　　An important feature of this chip is the scan-detection system, which operates with both frequency and signal amplitude data to minimize "false" tuning problems.

Supply Voltage (Pin #6)	+18 V max.
Recommended Operating Range	+6.5 to +16.5 V
Supply Current (No input signal)	25 mA typ.
	33 mA max.
Rf Sensitivity	2.6 μV rms typ.
	10 μV rms max.
Usable Sensitivity	5.6 μV rms typ.
	10 μV rms max.

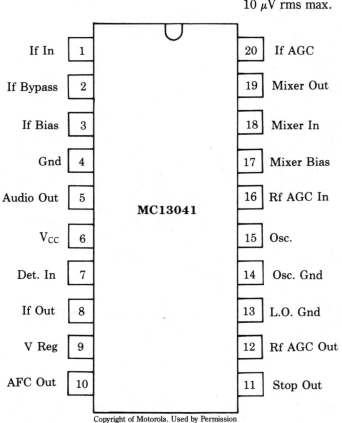

Left	Pin		Pin	Right
If In	1		20	If AGC
If Bypass	2		19	Mixer Out
If Bias	3		18	Mixer In
Gnd	4		17	Mixer Bias
Audio Out	5		16	Rf AGC In
V_{CC}	6		15	Osc.
Det. In	7		14	Osc. Gnd
If Out	8		13	L.O. Gnd
V Reg	9		12	Rf AGC Out
AFC Out	10		11	Stop Out

MC13041

MC13055 Wideband FSK Receiver

The MC13055 is a FSK (frequency shift keying) receiver, intended for use in rf data-link systems using carrier frequencies as high as 40 MHz. The FSK data rate can be as high as 2.0 M baud (1.0 MHz).

The MC13055 is similar to the MC3356 (discussed earlier in this section), except that this chip does not include the oscillator/mixer circuitry. On the other hand, the if bandwidth has been increased in the MC13055, and the detector output has been revised to form a balanced configuration.

Like the MC3356, the MC13055 features an on-chip received signal-strength metering circuit, and a versatile date slicer/comparator.

Max. Supply Voltage	+15 V
Recommended Operating Range	+3 to +12 V
Max. Power Dissipation	1.25 W
Total Drain Current	20 mA typ.
	25 mA max.
Input Sensitivity (40 MHz)	$20\mu V$

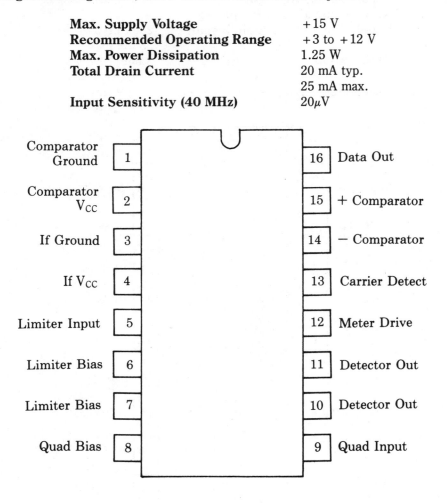

MC13055

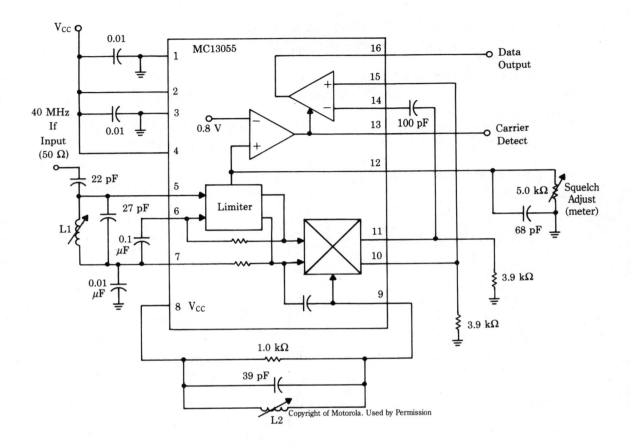

Copyright of Motorola. Used by Permission

455

MC44802 PLL-Tuning Circuit
with 1.3 GHz Prescaler

The MC44802 is a tuning circuit for use in television receivers. One 18-pin IC contains all the circuitry required for PLL (phase-locked loop) control of a VCO (voltage-controlled oscillator.)

The chip includes a high-frequency prescaler that permits handling of frequencies as high as 1.3 GHz. The high-frequency prescaler can be bypassed via software control, if it is not called for in a given application.

The 15-bit programmable divider stage in this device accepts input frequencies ranging up to 125 MHz.

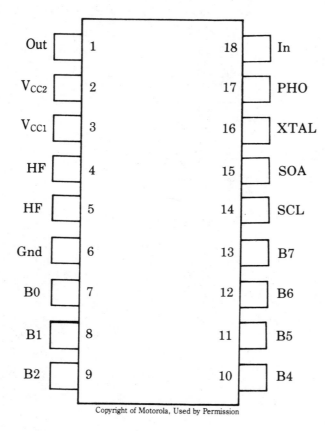

Copyright of Motorola, Used by Permission

MC44802

Supply Voltage
   V_{CC1}

6.0 V absolute max.
4.5 V min.
5.0 V typ.
5.5 V recommended operating max.

   V_{CC2}

36 V absolute max.
25 V min.
30 V typ.
35 V recommended operating max.

V_{CC1} Supply Current (V_{CC1} = 5.0 V)
60 mA typ.
90 mA max.

V_{CC2} Supply Current (Output Open)
0.8 mA typ.
2.0 mA max.

Clock Frequency Range
0 Hz min.
100 kHz max.

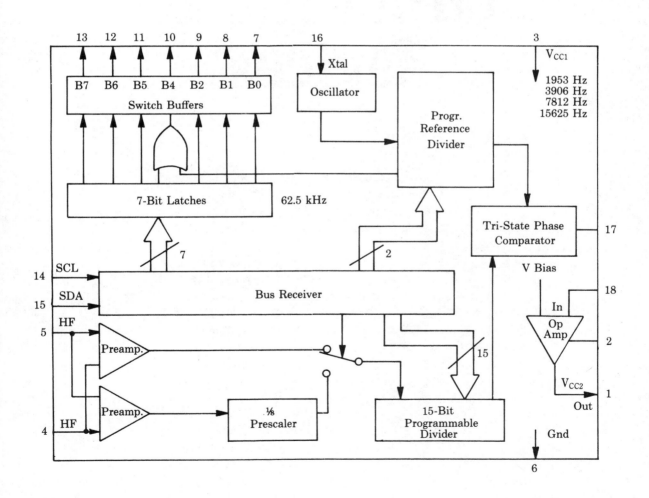

8
SECTION

Other linear devices

This remaining section covers a variety of linear ICs, which do not fit into the categories of sections 5 through 7.

For each of these devices, pinouts, a description, list of features, particular specifications, and absolute-maximum ratings are given.

To aid you in learning about the various ICs, a mini-glossary precedes our description of the devices in this section. Note that term definitions are given for the two types of devices: voltage comparators and voltage regulators. These mini-glossaries are similar to the operational-amplifier term list given in section 5.

Linear IC Listing

Voltage Comparator

bandwidth That frequency at which the voltage gain is reduced to $1/\sqrt{2}$ times the low-frequency value.

common-mode rejection ratio The ratio of the input common-mode voltage range to the peak-to-peak change in input offset voltage over this range.

harmonic distortion The percentage of harmonic distortion being defined as one-hundred times the ratio of the root-mean-square (rms) sum of the harmonics to the fundamental. % harmonic distortion =

$$\frac{(V2^2 + V3^2 + V4^2 + \ldots)^{1/2}\,(100\%)}{V1}$$

where V1 is the rms amplitude of the fundamental and V2, V3, V4, . . . are the rms amplitudes of the individual harmonics.

input bias current The average of the two input currents.

input common-mode voltage range The range of voltages on the input terminals for which the amplifier is operational. Note that the specifications are not guaranteed over the full common-mode voltage range unless specifically stated.

input impedance The ratio of input voltage to input current under the stated conditions for source resistance (R_S) and load resistance (R_L).

input offset current The difference in the currents into the two input terminals when the output is at zero.

input offset voltage That voltage which must be applied between the input terminals through two equal resistances to obtain zero output voltage.

input resistance The ratio of the change in input voltage to the change in input current on either input with the other grounded.

input voltage range The range of voltages on the input terminals for which the amplifier operates within specifications.

large-signal voltage gain The ratio of the output voltage swing to the change in input voltage required to drive the output from zero to this voltage.

output impedance The ratio of output voltage to output current under the stated conditions for source resistance (R_S) and load resistance (R_L).

output resistance The small signal resistance seen at the output when the output voltage is near zero.

output voltage swing The peak output voltage swing, referred to zero, that can be obtained without clipping.

offset voltage temperature drift The average drift rate of offset voltage for a thermal variation from room temperature to the indicated temperature extreme.

power supply rejection   The ratio of the change in input offset voltage to the change in power supply voltages producing it.

setting time   The time between the initiation of the input-step function and the time when the output voltage has settled to within a specified error band of the final output voltage.

slew rate   The internally-limited rate of change in output voltage with a large-amplitude step function applied to the input.

supply current   The current required from the power supply to operate the amplifier with no load and the output midway between the supplies.

transient response   The closed-loop step-function response of the amplifier under small-signal conditions.

unity-gain bandwidth   The frequency range from dc to the frequency where the amplifier open-loop gain rolls off to one.

voltage gain   The ratio of output voltage to input voltage under the stated conditions for source resistance (R_S) and load resistance (R_L).

Voltage Regulators

current-limit sense voltage   The voltage across the current-limit terminals required to cause the regulator to current-limit with a short-circuited output. This voltage is used to determine the value of the external current-limit resistor when external booster transistors are used.

dropout voltage   The input-output voltage differential at which the circuit ceases to regulate against further reductions in input voltage.

feedback sense voltage   The voltage, referred to ground, on the feedback terminal of the regulator while it is operating in regulation.

input voltage range   The range of dc input voltages over which the regulator will operate within specifications.

line regulation   The change in output voltage for a change in the input voltage. The measurement is made under conditions of low dissipation or by using pulse techniques such that the average chip temperature is not significantly affected.

load regulation   The change in output voltage for a change in load current at constant chip temperature.

long-term stability   Output voltage stability under accelerated life-test conditions at 125°C with maximum rated voltages and power dissipation for 1000 hours.

maximum power dissipation   The maximum total device dissipation for which the regulator will operate within specifications.

output-input voltage differential   The voltage difference between the unregulated input voltage and the regulated output voltage for which the regulator will operate within specifications.

output noise voltage   The rms ac voltage at the output with constant load and no input ripple, measured over a specified frequency range.

output voltage range   The range of regulated output voltages over which the specifications apply.

output voltage scale factor   The output voltage obtained for a unit value of resistance between the adjustment terminal and ground.

quiescent current   That part of input current to the regulator that is not delivered to the load.

ripple rejection   The line regulation for ac input signals at or above a given frequency with a specified value of bypass capacitor on the reference bypass terminal.

standby current drain   That part of the operating current of the regulator which does not contribute to the load current.

temperature stability   The percentage change in output voltage for a thermal variation from room temperature to either temperature extreme.

L-6-OV Series
6-Amp Overvoltage Protectors

The L-6-OV series of ICs are overvoltage protectors, designed to prevent, or at least limit damage to a load caused by an excessive power-supply output voltage. Essentially, the load is protected by the device automatically short-circuiting the output terminals of the power supply when the trip-point voltage limit of the IC is exceeded. The L-6-OV devices come in several standard trip voltages. The trip voltage for each device is fixed and cannot be adjusted with external circuitry.

The L-6-OV devices can be reset by interrupting the applied power and letting the case temperature drop below 71° C (if necessary). In most practical applications, an external heatsink will be required to maintain the protector's case temperature below the rated limit. Often the power-supply chassis itself will do just fine as the heatsink.

The L-6-OV devices are very simple to incorporate into almost any circuit that requires overvoltage protection. These ICs have just two active terminals—the positive and negative inputs.

Device	Nominal Supply Voltage	Trip-Point Voltage
L-6-OV-5	5 V	6.6 V ±0.2
L-6-OV-12	12 V	13.7 V ±0.4
L-6-OV-15	15 V	17.0 V ±0.5
L-6-OV-24	24 V	27.3 V ±0.8

For All L-6-OV Devices

Max. On-Stage Voltage	2.6 V
Max. On-Stage Current	6 A

Bottom View

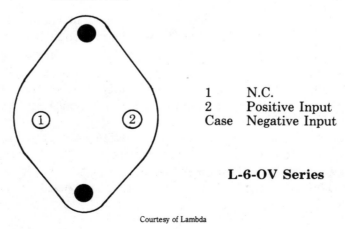

1	N.C.
2	Positive Input
Case	Negative Input

L-6-OV Series

Courtesy of Lambda

LM117/LM217/LM317 3-Terminal Adjustable Regulator

The LM117/LM217/LM317 are adjustable 3-terminal positive voltage regulators capable of supplying in excess of 1.5 A over a 1.2 to 37 V output range. They are exceptionally easy to use and require only two external resistors to set the output voltage. Further, both line and load regulation are better than standard fixed regulators. Also, the LM117 is packaged in standard transistor packages which are easily mounted and handled.

In addition to performing better than fixed regulators, the LM117 series offers full overload protection available only in ICs. Included on the chip are current-limit, thermal-overload protection and safe-area protection. All overload-protection circuitry remains fully functional, even if the adjustment terminal is disconnected. Features include:

- Adjustable output down to 1.2 V
- Guaranteed 1.5 A output current
- Line regulation typically 0.01 percent/V
- Load regulation typically 0.1 percent
- Current limit constant with temperature
- 100-percent electrical burn-in
- Eliminates the need to stock many voltages
- Standard 3-lead transistor package
- 80-dB ripple rejection

Normally, no capacitors are needed unless the device is situated far from the input filter capacitors, in which case an input bypass is needed. An optional output capacitor can be added to improve transient response. The adjustment terminal can be bypassed to achieve very high ripple-rejection ratios that are difficult to achieve with standard 3-terminal regulators.

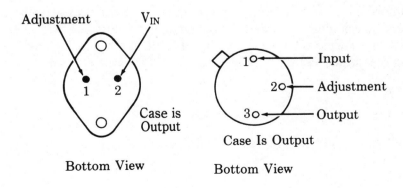

LM117

1.2 – 25 V Adjustable Regulator

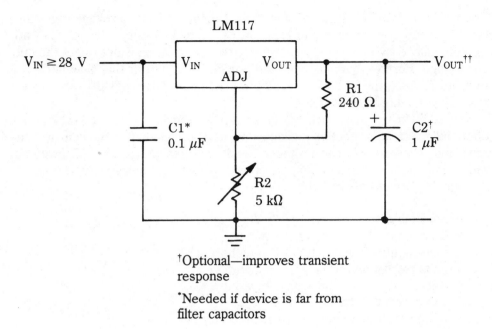

†Optional—improves transient response

*Needed if device is far from filter capacitors

$$^{\dagger\dagger}V_{OUT} = 1.25V\left(1 + \frac{R2}{R1}\right)$$

Besides replacing fixed regulators, the LM117 is useful in many other applications. Because the regulator is floating and sees only the input-to-output differential voltage, supplies of several hundred volts can be regulated as long as the maximum input to output differential is not exceeded.

Also, the LM117 makes an especially simple adjustable switching regulator, a programmable-output regulator, or by connecting a fixed resistor between the adjustment and output, a precision current regulator. Supplies with electronic shutdown can be achieved by clamping the adjustment terminal to ground, which programs the output to 1.2 V where most loads draw little current.

LM120/LM220/LM320 3-Terminal Negative Regulator

The LM120 series are 3-terminal negative regulators with a fixed output voltage of -5 V, -5.2 V, -6 V, -8 V, -9 V, -12 V, -15 V, -18 V, and -24 V with up to 1.5 A load current capability (LM320-5, LM320-5.2, LM320-6, etc.).

These devices need only one external component: a compensation capacitor at the output, making them easy to apply. Worst-case guarantees on output voltage deviation due to any combination of line, load, or temperature variation ensure satisfactory system operation.

Exceptional effort has been made to make the LM120 series immune to overload conditions. The regulators have current limiting, which is independent of temperature, combined with thermal-overload protection. Internal current limiting protects against momentary faults and thermal shutdown prevents junction temperatures from exceeding safe limits during prolonged overloads.

Although primarily intended for fixed output voltage applications, the LM120 series can be programmed for higher output voltages with a simple resistive divider. The low quiescent drain current of the devices allows this technique to be used with good regulation. They feature:

- Preset output voltage error less than ± 3 percent
- Preset current limit
- Internal thermal shutdown
- Operates with input-output voltage differential down to 1 V
- Excellent ripple rejection
- Low temperature drift
- Easily adjustable to higher output voltage

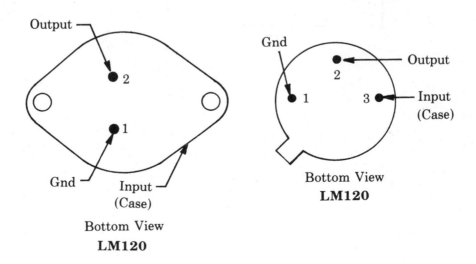

Bottom View
LM120

Bottom View
LM120

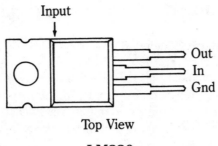

Input

Out
In
Gnd

Top View

LM320

Fixed Regulator

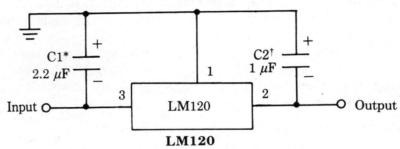

C1*
2.2 μF

+

−

3

1

LM120

2

C2†
1 μF

+

−

Input O

O Output

LM120

Input

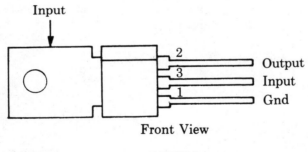

2 Output
3 Input
1 Gnd

Front View

LM320

LM122/LM222/LM322 Precision Timer

The LM122 series are precision timers that offer great versatility with high accuracy. They operate with unregulated supplies from 4.5 to 40 V while maintaining constant timing periods from microseconds to hours. Internal logic and regulator circuits complement the basic timing function, enabling the LM122 series to operate in many different applications with a minimum of external components.

The output of the timer is a floating transistor with built-in current limiting. It can drive either ground-referred or supply-referred loads up to 40 V and 50 mA. The floating nature of this output makes it ideal for interfacing, lamp or relay driving, and signal conditioning where an open collector or emitter is required. A logic-reverse circuit can be programmed by the user to make the output transistor either on or off during the timing period.

The trigger input to the LM122 series has a threshold of 1.6 V independent of supply voltage, but it is fully protected against inputs as high as ± 40 V, even when using a 5 V supply. The circuitry reacts only to the rising edge of the trigger signal, and is immune to any trigger voltage during the timing periods.

An internal 3.15 V regulator is included in the timer to reject supply voltage changes and to provide the user with a convenient reference for applications other than a basic timer. External loads up to 5 mA can be driven by the regulator. An internal 2 V divider between the reference and ground sets the timing period to 1 RC. The timing period can be voltage-controlled by driving this

Metal Can Package

Emitter

Logic 1
10
9 Collector

Trigger 2
8 Boost

LM122

V_{ref} 3
7 V^+

R/C 4
6 V_{adj}
5
7

Gnd

Top View

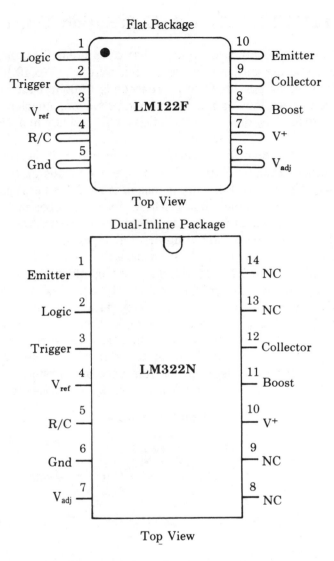

Flat Package

1 Logic
2 Trigger
3 V_{ref}
4 R/C
5 Gnd

LM122F

10 Emitter
9 Collector
8 Boost
7 V^+
6 V_{adj}

Top View

Dual-Inline Package

1 Emitter
2 Logic
3 Trigger
4 V_{ref}
5 R/C
6 Gnd
7 V_{adj}

LM322N

14 NC
13 NC
12 Collector
11 Boost
10 V^+
9 NC
8 NC

Top View

divider with an external source through the V_{ADJ} pin. Timing ratios of 50:1 can be easily achieved.

The comparator used in the LM122 utilizes high-gain pnp input transistors to achieve 300-pA typical input bias current over a common mode range of 0 to 3 V. A boost terminal allows the user to increase comparator operating current for timing periods less than 1 ms. This lets the timer operate over a 3 μs to multi-hour timing range with excellent repeatability.

The LM2905/LM3905 are identical to the LM122 series except that the boost and V_{REF} pin options are not available, limiting minimum timing period to 1 ms.

470

LM123/LM223/LM323 3-Amp, 5-Volt Positive Regulator

The LM123 is a 3-terminal positive regulator with a preset 5 V output and a load driving capability of 3 A. New circuit design and processing techniques are used to provide the high output current without sacrificing the regulation characteristics of lower current devices.

The 3 A regulator is virtually blowout proof. Current limiting, power limiting, and thermal shutdown provide the same high level of reliability obtained with these techniques in the LM109 1-amp regulator.

No external components are required for operation of the LM123. If the device is more than 4 inches from the filter capacitor, however, a 1 μF solid tantalum capacitor should be used on the input. A 0.1 μF or larger capacitor can be used on the output to reduce load transient spikes created by fast-switching digital logic or to swamp out stray load capacitance.

An overall worst-case specification for the combined effects of input voltage, load currents, ambient temperature, and power dissipation ensure that the LM123 will perform satisfactorily as a system element. Features are:

- 3 A output current
- Internal current and thermal limiting
- 0.01 Ω typical output impedance
- 7.5 V minimum input voltage
- 30 W power dissipation

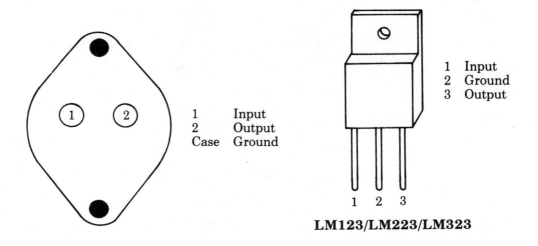

1	Input
2	Output
Case	Ground

1	Input
2	Ground
3	Output

1 2 3

LM123/LM223/LM323

LM139/LM239/LM339, LM139A/LM239A/LM339A, LM2901, LM3302 Low-Power Low-Offset Voltage Quad Comparator

The LM139 series consists of four independent precision voltage comparators with an offset voltage specification as low as 2 mV maximum for all four comparators. These were designed specifically to operate from a single power supply over a wide range of voltages. Operation from split power supplies is also possible and the low-power supply-current drain is independent of the magnitude of the power-supply voltage. These comparators also have a unique characteristic in that the input common-mode voltage range includes ground, even though operated from a single power-supply voltage.

Application areas include limit comparators; simple analog-to-digital converters; pulse, square-wave, and time-delay generators; wide-range VCOs; MOS clock timers; multivibrators and high-voltage digital logic gates. The LM139 series was designed to directly interface with TTL and CMOS. When operated from both plus and minus power supplies, they will directly interface with MOS logic, where the low power drain of the LM339 is a distinct advantage over standard comparators.

Supply Voltage Range:

LM139 series	2 to 36 V_{dc} or
LM139A series, LM2901	± 1 to ± 18 V_{dc}
LM3302	2 to 28 V_{dc}
	or ± 1 to ± 14 V_{dc}
Supple Current Drain	0.8 mA
Input Biasing Current	25 nA
Input Offset Current	± 5 nA
Offset Voltage	± 3 mV
Output Saturation Voltage	250 mV at 4 mA

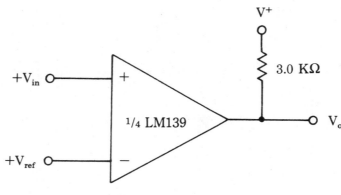

Basic Comparator

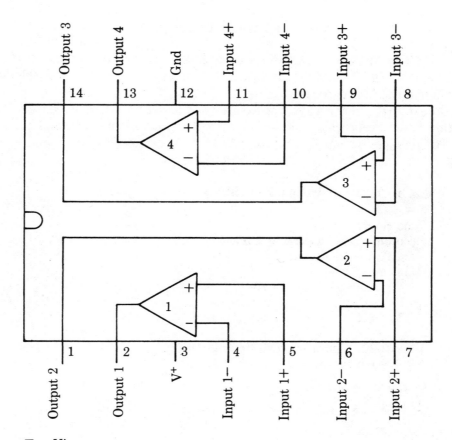

Top View

LM139

BA222 Monolithic Timer

The BA222 is a timer IC, similar in concept to the popular 555, discussed later in this section. Like the 555, the BA222 can be used in either monostable-or astable-multivibrator circuits.

An external resistor and capacitor are used to set the RC time constant of the timer over a very wide range—from a few microseconds up to several hours.

The time period equation for the BA222 is the same as for the 555:

$$T = 1.1RC$$

The BA222 is contained within a 7-pin SIP (single-inline package).

Max. Supply Voltage	+18 V
Recommended Operating Range	+4.5 to 16.0 V
Max. Power Dissipation	500 mW
Quiescent Current	
V_{cc} **= 5 V Infinite Load**	3 mA typ.
	7 mA max.
V_{cc} **= 15 V Infinite Load**	10 mA typ.
	15 mA max.
Monostable Operating Timing Regulation	1% typ.
Astable Operating Timing Regulation	2.5% typ.
Output Low Voltage	
V_{cc} **= 5 V** I_{sink} **= 5 mA**	0.25 V typ.
	0.35 V max.

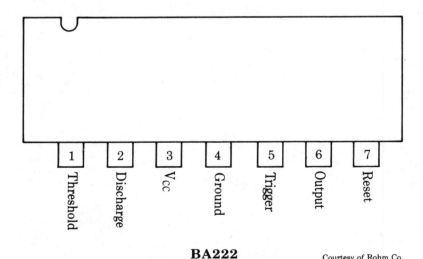

BA222

Courtesy of Rohm Co.

V_{cc} = 15 V I_{sink} = 100 mA   2.0 V typ.
                                            2.5 V max.
V_{cc} = 15 V I_{sink} = 100 mA   2.5 V typ.

Output High Voltage

V_{cc} = 5 V I_{source} = 100 mA   2.75 V min.
                                            3.30 V typ.
V_{cc} = 15 V I_{source} = 100 mA   12.75 V min.
                                            13.30 V typ.
V_{cc} = 15 V I_{source} = 100 mA   12.50 V typ.

BA225, BA226, BA235, BA236
Dual Monostable Timers

The BA225, BA226, BA235, and BA236 each contain two separate timers in a single IC package. Each timer section is similar to the one contained in the BA222, discussed earlier, except the pinouts for these devices are suited only for monostable-multivibrator applications. Astable-multivibrator circuits are not easily designed around these chips.

The basic time-period equation for this series of ICs is the same as for the BA222 and the popular 555 timer IC:

$$T = 1.1RC$$

The BA225 and BA226 are contained in 8-pin DIP (dual inline package) housing, and the BA235 and BA236 use a 9-pin SIP (single inline package) housing.

The BA225 and the BA235 are triggered by the leading edge of the input pulse, while the BA226 and the BA236 are triggered by the trailing edge of the input pulse. Otherwise, the specifications are the same for all four devices.

Supply Voltage	+16 V max.
	+5.0 V typ.
	+4.0 V min.
Power Dissipation	450 mW max.
Quiescent Current	1.5 mA typ.
	3.0 mA max.
Timing Regulation	1% typ.
	10% max.
Output Low Voltage	
(V_{cc} = 5 V I_{sink} = 5 mA)	0.5 V typ.
	1.0 V max.
Output High Voltage	
(V_{cc} = 5 V I_{source} = 5 mA)	3.0 V min.
	4.0 V max.

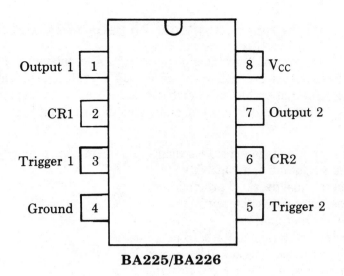

BA225/BA226

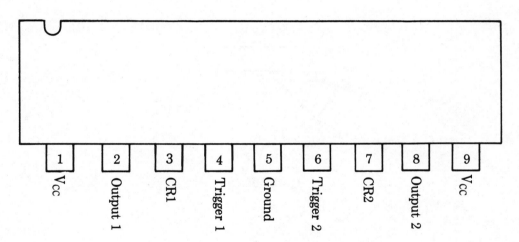

BA235/BA236

477

LM320L Series 3-Terminal Negative Regulator

The LM320L-XX series of 3-terminal negative voltage regulators features several selected fixed output voltages from -5 to -24 V with load current capabilities to 100 mA. Internal protective circuitry includes safe operating area for the output transistor, short-circuit current limit, and thermal shutdown. Features include:

- Preset output voltage error less than ± 5 percent over temperature
- 100 mA output current capability
- Internal thermal overload protection
- Input-output voltage differential down to 2 V
- Internal current limit
- Maximum load regulation -0.15 percent/mA
- Maximum line regulation -0.1 percent/V
- Output transistor safe-area protection

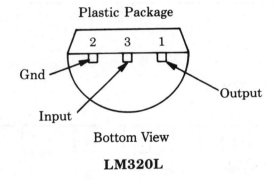

LM320L

LM340 Series Voltage Regulator

The LM340-XX series of 3-terminal regulators is available with several fixed output voltages, making them useful in a wide range of applications. One of these is local on-card regulation, eliminating the distribution problems associated with single-point regulation. The voltages available allow these regulators to be used in logic systems, instrumentation, stereo, and other solid-state electronic equipment. Although designed primarily as fixed voltage regulators, these devices can be used with external components to obtain adjustable voltages and currents.

The LM340-XX series is available in two power packages. Both the plastic TO-220 and metal TO-3 packages allow these regulators to deliver over 1.5 A, if adequate heat sinking is provided. Current limiting is included to limit the peak output current to a safe value. Safe-area protection for the output transistor is provided to limit internal power dissipation. If internal power dissipation becomes too high for the heat sinking provided, the thermal-shutdown circuit takes over, preventing the IC from overheating.

Considerable effort was expended to make the LM340-XX series of regulators easy to use, with a minimal number of external components. It is not necessary to bypass the output, although this does improve transient response. Input bypassing is needed only if the regulator is located far from the filter capacitor of the power supply. Features include:

- Output current in excess of 1.5 A
- Internal thermal-overload protection
- No external components required
- Output transistor safe-area protection
- Internal short-circuit current limit

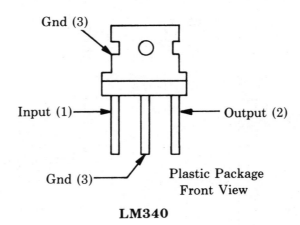

Plastic Package
Front View

LM340

555 Timer

The 555 timer is probably one of the most popular ICs ever. It was designed for use in both monostable-multivibrator and astable-multivibrator circuits.

The timing period of the 555 is set by a straightforward external resistor-capacitor combination, according to a simple formula:

$$T = 1.1RC$$

For reliable operation, the timing resistor should have a value between 10 kΩ and 14 MΩ, and the timing capacitor's value should be between 100 pF and 1000 μF. These values produce a practical timing range from a low of 1.1 microsecond up to a high of 15,400 seconds (4 hours, 16 minutes, and 40 seconds). The timer certainly has quite an impressive range, especially for such an inexpensive and easy-to-use chip.

Supply Voltage	+16 V max.
	+4.5 V min.
Supply Current	
V_{cc} = 15 V Infinite Load Output Low	10 mA typ.
V_{cc} = 15 V Infinite Load Output High	9 mA typ.
Power Dissipation	600 mW max.
Threshold Voltage	2/3 X Vcc
Threshold Current	0.1 μA typ.
	0.25 μA max.
Trigger Voltage	5 V typ.
Trigger Current	0.5 μA typ.
Reset Voltage	0.4 V min.
	0.7 V typ.
	1.0 V max.
Reset Current	0.1 mA typ.

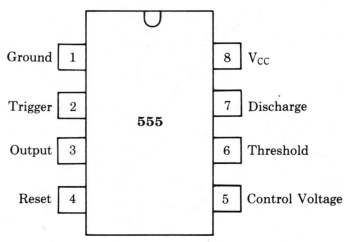

556 DUAL Timer

The 556 timer IC contains two 555-type timer sections. These two sections are independent of one another, except for the power-supply connections.

Each of the timer stages in the 556 is the same as the 555 timer, discussed earlier. These timers are designed for use in both monostable-multivibrator and astable-multivibrator circuits. The timing period of each timer section is set by a straightforward external resistor-capacitor combination, according to a simple formula:

$$T = 1.1RC$$

For reliable operation, the timing resistor should have a value between 10 kΩ and 14 MΩ, and the timing capacitor's value should be between 100 pF and 1000 μF. These values produce a practical timing range from a low of 1.1 microsecond up to a high of 15,400 seconds (4 hours, 16 minutes, and 40 seconds).

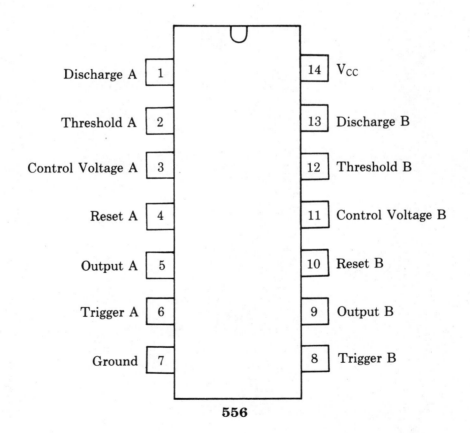

556

Supply Voltage	+16 V Max.
	+4.5 V Min.
Supply Current	
V_{cc} = 15 V Infinite Load Output low	10 mA Typ.
V_{cc} = 15 V Infinite Load Output high	9 mA Typ.
Power Dissipation	600 mW Max.
Threshold Voltage	$2/3$ X V_{CC}
Threshold Current	0.1 μA Typ.
	0.25 μA Max.
Trigger Voltage	5 V typ.
Trigger Current	0.5 μA typ.
Reset Voltage	0.4 V min.
	0.7 V typ.
	1.0 V max.
Reset Current	0.1 mA typ.

BA612 Large Current Driver

The BA612 contains five Darlington transistor arrays with input resistors to boost the current-driving capability of other circuitry.

Notice that all of the inputs are along the left side of the 14-pin DIP (dual-inline package) IC and all of the outputs are to the right.

Notice also that this chip has no V_{cc} supply-voltage connection. Power is "stolen" through the load.

Supply Voltage (Through Load)	30 V max.
Power Dissipation	550 mW max.
Output Current Driving Capability	400 mA Max.
Input Voltage	
Positive	30 V Max.
Negative	-0.5 V Max.

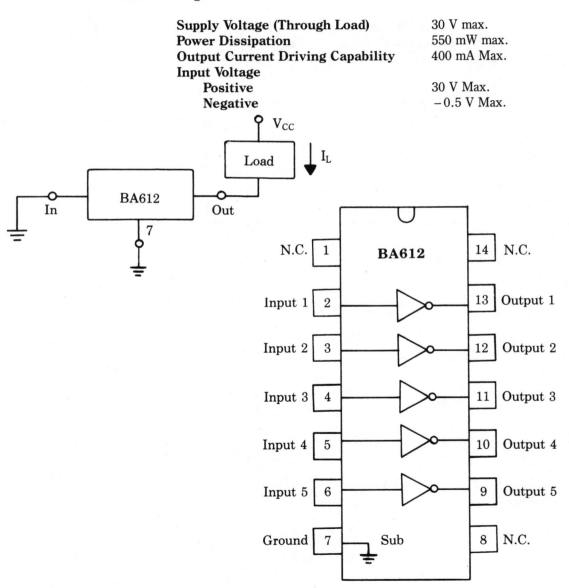

BA634 Toggle Flip-Flop with Reset

The BA634 is a toggle-type flip-flop circuit with a high noise margin. Its output circuitry features a totem-pole configuration. A reset pin is provided.

This chip is available in a five-pin SIP (single-inline package) housing. Unlike many other flip-flop circuits, there is only a small difference in the power consumption when the output is high or low. This characteristic permits an easier power supply design.

Supply Voltage	− 16 V max.
Power Dissipation	150 mW max.
Input Voltage	− 12 V min.
	0 V max.

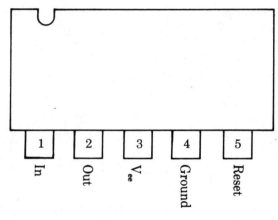

BA634

LM723/LM723C Voltage Regulator

The LM723/LM723C is a voltage regulator designed primarily for series regulator applications. By itself, it will supply output currents up to 150 mA, but external transistors can be added to provide any desired load current. The circuit features extremely low standby current drain, and provisions are made for either linear or foldback current limiting. Important characteristics are:

- 150 mA output current without an external-pass transistor
- Output currents in excess of 10 A possible by adding external transistors
- Input voltage 40 V max
- Output voltage adjustable from 2 to 37 V
- Can be used as either a linear or a switching regulator

The LM723/LM723C is also useful in a wide range of other applications such as a shunt regulator, a current regulator or a temperature controller.

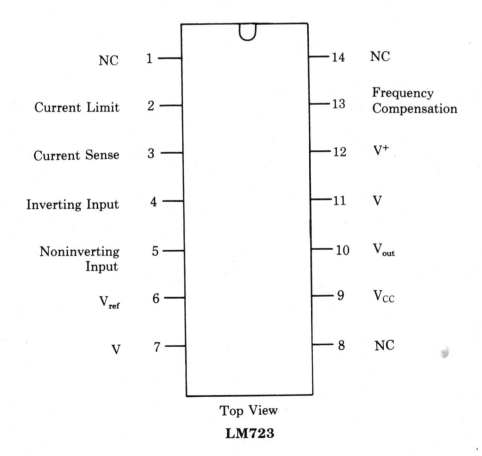

Top View

LM723

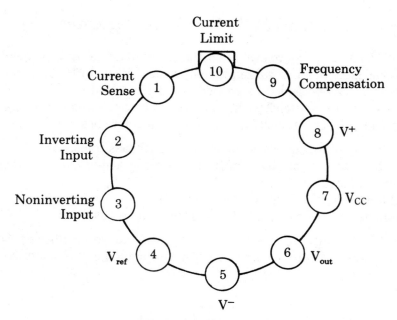

Note: Pin 5 connected to case.

Top View

LAS1000, LAS1100 150-mA Positive Voltage Regulator/Linear Controller

The LAS1000 and LAS1100 are voltage-regulator ICs capable of putting out currents up to 150 mA. These chips include safety features such as internal current limiting, electronic shutdown, and thermal shutdown. The LAS1000 and LAS1100 feature excellent temperature regulation and very low output impedance, providing superior performance and load regulation.

LAS1000

Input Voltage	5 V Min.
	40 V Max.
Output Voltage	2.63 V Min.
	38 V Max.
Output Current	150 mA Max.
Input/Output Differential	38 V Max.
Power Dissipation	800 mW Max.

LAS1100

Input Voltage	5 V min.
	50 V max.
Output Voltage	2.63 V min.
	48 V max.
Output Current	150 mA max.
Input/Output Differential	48 V max.
Power Dissipation	800 mW max.

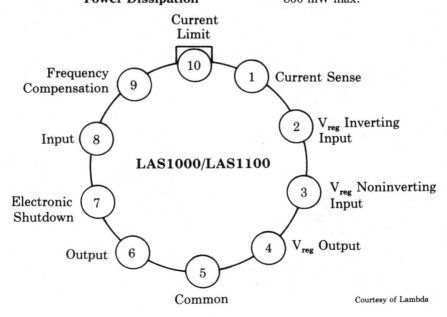

LAS1000/LAS1100

Current Limit — 10
Current Sense — 1
V_{reg} Inverting Input — 2
V_{reg} Noninverting Input — 3
V_{reg} Output — 4
Common — 5
Output — 6
Electronic Shutdown — 7
Input — 8
Frequency Compensation — 9

Courtesy of Lambda

487

UAA1041 Automotive Direction Indicator

The UAA1041 is designed for use with a relay in automotive signaling applications. While intended primarily for the direction (turn signal) indicators, this chip can also be used for other warning lamps, such as "handbrake on."

The UAA1041 features defective lamp detection, and overvoltage protection. It also features short-circuit detection and relay shutdown to minimize the risk of fire or other damage. The chip is internally protected against reversed battery connections.

Supply Voltage	18 V max.
	8.0 V min.
Overvoltage Detector Threshold	19.0 V min.
	20.2 V typ.
	21.5 V max.
Current (Continuous)	
Pin #1	+150 mA pos. max.
	−35 mA neg. max.
Pin #2	±350 mA max.
Pin #3	±300 mA max.
Pin #8	±25 mA max.
Current (Pulse)	
Pin #1	+500 mA pos. max.
	−500 mA neg. max.
Pin #2	±1900 mA max.
Pin #3	±1400 mA max.
Pin #8	±50 mA max.

```
   −V_cc  | 1        8 |  Start

   +V Bat | 2        7 |  Fault Det.

   Rly Out| 3        6 |  Fault Det.
                           On/Off

   Osc    | 4        5 |  Osc
```

Copyright of Motorola, Used by Permission

LAS1400 Series
3-Amp Positive Voltage Regulators

The LAS1400 series of ICs are voltage regulators designed to put out a well-regulated voltage at relatively high current levels—up to 3 full amperes.

Three fixed voltage regulators are in the LAS1400 Series:

LAS1405	5 V
LAS1412	12 V
LAS1415	15 V

A related device is the LAS14AU, which is a four terminal adjustable voltage regulator, with an output voltage ranging from +4 up to +30 volts. This chip also offers remote sense capability with a single external potentiometer.

Input Voltage	
LAS1405	30 V max.
LAS1412	30 V max.
LAS1415	35 V max.
LAS14AU	35 V max.
Power Dissipation (Internally Limited)	30 W max.
Line Regulation	1.0% Vo
Load Regulation	0.6% Vo
Quiescent Current	20.0 mA max.

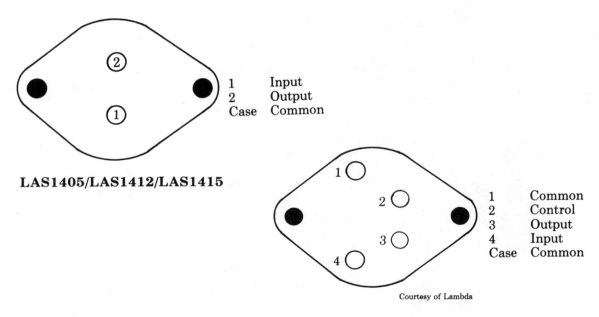

1	Input
2	Output
Case	Common

LAS1405/LAS1412/LAS1415

1	Common
2	Control
3	Output
4	Input
Case	Common

Courtesy of Lambda

LAS14AU

MC1455 Timer

The MC1455 is a monolithic timer, not entirely dissimilar to the popular 555 IC, discussed earlier in this section. In fact, the MC1455 is designed as a direct, improved replacement for the 555.

This chip can be used in both monostable multivibrator and astable multivibrator applications. In the monostable mode, the timing period is precisely set by one external resistor and one external capacitor. The timing periods (frequency and duty cycle) in the astable mode are precisely controlled by two external resistors and one external capacitor. The circuitry is similar to that used for the 555 timer. The same basic timing equation is used for the MC1455;

$$T = 1.1RC$$

Timing periods from a few microseconds up to several hours can be easily set up with this device. In the astable mode, the duty cycle is fully adjustable.

The output can be selected for either normally ''on'' (high) or normally ''off'' (low) to suit the individual application. The output of the MC1455 can source or sink up to 200 mA, or drive MTTL circuits.

Supply Voltage	+18 V max.
Recommended Operating Range	+4.5 V to +16 V
Supply Current	
V_{cc} **= 5 V Infinite Load**	3.0 mA typ.
	6.0 mA max.
V_{cc} **= 15 V Infinite Load**	10 mA typ.
	15 mA max.
Power Dissipation	680 mW max.
Discharge Current (Pin #7)	200 mA max.
Timing Error	1.0% typ.

1. Ground
2. Trigger
3. Output
4. Reset
5. Control Voltage
6. Threshold
7. Discharge
8. V_{cc}

G Suffix
Metal Package
Case 601-04

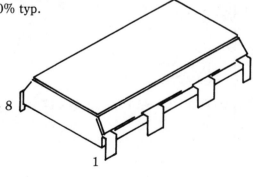

D Suffix
Plastic Package
Case 751-02
SO-8

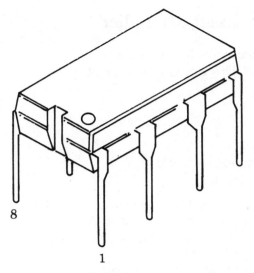

P1 Suffix
Plastic Package
Case 626-05

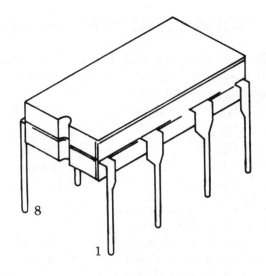

U Suffix
Ceramic Package
Case 693-02

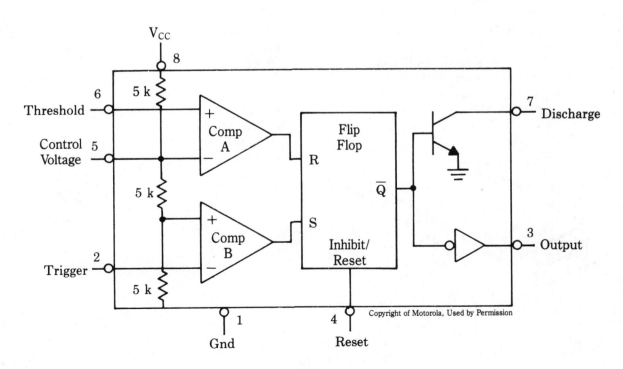

Copyright of Motorola, Used by Permission

MC1455

491

MC1494L, MC1594L Linear Four-Quadrant Multiplier

The MC1494L and MC1594L are linear four-quadrant multiplier ICs—the output voltage is the linear product of two input voltages. This chip offers excellent linearity in its operation.

Typical applications for this device include:

- Multiply
- Divide
- Square root
- Mean square

- Phase detector
- Frequency doubler
- Balanced modulator/demodulator
- Electronic Gain Control

In technical terms, the MC1494 and MC1594 are variable transconductance multipliers with internal level-shift circuitry and an on-chip voltage regulator. A pair of complementary-regulated voltages are provided to simplify offset adjustment and improve power-supply rejection.

Four external potentiometers can be added to the circuit to allow full manual adjustment over scale factor, input offset, and output offset.

Supply Voltage	± 18 V Max.
Power Dissipation	750 mW Max.
Maximum Error (X or Y)	
MC1494L	$\pm 1.0\%$ Max.
MC1594L	$\pm 0.5\%$ Max.
Input Voltage Range	± 10 V
Frequency Response (3-dB Small Signal)	1.0 MHz
Power Supply Sensitivity	30 mV/V typ.
Power Supply Current	
MC1494L	± 6.0 mA typ.
	± 12 mA max.
MC1594L	$+6.0$ mA, -6.5 mA typ.
	± 9.0 mA max.

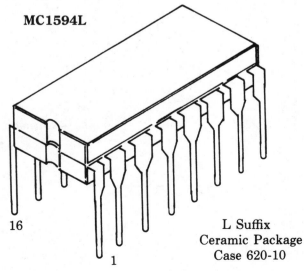

16

1

L Suffix
Ceramic Package
Case 620-10

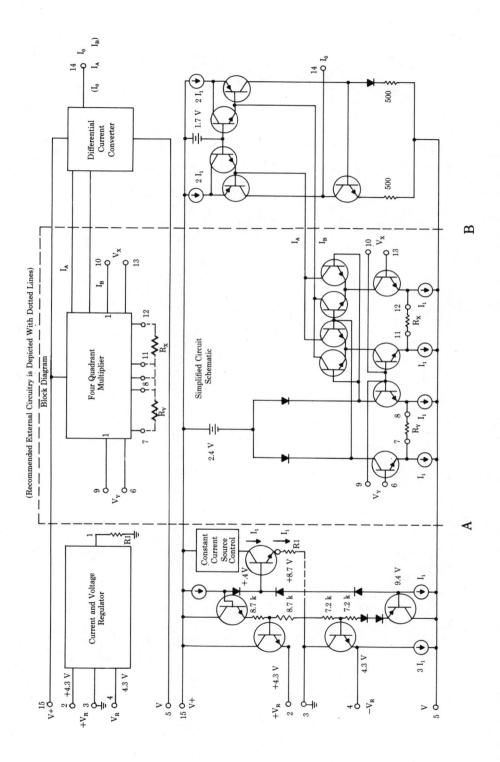

(Recommended External Circuitry is Depicted With Dotted Lines)

Block Diagram

Simplified Circuit Schematic

493

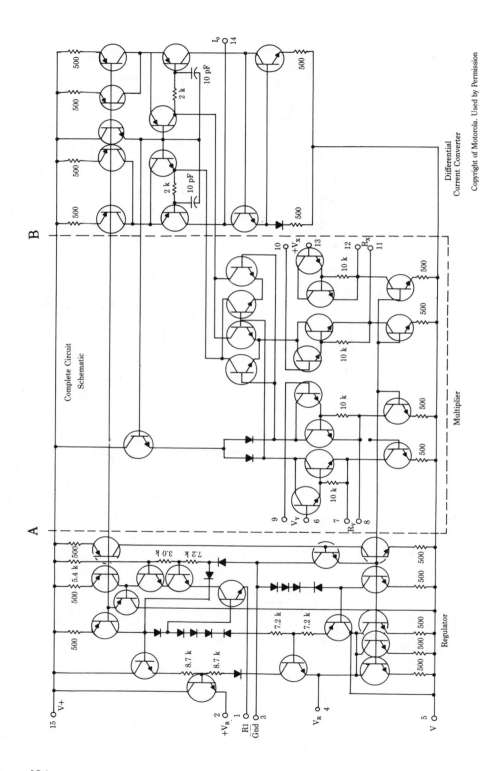

Complete Circuit Schematic

Differential Current Converter

Copyright of Motorola. Used by Permission

Multiplier

Regulator

BA1604 PLL Tone Decoder

The BA1604 is a tone decoder IC using PLL (phase-locked loop) circuitry. It is available in an 8-pin DIP (dual inline package) housing. This device operates with fine frequency selectivity.

The circuitry within the BA1604 includes;

- PLL
- Phase detector
- Buffer amplifier
- Voltage comparator
- Output logic driver

In operation, if the input signal has a frequency within the circuit's passband, the PLL will lock onto the input signal, and the phase detector's output voltage then drops. The transistors within the voltage comparator and output-logic driver stages are turned on by this.

The center frequency of the tone decoder is controlled by an RC time constant connected between pins #5 and 6. A wide range of frequencies can be used with this chip, from about 0.01 Hz up to 500 kHz. The center frequency can be controlled with an external resistor over a wide ratio—typically 20:1. The center frequency is highly stable. A current-controlled oscillator is used in the PLL. The detection bandwidth of the tone decoder can be adjusted between 0 and 14 percent.

The BA1604 can drive output loads up to 100 mA. The output signals from this device are directly interfacable with standard-logic (digital) circuitry. The BA1604 is a direct, pin-for-pin replacement for the 567 tone-decoder IC.

Supply Voltage	9.0 V max.	**Center Frequency**	0.01 Hz min.
	6.0 V typ.		500 kHz max.
	4.75 V min.	**Output Current**	100 mA max.
Power Dissipation	300 mW max.		

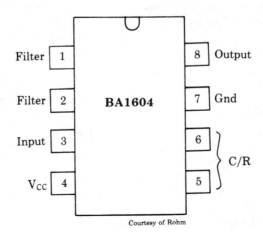

Courtesy of Rohm

LAS1900 Series
5-Amp Positive Voltage Regulators

The LAS1900 series is a group of relatively high-power voltage-regulator ICs. Each device in this series can handle currents up to 5 amperes.

Three fixed voltage devices are available:

LAS1905	+ 5 V
LAS1912	+ 12 V
LAS1915	+ 15 V

The LAS1900 series also includes the LAS19U, which is a four-terminal adjustable voltage regulator. The regulated output voltage can be adjusted between +4 and +30 volts. A single external potentiometer can be used to provide remote-sense capability.

Input Voltage	
LAS1905	+30 V max.
LAS1912	+30 V max.
LAS1915	+35 V max.
LAS19U	+35 V max.
Output Voltage	
LAS1905	+5 V
LAS1912	+12 V
LAS1915	+15 V
LAS19U	+ 4 V min.
	+30 V max.
Power Dissipation	50 W max.
Line Regulation	1.0% Vo max.
Load Regulation	0.6% Vo max.
Quiescent Current Line	5.0 mA max.
Quiescent Current Load	5.0 mA max.
Control Voltage (LAS19U Only)	3.6 V min.
	4.0 V max.

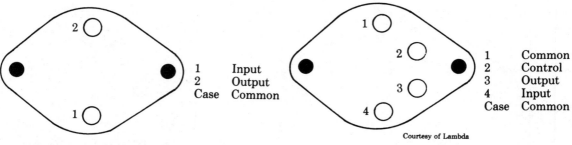

1	Input
2	Output
Case	Common

1	Common
2	Control
3	Output
4	Input
Case	Common

Courtesy of Lambda

LAS1905/LAS1912/LAS1915   **LAS194**

LM2905/LM3905 Precision Timer

The LM122 series contains precision timers that offer great versatility with high accuracy. They operate with unregulated supplies from 4.5 to 40 V while maintaining constant timing periods from microseconds to hours. Internal logic and regulator circuits complement the basic timing function, enabling the LM122 series to operate in many different applications with a minimum of external components.

The output of the timer is a floating transistor with built in current limiting. It can drive either ground-referred or supply-referred loads up to 40 V and 50 mA. The floating nature of this output makes it ideal for interfacing, lamp or relay driving, and signal conditioning where an open collector or emitter is required. A logic-reverse circuit can be programmed by the user to make the output transistor either on or off during the timing period.

The trigger input to the LM122 series has a threshold of 1.6 V independent of supply voltage, but it is fully protected against inputs as high as ± 40 V, even when using a 5 V supply. The circuitry reacts only to the rising edge of the trigger signal, and is immune to any trigger voltage during the timing periods.

An internal 3.15 V regulator is included in the timer to reject supply voltage changes and to provide the user with a convenient reference for applications other than a basic timer. External loads up to 5 mA can be driven by the regulator. An internal 2 V divider between the reference and ground sets the timing period to 1 RC. The timing period can be voltage controlled by driving this divider with an external source through the V_{ADJ} pin. Timing ratios of 50:1 can be easily achieved.

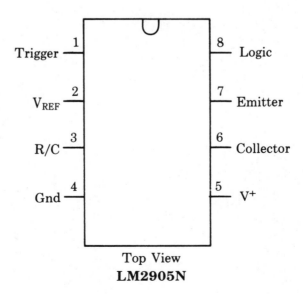

Top View
LM2905N

The comparator used in the LM122 utilizes high-gain pnp input transistors to achieve 300-pA typical input bias current over a common-mode range of 0 to 3 V. A boost terminal allows the user to increase comparator operating current for timing periods less than 1 ms. This lets the timer operate over a 3 μs to multi-hour timing range with excellent repeatability.

The LM2905/LM3905 are identical to the LM122 series except that the boost and V_{REF} pin options are not available, limiting the minimum timing period to 1 ms.

CA3000 Dc Amplifier

The CA3000 is a general-purpose amplifier used in Schmitt trigger, RC-coupled feedback amplifier, mixer, comparator, crystal oscillator, sense amplifier, and modulator applications. It comes in a 10-lead TO-5 package.

Max. Positive Dc Supply Voltage	+10 V
Max. Negative Dc Supply Voltage	−10 V
Max. Input Signal Voltage:	
Single-ended	±2 V
Common mode	±2 V
Max. Total Device Dissipation	300 mW
Typ. Input Offset Voltage	1.4 mV
Typ. Input Offset Current	1.2 μA
Typ. Input Bias Current	23 μA

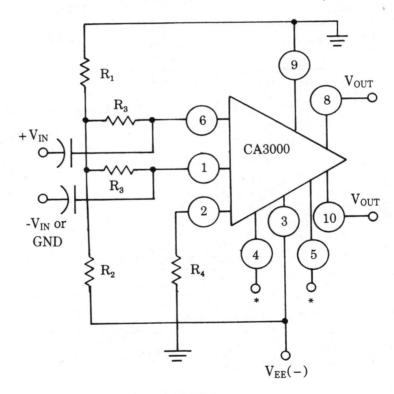

CA3000

CA3035 Ultra-High-Gain Wideband-Amplifier Array

The CA3035 is a general-purpose amplifier with three individual amplifiers used in remote-control amplifier applications, such as TV receivers. It comes in a 10-lead TO-5 package.

Max. Input Signal Voltage (single-ended)	1 Vp-p
Max. Supply Voltage	15 V
Max. Total Device Dissipation	300 mW
Typ. Quiescent Operating Voltage	2 V
Typ. Quiescent Operating Voltage	1.9 V
Typ. Quiescent Operating Voltage	4.9 V
Typ. Total Current Drain (R_{L3} = 5kΩ)	5 mA
Typ. Voltage Gain (f = 40 kHz):	
Amplifier 1, 2, 3	44 dB
Cascade	132 dB
Typ. Noise Figure (Amplifier 1)	6 dB
Typ. Sensitivity	100 μV

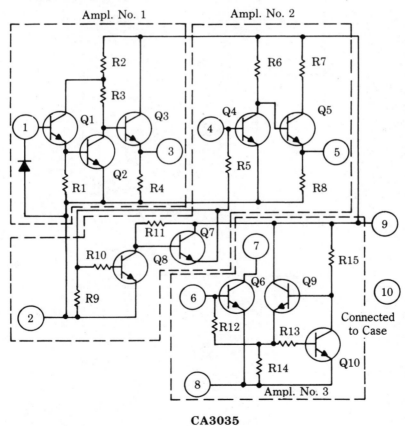

CA3035

500

CA3054 General-Purpose Transistor Array

As integrated circuits go, the CA3054 is a pretty simple device. It basically contains six npn transistors arranged for a number of general-purpose applications.

The six transistors on this chip are divided into two groups of three each. Each three-transistor combination is a simple differential amplifier with a constant-current transistor. The two differential amplifiers are electrically independent of one another, except for the chip's common-ground connection.

Each differential-amplifier stage can handle signals from dc (0 Hz) up to 120 MHz.

Collector-Emitter Voltage	15 V max.
Collector-Base Voltage	20 V max.
Emitter-Base Voltage	5.0 V max.
Collector-Substrate Voltage	20 V max.
Collector Current	
Continuous	50 mA max.
Input Offset Voltage	± 5 mV max.

Pin Connections

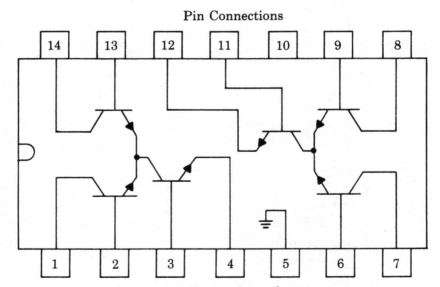

Pin 5 is connected to substrate
and must remain at the lowest circuit potential

CA3054

MC3325 Automotive Voltage Regulator

The MC3325 is a voltage-regulator IC designed primarily for automotive applications. It is designed for use in conjunction with an npn Darlington transistor in a floating-field alternator charging system.

This chip features overvoltage protection and automatic shutdown upon loss of battery sense.

Battery Sense: Threshold Voltage

on Pin #5	11.8 V min.
	13.45 V max.
on Pin #6	11.1 V min.
	12.75 V max.
on Pin #7	10.5 V min.
	11.9 V max.

Current

Into Pin #2	120 mA max.
Into Pin #3	20 mA max.
Into Pin #4	20 mA max.
Into Pin #5	50 mA max.
Into Pin #6	50 mA max.
Into Pin #7	50 mA max.
Into Pin #8	50 mA max.
Into Pin #9	50 mA max.
Into Pin #10	50 mA max.

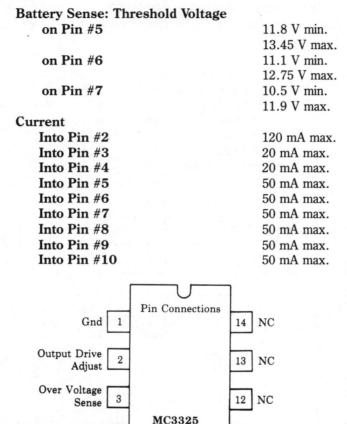

Copyright of Motorola. Used by Permission

MC3346 General-Purpose Transistor Array

As integrated circuits go, the MC3346 is a pretty simple device. It contains six transistors arranged for a number of general-purpose low-power applications.

Collector-Emitter Voltage	15 V max.
Collector-Base Voltage	20 V max.
Emitter-Base Voltage	5.0 V max.
Collector-Substrate Voltage	20 V max.
Total Power Dissipation	1.2 W max.
Collector Current (Continuous)	50 mA max.

Circuit Schematic

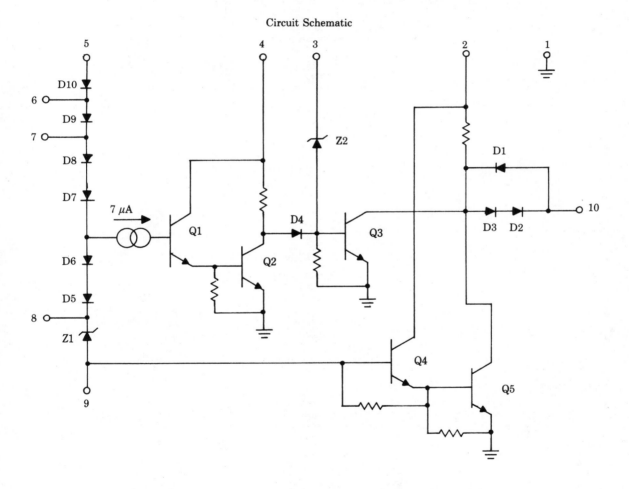

503

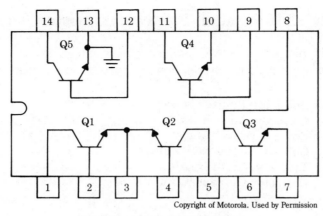

Pin 13 is connected to substrate
and must remain at the lowest circuit potential.

MC3346

MC3373 Remote-Control
Wideband Amplifier with Detector

The MC3373 is a wideband amplifier and detector intended primarily for use in infrared remote-control systems. This chip provides the necessary high gain and pulse shaping to properly couple the signal from an infrared-receiver diode to the tuning-control system logic.

Supply Voltage	15 V max.
	4.75 V min.
Power Dissipation	1.25 W max.
Supply Current	1.5 mA min.
	2.5 mA typ.
	3.5 mA max.
Input Frequency	30 kHz min.
	40 kHz typ.
	80 kHz max.

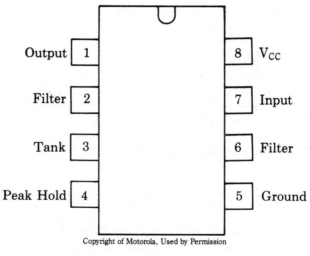

Copyright of Motorola, Used by Permission

MC3373

505

MC3397T Series-Switch
Transient-Protection Circuit

Transients, or brief, large-level noise spikes can be problematic in many circuits. They can interfere with correct signals, and in some cases can even cause permanent damage to some components. The MC3397T is an IC designed to prevent such problem transients from penetrating sensitive circuit areas.

Normally, this chip behaves like a saturated series-pass element with a very low voltage drop for load currents up to (and even exceeding) 750 mA. When, however, the MC3387T senses an overvoltage condition (typically above 17.5 volts), or a positive or negative high-voltage transient spike, the device will instantly switch to an open-circuit (off) state. Power to the load is interrupted by this open-circuit condition, and therefore, the load is isolated and protected from the potentially damaging effects of the excessive voltage.

As soon as the applied voltage returns to its normal (within a safe range) levels, the MC3397T will automatically switch back into its normal (on) state, reconnecting the power line to the load.

The on state for the MC3397T accepts voltages from 4 to 16 volts. This chip can withstand positive or negative voltage transients as high as 125 volts—plenty of "headroom."

Input Voltage	
Continuous	± 85 V max.
Transient	± 125 V max.
Minimum Operating Voltage	2.5 V typ.
	4.5 V max.
Power Dissipation	2.0 W max.
Output Current	Internally Limited

Timing Diagram

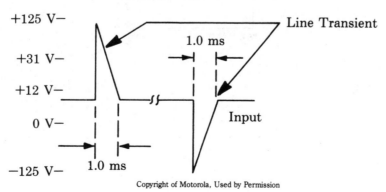

MC3397T

Block Diagram

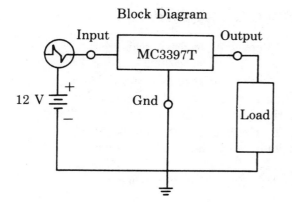

Input

MC3397T

Output

12 V

Gnd

Load

T Suffix
Platic Package
Case 221A-04

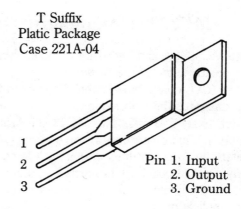

1
2
3

Pin 1. Input
2. Output
3. Ground

MC3399T Automotive High-Side Driver Switch

The MC3399T is a high-side driver switch that is designed to drive loads from the positive side of the power supply.

A TTL-compatible enable pin is used to control the output of this device. In the on state, the chip exhibits very low saturation voltages for load currents up to (at least) 750 mA. The MC3399T protects the load from high-voltage transients by switching into an open-circuit state for the length of the transient. When the applied voltage drops back to an acceptable level, the device automatically switches back to its normal on state.

As the name of this chip suggests, it is intended primarily for use in automotive applications.

Ignition Input Voltage
    Continuous — +25 V max.
    − 12 V max.

Transient
    T = 100 ms — ± 60 V max.
    T = 1.0 ms — ± 100 V max.
Input Voltage — −0.3 to +7.0 V max.
Power Dissipation — 2.0 W max.
Output Current — Internally Limited
Output Current Limit (V_o = 0 V) — 1.6 A typ.
2.5 A max.

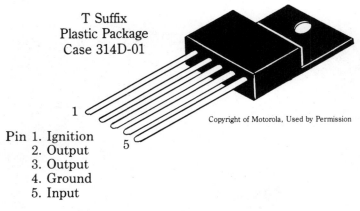

T Suffix
Plastic Package
Case 314D-01

1

Copyright of Motorola, Used by Permission

Pin 1. Ignition
    2. Output
    3. Output
    4. Ground
    5. Input

5

Heatsink surface connected to Pin 2.

MC3399T

MC3456, MC3556 Dual Timer

The MC3456 and MC3556 each contain two independent timer stages. Each of these timers can be used in either monostable-multivibrator or astable-multivibrator circuits. Basically, these chips are improved versions of the 556 dual-timer IC, discussed earlier in this section.

Each of the timer sections in these chips are equivalent to Motorola's MC1455 timer IC, also discussed earlier in this section. The timing period is set by a simple external resistor/capacitor combination. The formula for the basic (monostable) timing period is:

$$T = 1.1RC$$

Timing periods from a few microseconds up to several hours can be set up with MC3456 and MC3556.

Supply Voltage	
MC3456	+4.5 V min.
	+16 V max.
MC3556	+4.5 V min.
	+18 V max.
Power Dissipation	1.0 W max.
Supply Current	
MC3456 (V_{cc} = 5 V Infinite Load)	6.0 mA typ.
	12 mA max.
(V_{cc} = 15 V Infinite Load)	20 mA typ.
	30 mA max.
MC3556 (V_{CC} = 5 V Infinite Load)	6.0 mA typ.
	10 mA max.
(V_{CC} = 15 V Infinite Load	20 mA typ.
	24 mA max.
Discharge Current	200 mA max.

NOTE: Specifications are for both the MC3456 and the MC3556, except where noted.

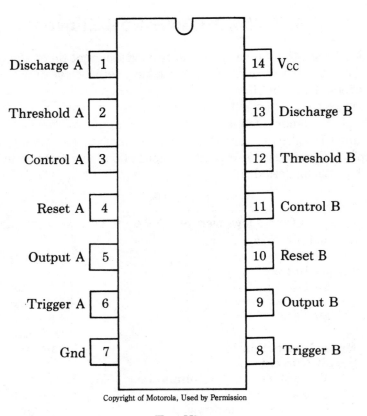

Discharge A — 1

Threshold A — 2

Control A — 3

Reset A — 4

Output A — 5

Trigger A — 6

Gnd — 7

14 — V_{CC}

13 — Discharge B

12 — Threshold B

11 — Control B

10 — Reset B

9 — Output B

8 — Trigger B

Top View

MC3456/MC3556

MC3484S2-1 2.4 Amp Solenoid Driver

The MC3484S2-1 is a solenoid driver IC, intended primarily for automotive applications, such as applying full-battery voltage to a fuel injector for rapid current rise in order to produce a positive-injector opening. When the load current reaches 2.4 amperes, the injector driver reduces the load current by a 4-to-1 ratio, and then operates as a constant-current supply, holding the injector open and reducing system dissipation. This chip is also suitable to many other solenoid-driving applications.

The MC3484S2-1 features two high-impedance inputs that can be driven by TTL or CMOS logic—permitting a variety of control options to suit various applications.

Battery Voltage	24 V max.
	4.0 V min.
Input (pin #1)	−6.0 V min.
	+24.0 V max.
Output Peak Current	1.7 A min.
	2.4 A typ.
	2.9 A max.
Output Sustain Current	0.5 A min.
	0.6 A typ.
	0.7 A max.
Output Voltage In Saturated Mode (1.5 A)	1.2 V typ.

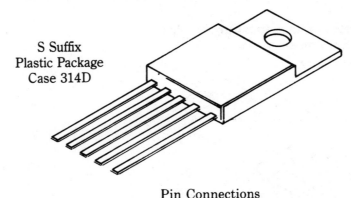

S Suffix
Plastic Package
Case 314D

Pin Connections
Unformed Package

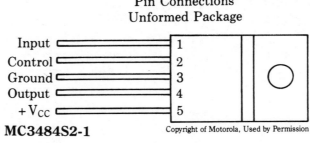

Input — 1
Control — 2
Ground — 3
Output — 4
+V$_{CC}$ — 5

MC3484S2-1

511

MC3484S4-1 4.0-Amp Solenoid Driver

The MC3484S4-1 is a solenoid-driver IC. It is a high-current version of the MC3484S2-1, discussed previously.

Like its smaller version, the MC3484S4-1 is intended primarily for automotive applications, such as applying full-battery voltage to a fuel injector for rapid current rise in order to produce a positive injector opening. When the load current reaches 4.0 amperes, the injector driver reduces the load current by a 4-to-1 ratio and then operates as a constant-current supply, holding the injector open and reducing system dissipation. This chip is also suitable to many other solenoid-driving applications.

The MC3484S4-1 features two high-impedance inputs that can be driven by TTL or CMOS logic—permitting a variety of control options to suit various applications.

Battery Voltage	24 V max.
	4 V min.
Input (pin #1)	-6 V min.
	+24 V max.
Output Peak Current	3.6 A min.
	4.0 A typ.
	5.2 A max.
Output Sustain Current	0.95 A min.
	1.0 A typ.
	1.3 A max.
Output Voltage In Saturated Mode 3.0 Ampere	1.6 V typ.

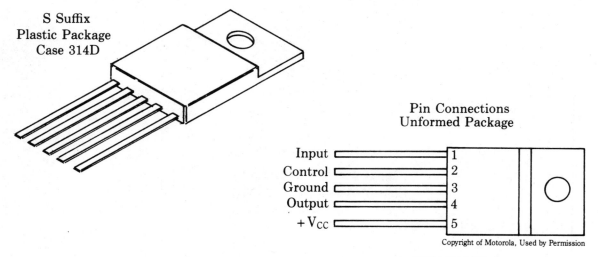

S Suffix
Plastic Package
Case 314D

Pin Connections
Unformed Package

Input	1
Control	2
Ground	3
Output	4
+V_{CC}	5

MC3484S4-1

LAS3800 500 mA Pulse-Width Modulator Controller

The LAS3800 is a high-performance switching-type voltage regulator in a 16-pin DIP (dual-inline package) IC. It is designed for use in fixed-frequency power-control applications, such as switching power supplies and motor controls.

The features of the LAS3800 include;

- Current-limit frequency shift
- High-speed current-limit comparator
- Output over-current protection
- Programmable dead-time and frequency-shift
- Uncommitted error amplifier

Input Voltage	40 V max.
Collector Supply Voltage	40 V max.
Source Current (Per Output)	500 mA max.
Line Regulation (V_{in} = 12 to 40 V)	0.01%/V max.
Standby Current	7 mA min.
	13 mA max.

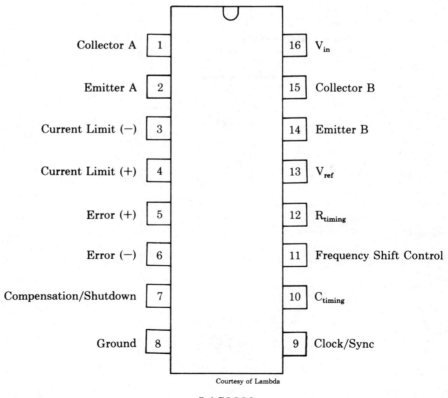

Courtesy of Lambda

LAS3800

513

3909 LED Flasher/Oscillator

The 3909 is a simple 8-pin oscillator IC. It is primarily intended for LED flasher circuits, but it can be used in many other low-frequency oscillator applications, too.

A simple external capacitor is used to set the frequency of the on-chip oscillator. The timing resistors are provided within the chip itself. This timing capacitor also provides a voltage boost, so pulses of over 2 volts are delivered to the external LED (or other load device), even with supply voltages as low as 1.5 volts.

Being inherently self-starting, the basic 3909 LED flasher circuit requires only the IC, a battery, the LED, and a timing capacitor.

A slow (pin 8) or a fast (pin 1) flash rate can be set up, depending on where the external timing capacitor is connected to the chip.

Supply Voltage	6.4 V max.
Power Dissipation	500 mW max.
Operating Current	75 mA max.
Peak Output Current	45 mA max.
Output Pulse Width	6 ms max.
Slow-Flash Frequency	1.3 Hz max.
Fast-Flash Frequency	1.1 kHz max.

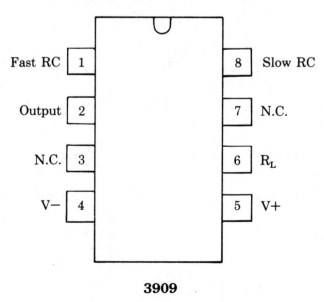

3909

BA6121 4-Output Switching Regulator

The BA6121 is a switching-type voltage-regulator IC. Its primary intended application is for use in VCRs. This chip features four blocks of switching regulators and a power-save pin to reduce current consumption. Each of the four switching-regulator blocks within the BA6121 contains an error-input pin.

The circuitry contained on this chip includes four PWM (Pulse-Width Modulated) switching regulator blocks with REF control, drivability control, and feedback-limiting pins.

Supply Voltage	18 V Max.
Recommended Operating Range	8 to 16 V
Power Dissipation	400 mW Max.
Sink Current	
Pin #5	5 μA max.
Pin #7	5 μA max.
Pin #8	10 mA max.
Pin #9	5 μA max.
Pin #11	30 mA max.
Pin #14	20 mA max.
Pin #16	5 μA max.
Drain Current	
Pin #1	1 mA max.
Pin #2	30 μA typ.
Pin #4	200 μA typ.
Pin #13	0.3 mA typ.
Pin #15	30 μA typ.

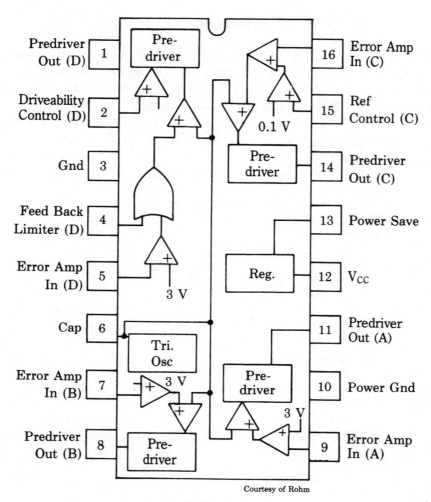

Courtesy of Rohm

BA6121

BA6139 Fluorescent Display Driver

The BA6139 is a monolithic driver for various types of fluorescent displays. This chip is available in a 16-pin LF package, requiring a minimum of space on the circuit board.

Seven channels are implemented on the BA6139. The discharge time constant can easily be varied by changing the value of an external resistor.

Supply Voltage	35 V absolute max.
Recommended Range	30 V max.
	24 V typ.
Power Dissipation	550 mW max.
Output High Voltage	23.0 V typ.
	22.7 V min.
Output Low Voltage	1.0 V max.
Output Current	10 mA min.

Dimensions (Unit: mm)

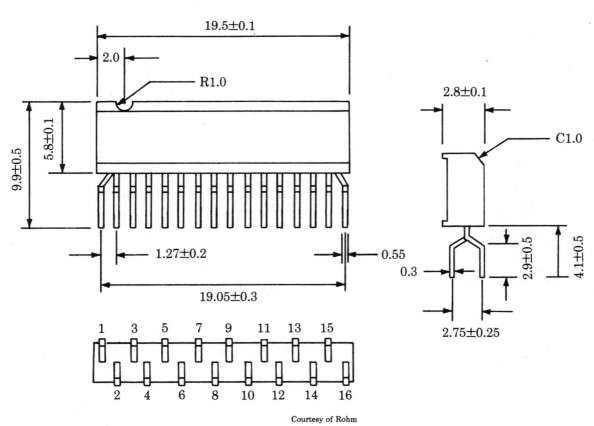

Courtesy of Rohm

517

Pin Connections

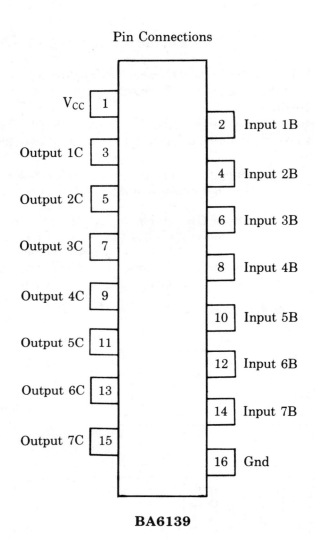

BA6139

BA6209 Reversible Motor Driver

The BA6209 is an IC designed primarily for use in VCRs to control reversible motors, such as the loading motor, the capstan motor, and the reel motor.

This chip features an internal surge suppressor, making it capable of withstanding brief bursts of current up to 1.6 A. Such current surges can frequently occur when a motor is stopping or changing direction.

The BA6209 automatically brakes the motor when the control inputs are both set high or low. The control pin (V_r, pin #4) accepts a control voltage, adjusting the motor speed over a wide range.

This chip is available in a 10 pin-SIP (single-inline package) housing.

Supply Voltage	
V_{cc1}	18 V max.
	6.0 V min.
V_{cc2}	18 V max.
Power Dissipation	2200 mW 2.2 W max.
Output Voltage	7.2 V typ.
	6.6 V min.
Output Current	1.6 A max.

Block Diagram

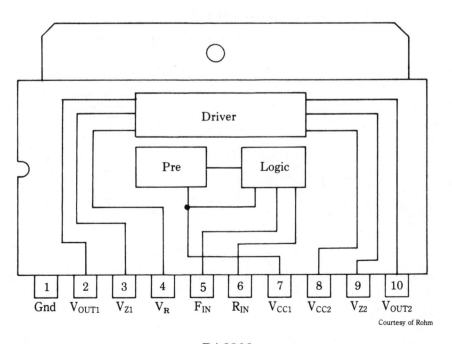

Courtesy of Rohm

BA6209

Dimensions (Unit: mm)

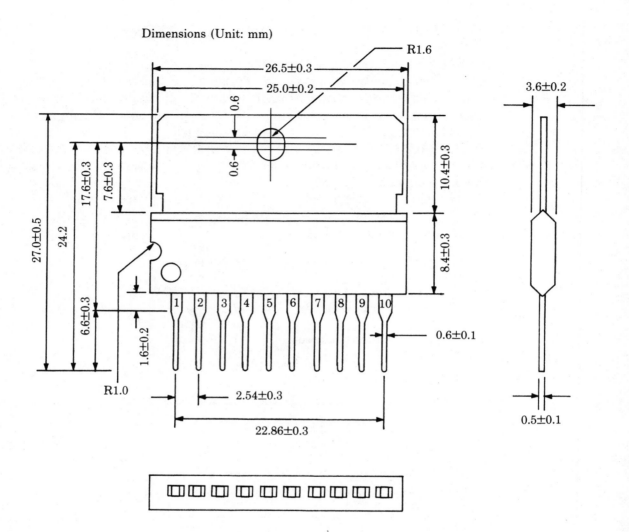

LSH6325P 2-Amp Dc-to-Dc Microconverter

The LSH6325P is a switching-type voltage-regulator IC within a standard TO-220-style package. With just an external choke and two external capacitors, this chip can be used as 5-volt dc-to-dc converter capable of handling currents up to 2 ampere at a minimum efficiency of 70 percent.

The output voltage can be programmed from 5 to 27 volts, although it is preset at 5.05 volts ± 1.5 percent.

Input Voltage	35 V max.
Preset Output Voltage	5.30 V max.
	5.05 V typ.
	4.80 V min.
Power Dissipation	Internally Limited

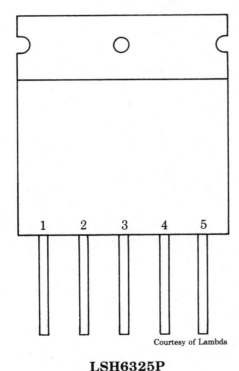

1	V_{sense}
2	E_O
3	Small-Signal Ground
4	Power Ground
5	Input
Tab	Small-Signal Ground

Courtesy of Lambda

LSH6325P

LSH6335P 3-Amp Dc-to-Dc Microconverter

The LSH6335P is a switching-type voltage-regulator IC within a standard TO-220-style package. With just an external choke and two external capacitors, this chip can be used as 5-volt dc-to-dc converter capable of handling currents up to 3 amperes at a minimum efficiency of 70 percent. Basically the LSH6335P is a heftier (higher current) version of the LSH6325P.

The output voltage of this device can be programmed from 5 to 27 volts, although it is preset at 5.05 volts ±1.5 percent.

Input Voltage	35 V max.
Preset Output Voltage	5.30 V max.
	5.05 V typ.
	4.80 V min.
Power Dissipation	Internally Limited

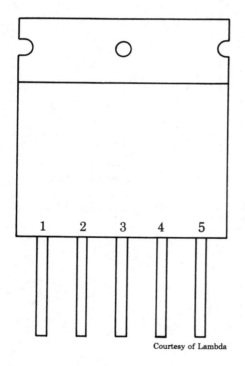

1	V_{sense}
2	E_O
3	Small-Signal Ground
4	Power Ground
5	Input
Tab	Small-Signal Ground

Courtesy of Lambda

LSH6335P

LSH6355P 5-Amp Dc-to-Dc Microconverter

The LSH6355P is a switching-type voltage-regulator IC within a standard TO-220-style package. With just an external choke and two external capacitors, this chip can be used as 5-volt dc-to-dc converter capable of handling currents up to 5 amperes at a minimum efficiency of 70 percent. Basically, the LSH6355P is a high-current version of the LSH6325P and LSH6335P, discussed earlier in this section.

The output voltage can be programmed from 5 to 27 volts, although it is preset at 5.05 volts ± 1.5 percent.

Input Voltage	35 V max.
Preset Output Voltage	5.30 V max.
	5.05 V typ.
	4.80 V min.
Power Dissipation	Internally Limited

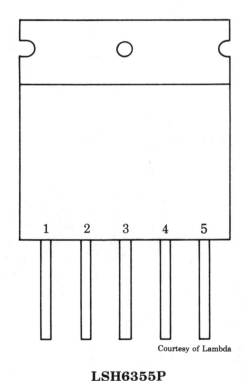

1	V_{sense}
2	E_O
3	Small-Signal Ground
4	Power Ground
5	Input
Tab	Small-Signal Ground

Courtesy of Lambda

LSH6355P

LSH6385P 8-Amp Dc-to-Dc Microconverter

The LSH6385P is a switching-type voltage-regulator IC within a 9-pin SIP (single-inline package) housing. With just an external choke and two external capacitors, this chip can be used as 5-volt dc-to-dc converter capable of handling currents up to 8 amperes at a minimum efficiency of 70 percent. Basically the LSH6385P is a high-current version of the LSH6325P, LSH6335P, and LSH6355P (discussed previously).

The output voltage of this device can be programmed from 5 to 27 volts, although it is preset at 5.05 volts ±1.5 percent.

Input Voltage	35 V max.
Preset Output Voltage	5.30 V max.
	5.05 V typ.
	4.80 V min.
Power Dissipation	Internally Limited

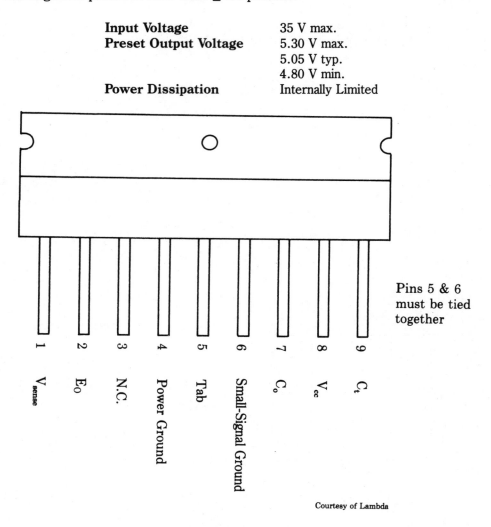

Pins 5 & 6 must be tied together

Courtesy of Lambda

LSH6385P

BA6993 Dual Comparator

The BA6993 contains two comparator stages in a single 8-pin DIP (dual-inline package) housing. These comparators are very easy to work with. Aside from the power-supply connections, each comparator has just three pins—the inverting input, the noninverting input, and the output. The power-supply connections are common to both comparator stages. Otherwise, the two comparators in the BA6993 are fully independent of one another.

The BA6993's comparators use open-collector outputs, permitting hardwired OR connections. Either a single-ended (+2 to +36 volts) or a dual-polarity (±1 to ±18 volts) power supply can be used with this chip.

Supply Voltage		
	Single Polarity	+36 V max.
		+2 V min.
	Dual Polarity	±18 V max.
		±1 V min.
Power Dissipation		500 mW max.
Differential Input Voltage		36 V max.
Voltage Gain		50 V/mV min.
		200 V/mV typ.
Output Sink Current		16 mA typ.
		10 mA min.

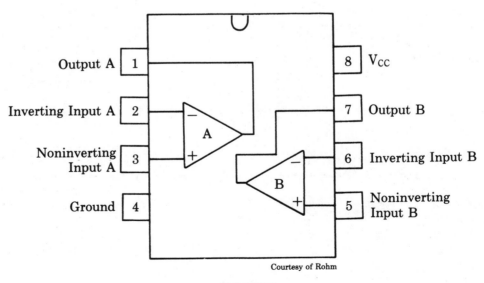

Courtesy of Rohm

BA6993

525

TCF7000 Pressure Transducer Amplifier

The internal circuitry of the TCF7000 consists of two low-power operational amplifiers. These two op-amp stages are identical, except amplifier A is a npn transistor driving an on-chip current source, and amplifier B is npn transistor with a pull-up resistor.

This chip is intended for use in automotive and industrial pressure-sensing applications.

Supply Voltage	20 V max.
	4.0 V min.
Supply Current	2.2 mA typ.
Short-Circuit Duration	Continuous
Common-Mode Rejection	100 dB typ.
	50 dB min.

Typical Application

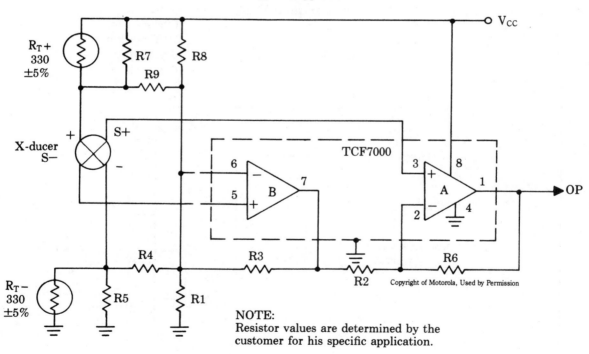

Copyright of Motorola, Used by Permission

NOTE:
Resistor values are determined by the customer for his specific application.

TCF7000

Pin Assignments

(Top View)

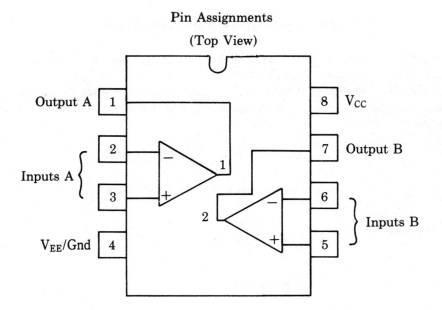

Output A   1

2   –

Inputs A {

3   +

1

2

V_{EE}/Gnd   4

8   V_{CC}

7   Output B

–

6

+

5

} Inputs B

7805 5-Volt Voltage Regulator

The 7805 is a popular and easy-to-use voltage-regulator IC. It has just three pins—input (1), output (2), and common or ground (3).

The 7805 is designed for a well-regulated output voltage of 5 volts. This voltage-regulator chip can handle currents over 1.5 ampere if adequate heat-sinking is provided.

Input Voltage	+35 V max.
Output Voltage	+5 V
Power Dissipation	Internally Limited

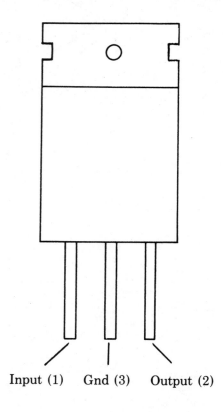

Input (1)   Gnd (3)   Output (2)

7805

7812 12-Volt Voltage Regulator

The 7812 is a popular and easy-to-use voltage-regulator IC. It has just three pins—input (1), output (2), and common or ground (3).

The 7812 is designed for a well-regulated output voltage of 12 volts. This voltage-regulator chip can handle currents over 1.5 ampere if adequate heat-sinking is provided.

Input Voltage	+35 V max.
Output Voltage	+12 V
Power Dissipation	Internally Limited

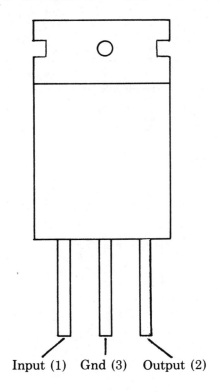

Input (1)   Gnd (3)   Output (2)

7812

7815 15-Volt Voltage Regulator

The 7815 is a popular and easy-to-use voltage-regulator IC. It has just three pins—input (1), output (2), and common or ground (3).

The 7815 is designed for a well-regulated output voltage of 15 volts. This voltage-regulator chip can handle currents over 1.5 ampere if adequate heat-sinking is provided.

Input Voltage	+35 V max.
Output Voltage	+15 V
Power Dissipation	Internally Limited

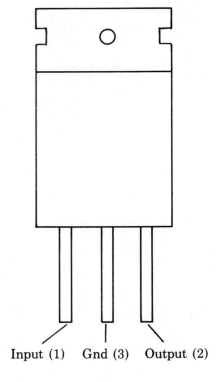

Input (1)   Gnd (3)   Output (2)

7815

LAS8091P 4-Channel Push-Pull Inverting-Output Driver

The LAS8091P is a 4-channel inverting-output driver IC intended for use with inductive loads, such as relays, solenoids, and capacitive loads up to 0.03 μF.

This chip is available in a 16-pin DIP (dual-inline package) housing with the four middle pins (4, 5, 12, and 13) connected together for heat-sinking.

Supply Voltage	36 V max.
Input Voltage	30 V max.
Enable Voltage	30 V max.
Power Dissipation	2.2 W max.
Output Current	
Source Mode	Peak Internally Limited
Sink Mode	440 mA max.

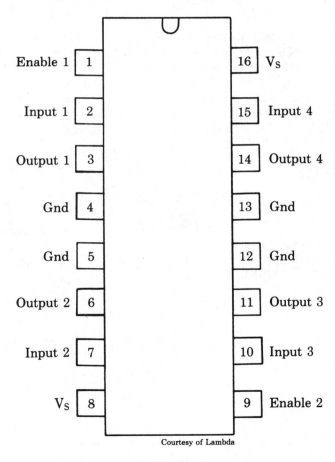

Courtesy of Lambda

LAS8091P

LAS8100 Series 3-Amp Peak
Switching Transistor Drivers

The LAS8100 series of ICs are designed to drive low-gain, high-current switching bipolar transistors, Darlington transistors, or FETs at their maximum switching speeds. These chips provide simple turn-on and turn-off and are compatible with TTL, CMOS, and NMOS digital circuits.

The LAS8100 is a single monolithic driver for switching transistors. It is available in a 4-pin TO-3 housing.

The LAS8100P is similar to the LAS8100, except it is housed in a special 5-pin TO-220 package. This chip is also a single monolithic driver for switching transistors.

The LAS8101 is a dual driver IC containing 2 monolithic drivers for switching transistors. It is effectively the equivalent of 2 LAS8100s in a single 8-pin TO-3 housing.

Supply Voltage	26 V max.
Power Dissipation	15 W max.
Output Current	
Source: Peak	3 A max.
Source: Continuous	1 A max.
Sink: Peak	3 A max.
Sink: Continuous	3 A max.

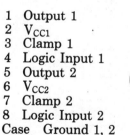

1   Output 1
2   V_{CC1}
3   Clamp 1
4   Logic Input 1
5   Output 2
6   V_{CC2}
7   Clamp 2
8   Logic Input 2
Case   Ground 1, 2

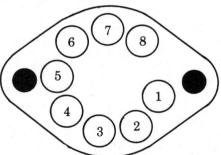

LAS8101

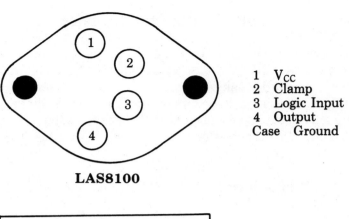

1   V_{CC}
2   Clamp
3   Logic Input
4   Output
Case   Ground

LAS8100

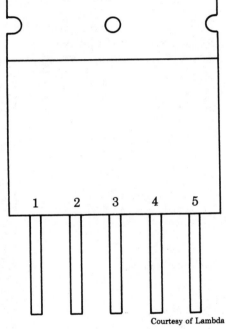

1   V_{CC}
2   Clamp
3   Ground
4   Logic Input
5   Output
Tab   Ground

Courtesy of Lambda

LAS8100P

533

BU8302A Tone/Pulse Dialer

The BU8302A is an IC designed for use in telephone systems. It functions as both a tone and pulse dialer. Its on-chip memory can store and redial the last number dialed for up to 17 digits.

The DTMF tones have their output amplitude internally regulated, and therefore are not affected by fluctuations in the circuit's supply voltage.

The BU8302A's internal master oscillator uses an external 3.58 MHz crystal or a ceramic resonator.

Supply Voltage	6.0 V max.
	2.5 V min.
	3.5 V typ.
Operating Current	1.0 mA typ.
	2.0 mA max.
Memory Retention Current	0.1 μA typ.
	0.75 μA max.

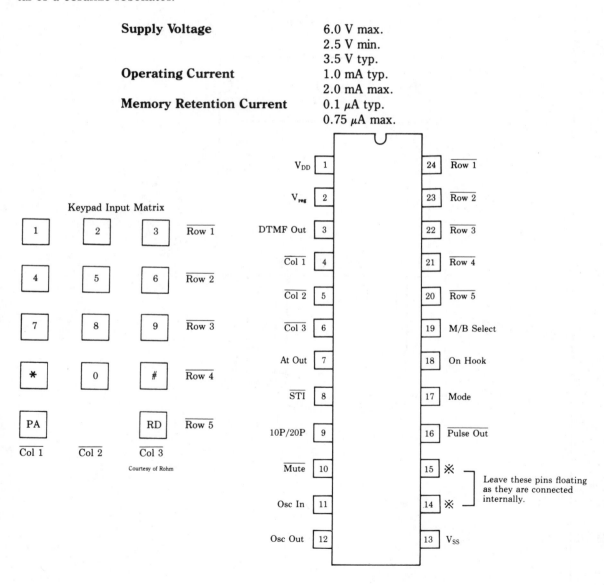

Keypad Input Matrix

1	2	3	$\overline{\text{Row 1}}$
4	5	6	$\overline{\text{Row 2}}$
7	8	9	$\overline{\text{Row 3}}$
*	0	#	$\overline{\text{Row 4}}$
PA		RD	$\overline{\text{Row 5}}$

$\overline{\text{Col 1}}$ $\overline{\text{Col 2}}$ $\overline{\text{Col 3}}$

Courtesy of Rohm

Pin	Name	Pin	Name
1	V_{DD}	24	$\overline{\text{Row 1}}$
2	V_{reg}	23	$\overline{\text{Row 2}}$
3	DTMF Out	22	$\overline{\text{Row 3}}$
4	$\overline{\text{Col 1}}$	21	$\overline{\text{Row 4}}$
5	$\overline{\text{Col 2}}$	20	$\overline{\text{Row 5}}$
6	$\overline{\text{Col 3}}$	19	M/B Select
7	At Out	18	On Hook
8	$\overline{\text{STI}}$	17	Mode
9	10P/20P	16	$\overline{\text{Pulse Out}}$
10	$\overline{\text{Mute}}$	15	※
11	Osc In	14	※
12	Osc Out	13	V_{SS}

Leave these pins floating as they are connected internally.

534

BU8304, BU8304F Tone/Pulse Dialer

The BU8304 and BU8304F are ICs designed for use in telephone systems. They function as both a tone and pulse dialer. An on-chip memory can store and redial the last number dialed for up to 17 digits.

The DTMF tones have their output amplitude internally regulated and therefore are not affected by fluctuations in the circuit's supply voltage.

The internal master oscillator in the BU8304 and the BU8304F uses an external 3.58 MHz crystal or ceramic resonator.

Supply Voltage	5.5 V max.
	2.5 V min.
Operating Current	1.0 mA typ.
	2.0 mA max.
Memory Retention Current	0.1 μA typ.
	0.75 μA max.

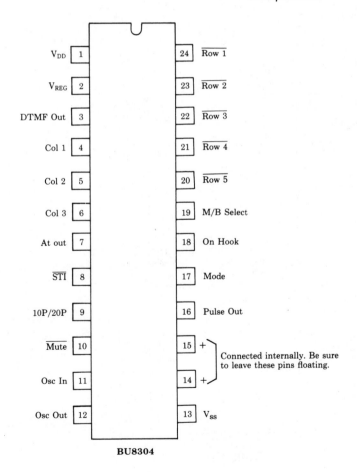

BU8304

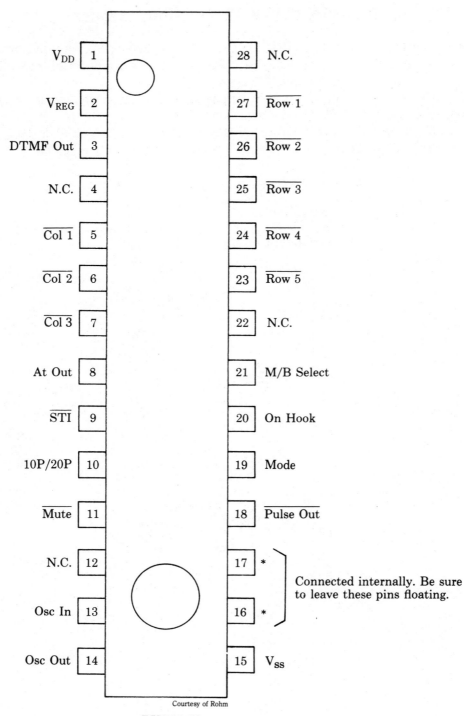

V_{DD}	1	28	N.C.
V_{REG}	2	27	$\overline{\text{Row 1}}$
DTMF Out	3	26	$\overline{\text{Row 2}}$
N.C.	4	25	$\overline{\text{Row 3}}$
$\overline{\text{Col 1}}$	5	24	$\overline{\text{Row 4}}$
$\overline{\text{Col 2}}$	6	23	$\overline{\text{Row 5}}$
$\overline{\text{Col 3}}$	7	22	N.C.
At Out	8	21	M/B Select
$\overline{\text{STI}}$	9	20	On Hook
10P/20P	10	19	Mode
$\overline{\text{Mute}}$	11	18	$\overline{\text{Pulse Out}}$
N.C.	12	17	*
Osc In	13	16	*
Osc Out	14	15	V_{SS}

Connected internally. Be sure to leave these pins floating.

Courtesy of Rohm

BU8304F

BA9101 8-Bit Successive Comparison A/D Converter

The BA9101 is an 8-bit analog-to-digital (A/D) converter in a 22-pin DIP (dual inline package) housing. The successive-comparison method of A/D conversion is used in this chip.

The circuitry within this device includes the necessary reference voltage and clock sources, so no external components are required for basic operations.

The BA9101 features tristate outputs that allow direct connection to a data bus. External control of conversion start, data read, and clock timings is supported.

Supply Voltage	
Pin #22	+6 V max.
	+4.5 V min.
Pin #1	−8.5 V max.
	−6.3 V min.
Power Dissipation	500 mW max.
Analog Input Voltage	0 to 5 V typ.
	±2.5 V typ.
Analog Input Resistance	3000 Ω typ.
	4000 Ω max.
	2000 Ω min.
Maximum Clock Frequency	400 kHz min.

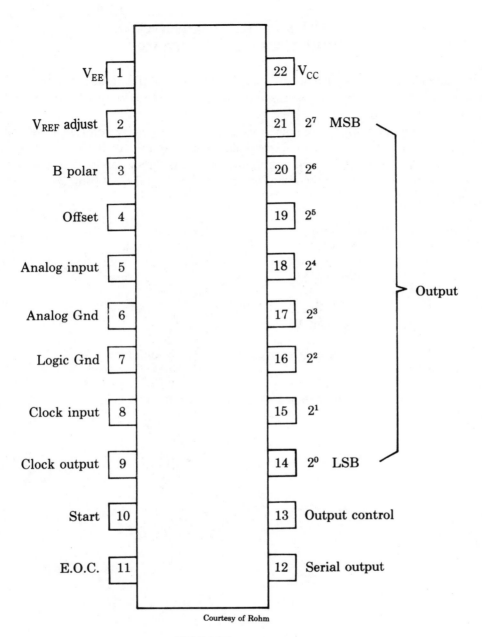

Courtesy of Rohm

BA9101

538

BA9201, BA9201F 8-Bit D/A Converter with Latch

The BA9201 and BA9201F are 8-bit digital-to-analog (D/A) converter ICs, complete with internal-reference voltage-source and input-data latch circuitry. An external reference voltage can be substituted for the internal reference voltage source, if desired in a specific application.

The input data latch permits the use of multiple D/A converters in appropriate systems.

Supply Voltage	
Pin #18	+6 V max.
	+4.5 V min.
Pin #1	−8.5 V max.
	−6.3 V min.
Power Dissipation	500 mW max.
Resolution	8 bits
Full-Scale Current	1.992 mA typ.
	2.10 mA max.
	1.90 mA min.
Input High Voltage	2.3 V min.
Input Low Voltage	0.8 V min.

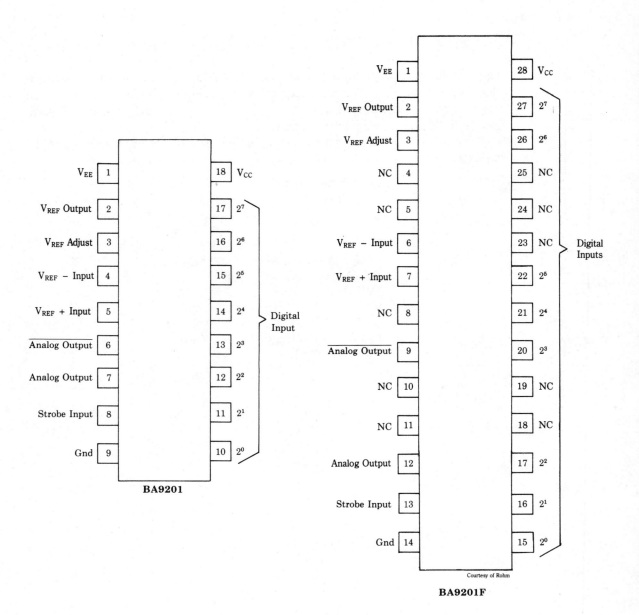

BA9201

BA9201 pin labels:
- 1 — V_{EE}
- 2 — V_{REF} Output
- 3 — V_{REF} Adjust
- 4 — $V_{REF} -$ Input
- 5 — $V_{REF} +$ Input
- 6 — $\overline{\text{Analog Output}}$
- 7 — Analog Output
- 8 — Strobe Input
- 9 — Gnd
- 18 — V_{CC}
- 17 — 2^7
- 16 — 2^6
- 15 — 2^5
- 14 — 2^4
- 13 — 2^3
- 12 — 2^2
- 11 — 2^1
- 10 — 2^0

Digital Input

BA9201F

BA9201F pin labels:
- 1 — V_{EE}
- 2 — V_{REF} Output
- 3 — V_{REF} Adjust
- 4 — NC
- 5 — NC
- 6 — $V_{REF} -$ Input
- 7 — $V_{REF} +$ Input
- 8 — NC
- 9 — $\overline{\text{Analog Output}}$
- 10 — NC
- 11 — NC
- 12 — Analog Output
- 13 — Strobe Input
- 14 — Gnd
- 28 — V_{CC}
- 27 — 2^7
- 26 — 2^6
- 25 — NC
- 24 — NC
- 23 — NC
- 22 — 2^5
- 21 — 2^4
- 20 — 2^3
- 19 — NC
- 18 — NC
- 17 — 2^2
- 16 — 2^1
- 15 — 2^0

Digital Inputs

Courtesy of Rohm

540

BA9221 12-Bit D/A Converter

The BA9221 is a 12-bit digital-to-analog (D/A) converter IC with a conversion time as short as 250 ns. This chip is also capable of multiplying operations. The primary intended application of the BA9221 is for use in digital audio systems or in other high-speed digital-to-analog control systems.

Supply Voltage	
V_{cc}	+7 V max.
V_{ee}	−18 V max.
Power Dissipation	600 mW max.
Resolution	12 bits
Full-Scale Current	3.999 mA typ.

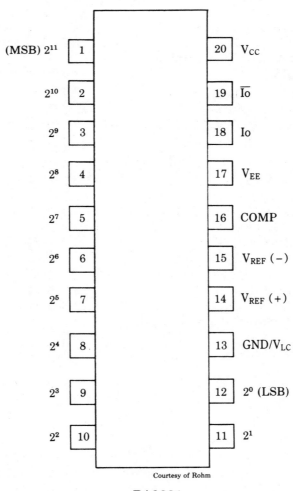

Courtesy of Rohm

BA9221

MC10319 High-Speed 8-Bit A/D Flash Converter

The MC10319 is an 8-bit analog-to-digital (A/D) converter IC designed for very fast data conversion. The circuitry used in this chip is known as a *flash converter*.

An internal Grey-code structure is used in this device to eliminate large output errors on fast-slewing input signals. The parallel three-state digital outputs of the MC10319 are fully TTL-compatible.

Within this chip are 256 parallel comparators across a precision input reference network. The outputs of the comparators are then passed through latches and into an encoder network to produce 8 parallel bits for the digital outputs and a single overrange bit.

Supply Voltage	
V_{cc} **Pin #15**	+7.0 V absolute max.
V_{cc}**(D) Pin #11 and 17**	+7.0 V absolute max.
V_{ee} **Pin #13**	−7.0 V absolute max.
Recommended Supply Voltages	
V_{cc}**(A)**	+5.5 V max.
	+5.0 V typ.
	+4.5 V min.
V_{cc}**(D)**	+5.5 V max.
	+5.0 V typ.
	+4.5 V min.
V_{ee}	−6.0 V max.
	−5.0 V typ.
	−3.0 V min.
Positive Supply-Voltage Differential	
V_{cc}**(D)**—V_{cc}**(A)**	−0.3 to +0.3 V
Power Dissipation	618 mW max.
Clock Frequency	25 MHz max.
	0 MHz min.
Resolution	8 Bits max.
Accuracy	9 Bits typ.
Analog Input Voltage	+2.5 V max.
	−2.5 V min.
Input Capacitance	50 pF

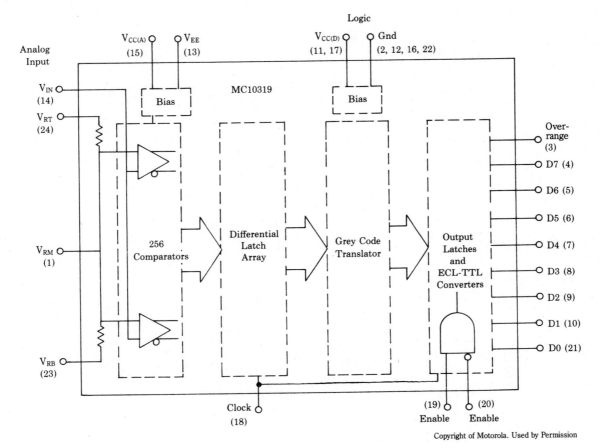

Analog Input

$V_{CC(A)}$ (15) V_{EE} (13)

Logic

$V_{CC(D)}$ (11, 17)   Gnd (2, 12, 16, 22)

V_{IN} (14)

V_{RT} (24)

MC10319

Bias

Bias

256 Comparators

Differential Latch Array

Grey Code Translator

Output Latches and ECL-TTL Converters

Over-range (3)

D7 (4)

D6 (5)

D5 (6)

D4 (7)

D3 (8)

D2 (9)

D1 (10)

D0 (21)

V_{RM} (1)

V_{RB} (23)

Clock (18)

(19) Enable   (20) Enable

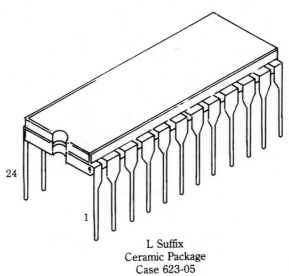

24

1

L Suffix
Ceramic Package
Case 623-05

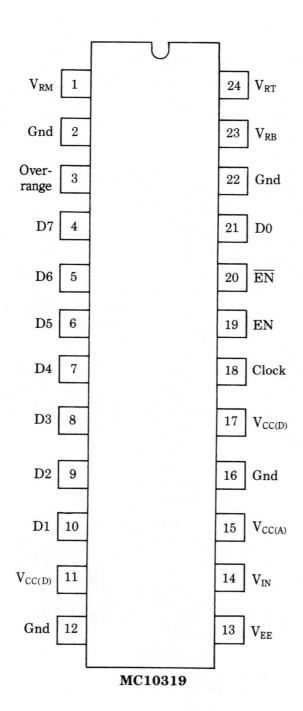

MC10319

544

MC33064, MC34064 Undervoltage-Sensing Circuit

The MC33064 and MC34064 are designed to monitor a voltage and react when it drops below a specific level. Their primary intended application is as reset controllers in microprocessor-based systems. Low-voltage detection with these devices is quite simple, requiring just a single external resistor.

The difference between the MC33064 and the MC34064 is in the acceptable operating temperature range. The MC34064 is suitable for most consumer applications. The temperature ratings for the MC33064 meet military specifications.

Power Input Supply Voltage -1.0 to $+10$ V max.
Power Dissipation   625 mW max.
Threshold Voltage   4.7 V max.
                   4.6 V typ.
                   4.5 V max.

D Suffix
Plastic Package
Case 751
(SO-8)

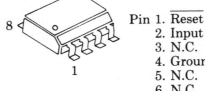

Pin 1. $\overline{\text{Reset}}$
2. Input
3. N.C.
4. Ground
5. N.C.
6. N.C.
7. N.C.
8. N.C.

P Suffix
Plastic Package
Case 29
(TO-226AA)

Pin 1. $\overline{\text{Reset}}$
2. Input
3. Ground

ORDERING INFORMATION

Device	Temperature Range	Package
MC34064D-5	0°C to +70°C	Plastic SO-8
MC34064P-5		Plastic TO-226AA
MC33064D-5	−40°C to +85°C	Plastic SO-8
MC33064P-5		Plastic TO-226AA

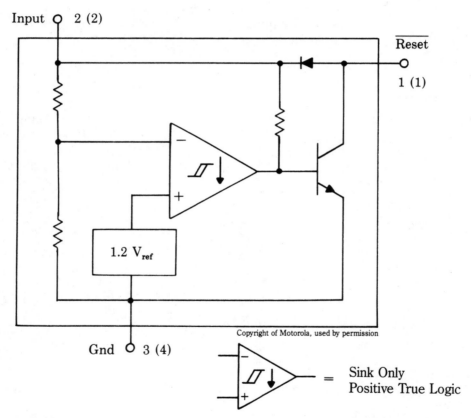

Copyright of Motorola, used by permission

Pin numbers adjacent to terminals are for the 3-pin TO-226AA package.
Pin numbers in parenthesis are for the D suffix SO-8 package.

MC33064/MC34064

546

MC33160, MC34160 Microprocessor Voltage Regulator /Supervisory Circuit

The MC33160 and MC34160 are specialized voltage-regulator ICs including supervisory monitoring circuits for use in microprocessor systems. Only a minimum of external components are required.

The circuitry within these chips include:

- 5.0 V, 100 mA voltage regulator with short-circuit current limiting
- 2.6 V bandgap reference
- Low-voltage reset comparator
- Power-warning comparator with programmable hysteresis
- Uncommitted comparator for microprocessor line synchronization or other applications

The MC33160 and MC34160 also feature a chip-disable input for low standby current and internal thermal-shutdown circuitry for over-temperature protection. The center tabs (pin # 4, 5, 12, and 13) of the 16-pin DIP housings for these chips are connected for heat-sinking purposes.

The difference between the MC33160 and the MC34160 is in the acceptable operating temperature range. The MC34160 is suitable for most consumer applications. The temperature ratings for the MC33160 also meet military specifications.

Supply Voltage	40 V max.
Supply Current	
Standby	0.18 mA typ.
	0.35 mA max.
Operating	1.5 mA typ.
	3.0 mA max.
Power Dissipation	1.0 W max.
Regulated Output Voltage	
	5.0 V typ.
	5.25 V max.
	4.75 V min.
Line Regulation	2.0 mV typ.
	20 mV max.
Load Regulation	4.0 mV typ.
	30 mV max.

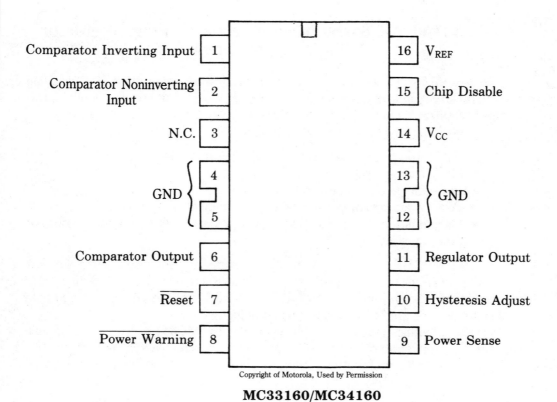

Comparator Inverting Input	1		16	V_{REF}
Comparator Noninverting Input	2		15	Chip Disable
N.C.	3		14	V_{CC}
GND	4		13	GND
	5		12	
Comparator Output	6		11	Regulator Output
$\overline{\text{Reset}}$	7		10	Hysteresis Adjust
$\overline{\text{Power Warning}}$	8		9	Power Sense

MC33160/MC34160

X9MME Digitally Controlled Potentiometer

The X9MME is an 8-pin DIP (dual-inline package) IC, which is a solid-state, digitally controlled substitute for a mechanical potentiometer. This device is ideal for digitally controlled resistance trimming.

    Within the X9MME is a 99-resistor array. Between each resistance element and at each end are tap points accessible to the digitally controlled wiper element. The wiper position is controlled by the following input pins:

- $\overline{CS}$ (Pin #7)   Chip Select
- $U/\overline{D}$ (Pin #2)   Up/Down Control
- $\overline{INC}$ (Pin #1)   Increment Wiper Movement Control

    A nonvolatile memory stores the last wiper position, which will be automatically recalled upon power up.

    Three devices are in the X9MME series. The X9103 has a 10 kΩ potentiometer, the X9503 has a 50 kΩ potentiometer, and the X9104 has a 100 kΩ potentiometer.

Supply Voltage	5.0 V typ.
Supply Current	25 mA typ.
	35 mA max.
Resistance	
X9103	10 kΩ max.
	40Ω min.
X9503	50 kΩ max.
	40 Ω min.
X9104	100 kΩ max.
	40 Ω min.
Wiper Increments	
X9103	101 Ω typ.
X9503	505 Ω typ.
X9104	1,010 Ω typ.

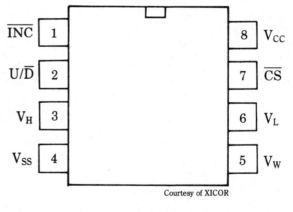

Courtesy of XICOR

X9MME

$\overline{INC}$	Increment — Wiper Movement Control
$U/\overline{D}$	Up/Down Control
V_H	High Terminal of Potentiometer
V_{SS}	Ground
V_W	Wiper Terminal of Potentiometer
V_L	Low Terminal of Potentiometer
$\overline{CS}$	Chip Select for Wiper Movement/Storage
V_{CC}	System Power

APPENDIX

Symbols
& definitions

DC Voltages

All voltages are referenced to ground. Negative voltage limits are specified as absolute values (i.e., 10V is greater than -1.0V).

V_{CC} Supply voltage: The range of power supply voltage over which the device is guaranteed to operate within the specified limits.

V_{CD} (Max) Input clamp diode voltage: The most negative voltage at an input when the specified current is forced out of that input terminal. This parameter guaranteed the integrity of the input diode intended to clamp negative ringing at the input terminal.

V_{IH} Input high voltage: The range of input voltages recognized by the device as a logic high.

V_{IH} (Min) Minimum Input high voltage: This value is the guaranteed input high threshold for the device. The minimum allowed input high in a logic system.

V_{IL} Input low voltage: The range of input voltages recognized by the device as a logic low.

V_{IL} (Max) Maximum input low voltage: This value is the guaranteed input low threshold for the device. The maximum allowed input low in a logic system.

V_M Measurement voltage: The reference voltage level on ac waveforms for determining ac performance. Usually specified as 1.5V for most TTL families, but 1.3V for the low-power Schottky 74LS family.

V_{OH} (Min) Output high voltage: The minimum guaranteed high voltage at an output terminal for the specified output current I_{OH} and at the minimum V_{CC} value.

V_{OL} (Max) Output low voltage: The minimum guaranteed low voltage at an output terminal sinking the specified load current I_{OL}.

V_{T+} Positive-going threshold voltage: The input voltage of a variable threshold device which causes operation according to specification as the input transition rises from below V_{T-} (Min).

V_T- Negative-going threshold voltage: The input voltage of a variable threshold device which causes operation according to specification as the input transition falls from above V_{T+} (Max).

Dc Currents

Positive current is defined as conventional current flow into a device. Negative current is defined as conventional current flow out of a device. All current limits are specified as absolute values.

I_{CC} Supply current: The current flowing into the V_{CC} supply terminal of the circuit with specified input conditions and open outputs. Input conditions are chosen to guarantee worst case operation unless specified.

I_I Input leakage current: The current flowing into an input when the maximum allowed voltage is applied to the input. This parameter guaranteed the minimum breakdown voltage for the input.

I_{IH} Input high current: The current flowing into an input when a specified high-level voltage is applied to that input.

I_{IL} Input low current: The current flowing out of an input when a specified low-level voltage is applied to that input.

I_{OH} Output high current: The leakage current flowing into a turned off open collector output with a specified high-output voltage applied. For device with a pull-up circuit, the I_{OH} is the current flowing out of an output which is in the high state.

I_{OL} Output low current: The current flowing into an output which is in the low state.

I_{OS} Output short-circuit current: The current flowing out of an output which is in the high state when the output is short circuit to ground.

I_{OZH} Output off current high: The current flowing into a disabled 3-state output with a specified high output voltage applied.

I_{OZL} Output off current low: The current flowing out of a disabled 3-state output with a specified low output voltage applied.

Ac Switching Parameters and Definitions

f_{MAX} The maximum clock frequency: The maximum input frequency at a clock input for predictable performance. Above this frequency the device may cease to function.

t_{PLH} Propagation delay time: The time between the specified reference points on the input and output waveforms with the output changing from the defined low level to the defined high level.

t_{PHL} Propagation delay time: The time between the specified reference points on the input and output waveforms with the output changing from the defined high level to the defined low level.

t_{PHZ} Output disable time from high level of a 3-state output: The delay time between the specified reference points on the input- and output-voltage waveforms with the 3-state output changing from the high level to a high impedance off state.

t_{PLZ} Output disable time from low level of a 3-state output: The delay time between the specified reference points on the input and output voltage waveforms with the 3-state output changing from the low level to a high impedance off state.

t_{PZH} Output enable time to a high level of a 3-state output: The delay time between the specified reference points on the input and output voltage waveforms with the 3-state output changing from a high impedance off state to the high level.

t_{PZL} Output enable time to a low level of a 3-state output: The delay time between the specified reference points on the input and output voltage waveforms with the 3-state output changing from a high impedance off state to the low level.

t_h Hold time: The interval immediately following the active transition of the timing pulse (usually the clock pulse) or following the transition of the control input to its latching level, during which interval the data to be recognized must be maintained at the input to ensure its continued recognition. A negative hold time indicates that the correct logic level may be released prior to the active transition of the timing pulse and still be recognized.

t_s Setup time: The interval immediately preceding the active transition of the timing pulse (usually the clock pulse) or preceding the transition of the control input to its latching level, during which interval the data to be recognized must be maintained at the input to ensure its recognition. A negative setup time indicates that the correct logic level may be initiated sometime after the active transition of the timing pulse and still be recognized.

t_w Pulse width: The time between the specified reference points on the leading and trailing edges of a pulse.

t_{rec} Recovery time: The time between the reference point on the trailing edge of an asynchronous input control pulse and the reference point on the activating edge of a synchronous (clock) pulse input such that the device will respond to the synchronous input.

Index